INDIA'S CHINA CHALLENGE

Advance praise for *India's China Challenge*

'Ananth Krishnan presents a gripping account of contemporary China, the country's stupendous progress and the dark side. His eye and intellect are probing, and he is an indomitable explorer. The effect is brilliant.'

– **Nirupama Rao,** Former Foreign Secretary and Ambassador to China

'Ananth Krishnan has managed to convey some penetrating insights on China in a most readable manner combining sharp analysis with an engaging familiarity and empathy with the country and its people. It is a welcome and timely departure from the gross stereotype imagery that passes for Chinese studies these days. It is a highly recommended read.'

– **Shyam Saran,** Former Foreign Secretary

'Ananth Krishnan has been covering China from China for over a decade. But he is not just an enterprising journalist. He has brought scholarly standards to his reporting on Chinese history, politics, military and foreign policy. In this book he tackles an issue of profound significance to India and indeed to the world. The expectation that PRC that expands as the People's Republic of China would also mean the Peaceful Rise of China has been belied. Of course, Ananth Krishnan provides Indian viewpoints forcefully. But what give value to this very timely book are the Chinese perspectives on India that he provides. The narrative is both racy and insightful.'

– **Jairam Ramesh,** MP, Former Union Minister and noted author

'It is such a joy to read Ananth Krishnan's book on China and India, a topic that will occupy much of our attention for years and decades to come. Ananth is one of the few rising stars in

India who have mastered the Chinese language and gained such deep and unique insights into the politics, society and economy of China that I cannot think of another person who would be in the same position to enlighten us on the two most populous countries and their inter-relations. For one, he has made more trips to my native hometown province, Hunan, than I have since 2009! Also, his writing is brilliant and a pleasure to read. Given the rising geopolitical and geoeconomic issues between India and China, this book is extremely timely and a must-read for anyone who wants to understand the present China challenge.'

– **Zhiwu Chen**, Chair Professor of Finance and Victor and William Fung Professor in Economics at the University of Hong Kong, Professor of Finance at Yale University (1999–2017)

'How should India relate to China? By being more like it: single party rule, surveillance society, state capitalism? Or being more of itself: diversity, debate, creative entrepreneurship? Our obsession with navel gazing has built a dangerous ignorance about China. Ananth Krishnan helps remedy that. He is that rare Indian who spent years in China, studying, interacting, reporting. His book is a most engaging, significant and timely read.'

– **Shekhar Gupta**, Founder and Editor-in-Chief, The Print

'Ananth Krishnan is one of India's most well-informed, astute, and prolific observers of China. During his decade in Beijing he enjoyed ringside seats to China's transformation, from the more disciplined and understated Hu Jintao to the dark, unbridled nationalism of Xi Jinping. *India's China Challenge* is brimming with insights into this dynamic chapter in China's history, and how it has fundamentally transformed the contentious China-India relationship.'

– **Jeff M. Smith**, Research Fellow, The Heritage Foundation

INDIA'S CHINA CHALLENGE

A JOURNEY THROUGH CHINA'S RISE AND WHAT IT MEANS FOR INDIA

ANANTH KRISHNAN

HarperCollins *Publishers* India

First published in hardback in India in 2020 by
HarperCollins *Publishers*
A-75, Sector 57, Noida, Uttar Pradesh 201301, India
www.harpercollins.co.in

2 4 6 8 10 9 7 5 3

P-ISBN: 978-93-9032-768-3
E-ISBN: 978-93-9032-769-0

Typeset in 10.5/13.7 Sabon LT Std at
Manipal Technologies Limited, Manipal

Printed and bound at
Thomson Press (India) Ltd

MIX
Paper
FSC FSC™ C010615

This book is produced from independently certified FSC™ paper
to ensure responsible forest management.

For Tara, Zhao Wen, and my parents

Contents

Introduction xi

PART I: POLITICS

1. In Mao's Shadow 3
2. The Rise of Xi 30
3. A Battle of Ideas 54

PART II: ECONOMY

4. The Manufacturing Miracle 73
5. From Countryside to Megacities 92
6. The Next Tech Giant 116

PART III: DIPLOMACY

7. Building a Chinese Order 137
8. Competition and Collaboration 157
9. Where China Meets India 171
10. From Doklam to Galwan 182
11. The China–Pakistan Nexus 202

PART IV: HISTORY

12. Original Sins 219
13. Ghosts of 1962 234
14. The Case for Settling 247

PART V: FRONTIERS

15. Tibet: Past and Present 267
16. Restless in Xinjiang 296
17. The Fight for Hong Kong 314

PART VI: PORTRAITS

18. Renewing Links 333
19. The Discoverer 337
20. The Treasure Hunter 345
21. The Interpreter 351
22. The Fan 357
23. The Green Warrior 362
24. The Dreamer 369

Epilogue: China After the Pandemic 376

Acknowledgements 389

Notes 395

Bibliography 415

About the Author 419

Introduction

I FIRST MOVED TO CHINA in the summer of 2008. My hope was to stay the summer and return with, at the most, a smattering of the language. This rather modest plan turned into an unexpected decade-long journey, which gave me a ringside seat of the country's phenomenal rise. I moved to Beijing in 2009 and lived there until August 2018, working as a reporter for *The Hindu* and then for *India Today*. My job gave me a privileged opportunity to travel the length and breadth of the country, beyond the glitzy skyscrapers of Shanghai and the grand avenues of Beijing that greet most visitors.

When I left for India in August 2018, I resolved never to write a book about China. There were two reasons for this. First, things changed so fast in the country that events often overtook even what I wrote for *India Today*, a weekly magazine. Where would that leave a book? Moreover, ten years may be just a blip in the life of a country. This is especially true for one with a history as long as China's.

But the longer I was back in India, the more my resolve began to weaken. The China that I encountered in conversations with people, in newspapers and on television was, in many ways, unrecognizable from the nation I had experienced. As a country, India grossly underinvests in trying to understand its most important neighbour. This is at every level, from the media to the business community to the government. When I left Beijing, there were only four Indian reporters based in China. There wasn't a single television channel from India that had set up a China bureau – not that this stopped them in any way from holding forth every night on the topic. In contrast, almost every European country, regardless of its size, seemed to have reporters in Beijing. The Indian correspondents could only marvel at the resources they had to pursue stories. If language is a barrier, we haven't done enough to surmount it.

One of the central challenges of writing this book was: how do you capture the diversity of more than a billion voices? How do you then wrap them up, with all their complexities, into one neat, easy argument, as books are required to do? My inability to answer this question was the second reason for my reluctance to write. Finally, I resolved that I wouldn't try. A note here on what this book isn't. It doesn't have a tidy argument to offer that captures the many changes unfolding in China. And it, by no means, offers a definitive history of the country's political and economic changes over the past decade.

This book is an on-the-ground perspective of a reporter, informed mostly by interviews with people I came to meet and know during my time in China. Throughout this book, you will find a range of Chinese voices: a veteran journalist chronicling hidden disasters of the Mao era; an industrial tycoon who left Silicon Valley to lead his country's economic transformation; a leading economist who went from being one of the architects of China's reforms to being vilified as a traitor; a leader of the Tiananmen Square protests who lives in exile and yearns to go home; a People's Liberation Army soldier who fought in the 1962 war, but spent the rest of his life fighting the government for a cleaner environment; an innovator who is using artificial intelligence to transform how Chinese companies work; and many more.

My aim in writing this book is to present some of the perspectives that I came across in my time there, to try to unpack some of these changes. My broader aim is to ask what China's many transformations mean for India. These pages reflect one person's subjective experience of living through these changes over the past ten years, changes that I have tried to make sense of in the only way that reporters know – by talking to people.

This is an account based almost entirely on interviews I conducted during the course of my time in China. It is also informed by the work of many scholars that I regularly turned to for wisdom and context. You will find a list of those works in the Bibliography, which I hope the reader finds useful for further exploration of the many themes this book touches upon, some only at the surface.

The title, *India's China Challenge*, might be interpreted in two ways – something that struck me only belatedly. The first, and the way I intended, refers to the challenges posed to India by China's rise. It might, however, also be interpreted as the challenge that India poses to China. After all, there is perhaps no other emerging country, one with a political system that couldn't be more different, that could potentially offer a credible alternative vision to China, as I argue in the section 'Diplomacy'. Whether India can actually do so remains uncertain. What is very certain though is the immediate challenge that our country faces from China, which is the focus of this book.

So, what is India's China challenge?

In Part I, I look at the political challenge of dealing with the rise of a one-party state – one that is now keen to offer its authoritarian–capitalist model to the world and shape global institutions in line with its own values. It is hence more important than ever to understand what those values are. Chapter 1 looks at the China model and how Mao's legacy continues to shape the country's politics. In Chapter 2, I look at the rise of Xi Jinping and the changes unfolding in China in the wake of his ascension, from the centralization of power to an increasingly prominent role for a political party that earlier preferred to pull the strings from behind the scenes. These are trends that the coronavirus pandemic, which even China's President Xi Jinping acknowledged had posed 'a major test of China's system and capacity for governance', has accelerated.[1] In Chapter 3, I look at the battle of ideas and the role of ideology in Chinese politics.

Part II examines the economic challenge – of both learning from China's remarkable and unique growth story, and navigating an increasingly lopsided economic relationship driven by Indian dependencies on Chinese manufacturing, an issue of increasing salience in the wake of the pandemic. Chapter 4 looks at the manufacturing miracle and how Chinese supply chains became so integral to the Indian economy. Chapter 5 examines how urbanization has transformed the country, and the lessons to be drawn from both the promises and perils of China's experience. In Chapter 6, I look at the emergence of 'tech China', and the contradictions of an innovation power bound by suffocating systems of censorship and surveillance, as well as the growing reliance on technology as a driver of both growth and governance – another trend that the pandemic has hastened.

Part III examines the third major challenge, which is manifested in India's difficult diplomatic and military engagement with China. Chapter 7 looks at the emergence of an increasingly assertive and confident China under Xi, and how it is looking to play an ever greater role on the world stage – in many ways to India's detriment. Chapter 8 examines the complicated dynamic of the India–China relationship, and how this sensitive balance is increasingly tilting towards competition and not cooperation. Chapters 9, 10 and 11 assess two of the most important drivers of that trend: the boundary dispute and a deepening China–Pakistan nexus.

In Part IV, I look at the challenge of history – of the unresolved boundary and the 1962 war – and why settling the question of the past is so crucial to this relationship's future. In Part V, I try to present a different perspective of China as seen from its restless frontiers, which convey a sense of a political model that is far less resilient – and far less confident – than it might appear to be on the surface.

Tying the four challenges together is what is in my view, perhaps the greatest challenge of them all: the conceptual challenge of reassessing how we think about and engage with our most important neighbour. This is a question I try to address throughout the book, as I make a case for re-examining some of our most deeply held conventional wisdoms on everything from the China model and the reasons behind its economic success, to the boundary dispute and the war.

During my time in China, I was fortunate to meet many people who helped me challenge my own deeply held views, and this book is filled with their voices. In the last part, 'Portraits', I share six of those voices – people who are in their own way defying convention. Their stories may appear disconnected, but binding them are surprising links to India.

Even as I write this in the summer of 2020, China is on the mind of many Indians. Two events – the COVID-19 pandemic and the most serious violence on the India–China border since 1967 – have only reminded us of the impact this neighbour has on our lives, albeit in the worst ways possible. As I write, India is still in the grip of confronting both crises. The prospect of a conflict with China no longer feels far-fetched and remote, but immediate and real. It shouldn't have to take multiple problems for us to pay attention to a country that impacts our lives in more ways than we realize.

My own China journey is not over. In many ways, I feel it has only just begun. When I left in 2018, I wasn't sure I was ever going to return, but by early 2020, I was given another opportunity to go back to report from Beijing. I readily accepted (going back, perhaps, would be the only way to ensure I didn't forget all the Mandarin I had invested so much time in!), although the coronavirus outbreak early in the year left me uncertain about when I would be able to do so.

If there is one thing that I take away from my time in China – or should I say, my first stint in the country – it is that the less time you spend in a place (or with a person), the more confident you are in your assessment of them. But the longer you get to know someone or a place, the more you discover about their many complexities and contradictions, layer by layer. At the end of your journey, you are left with more questions than answers. And that, actually, might not be a bad thing at all.

Chennai
June 2020

PART I

POLITICS

1

In Mao's Shadow

IT IS A HOT SUMMER morning in Beijing, and I am lost. I have just crossed Tiananmen Square, and the more-than-usual security presence suggests one thing: an important political anniversary approaches. It is a few days to go before 1 July 2011, a date marked on the calendars of every one of China's 90 million or so Communist Party members, journalists, school teachers, and perhaps every policeman and woman in town.

For days, the streets outside my home – a quiet and leafy residential community in the heart of Beijing where live retirees, bureaucrats and the young doctors who work in a nearby military hospital and became my daily ping-pong partners – have been lined by grandmas and grandpas, all sporting red armbands. They are the eyes and ears of every neighbourhood, recruited by the Communist Party of China (CPC) to keep a close watch on the streets every time a 'sensitive' event approaches. And this event, even by Chinese standards, is about as sensitive as they come. The CPC is preparing to mark its ninetieth anniversary, and I am facing a deadline.

I have headed west, past Tiananmen, in search of Mao. It's not the Mao who's on everyone's mind. The Mao I am looking for has been, for decades, one of China's most influential economists, one of the architects of its reforms. He also happens to be an outspoken political thinker, a rare voice in Beijing who speaks without fear or favour.

Mao Yushi is in his early eighties, but is perhaps even more active now than he was forty years ago, relentless in his writings, blog posts and regular messages on Weibo, the Twitter-like microblogging platform used in China. Twitter, Facebook and YouTube were all banned in 2009 with impeccable timing, two months after I first landed in China. The trigger for the ban was an outbreak of rioting and violence in Urumqi, in the western Xinjiang region, on 5 July 2009.

In 1993, Mao Yushi founded what is one of Beijing's most respected think tanks, the Unirule Institute of Economics, just as the country's economy was opening up. He has written more than a dozen books in China, most of which, unusual for an academic, have been popular bestsellers. One of his first books, *Economics in Everyday Life*, is perhaps still the most widely read explainer in China on capitalism and the market.[1] It made the case, to a still sceptical public, for why the liberalization of China's economy would improve ordinary lives.

The book was lapped up by a public unused to a frank and well-argued defence of capitalism. Mao's writings go beyond the domain of economic freedom. He has always made the case – as much as one can in China – for the importance of individual liberties for a nation's prosperity. It is no surprise then that he was hailed as 'one of the pioneers of the movement in China for civil society and freedom' when he was awarded the Cato Institute's Milton Friedman Prize for Advancing Liberty.

In the summer of 2011, Mao Yushi was back in the public spotlight, but for grimmer reasons. He had just penned an essay that had set China's internet on fire. 'Returning Mao Zedong to Human Form' was the provocative title. In the essay, he slammed the deification of Mao Zedong by the CPC, and ahead of the Party's anniversary, called for an open and public debate on Mao's legacy. It was time, he said, to stop whitewashing the disasters Mao had unleashed on the country, particularly during the 1958

Great Leap Forward and the decade-long Cultural Revolution from 1966. He was unsparing in his evaluation of China's most important founding father. 'In Mao Zedong's eyes,' he wrote, 'the people were just meat and muscle. They were tools he used to shout "Long Live". His thirst for power dominated his life, and to this end, he went entirely mad.'[2]

When I finally made it to Yushi's modest west Beijing apartment, hidden away in a tree-lined street a few blocks west of Tiananmen, his wife greeted me at the door. He was on the phone, she said. It hadn't stopped ringing since the essay was published. There were brickbats and bouquets, but mostly brickbats. The calls came so frequently that it became apparent there was an organized campaign of intimidation under way. The death threats and abuse were on an almost daily basis. What was striking was how many of the callers sounded so young, some perhaps still in their teens.

Mao Yushi's stature in China is such that the government chose not to directly confront him over the essay. He is still widely respected, particularly in economic and financial circles, for the important role he played in the reforms, which bought him some amount of leeway and protection against official action. I asked him why he wrote that essay when he knew of the trouble it would unleash. 'My view,' he told me, 'is that the legitimacy of the Party comes from success in conducting reform and opening up, and not because of Mao.'

As Yushi explained to me that morning over many cups of Oolong tea, in his view, what had enabled the Party to survive until its ninetieth birthday was not authoritarianism and iron-fisted rule, but, on the contrary, the corrective measures it had taken to retreat from authoritarianism. This was a lesson, in his view, that was not just about history but crucial to the political direction China should take in the future.

What worried him was that not many of his fellow citizens saw this. Needless to say, that was not how the Party portrayed it either. In the view of the Party, it was a strong, centralized leadership that had laid the foundation for China's rise – and provided a stark contrast to the messy, inefficient and chaotic democracies in China's neighbourhood. The Party, in Yushi's view, had been so successful in turning this history on its head that not just every schoolchild in China, but even observers of the country from around the world had now come to accept this as the conventional wisdom about its rise.

The China Model

Shanghai was my very first home in China, where I spent four months trying to learn as much Mandarin as I could before moving to Beijing. You cannot find two cities that are more different from one another. Each has its own charm and energy, and the debate about which is the better place to live in is an endless one for the loyal residents of each city, who also tend to not have the most favourable opinion of the other city's inhabitants. Shanghainese are seen in Beijing – and to be fair, in much of China – as being full of airs (and too 'Western'). Beijingers are viewed in the south as being crude and ill-mannered, known as they are for not beating about the bush. I tend to end up on the Beijing side of the debate, having fallen in love with the city's more rugged charm and its incomparable history. But Beijing is an acquired taste, unlike Shanghai, which can captivate you at first sight. And there are few more alluring sights than the gleaming skyline of Pudong, Shanghai's stunning financial district.

When you stand on the Bund, the old embankment on the western banks of the Huangpu river, the skyline descends on you and takes your breath away. The Huangpu runs right through the middle of Shanghai. On its west is old Shanghai, called Puxi (literally, west of the Huangpu). Puxi was where foreign powers, starting with the British, set up the old international settlement in the nineteenth century after the defeat of the Qing army in the Opium War (1839–42). The French Concession, with its cobbled footpaths and old European-style homes that have now been converted into trendy cafes and boutique shops, is probably one of my favourite places in China. Here, you can spend hours and hours endlessly strolling through parks and tree-lined streets. Pudong (east of the Pu) is on the other bank of the river, set up in 1993 as a special economic zone on what was then largely farmland.

Stroll among the tourists on the embankment today facing Pudong, and you will notice something curious. You will see most tourists with their backs turned towards the beautiful buildings of the Bund, from the old HSBC building to the art deco Peace Hotel, and instead, looking in the opposite direction.

This is no accident. The beautiful buildings of old Shanghai that line the Bund, mostly established by the British to house banks and trading companies, were built on a scale intended to wow the visitors who sailed up the Huangpu – and send a not-so-subtle message about who was in charge. Taking a cue from this, the financial heartbeat of New China was similarly built not just to wow but to shine so bright so as to cast a shadow on the Bund, and throw a painful colonial past into darkness.

Every evening, as night falls on the Huangpu, the buildings of Pudong light up. The 470-metre tall Oriental Pearl Tower, the tallest building in China when built in 1994, glistens pink, with its two massive, gravity-defying glass spheres – each 50 metres in diameter – that look as if they are suspended in mid-air. On its right, you will see the 492-metre 'Bottle Opener', as the Shanghai World Financial Centre is more popularly known, with good reason. The Bottle Opener dethroned the Pearl Tower as China's tallest building when it was unveiled in 2008. And then, furthest to the right, the tallest of them all, the 632-metre tall Shanghai Tower, which unseated the Bottle Opener in 2015. Three skyscrapers, three awe-inspiring symbols, for three decades of the China story since the economy began opening up in the early 1990s.

'When do you think India will get there?' was the question I perhaps heard the most often when taking in the view from the Bund in the company of visitors from India – whether they were visiting friends, family or colleagues on tour. To most visitors to China, from India or anywhere, their first experiences tend to be the skyline of Shanghai, a modern bullet train network that's now the world's longest, or the gleaming shopping malls of Nanjing Road in Shanghai or Wangfujing in Beijing.

That is precisely how the CPC likes it. The Party wants the world to see China as an economic superpower led by an efficient, capable and post-ideological regime that embraced economic liberalization. Today, this is an increasingly persuasive image, particularly when contrasted with the challenges democracies elsewhere are grappling with.

It is true that in the years since the economic reforms of the late 1970s and the opening up of the economy in the 1990s, the Party has retreated from many aspects of the private lives of Chinese. Work units no longer have to grant permission to marry. They are free to choose the jobs they want. Most can travel to any country of their choosing on holiday. And what came as a huge surprise to this citizen of the world's largest democracy, during my time in China, was the gradual discovery that the life of a young Chinese citizen is, in many ways, far less encumbered than that of her or his counterpart in India – as long as you stay away from politics. Barring the absence of political freedoms, young Chinese women and men, I found, broadly fare better when it comes to economic and social freedoms – to live their lives as they see fit, to start their own businesses, to work where they choose, and find their partners with far less societal or familial interference.

So compelling has been China's economic success story that we are now in the curious position where the business elites of India – and indeed much of the world – are often falling over each other to hold up as a shining example a one party-ruled authoritarian and political system that still, make no mistake, very much retains its Leninist DNA. The increasing admiration for Beijing's political model, particularly in the developing world, has coincided with two parallel events: China's stunning rise to a $14 trillion economy in 2019, the world's second largest, and the gradual turmoil seen engulfing much of the West, starting with the financial crisis of

2008 and culminating in the political turmoil unleashed by the rise of populism. China's seemingly steady onward march has provided a stark contrast.

Coupled with this expanding acclaim abroad is a growing confidence at home coursing through the veins of the Party leadership. Many in Beijing are increasingly convinced that the end of history isn't to be found in the liberal democracies of the West, but in the East, and more specifically, in the China model. In the words of President Xi Jinping at the Party's National Congress in 2017, the China model was 'blazing a new trail' and 'offering a new option for countries who want to speed up their development', with what he called 'a Chinese wisdom and a Chinese approach to solving the problems facing mankind'.[3]

During my time in Beijing, I found that this admiration abroad was only growing. China was the future, as seen in the awestruck eyes of the steady stream of government officials, businessmen and journalists on the ever-frequent junkets hosted by the Chinese government. But how accurate is this China model as imagined by the rest of the world – the increasingly pervasive impression of a regime run by far-sighted and post-ideological technocrats, carefully chosen by meritocracy, the stewards of the political system of the future?

There is nothing communist about this imagined China. This is a China that left Mao Zedong behind, a China that is the perfect blend of strong government and free market – an efficient and centralized government that 'gets things done'. Who wants democratic freedoms anyway, so the argument goes, when you have Louis Vuitton showrooms and Starbucks outlets at every corner, when economic liberalization has brought in the freedom to buy all that you need? But how true is this representation of China? Is it grounded in reality, or is it the case that for the frustrated citizens of messy democracies, whether in India or America, it is tempting to imagine the China model as what they want it to be, rather than what it really is?

The Party

There is one crucial detail that is missing in this widely prevalent caricature of how the country works – the beating heart that is at the centre of the China model, which is the CPC. Even if the Party has indeed retreated in many ways from the daily lives of the people, it remains as firmly in control over the political domain as it ever was. For those who don't live in China, that's sometimes not easy to see. A friend in Beijing once remarked to me that the greatest trick the Party ever pulled was to convince the world of its irrelevance – or at least, of the irrelevance of ideology in China today.

But, in fact, the Party is everywhere. It is in complete control and exerts its influence over every aspect of policy and decision-making, even if the Party is itself a black box. If you lift the veil and take a closer look at the nuts and bolts of China's political apparatus, you will see, as the journalist Richard McGregor puts it in his excellent book, *The Party*, something 'straight out of the Leninist playbook'.[4] An omnipresent political machine that keeps a tight grip on the three pillars key to its survival: personnel, propaganda and the People's Liberation Army (PLA), which is unique among militaries in owing its allegiance not to a state but to one political party.

To understand the degree of omnipresence, consider such a situation in India: the Indian National Congress or the Bharatiya Janata Party is not just the ruling party at the Centre, but controls every state government, appoints the heads of every Indian bank and major corporation (who will, of course, be party members), controls the Indian armed forces and appoints its generals, oversees every media organization and what they publish, controls colleges and schools, decides the curriculum that only teaches the party version of history, has a party cell in every company, whether public or private, and controls every level of administration, right from the top to the village and even your resident welfare association.

Welcome to one party–ruled China.

The fact is Mao Zedong would probably immediately recognize the blueprint and institutions he borrowed from Lenin and Stalin and passed on, regardless of the Louis Vuitton stores and Starbucks outlets. And this blueprint has broadly remained in place for close to 100 years since the Party's founding in 1921. As one professor in Renmin University in Beijing put it succinctly to McGregor, 'The Party is like God. He is everywhere. You just can't see him.'[5]

You can't see the Party because it chooses to stay out of view, and as a result, what visitors to China see are the institutions (which the Party controls from behind the scenes) that on the surface resemble those of any other country: a government and cabinet ministries, courts at all levels, a central bank, two houses of parliament, and of course, above them all, a president. Yet, even the president, largely for the purposes of global optics, dons this title only for the outside world. 'President' does not even exist within the lexicon of domestic Chinese politics. China's English-language media refer to 'President' Xi Jinping, but the domestic media translate the same title as the 'National Chairman', all aimed at conveying to the world a subtly different message about how this system really works. The title of National Chairman is itself the least important of the three crowns Xi wears. His position as the General Secretary of the Communist Party of China is what gives him his power, as does his being the Chairman of the Central Military Commission that controls the PLA. The Party, as always, comes first.

Mao's Legacy

For anyone trying to make sense of China and its political system, the experience should come with a warning sign: the process can leave you in a state of permanent cognitive dissonance. How does one make sense of the China that occupies our imagination – of the Shanghai skyscrapers, the high-speed trains, the shopping malls and the economic miracles – and the Maoist–Leninist political machine that continues to underpin it all?

One helpful place to start is where the journey of China's 'Chairman' began. 'Seeking truth from fact' are the words carved into the beautiful wooden archway that hangs above the entrance to the Yuelu Academy near Changsha, the capital of Mao's native Hunan province. One of China's four great centres of classical learning, this more than 1,000-year-old institution was founded in 976 CE, during the Song Dynasty (960–1279 CE). The four words carved into the door, read as '*shi shi qiu shi*' in Chinese, were taken from the second-century *Book of Han*, and inscribed onto the university's front door by administrators to serve as a moral guide to its elite students.

Yuelu was where twenty-four-year-old Mao Zedong picked up this phrase, which would later become one of the banners of his revolution. He was just out of college and struggling to adjust to the thriving intellectual climate of Changsha – a world away from his farming hometown of Shaoshan. On the winter's morning when I visited the academy, several groups of Chinese high-school students were on tour. The main attraction was a small, sparse room, decorated only by a rickety desk and a hard wooden bed. 'It was here that Chairman Mao studied,' the teacher leading the tour told them. 'It was here that he became so wise; so you must all study hard so one day you can become like the Chairman!'

Yuelu is the first stop on what has now unofficially become the Chairman Mao Pilgrimage Tour. The second stop is Shaoshan, his birthplace, which is a two-hour drive from Changsha, Hunan's bustling and modern provincial capital that rivals Beijing or Shanghai in its stunning infrastructure. A Maglev train that goes at 200 kilometres per hour runs through the city, connecting its modern South Railway station – an airport-like hub on China's bullet train route – with the international airport.

We left the city behind in search of Shaoshan and were very quickly on a road that is like any you will find in small-town China: immaculately paved, with four wide lanes and a steady procession of heavy haul trucks to keep travellers company. As we drove into the town, though, it quickly became clear this was no ordinary place. The small town's streets were lined by tour buses, while local Hunanese women, famed for their fiery temper (which, locals like to say, is only matched by the hot local cuisine) swarmed over visitors, hawking Mao keychains, Mao statues and Mao t-shirts. Pudgy Mao impersonators, dressed in green coats, wandered the streets offering to pose with tourists for 20 yuan (also known as Renminbi or RMB, meaning 'the people's currency').

Shaoshan's square was the main draw. A towering Mao statue, one of the largest in China, watched over the main square. Far removed from the bustling Mao-inspired local commerce that thrives on the city's edges, the square presented a solemn sight. Hundreds of Chinese from all over the country were there to pay their respects. For many, the experience was religious. The devotees – there is no more apt description – walked around the statue slowly, their heads respectfully lowered. They circled the statue four times, before kneeling in front of it. As they placed wreathes at Mao's feet, some uttered prayers. Some were moved to tears. The day I visited, I saw students, soldiers, serving government officials, and, most common of all, retirees.

'We are here to say thank you for what he has done for us,' one eighty-year-old man who had travelled all the way from northern Hebei told me. Tour over, I shared a cup of tea with Chen Yuxiang, a professor at the Marxism School of Hunan University, a modern institution that today inhabits the same campus once occupied by the Yuelu Academy. Chen explained to me that even now, there is a pervasive belief among most Chinese that Mao was a great man for the role he played in the communist revolution and the founding of the People's Republic in 1949.

Yet, for most of the world, the subsequent three decades of chaos that Mao unleashed, and his direct responsibility for the deaths of millions of people, both from the 1958 Great Leap Forward, the subsequent four-year famine and the decade-long Cultural Revolution (1966–76), is his abiding legacy. The puzzling thing about the continued deification of Mao in China is that the horrors of those three decades have been all but whitewashed –

not only from the Party propaganda and school textbooks, but also, it seems, from public memory.

More than politics, the fondness for Mao is also a question of nostalgia for many Chinese, especially those who grew up in the 1950s and 1960s. The Mao era was a time of hardship, but also, I have often heard from older Chinese friends, a simpler time, a time when they had something to believe in, unlike the no-holds-barred mad rush for prosperity that is defining the youth of their children. There was poverty, yes, but everyone was in the same boat, without the glaring inequalities of today. If you want a sense of this nostalgia, just pop into a park in almost any Chinese city on a Sunday morning, and you'll see dozens of older Chinese gathering and singing 'Red songs' in praise of the Chairman.

There is indeed genuine nostalgia, but there is also politics that plays a role in shaping this public memory of Mao. Communist Party propaganda continues to emphasize his achievements as the People's Republic's founding father while firmly clamping down on any discussion of the calamities of the 1950s and 1960s. This is important too, because for the Party, keeping alive this sentiment serves a crucial purpose in the absence of other ideological tethers that connect it to the people, particularly after the 'reform and opening up' of the Chinese economy and the whole-hearted embrace of capitalism.

The year I visited Mao's birthplace, there was more than usual interest in his life. The previous year, China had celebrated the sixtieth anniversary of the founding of the People's Republic in 1949. Local tourism officials in Shaoshan told me they expected a record 5 million visitors that year. The Mao tourism campaign is quite revealing about public perceptions of the Chairman. The appeal is as much to his role as founding father as an invocation of Chinese cultural and religious traditions, framing him more as some kind of divine presence in a blend of Maoism and mysticism.

One story that tour guides like to tell visitors is that when the Mao statue was unveiled in 1996, both the sun and the moon appeared together in the sky. Others like to say that this is the town with the most perfect feng shui in all of China, because of the specific positions and alignment of the mountains, lakes and fields. Just staying here, the story goes, will imbue your body with positive energy (plus, it explained the energy of the Chairman too). During my visit, I had an interesting chat with a young Changsha girl who worked in the town's booming entertainment industry – Hunan television is famous in China for its trendy reality television and entertainment shows – and carried on her pilgrimage a Louis Vuitton bag. She told me she wholeheartedly believed the feng shui theory and felt that her life had changed for the better after every visit to Shaoshan. On each trip, she made a sizeable donation. And, lo and behold, her prayers always came true.

For the Party, this adulation is only to be encouraged, because the veneration of Mao is useful to furthering its legitimacy even today. More importantly, it is also a justification for the Party's continuation of the Maoist–Leninist authoritarian system. Which is why China's leaders, in their speeches, always make it a point to stress that it was Mao's legacy – and not the economic reforms and opening up – that provides the bedrock of the regime's legitimacy. And any attempt to separate China's first three decades of Maoist chaos from the subsequent three decades of reforms under Deng Xiaoping is firmly squashed. In the Party's view – and a view that every schoolchild in China is taught right from primary school – questioning this fundamental principle is tantamount to heresy.

A Perpetual Struggle

Understanding Mao's beliefs is important in understanding the ideology that continues to inform the Party's views on politics today. Creating what he called 'a people's democratic dictatorship' was his mission soon after 'New China' was founded in 1949. In an essay he wrote shortly before the founding of the republic, Mao said he would establish a 'people's democratic dictatorship' that would 'deprive the reactionaries of the right to speak and let the people alone have the right'. And to critics who accused him of being dictatorial, he said he would reply: 'My dear sirs, you are right, that is just what we are.' He would be proud to be dictatorial, he said, to 'running dogs of imperialism, the landlord class and bureaucrat-bourgeoisie', but 'the rest of the people would enjoy the full range of freedoms'.[6]

Even that, however, would quickly prove to be an empty promise, just as his promise of democracy turned out to be when he led the communist revolution in the 1930s. Back then, the communist base in Yan'an was the promised land for idealistic Chinese intellectuals who wanted to fight for democracy. Tens of thousands of writers, artists and students descended on Yan'an to fight for the new revolution – and against what they saw as the autocracy and corruption of Chiang Kai-shek's Kuomintang Nationalist government. By the early 1940s, however, any semblance of democracy had been stamped out, with the first of many ideological purges beginning in the 1942 Rectification Movement that laid the groundwork for how Mao wanted to rule.

Perpetual struggle was at the heart of Mao's ideology. As the journalist John Garnaut writes, what Mao did was import the communism of Lenin and Stalin, and 'graft it' onto an existing ideological system with a long history.[7] Mao was fascinated by Chinese history and drew from communism to create a hybrid. He had a voracious appetite for history and ideological thought. As Li Rui, Mao's secretary, put it, 'He only slept on one-third of the bed and the other two-thirds of his bed was covered by books, all of which were thread-bound Chinese books, Chinese ancient books. His research was the strategies of emperors. That was how to govern this country. That was what he was most interested in.'

For Mao, as Garnaut argues, Joseph Stalin was the perfect ideological intermediary to interpret Marx and Lenin. When Mao first came across Stalin's 'Short Course on the History of Bolsheviks', he 'thought he'd found an encyclopaedia of Marxism and acted as if he'd discovered a treasure ... Stalin's problem was different to Lenin's. Lenin had to win a revolution but Stalin had to sustain it.' That was exactly Mao's problem too: 'to explain that they'd won the revolution but the long-promised Utopia of perfect equality had to be postponed.' The only way to resolve that contradiction was to ensure the revolution was unending, and, in Stalin's view, that required having an unending list of enemies, real or imagined, who needed constant purging.[8]

The first few decades of the People's Republic were marked by one campaign after another, all with the aim of strengthening Mao's control. His first major step was a nationwide land reform, with 40 per cent of cultivated land seized from landlords and redistributed. This did bring benefits to 60 per cent of the population: the gain per person was between one-sixth and half an acre, not substantial but still a boon to masses languishing in poverty. The Party record does not, however, remember that the redistribution was accompanied by unspeakable violence on a grand scale.

Indeed, the Party's campaign actively encouraged the violence, spurring peasants to take on their landlords, as it whipped up a revolutionary frenzy and fervour that also helped consolidate its support among the masses. Violent mass campaigns would later become a tried-and-tested method for Mao every time he felt his power being challenged. By some accounts, one out of every six family of landlords in China had one family member killed, many of whom were dragged into the street and beaten to death. At least 1 million deaths would mark the beginning of Mao's New China.[9]

Investigating a Disaster

The land reform would pale in comparison to the two biggest legacies of Maoism: the four-year-long Great Leap Forward (1958–62) and the Cultural Revolution (1966–76). In 1958, China's farmers, exhorted by Mao's delusions of propelling the country to rival the Soviet Union by becoming an industrial superpower overnight, were told to abandon their farming tools to manufacture iron in backyard furnaces. While the fields were idle, officials fabricated figures to please their Chairman by showing bountiful harvests. Today, schoolchildren in China learn that 1958 marked the start of 'three years of natural disasters', a time when the country faced unusual hardship but came together under the leadership of the great Chairman.

That is not how Yang Jisheng remembers those days. In 1959, when he was nineteen, his father died from starvation in front of his eyes. That is one reason why, for three decades, fighting this historical amnesia has become a mission for him. Yang is a veteran Chinese journalist and writer, who spent more than twenty-five years chronicling a remarkable account of the famine that is true to history – perhaps the only account of those years in China that is true to history. As a journalist with the Party's official Xinhua news agency, Yang managed to secure access to classified archives – on the pretext of researching China's grain policy – that exposed alarming facts about the famine and Mao's complicity. The product of Yang's painstaking research – which was, in unexpected instances, aided by Party cadres who shared a similar sense of indignation about the falsified official account of the period – is a 1,000-page treatise titled *Tombstone*, named in tribute to Yang's father. It was first published in 2008.[10]

By day, Yang was the editor of *Yanhuang Chunqiu*, one among a dwindling number of progressive and independent Chinese magazines. With a circulation of around 2,00,000, the magazine was read closely by the Beijing elite and carried a lot of weight in academic circles after its founding in 1991, just as reforms were taking off. Under relentless pressure from the authorities for their independent stance, they had moved into a cramped space in an apartment complex in central Beijing, where I first met Yang.

The desks were piled with books and old newspapers, resembling a newspaper office of the 1960s or 1970s. This was where some of the most meaningful journalism in China and reflections on Chinese history were being carried out, and it was a world away from the modern offices in gleaming skyscrapers occupied by China's favoured state media outlets such as the *People's Daily* and China Central Television.

Yang told me that even the Party's official history notes that the population of China decreased by 10 million between 1959 and 1960, when it should have actually gone up by 10 million. However, the official record puzzlingly notes that in the entire four-year period until 1962, a total of 16 million people died due to 'natural disasters'. 'The authorities have always been trying to avoid this part of history,' he told me.

Party officials had variously blamed natural disasters and the Soviet Union demanding the payback of loans as the main causes of the agricultural crisis. 'In my estimation,' Yang told me, '36 million people died. And this is a little conservative. It is not the highest estimate, and it's not the lowest estimate. But I think it is the closest estimate, because some things cannot be figured out.' This four-year period in China alone accounted for more than half of the total deaths from famine anywhere in the world throughout the entire twentieth century. And it is now but a footnote in China's public memory.

Hearing how Yang went about writing his account in a country that so carefully guards its history was fascinating. On his travels across China while covering stories for Xinhua, he quietly sought out local archives wherever he visited, on the pretext that he was researching grain policy. The official archives gave him a more accurate understanding of the agrarian crisis and how the government had responded to it in different counties.

'There were some natural disasters, because China is such a vast country, but nothing that was extraordinary in those years,' Yang told me. 'I was able to look at statistics from the department of public security, which had the household registration records, and also talked to the staff responsible for population statistics. My aim was not to do research county by county.' The biggest takeaway from his investigation was that he established that the Great Leap Forward was a systemic and structural failure, as he brought to light the remarkable scale of the tragedy in various counties where entire families starved to death. 'What has been consistent in the Party's different accounts of the famine over the years,' Yang said, 'is the denial of what was a systemic problem.' And that was entirely because of the system that Mao had built.

'The common people then were not even allowed to look for food, even when they were starving, because the Party said that doing so was being capitalist! Another problem of that period was over-centralized political and economic power. It is natural that hungry people should look for food. But the rights of people who were looking for food were denied. There was no market, so you could not buy food. And they refused outside aid. Begging for food was not an option, as other people were also suffering from hunger. They could only sit and wait for death, doing nothing. So in some families, all the family members died of hunger. At that time it was a totalitarian system – that is why Mao's wrong policy could be carried on for four years. This would not have been possible in a democratic country, as experts like Amartya Sen, who I quote in my book, have shown. If this was America, Britain or India, the wrong policy would have been opposed by the people. It could not have lasted four years.'

Yang was still haunted by the images and accounts that he came upon during his research, which was buttressed by oral histories from families from across China, who shared their stories with him. 'In some cases, people even began to eat people,' he said. 'There is a written record of these incidents of people eating people, of more than several thousand cases. When conducting interviews, I was first surprised and shocked. But after seeing case after case, so many cases, I became numbed.'

Yang interviewed a sixty-year-old migrant worker in Beijing who had lost two relatives during the famine. The man told him that his grandson, nineteen, had refused to believe how they had died because of what he had been taught at school. 'We should face this part of history directly, so we can learn from it and avoid such mistakes in the future,' Yang told me. 'We don't have communes today. We don't have food shortages today. But it is also about political systems. Learning about this period changed everything I thought I knew about political systems and about the over-centralization of power. If we do not tell this part of history, younger generations may never know. Then history will become myth.'

Does this history matter? In the view of the Party, it is a closed chapter and nothing is to be gained from reopening it. But in the view of those fighting to preserve the memories of the millions of lives lost, lessons will never be learned until the Chinese public comes to terms with these events. And unless they do so, people like Yang worry there will forever remain the prospect of history repeating itself.

Yang said the political loosening of the period of reform and the opening up of the economy encouraged him to pursue the project, starting in the 1980s and 1990s. But now, he believed, the trend towards openness is actually reversing. Today's China, in his view, is the most difficult period for historians and journalists since the days of the Cultural Revolution.

Yang's magazine finally shut down in 2016, four years into Xi Jinping's term. The reason, publisher Du Daozheng announced, was 'a decreasing tolerance' in the establishment for liberal ideas.[11] Yang, undeterred, has begun working on a book on Mao's second big disaster, the Cultural Revolution, the ten-year period of chaos from 1966.

Unending Revolution

Just as with the Great Leap Forward, there is rarely public discussion within China about the Cultural Revolution. But in 2011, just as the Communist Party prepared to mark its ninetieth anniversary – and also prepare for a once-in-ten-years leadership change the following year – an unusual but brief public debate surfaced. A Communist Party 'princeling' named Bo Xilai – whose father had fought alongside Mao – launched a campaign that year to venerate Mao and Cultural Revolution–era 'Red' ideology in the city of Chongqing, in China's southwest, where he served as the Party boss.

Under Bo's 'Road to Revitalization' campaign, Chongqing's residents were bombarded with thirty-five 'Red songs', which played non-stop on television and radio stations. Newspapers were ordered to print the lyrics. Public performances of 'Love the Red Flag' were staged, while regular programming of soap operas was stopped, replaced by broadcasts of Red rallies that Bo presided over. The unlikely list of honoured guests invited to preside over these controversial rallies, along with Bo, included a certain Henry Kissinger. Students in Chongqing were sent to work in the countryside – just as Mao had decreed in the mid-1960s. As Bo himself put it memorably, 'Red songs won public support because they depicted China's path in a simple, sincere and vivid way. There's no need to be artsy-fartsy ... only dilettantes prefer enigmatic works.' [12] Bo also launched a massive anti-corruption campaign to 'smash the black', as the mafia was referred to, but used it to also neatly eliminate all of his political rivals as he purged some 1,500 officials, some of whom he had executed.

Bo's apparent motivation was to push himself into the national spotlight – and onto the new Politburo Standing Committee that was set to take control in the once-in-ten-years leadership Congress in 2012 – but his power grab ultimately ended in disaster. A falling out with his right-hand man, the police chief of Chongqing, Wang Lijun, triggered a chain of events that finally exposed the role of Bo and his wife in the death of their British businessman friend and fixer, Neil Heywood. Bo was sent to prison. Some of his politics, however, endured, even if the direct invocation of the Cultural Revolution was deemed a step too far for the Party leadership. The then premier, Wen Jiabao, even publicly chided Bo in a rare open criticism of a Politburo member, telling him to remember the Party's consensus on turning the page over the Cultural Revolution.

For many people in China, Bo's exploitation of a still-open wound brought back unresolved memories. Among them was Wang Youqin, who in the year 2000 had opened a website to serve as an online memorial for the mostly forgotten victims of the violence unleashed by Mao's Red Guards. I first heard about her when I came across a remarkable documentary by the Chinese filmmaker Hu Jie, called *Though I am Gone*, in which he tells the story of the very first victim of the Cultural Revolution, who happened to be Wang's high school teacher in Beijing. The documentary is banned in China.

I met Wang one day in west Beijing, not far from her old high school. Within weeks of opening the online memorial, she told me, she began receiving hundreds of emails from across China, from husbands and wives and sons and daughters who had lost their loved ones and wanted their stories recorded. One woman wrote in with an old photograph of her mother, a high-school teacher in Hunan, who was brutally killed by her students. In 2002, just two years after she opened her online memorial, the emails stopped suddenly – the Chinese government had blocked her website.

In May 1966, Mao had issued a circular calling for a 'Great Proletarian Cultural Revolution' and declaring war on all 'counter-revolutionaries'. Two months on, no one quite knew what Mao really meant by 'counter-revolutionary', which apparently included anyone who was deemed a 'Capitalist roader', 'Rightist', 'intellectual' or 'landlord' – essentially anyone that an increasingly paranoid Mao perceived as a threat to his bid to consolidate total power.

Wang told me the Party's attempts to draw a line over this period of history hasn't helped heal wounds. After Mao's death, leaders like Hu Yaobang and Deng Xiaoping, who himself suffered during the revolution, embarked on what she describes as history's greatest ever exercise of rehabilitation. It was, however, both limited and far from enough. Families of victims were given 420 yuan and a letter saying their loved ones had been 'wrongly' punished. That was about it. The Party felt that looking forward, and burying history, was the easiest way to heal the scars. Mao, who in Wang's view bore direct responsibility for the millions of deaths, is after all still celebrated as a national hero, whose portrait hangs at Tiananmen Square, with history rewritten to blame only his associates and 'The Gang of Four'.

Wang was only thirteen when the first 'struggle sessions' began at her school in Beijing. Her school happened to be the first school in China where the student-led violence began. She was old enough to feel outraged at watching her teachers face daily humiliation. Teachers have, through much of Chinese history, enjoyed unquestioned respect in society. Yet, within a matter of a few weeks, the centuries-old belief had been so easily turned on its head – such was the power of Mao. In one session, she recalled, she watched her beloved teacher, Bian Zhongyun, being beaten. The Red Guards, led mostly by the older students, all of whom were girls, improbably accused the very same teacher who had taught them, day after day, year after year, of plotting a coup d'état against Mao. Disgusted by the scene, Wang left.

Hu Jie's documentary powerfully tells the story of how the Cultural Revolution began, and within weeks, turned the lives of one Beijing family upside down. The revolution had begun with the mobilization of the capital's students. They were, after all, an easy group to organize, and their teachers – who, Mao deemed, were 'intellectuals' – were an easy target to kick-start a political campaign. Mao's increasingly influential wife, Jiang Qing, had summoned Beijing's students to a mass rally, where they had been organized into cohorts of Red Guards, and encouraged to weed out 'class enemies' in their schools and neighbourhoods. She told them to spare no one. Jiang had openly incited violence, assuring them, as the documentary notes, that 'it served them right if bad people are beaten by good people'. Exhorted by Jiang, the older students from Bian's school – many of whom were daughters of top Party cadres – leapt into action. They began organizing struggle sessions aimed at discovering the 'enemies' in their midst. The students declared that Bian, their vice principal, was 'born into a big landlord's family'. So she became their first target.

When Bian and her husband came home one evening, they found that students had broken into their apartment. Their rooms had been ransacked by Red Guards in search of 'evidence' of their 'landlord' status. Threats were posted on every door. 'Upright your pig's ears and listen carefully!' said one message to Bian. 'We'll hack you to pieces if you dare act wantonly against our will!' Another taunted her about previous struggle sessions. 'On the struggle meeting with the shouting of accusations, you trembled all over, legs paralysed, holding a tall hat in your hands, having been poured with cold water, with mud in your mouth, just like a pig in the water!'

In Hu Jie's film, Bian's husband, Wang Jingyao, recalls the events of 5 August 1966, telling Hu he wanted to speak out 'to keep the record of history true to history'. That morning had begun like any other. Bian got dressed and bade goodbye to her husband with a matter-of-fact handshake. But as she stepped out of their small apartment that day, Wang had a feeling that his wife should never have left. The first struggle session, a few days before, had quickly gotten out of hand. Jiang Qing's incitement had appeared to whip up the impressionable young girls. One woman leapt out of the crowd onto the stage where Bian faced their accusations, grabbing her hair and hitting her. No one intervened. At the next session, a crowd of students, some armed with wooden bats, lunged at their teachers, swinging at them without holding back. But even Wang Jingyao was unprepared for what would unfold on 5 August. When Bian had come home the evening before and showed her husband the bruises on her back from the beatings that day, Wang suggested they immediately leave Beijing. But Bian was unfazed. 'I have done nothing wrong,' she told him. She insisted on going back to school the next day.

On the morning of 5 August, the Red Guards organized a parade across the middle school. That afternoon, Wang Youqin saw her classmates dragging a group of teachers across the playground, dousing them in black ink. Some students, Wang saw, had broken into the carpenter's room, and emerged with the legs of chairs and planks of wood with nails protruding from their ends. Wang saw her vice principal lying on the ground, down by a group of students and covered in ink. Bian was forced to scream, 'I'm a capitalist roader! I deserve the beatings!' The girls set about attacking her, parading her around the school and beating her with wooden clubs. Bian was finally dragged to the girls' washroom.

Barely conscious and bleeding, she was given a broom and asked to clean the floor. She was left there to die. When found by another teacher, the vice principal was already dead, bleeding and foaming at the mouth, the first victim of Mao Zedong's Great Proletarian Cultural Revolution.

Memories that Linger

Wang Youqin introduced me to Bian Zhongyun's husband, Wang Jingyao. When we met one July afternoon in 2011, he had recently turned ninety but looked a healthy sixty-five. He lived in a small apartment in west Beijing, not far from his wife's middle school. A portrait of Bian hung below a print of *The Last Supper* in his small living room. He was reluctant to talk about his wife. The forty-fifth anniversary of her death was approaching. The country, he said, had no interest in his story; this was a history that had no place in China today, a history that would soon be forgotten. In the summer of 1966, Bian's story was, unbelievably, far from unique: hundreds, if not thousands, of Chinese school teachers faced the same fate in the first days of the revolution. Tens of thousands of others also took their own lives in that decade, humiliated and denounced without reason. But the victims of the Cultural Revolution are now all but forgotten.

Wang Youqin has spent her life trying to right this wrong. Over the past decade, she has travelled across China, interviewing more than 1,000 families who had lost their loved ones. She has documented the stories of close to 700 victims in a remarkable personal history of that turbulent decade. 'People want justice,' she told me. 'They want to talk. But they cannot because they are still in fear.' Today, very few of the victims or the perpetrators of the crimes want to confront the past. In recent years, a few of the Red Guards have sought out the families of their old teachers to apologize. They are, however, in a minority.

'The victims,' Wang said, 'will become our next terracotta warriors – silent, with forgotten stories.' What was particularly traumatic about the tens of thousands of deaths, Wang felt, was that they took place in schools and homes, carried out by people who knew each other, and who had to go back to their torn-apart lives as if nothing had happened once the horrors ended. 'Mao mobilized people to turn against each other,' she said. 'This was not like Stalin's labour camps or Hitler's death camps, where the state was the perpetrator.' Here, ordinary people became murderers as they turned on one another.

A few years ago, Wang ran into Song Binbin, a Red Guard leader from her middle school, who, Wang said, was present at Bian's struggle sessions. Shortly after Bian's death, Song was given the honour of presenting a red armband – the Red Guards' badge – to Chairman Mao. The photo of Mao and Song is one of the most iconic images from the time, and is one that many Chinese would recognize. 'Does your name [Binbin] mean "courteous"?' Mao famously asked her. 'Yes,' she said. 'Be violent!' he told her.

While the photo went on to become one of the most famous portraits of the Cultural Revolution, few are aware of Song's backstory. Song refused to talk to Wang about those days or of Bian's death. When Bian's old middle school recently celebrated its ninetieth anniversary, Song was, in fact, honoured as an outstanding alumnus. The picture of her, as a young Red Guard, with Mao was put up at the same playground where Bian was beaten to death. It still stands there today. When that photo was put up, Wang told me, Bian's husband was enraged. He wrote a letter expressing his distress, saying it was an insult to the memory of his murdered wife. 'Song's red armband,' he wrote, 'was soaked in [his wife's] blood.' However deep the history is buried, Wang reflected, the memories will linger.

Lessons from the Past

Why do people like Mao Yushi, Yang Jisheng and Wang Youqin fight to preserve the record of events long done and dusted? And why does the Party go to great lengths to silence these voices?

One shared belief unites both those who are fighting this historical amnesia and those who want to keep it buried. It is a belief that this is not just a debate about history, but a conversation that will determine the direction of China's future.

This battle over history sheds light on why Mao's legacy is so important to the Party. To this day, the philosophy known as 'Mao Zedong Thought' remains one of the key guiding ideologies for the Party. Mao's legacy, even with all of its horrors, isn't seen as a black mark. It is seen as something to be venerated. As the Party Constitution puts it in its second paragraph, 'Marxism-Leninism, Mao Zedong Thought, Deng Xiaoping Theory, the Theory of Three Represents, the Scientific Outlook on Development, and Xi Jinping Thought on Socialism with Chinese Characteristics for a New Era' are its 'guides to action'.[13]

The latest ideology was enshrined in the Party Constitution at the nineteenth Party Congress in 2017, which bestowed on Xi Jinping two unique honours that cemented his place as the Party's tallest leader since Mao and Deng. It not only elevated his ideological contribution while he was still ruling, but did so by specifically naming him – an honour denied to his two predecessors, Jiang Zemin and Hu Jintao, the third- and fourth-generation leaders of the Party.

A widely held view outside China is that one of the biggest consequences of the forty years of reform and opening up was that economic liberalization meant an abandoning of all that Mao stood for. But that is not at all how many inside China see it. On the contrary, even after those forty years, many elements of 'Mao Zedong Thought' are still at the core of the Party's DNA. His ideology is invoked by the Party at every major event, and enshrined at the core of its Constitution. And, as many people assume wrongly, it's not just done in name.

The fourth paragraph of the Constitution leaves no doubt as to Mao's continuing relevance:

> With Comrade Mao Zedong as their chief representative, Chinese Communists developed Mao Zedong Thought by combining the basic tenets of Marxism-Leninism with the actual practice of the Chinese revolution. Mao Zedong Thought ... is a crystallization of the collective wisdom of the Communist Party of China. Under the guidance of Mao Zedong Thought, the Communist Party of China led the Chinese people of all ethnic groups in the long revolutionary struggle against imperialism, feudalism, and bureaucratic capitalism, securing victory in the new democratic revolution and founding the People's Republic of China, a people's democratic dictatorship.[14]

Even forty years after economic reforms, the core beliefs of Mao remain non-negotiable guiding tenets for the Party's leadership. This is a belief in perpetual struggle, aimed to ensure the retention of power, whatever may be the cost. Mao's belief in this endless struggle had disastrous consequences for the country, but it also ensured his grip on power. The economics may have been abandoned, but not the politics.

Few people understand this dichotomy better than the Chinese leader currently at the helm, the latest entrant tasked with keeping alive the contested legacy of the Chairman. The suit-wearing top leadership of the Party may have shed many of Mao's beliefs that brought China to ruin. Yet, they have also held on firmly to many of the fundamental founding principles for the Party that Mao envisioned, and have gone to great lengths to protect his legacy, which is seen as constituting a vital part of the Party's right to rule China. We often pay attention, rightly, to the remarkable changes that the country has seen since the early 1980s. But when you focus only on what's changed, you forget to look at what hasn't.

2

The Rise of Xi

THE WINTER OF 1968, TWO years into the Cultural Revolution, was a time of great uncertainty in Beijing. Lives had already been upended, families torn apart. And things were about to get even more chaotic. On 21 December, the *People's Daily* announced it would be 'absolutely necessary for educated youth to go to the countryside to get re-educated by the poor'. And a young fifteen-year-old Beijing resident named Xi Jinping began to pack his bags.[1]

Xi would join 17 million other youth – many just young children – as they left their families behind.[2] Some of them, like him, had already seen their lives turned upside down; so in some strange sense they were keen to leave. Many years later, Xi would reflect, 'Everyone was crying. I was laughing. My family who had accompanied me to the train had asked why, and I told them, I'd cry if I wasn't leaving. How can I be sure I have a future here? So don't cry. And then, their tears turned to laughter.'[3]

During the Cultural Revolution, Xi's father, like many others, had joined the long list of Mao's imagined enemies. He was dubbed a class enemy and suffered humiliating public struggle sessions at the Workers' Stadium in Beijing, which today hosts packed football matches every weekend and is home of the popular club Beijing Guo'an. With his father sidelined, the younger Xi was told, as he put it later, 'You deserve to be shot a hundred times!' Even in those dark times, he found some humour in that curse, wondering to himself, 'I thought there was no difference between being shot once and being shot a hundred times. Why should I be afraid of that threat?'[4]

Xi hailed from the Party's aristocracy – a 'princeling'. His father, Xi Zhongxun, was part of a group of communist leaders known as the 'eight immortals', revolutionaries who emerged as influential state leaders after the founding of the People's Republic. That was until his purge. Like other princelings, the younger Xi grew up in the heart of Beijing, in the elite compounds reserved for top leaders. He was sent away from this upbringing to a world that was unrecognizable – a small, dusty village called Liangjiahe in northwestern Shaanxi. His father was a Shaanxi native, but Xi was a Beijing boy.

Despite his initial optimism, Xi quickly found out that the countryside was not what he'd imagined it to be. He spent his days digging pits to lay water pipes. Three months was all he survived, and he went back to Beijing. But with the city in turmoil and his family among those that were in the firing line, he returned to Liangjiahe on his family's advice.[5]

In Xi's Footsteps

I followed the road to Liangjiahe that young Xi would have taken. Today, it's National Highway 211, a wide expressway full of trucks, and it runs from the old communist base of Yan'an, which is now the centre of the oil industry in Shaanxi. Yan'an's other big draw is tourism, because of its past as the revolutionary base for the communists from 1936 until 1948, and like Mao's hometown of Shaoshan, it is cashing in on the renewed interest in 'Red tourism'.

The highway takes you through cornfields, winding through red loess mountains and past small villages. Liangjiahe is located in a narrow valley sandwiched between sandstone-coloured mountains. Its residents live, as they did four decades ago, in cave homes that have been carved out of the hills. They make a living tending the cornfields. The only major difference, forty years after Xi's time there, is that there are no young hands in sight – only farmers in their sixties and seventies, who watch over the fields, while their children are away working in the booming urban centres of Xian and Yan'an.

The few villagers I spoke to recalled Xi's time in Liangjiahe and Yan'an fondly. 'He was like any one of us,' said one lady in her eighties. 'He could eat bitterness,' she said, using a very popular phrase – *chi ku*, meaning 'eating the bitter' – that describes the tolerance Chinese people have for hardship.

The villagers knew that he was no ordinary youth. His father, Xi Zhongxun, was one of Shaanxi province's most famous sons – a Communist Party revolutionary who rose to the position of vice premier after the People's Republic of China was founded. 'He was no different from the others,' recalled one farmer who knew Xi. 'At that time, even he did not have corn to eat here and survived eating the skin of wheat!'

On returning to Beijing in 1975, Xi joined the elite Tsinghua University. When his father was rehabilitated, as millions were following the death of Mao and the end of the Cultural Revolution, Xi was once again a princeling. His father's legacy and connections paved the way for his steady rise up the Party ranks. Xi would spend three valuable years working in the General Office of the Central Military Commission, the PLA's top ruling body, forging key connections with the powerful military.

Xi was set for a higher-profile posting, but in 1982, he made the surprise decision of leaving Beijing and returning to the countryside, working as a Party official in a poor county in Hebei province called Zhengding. It turned out to be a politically astute move, insulating him from possible criticism that his princeling status gave him only plum postings. From Hebei, he moved to the booming coastal provinces of Zhejiang and Fujian that were at the heart of China's opening up.

Both Xi and the vast Party propaganda apparatus he commands pointedly highlight his time in Liangjiahe as a turning point in his life. When Xi arrived in Liangjiahe in 1969, he was 'anxious and confused', he recalled in an essay he wrote in 1998. But when he left the 'Yellow earth' of Shaanxi province seven years later, he reflected, '... my life goals were firm and I was filled with confidence'. The seven years he spent in Liangjiahe, Xi later reflected, profoundly shaped his political outlook. 'During my seven or eight years in Shaanxi,' he said, 'I got to know what pragmatism was, what seeking truth from facts was, and what the general public was. It is something that will benefit me throughout my life.'[6]

A War on Corruption

With a membership of around 90 million, the Communist Party was, at the time of Xi's ascension, the world's largest political organization.[7] In its six decades as China's ruling party, it has presided over bloody wars, a four-year-long famine that claimed 30 million lives, a decade of turmoil unleashed by Mao during the Cultural Revolution, and thirty years of unprecedented economic growth. The Party arguably faces no serious threat to its rule and continues to enjoy legitimacy derived from three decades of growth.

Yet, the Party leadership remains mindful – some might say paranoid – about threats to its rule. The highest echelons of the Party remain as opaque as ever – the leadership leads cloistered lives and has near-zero interactions with the press – and what we know about it is gleaned from official speeches and pronouncements that the propaganda apparatus churns out on a daily basis. If in the past it was the staid pages of the *People's Daily* that did the job, today it is a multi-billion dollar, multi-pronged and multilingual PR machine, operating on every platform, from WeChat at home to Twitter and Facebook abroad (ironically banned in China).

Of all the threats to its rule, the Party knows there is none bigger than corruption. In China, the corruption of the Party elite is no secret: people here are well aware that corruption greases the wheels of politics and business. As the country has boomed, so have the corrupt. The scholar Minxin Pei writes, 'The emergence and entrenchment of crony capitalism' in China is in some sense 'a logical outcome of Deng Xiaoping's authoritarian model of economic modernization, because elites in control of unconstrained power cannot resist using it to loot the wealth'.[8]

The problem has grown to such an alarming scale that it won't be an exaggeration to say that many in the Party see it as the single biggest danger to its survival. So when Xi took over as the general secretary in November 2012, one of the first things he did was to send a strong signal that he and the Party were serious about combating the problem. Xi pledged that he would bring down not only the 'flies', or lower officials, that the Party, from time to time, purged to show it took the problem seriously, but the corrupt 'tigers' that roamed free among the Party elite.

At the time, Xi's declaration was met with cynicism among most people I knew in Beijing. After all, the Party has generally been careful to protect its own. Surely Xi would not rock the boat? When he came to power, there were no 'tigers' fiercer than Zhou Yongkang, who was the Party's security czar until his retirement as part of the once-in-ten-years leadership change in 2012. He also sat on the Politburo Standing Committee under Hu Jintao, one of the nine men who ruled China (there were always men on the Standing Committee).

During the course of a year, Party investigators sent by Xi methodically went after Zhou's cronies, starting in the Sichuan province and working their way through the oil industry – his bases of power. Then came the bombshell: the Party announced it was investigating Zhou – the first ever member of the elite Standing Committee to face corruption charges. What better way to signal that Xi meant business – and in the process, eliminate an official who was also known to be a political rival?

Xi's Politburo made it a point to lay out Zhou's many offences in great detail. It accused him of 'taking advantage of his posts to seek profits for others and accepting huge bribes personally and through his family'. The statement spared no detail: it said Zhou kept many 'mistresses', and 'traded his power for sex and money'. He was accused of amassing huge assets from businesses 'resulting in serious losses of state-owned assets'. The sordid details made for gripping reading for a Chinese public that has grown weary of official corruption.[9]

Tales of Graft in China and India

I have often thought of how corruption in China compared with that in India. In two very different societies with different political systems, a common cancer proliferated. Considering the opacity that still shrouds the political elite in China, and the larger size of its economy, the world's second largest, it is likely that the scale of corruption there dwarfs India's. Chinese authorities have themselves estimated that as much as 800 billion yuan (Rs 8 lakh crore) may have been taken out of the country as ill-gotten wealth. The Rs 4,479 crore supposedly stashed by 339 Indians in Swiss banks pales in comparison.[10]

There are far fewer checks and balances in China, especially in the still murky state-run sector, where the lines between Party, politics and business are blurred. Zhou Yongkang was a case in point: he leveraged his political connections to amass wealth in one of the most lucrative state-dominated areas of the economy – the petroleum industry. And he was by no means an exception.

As an outsider, I didn't often get a glimpse of this hidden world of wealth, but on the rare occasions that I did, my jaw would drop. I would hear many stories from a friend who worked in helping high net-worth Chinese emigrate to the US, Canada and Australia. He told me his main business wasn't in Beijing, Shanghai or Guangzhou, but in small towns in Hebei or Jiangxi one may have never heard of. In these places, local-level officials or well-connected businessmen had rapidly amassed fortunes – mining was one common source, while real estate millionaires were ubiquitous – and wanted to get their fortunes out of China just as rapidly, and move their families abroad. Such emigration was common even prior to Xi's ascension – a reflection of the confidence of Chinese elites in their political and legal system. The arrival of Xi, and the subsequent crackdown on corruption, only hastened such plans.

One such small-town businessman became an unlikely acquaintance, introduced to me by a common friend. He had made a fortune as one of the biggest real estate players in Beidaihe, a seaside town east of Beijing off the Bohai Sea that's famous as a getaway for the Party elite. I won't forget in a hurry the evening we first met.

Our common friend sent me the address of a restaurant I hadn't heard of, somewhere in north Beijing, near the Bird's Nest stadium. I entered a private room to see my new acquaintance stacking bottle upon bottle of some of the most expensive and hard-to-find Chinese Moutai liquor from Guizhou. I didn't have the heart to tell my host that I preferred to not eat meat as dish upon dish was wheeled in, but I had to draw the line when a massive sea cucumber was placed right in front of me. 'Do you not like to eat it?' he asked. As I stammered, my friend nudged me and said this was by far the most expensive item on the menu. Left with no choice, I had to eat the whole thing, piece by piece. Washing it down with 60 per cent strong alcohol didn't help.

Once dinner was over, we were driven to the villa of a fairly well-known artist who lived close by. The Beidaihe tycoon wasn't wasting a minute of his Beijing visit and wanted to go back with a new painting to add to his collection. It must have been past midnight – after much of the liquor collection had been consumed – when we showed up at the artist's house, who seemed to have just rolled out of bed. He led us down to his basement and showed us some of what was on offer, laid out on a table.

My friend, however, had his eye on a painting that was up on the wall, already framed. That wasn't for sale, he was told. 'I'll pay what you want!' he insisted, offering an extraordinary amount, before proceeding to grab the painting and smash it on the ground.

He extracted the canvas from the debris, rolled it up under his arm, and coolly walked out of the door.

That the scale of graft in China dwarfs that in India is no reason for us to feel sanguine. Corruption in the two countries is, in some sense, two different beasts. In the decade I spent in China, I noticed that corruption is far less of an everyday problem. One reason that the Party – despite the prevalence of so many corrupt officials at the top – still enjoys widespread legitimacy is that it has ensured the efficient (and usually painless) delivery of basic services. Whether it's getting your electricity connection or gas supply or driver's license, the system generally works (and without extra banknotes to move things along).

As the Party-run newspaper *Global Times* once observed of corruption in the two countries, 'The game is the same, only the rules are different.' A Chinese engineer based in India put it succinctly to the paper: 'In India, people are more blatant about asking for a bribe. They will tell you to your face how much it will take to get a license stamped. In China, things are more subtle – you have to guess what's required.'[11] Or to borrow from Xi's vocabulary, in China, the tigers may be much fiercer (and far wealthier), but in India, the flies are overwhelming. And for the man on the street, flies tend to be a far greater nuisance than the tigers you'll probably never have to encounter.

Xi's corruption campaign made itself felt in some unexpected ways. One November morning, elite investigators of the Party arrived at the Beijing home of a PLA general. Zhang Yang – for years one of the top-ranking PLA generals, who served on the Central Military Commission (CMC) under Hu Jintao – had for several weeks been questioned by investigators for corruption, although he hadn't been formally charged. But when the investigators showed up at his Beijing home that day, they found that he had died by suicide.

What was perhaps most surprising about General Zhang's suicide is that it was by no means rare. Between 2012 and 2017 –

Xi Jinping's first term – 158 Chinese officials committed suicide, according to official figures. Insiders believe the actual number may be far higher, considering the number of 'natural' deaths of many officials who were being investigated or were under detention.

This is perhaps the biggest spate of suicides of top Communist Party officials in China since Mao Zedong's Cultural Revolution (1966–76), when tens of thousands took their own lives after humiliating public struggle sessions by the Red Guards. Since 2009, at least 243 officials have died by suicide, according to a study conducted by the official Chinese Academy of Social Sciences (CASS). What is striking is that eighty-five of these cases were in the four years before Xi's ascension in late 2012, or around twenty-one a year. In the four years that followed, during which a mass campaign against corruption dominated Chinese politics and thousands of officials were purged, that number doubled. In this time, 158 suicides, or thirty-nine a year, were recorded.[12]

'It is stressful to be a Party official these days,' Maya Wang, a researcher at Human Rights Watch in Hong Kong, who has studied the Party's corruption crackdown, told me. She noted that 'many of those who kill themselves are under some form of investigation, and one reason, people speculate, is that if they take their own lives, the investigations stop', and they can thus protect their associates, families and their assets.

This sweeping campaign unleashed by Xi was supervised by his right-hand man, Wang Qishan, who he picked to head the Central Commission for Discipline Inspection (CCDI). Under Wang, the Party expanded the scope of investigations as well as the Party's unique extra-judicial practice for probing officials that is called 'Shuanggui'.

While under investigation – which usually ends in conviction, as the CCDI rarely begins probes until a dossier of usually impossible-to-overturn charges is readied – officials are not imprisoned, but kept at home, as in the case of the PLA general, or in hotels or undisclosed locations used by the CCDI. During this time, they are kept in a black hole of sorts for months, with their families in the dark about where they are detained, until they are finally transferred to a prison and the legal process begins. The courts, of course, answer to the Party, which has by then already decided the verdict.

Shuanggui, noted a December 2016 Human Rights Watch study on the opaque system, relies on 'getting confessions by placing those accused under huge psychological stress'. 'The indefinite isolation of Shuanggui, which itself can amount to torture, causes detainees' minds to collapse after three to five days and answer everything you ask,' a CCDI officer was quoted as saying in the report. The study cites a former Party official, Yang Zeyu, who was put under Shuanggui in December 2015. 'The judge in charge of my case told me, in private, that right now we have to fight corruption, so we need to employ these illegal and extraordinary channels. Otherwise, we cannot catch the bad guys.'[13]

The PLA, which has emerged as one of the targets of Xi's corruption crackdown, has thus grappled with a string of suicides. General Zhang was the third senior officer to take his own life under a cloud of suspicion. His death was followed by those of naval officer Senior Captain Li Fuwen, and Major General Chen Jie, a senior political commissar in the PLA's southern command.

Xi has now overhauled the investigative apparatus, with the CCDI replaced by a more powerful National Supervisory Commission. What this means for the Shuanggui system is unclear; some have suggested that moving the investigatory body out of the opaque CCDI to a national-level commission could bring some transparency to the process. 'Setting up the commission could be positive, but I would be sceptical,' Maya Wang of Human Rights Watch told me. 'The CCDI is mostly transforming an unlawful abusive system to something that is codified in law but equally abusive. This does not mean more fairness or transparency but more top-down control.'

End of Collective Leadership

If the struggle against corruption was the defining theme of Xi's first five-year term, the second major campaign was aimed at enforcing Party discipline more strictly. When the National People's Congress, China's rubber-stamp legislature, confirmed Xi as president in March 2013, the 3,000 or so delegates 'elected' him in a landslide. There was only one dissenting vote, leading some to question, perhaps only half-jokingly, if it came from Xi himself. The voting pattern would portend how Xi would tighten his grip after taking charge. Under him, the Party issued new regulations that barred its more than 90 million members from making 'irresponsible remarks' about government policies. One state media editorial called on all Party members to 'conform to Xi' – language not seen since the Mao years.[14]

Xi has transformed the Party in many ways since taking over as general secretary in 2012, and much of how he rules can be seen as a reflection of his own life story. Even though the Party today might be unrecognizable from the guerrilla organization headed by Mao in the hills of Yan'an, what is striking is not how much has changed but how much hasn't. Xi, more than many others in the system, has a deeply personal grasp on the arbitrariness of power in what is a brutal and winner-takes-all system. In fact, he once recalled that he had to apply no less than eight times before getting into the Communist Youth League, and then again apply ten times before the Communist Party accepted him – all because of his family history and the purging of his father. 'Where is the verdict against my father?' Xi had asked. 'When a fault is committed, there is a verdict. But where is the one against my father? Did you obtain the documents from the central government? If not, convey my request. Who do you think I am? What have I done? Have I written or chanted counter-revolutionary slogans? I am a young man who wants to build a career. What is the problem with that?'[15]

The lesson Xi seems to have learnt from his father's story may seem counterintuitive. Institutionalizing the exercise of political power is not seen as the answer to curbing its excesses. Wielding it is. And since taking over as the general secretary of the Party in November 2012, Xi has proved far more adept and skilful than his predecessors, Jiang Zemin and Hu Jintao, in exercising power.

Within five years of taking over from Hu, Xi established himself in the Party lexicon as its third great leader, after Mao and Deng. In a short span of time, he has dismantled the collective leadership system that restrained both Jiang and Hu. The former, for instance, worked in the shadow of Deng, while Hu had to contend with Jiang. Xi has no such constraints, and demonstrated this by removing the two-term limit that Deng had put in place to ensure stable successions. Indeed, it was this model of collective leadership put in place by Deng that arguably allowed China to escape the fate of other authoritarian countries ruled by the whims and fancies of a single dictator.

Xi has dramatically restructured the Party–state apparatus, giving the Party a greater say in running the country, and breaking down the walls between the Party set-up and the state machinery that, in the past, gave China's bureaucrats a veneer of insulation in running government and policy. Now, the Party is back.

China's political and governance model can be understood as a '6+1+2' system, as Zhu Guanglei, a Chinese scholar on governance, puts it. The '6' major groups are the Party's Central Committee, the Central Commission for Discipline Inspection (CCDI), the National People's Congress (NPC) or the lower house of parliament, the State Council or the government's cabinet, the Central Military Commission, and the Chinese People's Political and Consultative Conference (CPPCC), the largely ceremonial political advisory body or the upper house of parliament. The '1' refers to the president, and the '2' refers to the judicial branch, comprising the Supreme People's Court and Supreme People's Procuratorate (prosecutor).

Zhu describes the Party–state dynamic as a balance of 'multi-systems' and 'one main line', which refers to the CPC. What this means is you have a parallel structure that runs from the highest level to the smallest village, one for the Party and one for the government, with the important caveat that the government agencies are 'parallel to the CPC committee of the same level and are subordinate to the ruling party system'. This was, however, in theory, and the government departments were broadly left to their own devices to execute the mandates of the Party, which stayed in the background.[16]

This has changed under Xi, who has brought the role of the Party to the fore. His restructuring of the Party–state machinery has concentrated more administrative power in the hands of the Party, at the expense of the government, which generally functions with a little more transparency than Party organs do (or, to be more accurate, with a little less opacity).

This has reversed a two-decade-long shift that saw a somewhat diminished role for Party bodies. Xi has centralized power by setting up a number of Leading Small Groups (LSGs) that now decide policy on everything from national security to economic reforms. For instance, in the past, economic affairs were largely handled by the premier, who heads the State Council or cabinet, but now, decision-making is by the president. Xi heads the LSG for comprehensively deepening reform, which is now the most important body in setting policy, as well as LSGs for national defence and internet security. According to unconfirmed reports, Xi even heads an LSG on matters related to the South China Sea, underlining how he is now dictating policy directly on matters previously handled by bureaucrats. A one-party state is now a one-man show.

Bridging the Left and the Right

The Xi era is also seeing a narrowing of the already constrained spaces for political debate in China. These limited areas were in the past useful for generating feedback within the leadership – for instance, in testing the waters for new policies. One such institution is the Party-controlled state legislature. Since the founding of the People's Republic in 1949, the 'Two Sessions', referring to the annual convening of the upper and lower houses, have functioned more as elaborate political theatre, aimed at lending legitimacy to the Party, rather than acting as a real parliament. This was not, however, their original purpose.

When the Party came to power in 1949, Mao secured the support of other Chinese political parties by promising them a 'multi-party' set-up in which they would have their say, as the very name of the upper house, the Chinese People's Political Consultative Conference (CPPCC), suggests. Remarkably, these political parties continue to exist in China today as functioning members – at least in theory – of the upper house, although they exist merely to provide the illusion of a multi-party system. These include the rather improbably named China Democratic League and the China Association for Promoting Democracy, which do little else other than endorse the Party's decisions.

While the National People's Congress, which is the legislature, and the CPPCC, which acts as an advisory body, have largely functioned as nominal bodies, rarely turning down government bills, the sessions have at least provided a small but confined space for debate, as well as a rare window to discuss taboo issues. In recent years, for instance, during the annual March meetings, academics have called for pushing stalled political reforms, laws to publicize officials' assets, and greater checks on Party power – sensitive issues that the media is otherwise reluctant to broach. The Two Sessions also offered a rare opportunity every year for journalists to interact with Chinese parliamentarians, even if these interactions were often uninspiring. There were, on the rare occasion, some fireworks too.

My abiding memory of covering the parliament was from the spring of 2012, when Bo Xilai, then the under fire Chongqing Party secretary, held a no-holds-barred press conference shortly after his attempt at a power grab ended in ruin. A disgraced Bo had arrived in Beijing for the year's session, barely a few weeks after his police chief had fled to the US Consulate of all places, in the city of Chengdu, and spilled the beans on murder and corruption involving the Bo family. The episode was a major embarrassment for the leadership. His father, Bo Yibo, was like Xi's father: a famed communist revolutionary figure and an associate of Mao. Somewhat of a hardliner, Bo Yibo often clashed with the more moderate Xi Zhongxun, a rivalry that, many in China believed, was inherited by their sons.

I recall watching Bo Xilai's aides staring in horror as their boss held forth at that press conference for three hours. Bo was all but publicly making a case for his political future – unthinkable for China's Communist Party, which likes to keep such matters behind closed doors – and saying how his 'Chongqing model' of governance was showing the way for China's future. Curiously, Bo had to repeatedly stop his monologue and leave the room for telephone calls (presumably from the Party leadership telling him to shut up, someone suggested), but he would return unperturbed and carry on. A few days later, on the last day of the parliament, Bo was publicly chastised by Wen Jiabao, the then premier, before being summarily sacked the very next day. He is today serving a life term in a prison in Beijing's suburbs.

The purge of Bo ended a heated ideological debate that was convulsing China in the months before Xi's ascension. The former had emerged as the poster boy for what was being called China's 'New Left', not only for the 'Road to Revitalization' campaign that harked back to Mao's politics but also for what was being touted as his 'Chongqing model' of governance, which envisaged a greater role for the state. Bo's low-income housing projects in Chongqing and agricultural reforms had won him admiration among the left.

The New Left intellectuals were staunch critics of China's embrace of capitalism and the free market, and the growing inequality and corruption that had emerged in the years after reforms. Prominent among them were the academics Cui Zhiyuan and Wang Hui of Tsinghua University, and Wen Tiejun at Renmin University, who were strong critics of China's reforms process. The right in the country broadly referred to those who were pushing for both market reforms and a more liberal politics – in short, for a retreat of the state. The New Leftists themselves resented the label, seeing it as something 'right-wing radicals use ... to discredit us, make us look like remnants from the Maoist days'.[17]

He put a firm end to this brewing left–right divide. His politics appeared to smartly borrow from both camps. If Bo Xilai spoke, as we have seen, of a Mao-inspired 'Road to Revitalization', Xi made the 'Road to Rejuvenation' a major theme of his political message. He also borrowed from Bo's playbook a hard line on corruption. Bo had launched a 'smash the black' campaign in Chongqing to both neatly eliminate his rivals and tighten his grip over his municipality. As for the right, Xi's message on discipline quickly put an end to debates about constitutionalism and greater political freedoms that the group was championing in the lead-up to the 2012 leadership transition.

Very quickly, both left and right fell in line. A year into Xi's first term, I travelled to Beijing's suburbs to meet Wen Tiejun of Renmin University. When not in the classroom, Wen and his students run a commune in a farm outside Beijing. His students plant vegetables, tend to the chickens, and run a small donkey farm. The ideological debates were already a thing of the past by then. 'We need to go beyond ideology, beyond concepts such as left or right,' Wen told me. 'I am not trying to fight the mainstream, but only trying to give another voice, so people can decide what is in their interest.'

Wen was of the view that Xi was taking the arguments of the left seriously, in terms of bridging the urban–rural divide. 'The coastal areas developed faster. A lot of industries were set up for export to the West. Now, their market [for exports] has declined, so we have no choice but to invest inland.' He hoped the next decade under Xi would bring 'a new kind of rural–urban integration' that would help bridge the widening divide between the cities and countryside. Whether or not that gap would be overcome, what Xi did bridge was a growing political divide, stamped out firmly with his enforcing of Party discipline.

The drama of 2012 seems a distant memory. Party discipline is the watchword now. When Jiang Hong, a well-known academic, gave an interview to a magazine in the spring of 2016 before the annual sitting of China's parliament, he was doing what the Party-appointed Members of Parliament have done for years: testing the waters ever so gently. In the interview, Jiang had expressed his worry that MPs in China were increasingly fearful of 'talking too much'. Encouraging them to speak out, he reminded them that the Party had 'a tradition of hearing different opinions', and that free speech was 'enshrined in the Chinese Constitution' (although, he chose not to add, limited in reality). Soon after the interview was published on the website of the magazine *Caixin*, the article vanished, leaving some to wonder if the Party was now censoring even its own MPs. The magazine published a brief statement declaring that the internet censorship authority had taken the article down. And that statement too was promptly censored.

The already rubber-stamp NPC is now all but defunct, and the already remote likelihood of political liberalization has receded further. In the past, some Chinese intellectuals had seen the NPC as a potential vehicle for future political reforms. That prospect is fast diminishing. Currently, China only permits elections for delegates at the lowest levels of village and township governments. But even these affairs have been tightly controlled by the Party, with independent (non-Party) candidates in recent campaigns facing intimidation and threats. One of them was Qiao Mu, a professor teaching journalism at the Beijing Foreign Studies University. He told me he was forced to stop teaching when he contested the local elections in Beijing's Haidian district – an entirely legal act – against his university's president, who was backed by the Party. Qiao was made to vacate his office, and was exiled to the library. He finally emigrated to the US, where he lives today.

Red Families

During one parliament session in Beijing, I met with an MP called Li Hongta. Like most of his fellow MPs, he had flown into Beijing for the session and had spent his entire two weeks in the city cloistered in one of the big state-run hotels on Chang'an Avenue, the Avenue of Eternal Peace. This runs right down the heart of Beijing towards Tiananmen Square and the Great Hall of the People, the massive complex west of the square where the Parliament convenes.

Few people know more about the Party's history than Li. His grandfather, Li Dazhao, had founded the Communist Party of China in 1921 along with Chen Duxiu. Li Hongta sits on the upper house's social welfare and social security committee. When I asked him about the political tightening, he, unsurprisingly, wholeheartedly defended Xi's governance and leadership style. I asked him whether it wasn't true that the parliament, for instance, was just one big show with little substance. 'If you're asking if the Two Sessions are just mere formalism and have no real bearing, then how do you think we can explain to the public why we are even meeting every year for so long?' he countered. I asked him what his grandfather, a rebellious intellectual, would have made of Xi. He looked me straight in the eye and answered, without missing a beat, 'He would have approved.'

The support of the Party's illustrious 'Red families' has been one major factor explaining Xi's rise up its ranks. One glue that tethers Xi and the other members of the 'second Red generation' – or 'Hongerdai' as they are called in China – is their shared sense of being inheritors of Mao's revolution. As one Hongerdai put it to me, they saw the technocrat leaders of the previous generation, who did not descend from the first generation of communist leaders, as mere stewards and managers who were looking after their family asset.

This sentiment explains why Xi, more than his predecessors, has fixated on the issue of ideology as a coherent and binding element to keep the Party and its members in line. This was made clear in one of his very first speeches, made behind closed doors to Party officials in January 2013. It was delivered during what was called Xi's 'Southern Tour', invoking Deng Xiaoping's famous 'Southern Tour' of 1992 that set the stage for China's opening up. The text of the speech was obtained by the veteran journalist Gao

Yu, who was subsequently jailed for seven years for stealing state secrets.

In the speech, Xi emphasized a startlingly different message from Deng's in 1992. 'Why did the Soviet Union disintegrate?' Xi asked.

> Why did the Soviet Communist Party collapse? An important reason was that their ideals and beliefs had been shaken. In the end, 'the ruler's flag over the city tower' changed overnight. It's a profound lesson for us! To dismiss the history of the Soviet Union and the Soviet Communist Party, to dismiss Lenin and Stalin, and to dismiss everything else is to engage in historic nihilism, and it confuses our thoughts and undermines the Party's organizations on all levels.[18]

Two key lessons from the Soviet Union, in Xi's view, were ensuring the Party's control over the army – and thus preventing the emergence of a 'neutral' army – and resisting any attempt to introduce 'Western' political reforms. 'Why must we stand firm on the Party's leadership over the military?' he asked.

> [B]ecause that's the lesson from the collapse of the Soviet Union. In the Soviet Union, where the military was depoliticized, separated from the Party and nationalized, the Party was disarmed. A few people tried to save the Soviet Union; they seized Gorbachev, but within days it was turned around again, because they didn't have the instruments to exert power. Yeltsin gave a speech standing on a tank, but the military made no response, keeping so-called 'neutrality.' Finally, Gorbachev announced the disbandment of the Soviet Communist Party in a blithe statement. A big Party was gone just like that. Proportionally, the Soviet Communist Party had more members than we do, but nobody was man enough to stand up and resist.[19]

The second key lesson, Xi said, was to resist the persistent clamour for political liberalization, which has a not-insignificant constituency in China, particularly among the liberal intelligentsia.

Xi's speech reminds us how the world often misperceives the Chinese leadership when they speak of 'reforms', assuming its endgame is a liberal democratic state. On the contrary, when the Party speaks of reform – or when Xi speaks of reform – it is referring to reforming the CPC machine to strengthen its capacities for one-party rule, not to make it democratic. Xi said, 'Some people define reform as changes towards the universal values of the West, the Western political system, or it will not constitute "real" reform.'

> This is a stealthy tampering of the concept and a misunderstanding of our reform. Of course we must uphold the banner of reform, but our reform is reform that keeps us moving forward on the path of socialism with Chinese characteristics. We will walk neither the closed and rigid old path, nor the evil path of changing the flag ... We are still in the early stage of socialism, and we must do whatever we can to realize the goals of the current stage. But if we lose sight of our vision as communists, we will lose our direction and succumb to utilitarianism and pragmatism ... The great renewal of the Chinese nation has been the greatest dream of the Chinese nation over the last couple of hundred years. The 'Chinese Dream' is an ideal. But of course, as communists, we should have a higher ideal, and that is, communism.[20]

A Question of Timing

The year of Xi's ascension, 2012, was a tumultuous one in Chinese politics. The Bo Xilai scandal had exposed a split in the leadership, while there were grumblings among the Party elite that Hu Jintao's staid style had led to a drift, both in policy and leadership. There was a yearning for change.

And Xi made the most of it. In one sense, as the scholar Cheng Li writes, Xi was 'lucky enough to arrive at just the moment in history when his consolidation of power – to upset the inertia and possibly even prevent a split of the CPC leadership – was appealing to the Chinese public and most other Chinese leaders'. What helped him in this quest was his 'assembly of strong loyalist networks' in the Party, particularly among his fellow Hongerdai. This gave Xi the space to carry out 'bold political moves ... endorsed by the political establishment, but only as urgent, ad hoc measures to safeguard Communist Party rule.'[21]

Xi was the right man, at the right place, at the right time, Zhang Lifan, a historian and follower of elite Party politics, who lives in Beijing, told me. Zhang keeps a close eye on the political elite. He is, in some sense, one of them. His father, Zhang Naiqi, founded the China National Democratic Construction Association, one of China's eight officially recognized political parties (all of which essentially follow the CPC).

Zhang outlined to me how Xi was able to skilfully master the system. 'Before he came to power, there were many negative feelings about the collective leadership system inside the Party. Every member of the Politburo Standing Committee had their own power, their own opinion, and no one was taking responsibility. They wanted a strongman to take charge and change this situation.' They perhaps got more than they bargained for.

Zhang says key to Xi's ascendancy – and ensuring the support of the Party families – was his use of the anti-corruption campaign. Almost every family, he said, would have something to hide, so when Xi went after the first few big 'tigers' who were his political rivals, everyone quickly fell in line. 'Many families are afraid of being caught,' Zhang said, 'and do not dare to fight him. This allowed him to centralize power rapidly.'

If Xi's accumulation of power was seen by many in the Party as necessary to counter growing challenges, in Zhang's view the solution to the problem itself posed the biggest risk. Leaving aside the question of political succession, which had been given some stability through the collective leadership model and through the imposition of term limits, there is now the problem of personal accountability. 'The consequence of centralization is that all responsibilities fall on you too,' Zhang said. 'If you do well, everyone will support you. But from a rational point of view, if you want to disperse the risk, you need to give up some of your power.'

According to the historian, the biggest threat to Xi is the economy. He sees the basic compact between the Party and the people, of delivering growth in return for acceptance of Party rule, as the ultimate guarantor of the CPC's power. 'It does not matter if the Communist Party's leadership changes – the economy has to keep growing if the Party wants to keep power,' he said. 'One character of the Chinese people is that they don't care about high-level political fights, but they care about their livelihood.'

Zhang is right that the Party has to keep delivering on the economic front to keep up the grand bargain it struck with the people of China after Tiananmen. This explains why the Party under Xi has been searching for other sources of legitimacy, such as through Xi's 'Chinese Dream' campaign that highlights the country's 'rejuvenation' as a source of national pride.

This sentiment, for Xi, is a powerful force to tap. Not far from where the general secretary spent his years in exile is an old communist base called Yangjialing, where Mao established his headquarters, just outside Yan'an city. It was in here that the Party launched the revolution that brought it to power. For twelve years, Mao Zedong, Zhou Enlai and other leaders lived there, carving out homes in the caves of Yangjialing's loess mountains, which provided them protection from Japanese air raids.

During one visit to the caves, I ran into the eighty-two-year-old patriarch of the Zhang family, who had travelled 700 kilometres with three generations of his clan – ten hours on a cramped sleeper bus – to pay their respects to the communist revolutionaries. I sat with him on a park bench as he took in the swirling crowds of mostly young tourists, all snapping photos outside the cave homes once inhabited by Mao and Zhou Enlai, the former premier.

My companion was amused by the chaos and commotion, expecting a far soberer scene at a site of such historical significance. A young Chinese couple sat posing, sporting wide grins, on the foot of a bed where Zhou Enlai once slept, making V signs for the camera. They wore matching bright yellow shirts, and the girl carried a Louis Vuitton handbag.

Outside the cave, the leader of a tour group bellowed instructions into a megaphone. 'Travellers from Hunan! Red caps! Stand on the left! Shaanxi! Yellow caps! Stand on the right!' A group of tourists posed in front of a photograph of a young Mao taken by the journalist Edgar Snow. A sign above the photograph read '*tong xin, tong de*' – of one heart and one mind, a call to unify the Party. Nearby, half a dozen hawkers had set up shop, selling everything from 'Mao Zedong cigarettes' ('Only 30 yuan for a taste of the Yan'an spirit!') to posters of Mao, Zhou Enlai and the former President Liu Shaoqi, who was later purged by Mao ('Mao Zedong, only 50 yuan! Zhou Enlai, 40 yuan! Liu Shaoqi, 35 yuan!').

My companion told me he joined the Party in his twenties and had been a member for more than half a century. He lived through the famine triggered by the Great Leap Forward and survived the turmoil of the Cultural Revolution. Rehabilitated in the late 1970s, he was given a job as a low-level government official in the province of Shaanxi. There, he told me, he witnessed first-hand the turnaround in the country's fortunes. When he grew up, his family didn't have enough to eat. He had relatives who lost their lives to the famine.

His son isn't extraordinarily wealthy, but is comfortably well-off; he works at a bank in the provincial capital and sends his son to a private school. The Zhang family goes on two holidays every year. Their story is par for the course, reflecting the rise in prosperity in just one generation. 'Are our lives better now?' he repeated the question I posed to him. 'Those days were hard, no doubt. Today, we do not lack anything. I can eat meat every day.' He then paused and reflected. 'But if I had to answer your question,

I would say those days were better. We had less, but we felt more satisfied.' He had a sense of longing for a time when there was some meaning, even if the meaning came from the misguided revolution that Mao sold them. That, he felt, was missing in post-Mao China. This sense of vacuum is widely shared by many of his generation: a sense that China has, despite all its prosperity, lost its way, become a country without a sense of purpose, a society without a moral compass. And Xi hopes to fill this vacuum. Whether he is able to do so will, more than anything else, determine the success or failure of his grand project.

3

A Battle of Ideas

IN THE SPRING OF 2013, when Xi Jinping was four months into his leadership of the Party and was just one week into his presidency, I received an unusual invite. It was to a commemoration, on 15 April, of the twenty-fourth death anniversary of Hu Yaobang, the former Party general secretary whose demise sparked the unprecedented demonstrations that led to the Tiananmen Square protests in 1989. Hu is beloved by liberal and progressive elites in the China, although his ideas for a more moderate and open political system have been confined by the Party to the dustbin of history. Unlike previous leaders like Mao or Deng Xiaoping, Hu is rarely mentioned in state media today. His death anniversaries, given the sensitivity and the memory of 1989, aren't usually celebrated. But April 2013 was an unusual time in China.

In the weeks leading up to 15 April, a number of commentaries appeared in Chinese newspapers discussing Hu's legacy. 'Now that we are allowed to celebrate Hu Yaobang again, are times changing?' someone wondered on Weibo, China's Twitter equivalent, after one such article appeared in a Shanghai newspaper. An article was one thing; an event was something else.

I made my way to the venue – a small museum located in the corner of Beijing's massive Chaoyang Park – which was already packed by the time I got to the door. A hush descended when the star of the evening entered – Hu Yaobang's eldest son, and for many liberals in China, the great white hope and carrier of his father's legacy.

Hu Deping held the room in rapt attention as he spoke for an hour, showing rare photographs from his father's life. One photo, in particular, drew a gasp from the crowd. It was from 5 February 1980, and Hu Yaobang was on an inspection trip to the mountainous and poor province of Guizhou to see how reforms could help bring development. He was in the company of two young officials. One was the Secretary of Guizhou's provincial Party committee, named Hu Jintao, and the other a vice director in the Party's General Office, named Wen Jiabao.

The mood in the auditorium that evening was upbeat. After the talk, someone in the audience asked Hu Deping about democracy and the rule of law. Deping was always careful to not talk too directly about the present, and used the trick now perfected by Chinese scholars who point to moments in history as an indirect way to talk about sensitive current issues. 'We all care about this issue,' he replied thoughtfully. 'We should rule the country by law and treat the Constitution as if it is sacred.'

He told a story about Emperor Han Wendi from the Han Dynasty (206 BCE–220 CE). The emperor was on his horse during a trip when a passer-by accidentally startled it. Enraged, an accompanying official demanded the person pay a fine. The emperor, however, insisted that the matter be left to the law, and that no punishment be imposed without a sentence. 'Democracy,' Hu said, 'should start from law. And, in my view, democracy, law and freedom are closely related.'

A month before Xi took the reins of the Party in November 2012, Hu penned an essay making the case for China to move towards constitutionalism as a guiding political model.

> Some of the rights included in our Constitution have not been backed up by written laws that make sure they are guaranteed. In the political, economic, social, cultural and

> other fields there are still many cases in which the civil rights awarded by the Constitution are either damaged or disrespected and some of these cases are very serious. The existence of these problems not only harms the healthy development of the country and violates the rights of the people, it also damages both the position and the ability to govern of the Communist Party of China. For a state with a Constitution but in which constitutional governance is not practised, the document simply contains empty words on a sheet of paper.[1]

The Party, Hu went on, had 'learnt a profound lesson from history about what happens when we as a nation disregard the Constitution, put aside the Constitution, damage the authority of the Constitution and do not rule the country in accordance with the Constitution or the law'. 'The disaster of the Cultural Revolution was so painful, the country, the people and the Party all suffered heavy losses, and one of the fundamental causes of all this turmoil was that the Constitution and laws became empty words. We need to make sure that this lesson remains etched deep in our minds,' he concluded.[2]

The article generated a lot of debate in Beijing. The battle of ideas between the liberals and the Party conservatives was a relentless tug of war, and here a shot had been fired. Rumours surfaced in Beijing that Hu had paid a visit to the home of Xi – a fellow princeling – a few months before his Party ascension. And the event that spring evening only lent weight to a growing perception of a decisive shift in this battle of ideas. That was certainly the mood in the room.

How wrong it turned out to be.

Document Number Nine

One single document, issued just five months after Xi took over as Party general secretary and around the time of Hu Deping's evening speech, laid out in the clearest possible terms that this battle of ideas was all but over. At the time of its release, 'Document Number Nine' attracted little attention, in China or abroad, but it's perhaps the clearest marker yet of the political direction in which China is heading under Xi. The Central Committee–issued document, titled 'Communiqué on the Current State of the Ideological Sphere', lays out a detailed overview of what the Party sees as its biggest political threats and the action it plans to take to address them.[3]

A Communist Party document is perhaps an unlikely source to help dispel the widely pervasive – and misplaced – notion outside China that the Chinese people are somehow uniquely uninterested in democratic freedoms. But Document Number Nine does just that. Its authors seem to be convinced that it's the receptivity of the Chinese population to the idea of 'universal values' that carries the biggest threat to continuing Party rule. To that end, it called for an all-out campaign to stub out any cries for pushing universal values in China (which, it should be noted here, wouldn't be necessary if the locals were as uninterested in such ideas as many people in the rest of the world seem to believe).

The main message from Document Number Nine was that the current 'ideological situation' facing the Party was 'a complicated, intense struggle'. Among the most dangerous trends it identified were the promotion of Western constitutional democracy as 'an attempt to undermine the current leadership', pushing 'universal values' which, in its view, was a Western concept, and promoting civil society 'in an attempt to dismantle the ruling party's social foundation'.

The document underlined why the question of history is so important to the Party – and why voices like Mao Yushi and Yang Jisheng believe it is so inextricably tied to the question of China's political future. The communiqué came down firmly against questioning the official narrative on historical events, particularly in assessing Mao's legacy. As the document put it:

> The goal of historical nihilism, in the guise of reassessing history, is to distort Party history and the history of New China. This is mainly expressed in the following ways: Rejecting the revolution; claiming that the revolution led by the Chinese Communist Party resulted only in destruction; denying the historical inevitability in China's choice of the Socialist road, calling it the wrong path, and the Party's and new China's history a 'continuous series of mistakes'; rejecting the accepted conclusions on historical events and figures, disparaging our Revolutionary precursors, and vilifying the Party's leaders. Recently, some people took advantage of Comrade Mao Zedong's 120th birthday in order to deny the scientific and guiding value of Mao Zedong thought. Some people try to cleave apart the period that preceded Reform and Opening from the period that followed, or even to set these two periods in opposition to one another.

In the view of the Party, as the document makes clear, maintaining ideological control is a life-or-death struggle. This has also been a constant theme of Xi Jinping's speeches to Party members. As the Chinese scholar Li Junru has observed, calling for an 'unswerving adherence' to the Party was perhaps the most recurring theme of all of Xi's talks over the first five years of his presidency, and he made at least five speeches on the subject of ideology. Most notably, in 2015, Xi came out with what he called a 'three stricts and three earnests rule' for Party members: to be strict in 'self-development, exercise of power and self-discipline' and earnest in 'making plans, opening up new undertakings and upholding personal integrity'.[4]

In another speech, he outlined what he called 'five symptoms' of Party officials showing 'a lack of backbone'. These symptoms, in Xi's view, ranged from scepticism about communism and a 'yearning' for Western political systems to the 'worship of the Buddha':

> Some are sceptical about Communism, considering it a fantasy that will never come true; some do not believe in Marxism-Leninism but in ghosts and gods, and seek spiritual solace in feudal superstitions, showing intense interest in fortune-telling, worship of Buddha and god's advice for solving problems; some have little sense of principle, justice, and right and wrong, and perform their duties in a muddle-headed manner; some even yearn for Western social systems and values, losing their confidence in the future of socialism; and others adopt an equivocal attitude towards political provocations against the leadership of the CPC, the path of socialism with Chinese characteristics and other matters of principle, passively avoid relevant arguments without the courage to express their opinions, or even deliberately deliver ambiguous messages.[5]

These are views that China's leaders rarely express to the world, particularly when it comes to their distaste for what Xi calls 'seeking spiritual solace'. But, as one Beijing friend often reminded me, to really try and understand what China's leaders think, pay more attention to what they say at home, especially when they don't say those same things abroad.

Controlling the Classroom

Xi's first five years brought about a dramatic transformation in China's intellectual landscape. And nowhere did I see this more clearly than on university campuses in Beijing. Since the early 2000s, the opening up of China's economy also meant an opening up of its universities, which began to forge greater links especially with the West. With this came a massive improvement in the quality of China's higher education institutions, some of which are now among the best in Asia. It also brought about a space for debate. Yet, the strange irony is that even as the global footprint of Chinese institutions is expanding, at home that space is now being squeezed.

In November 2015, China's State Council, or cabinet, announced a plan to 'develop world-class universities and first-class disciplines' to make the country's schools more competitive globally. The focus is on improving the quality of faculty and research, a key determinant in most rankings, with the aim of getting universities into the world's top 15 by 2030.

On a Saturday morning in 2016, I travelled to Xi's alma mater, the elite Tsinghua University in west Beijing, where some of China's top educators had gathered. The occasion was the launch of the latest ambitious initiative in China's drive to build the 'Ivy League of the East' – a network of world-class universities that would attract top foreign minds, and perhaps more importantly, stem the flow of Chinese talent to the West, a problem that has, as in India, plagued its research institutions.

At the centre of this drive is Tsinghua University, the country's top-ranked educational institution that is not only Xi's alma mater but also that of his predecessor Hu Jintao. I was there to witness the unveiling of a new $400 million scholarship programme, modelled on the University of Oxford's famed Rhodes Scholarships, aimed at tapping the best Chinese and foreign talent. In attendance was Liu Yandong, a member of the Communist Party's Politburo, who was at the time the top official in charge of education policy. Also present was the American billionaire and Blackstone CEO Stephen Schwarzman, who donated $100 million for setting up the programme to be based at the newly built Schwarzman College at Tsinghua, a stunning building with every modern facility, designed in ancient Chinese style.

Schwarzman and Tsinghua University turned to David Li Daokui to head their 'Rhodes' programme. Li is a Harvard-educated economist who returned to China to become one of its most influential scholars, advising the government on policy and heading Tsinghua's finance department. He told me that he was optimistic about where China's education sector was going.

Tsinghua, and a number of Chinese universities, had made great strides in opening their doors to the world and becoming more global, which he believes goes some way in explaining their recent rapid rise up global university rankings. That year, three universities figured in the top 50 for the first time, with Tsinghua at 24.

'It is still relatively early, but we're making good progress,' said Li. 'There are two aspects to this, faculty and students. On the faculty side, many schools in Tsinghua already have recruited top non-Chinese academics to teach. In the finance department, which I was heading, we attracted the world's best insurance expert from the US, who now holds a chair. We are competitive in terms of pay, and that is often the bottom line.' On the student front, the record is mixed. The total number of foreign students in China has tripled in the past decade to around 4,00,000, but few campuses are truly international and language remains a barrier. The Schwarzman programme, Li said, hoped to change that. Around twenty of its 110-strong first batch are Chinese. Its scale is small, but the hope is to create the culture of an international classroom. 'Our programme is an accelerator in this regard,' he said. 'What we are also doing is putting pressure on the university to be more international, and to be bilingual.'

Taking a leaf out of the country's economic reforms, where foreign companies were encouraged to set up joint ventures in the 1990s in exchange for allowing their partners to absorb their technology and experience, Chinese universities have been far more aggressive than India's in courting global partnerships. Ironically, China's Party-controlled education system has in many ways been more flexible than India's, arranging numerous joint degree programmes and pushing every major university to have a top global partner. It has also welcomed foreign universities to set up campuses in China. New York University has a campus in Shanghai, established with East China Normal University, while Johns Hopkins has opened a graduate school in Nanjing.

Peter Salovey, the president of Yale University, had travelled all the way to Tsinghua for the launch of the Schwarzman programme.

He told me that key to the success of China's universities going global was their embrace of such partnerships. His university already had a number of partnerships with Chinese schools. With Tsinghua, it offers a dual degree master's programme in environmental sciences, where Tsinghua offers its engineering expertise while Yale contributes on the policy side. Students will receive master's degrees from both. Yale has similar partnerships with Peking University for nanotechnology and Shanghai Jiao Tong University for bioinformatics.

'Part of the success of Chinese universities will be building these kind of partnerships with top universities throughout the world,' Salovey said. 'That will make it more likely that students from around the world will come here to join incredibly talented Chinese students on these campuses, and create universities that are more international in flavour over time. I see that happening.'

Yet, adopting global standards is far from a straightforward process in China's strictly controlled education system, where Communist Party secretaries on campus are even more powerful than university presidents. This is less of a problem in the sciences or economics, but foreign students in any department will still find censored internet with no access to Google, Twitter or YouTube – hardly convenient for an academic environment (although software to scale the 'Great Firewall' of China – as the system of internet restrictions is known – is widely available).

'I joke that we are a special education zone,' Li told me. 'I told our faculty and students that within the Schwarzman College they will have 100 per cent academic freedom as understood in most other countries. Everything can be discussed here. Our scholars come here to understand. They don't come here to provoke a revolution. They don't plan to go to Tiananmen Square to protest. They come here to learn.'

But the rest of Tsinghua's students aren't given this privilege. 'As for the whole university, that is a complicated issue,' acknowledged Li. 'The university has its own ideas and systems.' At the same time, he hopes the push to go global will have a trickle-down impact and bring greater openness to other campuses. 'It is possible especially with other international programmes. For instance, Tsinghua's global MBA and public policy programmes are also adopting the same policies, so it is a step-by-step process.'

Not everyone shares his optimism. Qiao Mu, the professor who emigrated to the US after standing for polls as an independent candidate, told me he saw a huge contradiction between plans to open up the education sector and a crackdown at home. While embracing Western faculty and research methods, the Party is at the same time waging a war against 'Western ideas' that it sees as threatening. Party committees are enforcing a stricter control in university classrooms, and space for academic research in the humanities is shrinking.

Academic freedom may not be much of an issue in the sciences, where China is taking the lead, but here too there are other challenges when it comes to research. One reason for its surge in global rankings is a massive increase in funding. In 2012, Beijing spent 1 trillion yuan (around $150 billion) on research programmes. In that year, the number of full-time researchers in China had grown to 3,14,000, up by one-third from 2005. The number of published articles rose by 54 per cent to 1.1 million, while patents rose eight-fold to 66,755. But quantity doesn't mean quality. Zhang Jie, who heads the fourth-ranked Shanghai Jaio Tong University, lamented in one widely cited essay that the quality of research was 'sluggish' in part because of 'ossified practices in evaluation' and a system that rewarded 'quantity over quality'.[6]

Yi Pi, one of my close friends in Beijing, works in a medical research start-up. He returned to China after completing a graduate programme at Duke University. Yi largely agreed with Zhang's assessment. In the US, he told me, there was much greater support for research. 'We need to fully embrace their methods when it comes to teaching and research,' he said. There are other smaller practical challenges as well, such as not having access to resources such as Google Scholar, which is blocked in China.

The Memory of Tiananmen

Across the street from the Tsinghua University campus is its great rival, Peking University. If Tsinghua has produced some of China's brightest engineers and financial brains – not to mention, at least two Party General Secretaries – Peking University, or Bei Da as it is known, has occupied a unique space in China's political history. Since its founding in 1898, the university has played a key role in its country's cultural evolution. In the second decade of the twentieth century, the students propelled the New Culture Movement, and subsequently led the marchers to Tiananmen for the transformative 4 May 1919 protests that swept the country and energized nationalists, opposing the government's acceptance of the Treaty of Versailles that ceded parts of China to Japan. China's great writer of the twentieth century, Lu Xun, who spent time at Bei Da, wrote famously that the university had an indomitable spirit that could never be extinguished.

Seventy years after the 'May Fourth movement', it was Bei Da's students who drove forward the pro-democracy protests that convulsed the country in the summer of 1989, in part mobilized by the death of former leader Hu Yaobang in April of that year. The students ignited a nation, inspiring people across social divides, as they demanded free speech and an end to the rampant corruption. Their protests, as the world knows, came to a tragic and brutal denouement on the night of 3 June, as Deng declared martial law and sent in the PLA to clear Tiananmen Square of protesters. Hundreds, if not thousands, were killed that day. Contrary to popular opinion, few deaths occurred in the square itself, which had been vacated largely before the troops moved in. It was ordinary Beijingers in ordinary neighbourhoods who were shot and killed as the troops fired at will and moved in to take control of the contested capital.

One evening in late May 2009, a few days before the twentieth anniversary of Tiananmen would come and pass in utter silence in Beijing, I went to Bei Da to dine with a few students who were happy to share their thoughts about what happened in Tiananmen

Square. The subject of the protests is taboo in China today. They find no mention in textbooks, the media or in public debates. Like the Great Leap Forward or Cultural Revolution, it's an event the Party would rather forget – in many ways the chapter of history it would like to forget the most. If one does see, from time to time, some amount of reflection on the Great Leap Forward and the Cultural Revolution, none whatsoever on 1989 that questions the Party's 'conclusion' is tolerated. In the Party's view, the young protesters, who in fact saw themselves as nationalists and patriots attempting to cleanse the country, were 'counter-revolutionaries' and 'rioters'. The Party is so concerned about public debate on 1989 that even small private gatherings ahead of the anniversary are disrupted.

The Party's relentless silencing has been effective. 'China was in chaos, the Party had no choice,' one student told me over dinner that evening. These were not students who were clueless about what happened on the night of 3 June. They all had software that allowed them to scale the 'Great Firewall' with ease to watch YouTube videos from 1989. Yet, despite all the information they had access to, they still found the Party's rationale persuasive – if only because of the decades of prosperity that have followed 1989. I won't easily forget the words of one young girl at Bei Da who told me, very calmly, 'I would have done what Deng did.' Lu Xun was wrong about the Bei Da spirit; 1989 had crushed it.

What is most difficult to grapple with when it comes to the memory of Tiananmen, as writer Louisa Lim notes, is that the 'legacy of 1989 has not been all dark'. The decisions that stemmed from that year transformed China and brought prosperity to millions, and propelled the country's military and economic resurgence. Deng Xiaoping opened up the Chinese economy, embarked on economic reforms, and dramatically altered the role of the Party: it retreated from the lives of China's citizens in many ways, and gave them the freedom to pursue their lives and livelihood as they chose fit – to work, to choose their own jobs, to travel overseas. 'People shifted focus,' writes Lim, 'devoting their energies to buying apartments, setting up companies, and navigating the myriad of new opportunities offered by the economic liberalisation that was changing the world around them. All this happened not despite Tiananmen, but because of it.'[7]

Confronting the past has been traumatic and difficult even for those on the other side of the divide, like the former PLA soldier Chen Guang, who was among the troops on the streets of Beijing that night. 'Many have risen to positions in the government because they participated in the "suppression of counter-revolutionary turmoil", as the government calls it; some were promoted,' he told Lim. 'They didn't think it was a bad thing at all,' added Chen, now an artist whose works derive from his trauma and guilt. He is among few people who want to confront, rather than bury, this national memory, at great personal cost. 'They felt it was necessary,' he said of the leaders. 'To this day, they feel it was necessary.'[8]

That Tiananmen cannot be separated from China's subsequent success is what troubles people like Chen. The cost of the bargain is that many may never be given due justice, as the Communist Party still labels them 'rioters'. People like twenty-year-old Xiong Zhiming, shot by the PLA as he tried to rescue a female classmate. Like Wu Guofeng, also twenty, shot in the back of his head as he was riding his bicycle, camera in hand. Like Chen Yongting, yet another twenty-year-old, shot on the square, the first from his village in western China to go to college.

None of them are remembered today on the grand square. One afternoon when I visited it, a tour guide, leading visitors from around the world, described it as 'a symbol of national pride'. Young Chinese, in designer clothes, posed in front of the Mao portrait that hangs on Tiananmen gate. A video playing on newly set up screens on the square proclaimed President Xi Jinping's vision of a 'Chinese Dream' of national rejuvenation and prosperity. Old retirees from the provinces toured the square, rightfully proud of their country's resurgence.

It is possible that Tiananmen may be entirely forgotten by the current generation of young Chinese. Those who are fighting to preserve the truth – and the stories of those who lost their lives that night – are relegated to the fringes of society. The student leaders of 1989 are mostly in exile, in Taiwan or in the US, their influence fading to near oblivion. Ahead of Tiananmen's twenty-fifth anniversary in 2014, I travelled to Taipei to meet Wu'er Kaixi, the most charismatic of the student leaders. Back in 1989, the image on television had stunned a nation: a young student with unruly hair, voice raised, interrupting Premier Li Peng mid-sentence, scolding him on live television during a meeting in the Chinese parliament building that he attended wearing his hospital pyjamas.

Wu'er Kaixi rose to fame during the turbulent summer of 1989, becoming the face of the student movement. His meeting with Li Peng, on 18 May 1989, was at first seen as a great victory for the students, who were campaigning for dialogue to bring political reforms and an end to corruption. But barely two weeks later, it would end in tragic failure. Wu'er fled to Hong Kong, named number 2 in the 'most wanted' list of twenty-one student leaders the Party was hunting, behind fellow student leader Wang Dan. He never returned to Beijing, and today lives in exile in Taiwan.

Since 2009, Wu'er has made four attempts to return to China: boarding flights in Taipei and Tokyo, and trying to cross over from Hong Kong. He was prevented from doing so on every occasion, leaving him in the unique position of being a 'most wanted' fugitive who has, ironically, been pushed away despite his best attempts at turning himself in. What he wants, more than anything else, is a public trial in China that would reopen the debate on 1989.

'The Chinese government is afraid to have me back,' Wu'er told me. 'In 1989, we called for a dialogue, that is the slogan we introduced. They answered our demand with tanks. That dialogue never really occurred. I still want that, even if it has to happen in a Chinese courtroom, even if it is in the form of an indictment.' Over two decades on, he said, he was homesick. 'Living in exile has become a mental torture; it has become intolerable,' he said. 'I have not seen my parents for twenty-five years'.

What makes Wu'er's story even more striking is that he is an ethnic Uighur, the Turkic minority group that is native to China's western Muslim-majority Xinjiang region. His parents live in the regional capital, Urumqi. He cannot stop worrying for their safety, and has little knowledge of their whereabouts. In 2016, around a million Uighurs were placed in what China called 'training' centres, which were broadly camps, where they were forcibly interned in what the government framed as an 'anti-extremism' campaign.

Wu'er told me that for the students in 1989, one of their biggest symbols of inspiration was Mahatma Gandhi. They saw fasting as a powerful, non-violent method to make their case for reforms, unite the nation and win its support, and pressure the Party to have a dialogue. The tactic helped re-energize the movement in May 1989, when the protests appeared to have run their course. 'India earned its independence with an amazing struggle led by Mahatma Gandhi on a moral level,' he said. 'A non-violent movement completely shook the world.'

Looking back today, Wu'er believes the deal the Party struck with the people following the opening up of 1992, giving a certain degree of economic freedom in exchange for political submission, cannot last forever. 'Once you give people economic freedom, they will become a little bit more powerful and want more freedom,' he said, as the people would want 'rule of law and fair competition' to protect what they've made.

The Great Revival

The Party is well aware of this risk, which explains much of what drives Xi's thinking – from the relentless struggle on the ideological battlefield to campaigns aimed at ensuring the its grip doesn't, even for one second, slip. Many intellectuals in China have a dim view of the direction in which the country's political future is heading, and few have better captured their sense of anxiety than Xu Zhangrun. A professor in Tsinghua University, Xu penned a searing essay in the summer of 2018 that set China's internet alight, of course before it was scrubbed by the censors. Xu argued that Xi had upended several basic political principles that characterized China's post-reforms era, the first of which was a sense of basic security and stability that was a source of the Party's legitimacy. 'Most people were willing to put up with the existing political arrangements, in other words: "You hold onto the reins of power; I'll enjoy my personal life."'[9]

The other key principle that was now buried was the set ten-year term limit for the post of president, which many in Beijing saw as a key factor that enabled successful transitions of power over two decades. 'So, everyone came to believe that now, no matter who you are or what you do [that is, regardless of how bad or incompetent Party and state leaders might prove to be], at most you'll only be in power for ten years,' Xu wrote. 'People were hopeful that China would continue to move in the direction of becoming a normal, and normalised country, one in which both property rights and human rights would, over time, be granted appropriate expression in, and protection by, the Constitution.'[10]

Xu's essay, I heard from many in Beijing, was by no means an outlier but reflected the unease among many Chinese intellectuals about the political direction under Xi Jinping. In the wake of the Party's initial handling of the COVID-19 pandemic and the cover-up in Wuhan, Xu, the real estate tycoon Ren Zhiqiang, and other public figures voiced strong criticism of what they saw as a political climate that was taking China backwards, not forwards.

That is not how the Party sees it. In its view, the changes made in the Xi era are key to its survival – and for what it likes to call the 'Great Rejuvenation of the Chinese nation'. Scholar and legal theorist Jiang Shigong of Peking University's Law School, who has emerged as one of the more influential intellectuals in the Xi era, captured this view in a widely circulated January 2018 essay. He explained why the Party had declared the start of a 'new era' under Xi, which he saw as the fourth phase of the Communist Party's evolution. The first was the twenty-eight-year period as a revolutionary party until the founding of the People's Republic of China (PRC) in 1949. The second phase was from 1949 until 1978, which he rather generously describes as the period of 'standing up' – despite the calamitous Maoist turmoil – leading to the period of 'getting rich', which marked the start of the third phase of the reform era. Now, Jiang says, is the transition from 'getting rich' to 'becoming powerful', a phase he expects to last until the 100-year anniversary of the PRC in 2049. This is incidentally by when, according to Xi, China would have accomplished its 'Great Rejuvenation', including establishing what the president calls a 'world-class' military force. Jiang writes that Xi's ascension happened 'at a moment of historical crisis', presumably referring to the stasis of the Hu years, corruption and an eroding sense of legitimacy for the Party. The most interesting part of Jiang's essay is his understanding of how the Party under Xi is looking to renew its legitimacy. The idea, he says, is to turn to 'the brilliant political imagination of thousands of years of Chinese civilisation [to] successfully fill the spiritual vacuum left by the weakening of the Communist vision'.[11]

In Jiang's view, what he calls 'nationalist political confidence' is a 'spiritual force consolidating the entire Party and the people of the entire nation'. A sense of 'national self-confidence and feeling of pride' are the Party's biggest asset, in his view, which would lead Xi to adopt a strong nationalist governing philosophy. This explains why Xi's first big campaign after taking over was selling a 'Chinese Dream' of rejuvenation. 'From this perspective,' Jiang writes, 'the great revival of the Chinese nation is not only an economic and political revival, it is also the revival of a new tradition of political education supported by a political system and by core values, that will result in the great revival of Chinese civilization.'[12] One compelling reason for Xi's emphasis on ideology is the awareness that the basic post-Tiananmen compact has a shelf life. Behind many of his campaigns, which suggest he is turning to nationalism as an important source of legitimacy and unity, is one key realization: economic growth cannot forever remain the source of the Party's legitimacy.

PART II

ECONOMY

4

The Manufacturing Miracle

THE DEEP PENETRATION OF CHINESE manufacturing in the daily lives of Indians is on stark display in the Yijie crafts company, a small shop owned by Zhao Qingfeng. Hidden away in the maze that is the world's largest commodity market in Yiwu, a bustling trading town in the eastern coastal province of Zhejiang, the shop houses paintings and statues of more than half a dozen Hindu religious deities. On one shelf is a Tanjore-style painting of baby Krishna. Another carries the distinctive image of Saraswati on a lotus, a common sight in many Indian homes. These paintings, crafted almost perfectly, were produced not in Coimbatore or Chennai but in Cangnan, one of the many factory towns that dot the green Zhejiang landscape.

Zhejiang, one of the earliest regions in China to embrace economic reforms in the 1980s, is famous in the country for its entrepreneurs. Where there's a business opportunity, people in China like to say, you'll find the businesswomen and men of Zhejiang. Entrepreneurs like Zhao Qingfeng, who today finds himself running a business catering to people who live in a country he has never visited and who follow a religion he knows next to nothing about. From Cangnan's factories, the gods and goddesses make their way to the sprawling Yiwu commodity market.

If there's a 'Made in China' product in an Indian home, chances are it has passed through Yiwu at some point along its supply chain. Every statistic about Yiwu is staggering. The commodity market, one Yiwu government official told me, stretches over 5.5 million square metres – the equivalent of 750 football fields. I asked him how many days I would need to spend in the city if I wanted to visit the entire market. 'If you spend three minutes at a booth and eight hours a day visiting,' he said, 'it will take you a whole year.'

I made three visits to Yiwu over a span of five years, and I came away with the feeling that I'd only just scratched the surface. Strolling through the market by day was a source of endless fascination. In the evenings, I would wind up at one of the dozen or so Indian restaurants in the city, all of which do thriving business. No surprise, considering you cannot walk 10 yards through the Yiwu market without stumbling across a trader from India. To be sure, there are traders from all over the world – from the Middle East, Africa, Russia and Europe – all here seeking 'Made in China'. But for many of Yiwu's suppliers, it's trade with India, above all, that drives their businesses.

Every year, Yiwu officials told me, around 4,00,000 Indian businessmen descend on the city, accounting for three out of every four foreigners. In 2015, when I visited, there were around 250 Indian trading companies with permanent partnerships in Yiwu city, where around 1,000 Indians now reside permanently. That year, Yiwu shipped $1.8 billion worth of goods to India – more than to any other country – out of its total exports of $34 billion.[1]

Make in China, Buy in India

'The mountains are high, and the emperor is far away' is a Chinese saying you see quoted so often that it's become a cliché. You only need to visit a town like Yiwu to see that it is, nonetheless, quite true. Yiwu is a world away from Beijing. If the political capital can feel claustrophobic, this southern town feels like a veritable Wild West.

Yiwu is a gritty town, where businesses appear to rise and fall every other week. Deals are struck with the shake of a hand. Contracts can mean nothing. The city was in the news for the wrong reasons in 2012 when two Indians, Deepak Raheja and Shyamsunder Agarwal, were held hostage by locals after their company allegedly defaulted on payments of 10 million yuan (around $1.5 million).[2] These cases make the news, but they are outliers. You only need to see the steady stream of incoming businessmen (and they are mostly men) to see that the Yiwu model works.

There are traders from every corner of India patrolling the dimly lit corridors of the market, looking for bargains. One afternoon, I spotted a trader from Rajasthan procuring cartons of 'authentic' Rajasthani jewellery from a Chinese entrepreneur, jewellery that will be sold to unwitting foreign tourists in Jaipur. There are men from south India ordering pipes and electrical lights. A trader from Chennai said there was now a factory in Zhejiang that was producing 'authentic' Kanchipuram silk saris. In fact, Kanchipuram weavers had reportedly even been flown in to Zhejiang by an enterprising Chinese company for their brains to be picked. The saris were now being sold in Tamil Nadu, again to unsuspecting buyers. Investigations into this company's whereabouts, however, proved fruitless. There is a bit of Indian selling too. A trader from Delhi was negotiating prices for incense sticks with a tough Chinese woman entrepreneur. Was there actually a market for 'Made in India' in China today? 'Maybe only incense sticks,' she shrugged. 'Some Buddhists in China like to buy them.'

Wang Yifeng is one of Yiwu's most successful entrepreneurs. He started out on the factory floor but made a fortune when he started making artificial jewellery, which is one of the city's big businesses purely because of the Indian demand. That a city with no history in designing or producing jewellery is now one of the biggest centres of the trade underlines the resourcefulness of Yiwu's entrepreneurs. The market exports several hundred million dollars' worth of artificial jewellery to India and the world every year – in India they are sold everywhere, from Rajasthan to Andhra Pradesh.

There's nothing you can't find in the Yiwu market – that is, if you manage to locate the store that stocks what you're looking for. It takes me more than an hour one afternoon to locate He Hailuo, a prominent local businessman, who is one of the biggest exporters of Christmas decorations to the US, Europe and South Asia. Yiwu alone accounts for 60 per cent of world trade in Christmas decorations, and was once described by the BBC 'as the city where Christmas is made and sold'.[3]

He Hailuo's massive store on the fourth floor of the Yiwu market is packed with Christmas trees, lights and decorations. I visit just as a large shipment to India is readied. In between last-minute checks of consignments, he tells me it's not all smooth sailing. His biggest concern is rising wages – now far higher than in neighbouring Vietnam and Thailand – that threaten to undercut one of the key elements of Chinese competitiveness. At the same time, he is convinced that the supply chain in China is so deeply integrated and well oiled that it will be a long time before production moves en masse to Southeast Asia (not many in China look at India as a credible option).

'Some companies are moving to Vietnam,' he said. 'But where else would I have fifty suppliers and such a smooth supply chain?' From factories in Zhejiang and nearby Jiangxi, where labour is still cheap, goods are transported on four-lane expressways. There are no inter-provincial barriers or tax changes or hold-ups. The goods are then shipped from Ningbo, Shanghai or Guangzhou – ports with capacities unrivalled anywhere else in the world.

It's no surprise that India imports more goods from China than any other country, worth around $75 billion out of a two-way bilateral trade of $93 billion in 2019.[4] After China, the most imports come from the US, Saudi Arabia and the United Arab Emirates, which together account for a little less than what China alone sells to India. It isn't only the Yiwu type of 'Made in China' goods that are driving imports. Just as the country's manufacturing is moving up the value chain, so are the kinds of goods India is buying.

The largest imports today are electronics, electrical machinery, heavy equipment and chemicals. China accounts for around 75 per cent of India's telecom equipment imports. Three in every four Indian power plants use Chinese equipment. Between 70 and 80 per cent of all Active Pharmaceutical Ingredients (APIs), a key import for India's pharmaceuticals industry, come from China. All of this explains why, year after year, occasional social media campaigns to boycott China goods fall flat. Contrary to public imagination, we import far more than plastic buckets and cheap toys.

That it is cheaper for Indian companies to send designs to a factory in rural Zhejiang and have products – whether a baby Krishna painting or custom-made furniture or children's toys – shipped to Kolkata or Mumbai, rather than have them made in India, is both an illustration of the success of the China supply chain and the failures of Indian manufacturing. Yiwu presents a snapshot of what China's manufacturing did right – and why India continues to be in its tight embrace.

The Right Lessons

The conventional wisdom in India about China's economic miracle is that it was largely the result of one factor more than anything else: a centralized, efficient and heavy-handed state that was able to carry out infrastructure projects with a speed that India can only dream of, whether it was to build highways, skyscrapers or Special Economic Zones (SEZs).

When we look at the success story of China's economy, it's skyscrapers and SEZs that come to mind. But most of what we associate with China's economic take-off – the export and infrastructure boom – largely came in the 1990s and 2000s. The start of the country's economic miracle – and the greatest period of poverty reduction in its history – actually came in the preceding decade. The 1980s of China are, however, almost entirely absent in the world's imagination and understanding of its growth story. This matters because if we look at the 1980s, we draw entirely different lessons from what China got right.

It wasn't top-down, state-led infrastructure that first propelled economic growth, but greater decentralization and bottom-up economic entrepreneurship, starting in places like Zhejiang. One of the most important – yet, most forgotten – elements in kicking off the growth story was the role of rural entrepreneurs, starting in the 1980s. As the research of Massachusetts Institute of Technology economist Huang Yasheng has shown, this began 'first by dramatically improving agricultural yields and then by starting many small-scale businesses in food processing and construction materials'.[5]

Following the end of the commune system and Deng Xiaoping's market reforms in 1978, China's growth was propelled by a groundswell of millions of Township and Village Enterprises (TVEs), which were mostly private enterprises that 'produced a powerful surge of strong and balanced growth'. Most of the TVEs were run by private entrepreneurs who found a way, through these rural-based enterprises, to increase their income and go beyond agriculture. And until the mid-1990s, these rural entrepreneurs accounted for 30 to 50 per cent of all private sector activity in urban China.[6]

By 1985, there were 70 million people working in all rural enterprises. What we tend to forget is none of China's subsequent infrastructure boom would have been possible without this rural revolution. As Huang Yasheng writes, 'Many observers failed to ask a basic question: "Where did the government of such a low-income country get the money to finance all this impressive urban infrastructure?" The answer: rural China.'[7]

On one visit to Yiwu, I met Pradeep Shetty, a Mumbaikar, who is one of the longest-residing Indian businessmen in the city. Shetty is a leading figure of the resident Indian community, and has been trading with China since 1994, when he moved to

Hong Kong. He sources a variety of goods from China, including electrical items, bags, luggage and jewellery, and is one of the biggest suppliers of sunglasses to the US market for many brands. He also has a factory in Zhejiang province where he produces clothes for export. Shetty is an Indian who is making in China for the world.

'It's unbelievable,' he told me over dinner in one of Yiwu's Indian restaurants. 'You have thousands of Chinese employed merely to design artificial Indian jewellery. A friend from Mumbai orders twenty-five to thirty containers every month. And it's the same with toys. The Yiwu story is something of a miracle.'

Shetty told me that Yiwu was historically a poor town. It was cut off from the rest of Zhejiang, surrounded by mountains. Most of its inhabitants were farmers. When China's reforms began in the 1980s, many left for nearby provinces to find work in factories. They would return home once a year with all the unsold goods of their places of work. In the 1960s and 1970s, farmers could not do any kind of business, for it was disallowed as capitalist activity. After the reforms, TVEs began to mushroom. Much of Yiwu's entrepreneurship owes its antecedents to these TVEs. In the early 1990s, these enterprises were perfectly placed. 'Traders from the Middle East first started coming here to buy this stock in bulk,' Shetty said. 'Trade then took off from there. The rest is history.'

Two factors were key in enabling this transformation: the human capital that was able to seize the opportunity from Deng's reforms, and the willingness of the central government to decentralize and allow local governments to experiment with policy, which would have been sacrilege under Mao. The first generation of rural entrepreneurs 'were far better educated than their non-entrepreneurial peers'. Despite the political chaos of the Mao years, the communists in their first decade of rule were able to do more than India did in establishing health services. As early as 1965, China boasted better basic education and longer life expectancy for its citizens than India did, which has been suggested as one reason why many Chinese in the countryside turned to entrepreneurship in the 1980s, while only few in India did.[8]

The popular perception is that centralization was a key factor in propelling China's growth – and one big advantage over federal and democratic political systems, such as India's. The evidence actually suggests the opposite. The Party under Deng Xiaoping carefully studied the Soviet Union's collapse and drew at least four key lessons.[9] The first was to avoid the political liberalization and political reforms pushed by Gorbachev that were seen to have weakened the Communist Party's grip. The second was the need for sustained economic growth and market reforms.

Two other takeaways warned of the 'too centralized decision-making' that slowed down development, and rigid propaganda and information systems that did not allow officials to receive accurate information. Implementing these changes was by no means a straightforward process. While the general impression is that China's reforms were a linear process – that Deng snapped his fingers in 1978 and growth took off – the reality was anything but that simple. There was a reason why the reforms process was described by Deng as 'crossing the river by feeling the stones'. A franker assessment, as one official put it, was 'walking a tightrope over a bottomless pit – and the rope behind you is on fire'.[10]

Even though the 1980s reforms were successful in removing the shackles that had restrained Chinese people through the Mao years, the liberalization – which was not just economic, but also political in a period of unprecedented openness – initially led to inflation, corruption and discontent, culminating in the pro-democracy student movement, the Tiananmen Square protests, and the brutal crackdown by Deng in 1989. After Tiananmen, as China faced both economic and political isolation, the widespread expectation was that with the collapse of the Soviet Union, the Communist Party of China would follow suit. Deng realized the need for shock therapy to revitalize the economy, but the problem was that after Tiananmen, the conservatives, most opposed to market reforms, held sway.

Often, Deng faced considerable resistance from those within the Party opposed to market reforms, such as the powerful Chen Yun. Deng was fortunate to have trusted lieutenants to push the process at various stages, often drawing on the success of bottom-up cases before scaling up. The liberally inclined Zhao Ziyang, who was general secretary until Tiananmen, was followed by Zhu Rongji, who served as the first vice premier and then as the premier under Jiang Zemin, who was basically in charge of running the economy after Deng's famous 'Southern Tour' of 1992 began the opening up process.

Zhu pushed the massive reform of state-owned enterprises (SOEs) and the momentous privatization of the housing market, and steered China through the process of accession into the World Trade Organization (WTO), which would both be hugely significant decisions. The number of SOEs reduced from 2,62,000 in 1997 to 2,10,000 in 2008, with employment in the state sector falling from 113 million – 60 per cent of total urban employment in 1995 – to 64 million in 2007, just 20 per cent of urban jobs. The housing privatization programme starting in 1998, under which SOEs had to sell housing to their occupants at a discounted value, was by some measures one of the greatest wealth transfers in history, valued at $540 billion or one-third of the country's GDP when it was completed.[11]

The World's Factory

If Yiwu is a nerve centre of the supply chain, Dongguan is the heartbeat of Chinese manufacturing. Through the early 2000s, it was among the most prosperous manufacturing hubs in the world. Between 2003 and 2006, its economy grew at close to 20 per cent annually. Today, the city has twenty-three five-star hotels, all built in a fifteen-year time span. Few other cities better illustrate the breakneck growth of 'Made in China'. In the summer of 2015, when I decided to visit the factories of Indian companies that had a presence in Dongguan, it was, however, in an unusual slump. The evening I arrived, the usually bustling city centre was a ghost town. And the reason wasn't quite what you'd expect.

Besides being one of the largest centres for manufacturing, Dongguan also has the rather unseemly reputation of being one of the biggest centres for prostitution in China, its 'sin city'. Prostitution is illegal in the country, but in reality, widely prevalent, and particularly so in the southern cities that first embraced the reforms and opening. The authorities' approach is in some sense emblematic of the flexibility and pragmatism of the reform era. Since it was a source of substantial income and employment, local governments (many of whose officials were among the most regular patrons of the 'KTV' karaoke parlours, where more than karaoke is usually on offer) were happy to look the other way.

Yet, they were, from time to time, forced to carry out crackdowns to show that the Communist Party took the problem seriously. (After all, prostitution had been banned entirely by Mao.) The crackdown when I visited the city in 2015, however, was different. A huge team of 6,500 police raided 2,000 entertainment venues, underlining the scale of the business. By some accounts, between 5,00,000 and 8,00,000 people in Dongguan worked in the business – that's one in ten of the migrant population.[12] The city is now trying to shed this image of sleaze. 'Many wives feel anxious whenever their husbands take business trips to Dongguan,' as the Party secretary of the city put it. 'It's disgraceful.'[13]

I drove out of the city to the factory of Wipro Consumer Care & Lighting in the suburbs. I was greeted by Nagender Arya, who headed the company's East Asia, Middle East and Africa operations. A dizzying range of products rolled off the assembly line, from shampoos and lotions to soaps that are being used in homes from the Philippines to India and Africa, all made in Dongguan. Arya told me he had drawn two main lessons from the manufacturing hub's experience. 'They had built the infrastructure before the manufacturing set-up came,' he said. 'So this made everything possible. That's on the hard side. On the soft side as well, they got it right. They have pretty fast clearances for most manufacturers, and a lot of support from the local government, whether it is a local company or a multinational player.'

One of the most common observations I came to hear during visits to dozens of companies over the years – Indian, Chinese or others – was the eagerness of local governments to do business, and to make doing business easier. There were at least two reasons for this. For one, a key metric of assessing local officials' performance was the amount of foreign investment and the number of foreign enterprises they were able to attract. The second was the encouraging of inter-provincial competition for foreign investment. If Guangdong made you an offer, Zhejiang might make you a better one, throwing in, for instance, free land.

Down the expressway from Dongguan, towards the bustling provincial capital, Guangzhou, is another massive Indian factory where Essel Propack makes tube packaging. Starting with a small $2.5 million investment, the company now has five factories in China. Murugappan Ramasamy, who heads the company's international business wing, told me the single biggest factor behind the company's expansion was 'the speed of single-window clearances'. Connectivity helps too. An eight-lane expressway links the factory to the Guangzhou port, which is one of the world's busiest. In fact, five of the top ten busiest ports in the world today are in China.

The year I visited Guangzhou, I learned that every month, India ships up to 9 million tonnes of iron ore to China – by far India's biggest export. Much of the ore from the mines of Karnataka and Orissa eventually finds its way to the Guangzhou port, and then further up to factories such as Su Jianguo's on the city's suburbs. At the Guangzhou Sea Link Industrial Corporation, the ores from India are efficiently processed into myriad objects, from casters (a special kind of wheel used in shopping carts, wheelchairs, airport trolleys and even trucks) and locks to door closers and handrails for airport terminals.

The locks that roll off Su's assembly line bear a familiar label for an Indian eye – the brand name 'Godrej' is prominently etched into the steel. Every year, 10 million locks are packed into 1,000 crates, which make their way from Guangzhou's sprawling state-of-the-art port, across the Indian Ocean, to Godrej's warehouses, and eventually, to Indian homes. Su's handrails, meanwhile, adorn the shiny escalators at the new Bengaluru airport, while his door closers ensure the airport terminals in Hyderabad stay climate-controlled.

Every year, Guangzhou Sea Link ships $4 million worth of goods to India. And it isn't just low-end locks and accessories that southern China makes for India using ores and natural resources from the country. A few hours down the eight-lane expressway from Su's factory lies Shenzhen, where telecom giant Huawei is based. Huawei sells millions of dollars of telecom equipment to India every year – equipment that has helped fuel India's telecom revolution. And, 100 kilometres north is the base of one of China's biggest power companies, Shanghai Electric, which only in 2010 signed a record $8.3 billion deal to sell thirty-six power generators to Reliance Power.

'Chinese companies are realizing that India is perhaps our most important market in the next few decades,' Su told me in his Guangzhou office, which is stacked with a range of goods he ships to India. On one shelf are paperweights with an image of goddess Saraswati rendered perfectly. Another has glass idols of the god Ganesh. 'Earlier, we were all focused on Europe and the United States. But without a doubt, we need the Indian market.'

Su was part of the first generation of entrepreneurs unleashed by Deng's reforms. His company opened its first factory in Guangdong province, where the reforms began, in 1981. Following the financial crisis in 2008–09, Su told me, he began to notice a gradual change in local factories' patterns of production, the focus shifting from the West to emerging markets, such as India and Southeast Asia.

The rising Indian demand for Chinese goods propelled the country to become India's largest trade partner. But Su believes this trend isn't going to last forever. He has raised workers' wages by 30 per cent in the past twelve months, in keeping with the rest of Guangdong province. Rising labour shortages, in part driven by demographic changes, and a growing demand for higher wages among an increasingly assertive workforce have reduced Chinese competitiveness. 'The export model is changing,' Su said. 'This trend of China exporting to India, and the world, will not continue forever.' In fact, he told me, he was already considering shifting his production base out of Guangdong. His preferred destination was India.

Workers of the World

More than the infrastructure, it was labour that cropped up, in many of my conversations with factory owners, as the single most important aspect of the China model. And what was the biggest surprise to me was that, contrary to widespread belief, it wasn't just about labour being cheap. That was certainly the case in the early 1990s when the boom began. The initial phase of China's factory boom in the south and southeast of the country was largely driven by the influx of millions of migrant workers from the provinces into the hubs of development. It was, essentially, the abundance of cheap labour that laid the foundation for the nation's export-led growth and the unmatched competitiveness of 'the China price'. Back then, the factory towns presented a way out of poverty and a better future. By the time I had my first experience of China's factory towns in 2010, the situation was very different. I was surprised by how fast wages were rising, as I heard from people like Su. What came as an even greater surprise were the frequent reports of labour unrest and strikes that suggested a shift in the balance of power between workers and factories.

For decades the balance of power had been steady. As counterintuitive as it may seem, labour in 'communist' China is hardly empowered. In a strange irony, the labour movement and unions in India have more agency than they do in China. The Party maintains a tight leash on labour unions, fearing instability at the grassroots. The official All China Federation of Trade Unions is widely seen as representing the interests of the Party over the workers.

As Geoffrey Crothall, who studies China's labour trends at the Hong Kong–based China Labour Bulletin (CLB), told me, 'The problem is that the All China Federation of Trade Unions essentially does not have the power to make its own decisions. It is completely reliant on the Party to tell it what to do. It cannot become more pro-worker unless it gets the go-ahead from Beijing. The Party has to tell the union in no uncertain manner, "Your job now is to represent workers, and not act as a third-party facilitator." Whether or not the Party is willing to make the adjustment remains to be seen.'

One generation forward, economic and social contexts, as well as aspirations, are much different. The abundance of cheap labour has dried up. The current generation is better educated and not looking for factory jobs. 'Migrant workers are no longer so constrained for choice when it comes to finding employment,' Crothall told me. 'Now, if a company does not pay good wages, you can possibly go a few kilometres down the road to another town, or even go back home to work on your land.'

What's interesting is that even if wages are rising, and some companies (including Chinese ones) have moved factories that produce lower-value goods – such as clothes and toys – to Southeast Asia, many others are staying put. These are mostly the ones that want skilled labour.

In 2017, Tim Cook, the CEO of Apple, which does most of its manufacturing in China, laid to rest the myth that the only attraction about Chinese labour was cost. 'There's a confusion about China,' he said. 'The popular conception is that companies come to China because of low labour cost.' The real reason, he said, was 'the skill, and the quantity of skill in one location and the type of skill it is'. Cook credited the education system in China, and in particular, vocational training, which the country does on a massive scale. 'In the US you could have a meeting of tooling engineers and I'm not sure we could fill the room,' Cook said. 'In China you could fill multiple football fields.'[14]

China did get its policies and priorities right – in its investments in rural areas, health and education, by developing the vocational institutions that Cook refers to, and by making the right moves to decentralize and experiment at the local level. But the country also had, in many ways, the luck of being at the right place at the right time.

The Decoupling Debate

The border clash with China and the COVID-19 pandemic in 2020 ignited a debate in India about the dependence on Chinese manufacturing, and what could be done to loosen this tight embrace. With rising public anger in the wake of the border clash, social media campaigns called for boycotting Chinese goods, while Indian ministers made pledges to stop major Chinese imports, such as power equipment, although they did not offer clear alternatives.[15]

While the border incidents served as the trigger for the debate, the issues that it raised were not new. The rapid growth in bilateral trade in the 2000–14 period had been hailed by both sides as the most significant bright spot in an otherwise troubled relationship. But the impressive trade volumes masked deep structural problems. The lopsided trade balance had become an increasing source of tension. While imports of Chinese equipment and machinery soared, India's volume of exports to China has remained low, restricted to raw materials, such as low-grade ores, cotton and chemicals. Indian companies, particularly in the IT and pharmaceuticals sectors, have complained of a range of non-tariff barriers that have limited their access to the China market.[16]

In the year 2019, China accounted for 73 per cent of telecommunication equipment, 82 per cent of semiconductor devices, 81 per cent of antibiotics, and 75 per cent of active pharmaceutical ingredients.[17] Forced to retaliate on account of growing discontent from domestic manufacturers unable to compete with Chinese costs, India has imposed anti-dumping duties on ninety-nine products imported from China, and initiated other anti-dumping investigations targeting it more than any other country. Of the ninety-nine imposed duties, forty were on chemical imports, eleven on steel, ten on glass, eight on fibres and yarn, and five on electrical and electronic items and accessories.[18]

Despite the emotive appeal of boycott campaigns, it would be impossible to reduce dependencies overnight, Amitendu Palit, an economist at the National University of Singapore and the author of *China-India Economics,* told me.[19] 'China is by and large widespread across different concentrations. To that extent, it's going to be a difficult choice for India to get out of this dependence and search for alternative partners,' he said. 'What we are seeing in terms of India's trade engagement is the fact that for a variety of reasons, its dependence on imports is getting localized, in the sense that there is not a wide diversification of countries from which it is sourcing its imports. For example, if you look at critical medical supplies, which India has been importing for frontline healthcare workers in the COVID-19 battle, most of these come from China, which is one of the top sources, but, on the other hand, there isn't a very widely diversified source of countries from which India can actually import these either. This essentially means that aside from China, there are probably three or four countries of the world on which India's dependence is increasing.'

With China's centrality to global and regional supply chains, it would be far from easy for companies to relocate en masse. Supply chains had become sophisticated, requiring a whole range of suppliers, each with niche expertise. And, in China's case, the proximity of a huge market was another draw. 'When we look at value chains today, let's say in a post COVID-19 situation, the emphasis on the part of businesses is to make these chains shorter, more resilient, more durable, and locate them closer to the final demand markets,' Palit said. 'This is where we often overlook the importance of China. It continues to remain a major source of final demand. As a result of which, physically shifting supply chains out of the Chinese geography is going to be pretty difficult.'

Can China's manufacturing success story be recreated? That's the question that emerging economies everywhere in the world are asking. As the reforms unfolded, there were two huge advantages particular to China – location and timing – that suggest the prospect of any other country replicating its model is unlikely. China had the example of its East Asian neighbours, Taiwan, South Korea and Japan, to follow, and perhaps most important of all was the Hong Kong factor. As the economist Chen Zhiwu, who heads the Asia Global Institute at the University of Hong Kong and was previously at Yale University, put it to me, 'People often ask me, "Why did the Chinese economy grow so fast after 1978 and especially after the 1990s, but India's didn't?" I reply that's because India does not have a Hong Kong. In 1980, India's per capita GDP was almost twice that of China. By 1991, it was flat, and today it's about half of China's. India suffers from not having a free economy and free port like Hong Kong to facilitate its economy. China was fortunate to have this bridge to the world.' A bridge not just for financial capital, but human capital. 'It was precisely through Hong Kong that successful Chinese in the West could easily bring capital, technology and even their own human capital back to China in the 1990s. I think about the many Indians who are successful in the US, in big tech companies or my colleagues at Yale University, for whom it's not so easy to go back, because India doesn't have a Hong Kong.'

Then there was the timing. China was able to recognize and exploit the opportunities just as global production chains were forming through the opening of the early 1990s, and subsequently following its accession to the WTO in 2001. The infrastructure it was able to create through the 1990s enabled 'a unique and probably unrepeatable combination of low developing country labour costs and good, almost rich country infrastructure'.[20] The big difference from the East Asian experience, however, was the role of Foreign Direct Investment (FDI) flows, which averaged at

3 per cent of China's GDP from 1985 to 2005, compared with only half a per cent for South Korea and Taiwan (and even less for Japan) during their economic booms. As also the role of foreign firms, which played a major part in the export industry, accounting for as much as one-third of exports since the 1990s (a share that rose to more than half in 2005) and more than three-fourths of high-tech exports. The benefits for the country included absorbing their technology, which they willingly shared for access to the China market.[21]

For countries like India hoping to replicate the China story, what adds to their challenge is that the world has changed, Biswajit Dhar, an economist at the Jawaharlal Nehru University in New Delhi, told me. 'Global value chains today are looking quite different, and the data suggests that they are in fact becoming more local,' he said. 'Countries are depending more on their own economies rather than on global markets. This is an impact of the great recession of 2008. So, I don't think that the strategy that China followed, when a large part of the demand came from global markets, can work. It was a global market–driven industrialization strategy, an export-driven strategy, but that is not going to be a reality any more. Unfortunately, that possibility has now passed.'

The question India needs to ask, in Dhar's view, is why there had always been a huge gulf in FDI inflows between the two countries, despite the fact that on most indicators, India is a far more open economy when it comes to policies and regulations. 'The claim Indian governments often make that we are one of the most open regimes is actually true,' he said. 'But why is it that FDI is still not interested in coming here and we are not getting investment in the sectors that we're looking for? I think the reason is clear, and it is that there are skill-set problems in India. Foreign investors get into the sectors where there are acknowledged skills, for instance in information technology. But we don't have similar skill sets in manufacturing. There is a view that since wage rates are lower [than in China], investment is going to come here. That's not true. We all know that it's actually productivity-linked wages that matter, and productivity in India is pretty awful.'

Many of the factors that enabled China's manufacturing rise were unique to its condition, which make it hard to replicate. That doesn't, however, mean we should discount the policies that laid the foundations for the country to seize the advantage when the external conditions proved ripe. What we do know for sure is that many of China's policies, such as investments in health and education, and the rural reforms of the 1980s, underpinned everything that was to follow. No amount of throwing money into the construction of highways and skyscrapers would have yielded dividends without that foundation. Perhaps the most important takeaway, as the economist Huang Yasheng puts it, is that human capital, not physical capital, is the more critical enabling factor in economic growth. And that has been China's advantage over India, not the length of its highways.[22]

5

From Countryside to Megacities

IN THE WINTER OF 2011, I travelled with the Ni family from Beijing to their village in the south, in Anhui province. Every year, the couple makes the long journey back for the Chinese Lunar New Year, which falls either in January or February. I took the high-speed train – as China calls its bullet train network, which is the world's longest – to the nearest stop, from where the village was a one-hour bus ride away. The high-speed train track actually passes right through their village – barely a few hundred metres from their family home. When I got to the village, I was presented with the rather stunning image of a bullet train whizzing past snow-covered fields.

The Ni family had a two-storey, stand-alone house with a small backyard, where ducks and chicken roamed. It was ten times the size of their Beijing home – a shared space where they had only one room, and had to share the bathrooms and kitchen with two other Anhui migrant families. In Beijing, it was common for them to constantly move. They were often at the mercy of their landlords on short-term leases (with no written contract), and, from time to time, the city would embark on eviction drives to 'clean up the city', which meant demolishing the neighbourhood clusters where migrants lived to make way for developments.

The Ni family's village, sitting near the Chaohu lake, had a mix of older abandoned homes and some gleaming three-storey houses. In most homes, as was the case with the Ni family, the grandparents looked after the house and managed the land. The Nis' sixteen-year-old son went to a high school in a nearby town. He stayed at the boarding school during the weekdays, and came home to his grandparents for the weekend. His mother told me that leaving their son behind when he was two years old was the hardest decision they made. She guessed that since she left, over the fourteen years (or 5,000 or so days) they had been apart, they must have spent not more than 300 days together. They talked on WeChat every week, but as he grew older, they had drifted apart. He confided more in his grandparents.

Leaving their son behind is an extraordinary sacrifice to better their lives, and is one that hundreds of millions of Chinese have had to make. The Nis couldn't afford a school in Beijing. China offers free education for nine years, but only in your registered hometown. The household registration, or *hukou* system, a legacy from when the country had a planned economy, entirely determines a Chinese person's access to resources. It is kind of an internal passport, and, in many ways, a *hukou* identity is even more important than national identity.

The week that I visited the village, the usually empty gravel road – the village is still waiting for good roads – was full of cars of those who had come home for the holiday. They all bore different license plates – Beijing, Shaanxi, Jiangsu and Hebei – showing how far and wide the village's residents have spread across China. Over a few days at the Ni house, we met a cross-section of the village's residents. The only thing that united most of them was that they had all given up work in the village. In some cases, their older parents tilled the land, but most have leased out their farmland, some to companies that are taking forward China's plans to mechanize agriculture, and others to farmers from nearby villages and counties.

Their stories were all different. There were labourers, truck drivers and wealthy businesspeople. They came from the same village, had the same education, but ended up with extremely different experiences of China's boom – a microcosm of how unpredictable the transformation has been. The Nis, for instance, faced a daily struggle to save enough in Beijing to send home, moving jobs from construction to truck driving. One afternoon, one of their neighbours popped in to say hello, bearing a gift of fresh fruit for the new year. She cheerily walked in and plonked her brand-new Louis Vuitton bag on the table. She kept her fur coat on – it was freezing in the Ni home without heating.

After she left, I was told how she had made a fortune by starting a construction business in the nearby city of Tonglin. Her son, I heard, was studying in Australia. The Nis' sixteen-year-old son, who was engrossed in a computer game, lifted his head for a second in surprise. His father told me he often wondered how some struck gold, while others didn't. 'I think about this a lot,' he said. 'My friend and I moved to Beijing at the same time. I started driving trucks, and I am still doing that all these years later. He started selling snacks and now has a lot of money. I don't know if it's luck. Or maybe some people are just fated to do better than others.'

The Urban Wave

In 2012, China's economy reached a key turning point. Its 700 million urban population for the first time exceeded the number of rural Chinese. That number will touch 1 billion in the next decade. Remarkably, in 1950, India was more urban than China, with 17 per cent of its population living in cities, compared with China's 13 per cent. In the fifty-five years that followed, China urbanized far more rapidly, with a 41 per cent urbanization rate compared with India's 29 per cent. The gap will only continue to widen. By 2025, China's urban population will reach 64 per cent, compared with 38 per cent in India.[1]

This wave of urbanization has played a huge role in China's economic transformation, which began in the countryside. Chinese officials often note proudly that their cities, unlike those in India or Mexico, don't have slums. The *hukou* restriction is one reason. It disincentivized migrant workers to move with their families, often occupying temporary housing on the sites they worked, for instance. But that is only part of the story. Considering that there are more than 250 million migrants in China's cities, despite the *hukou* restrictions, it is also about urban planning.

The teeming municipality of Chongqing is a great example of China's urbanization experiment. If the growth of the world's great cities in history has been powered by the often unplanned and spontaneous movement of people from the hinterlands – or even from across oceans – the migrants who helped build the world's New Yorks and Mumbais, layer by layer, with their own dreams and ambition, then the Chongqing experiment turned that logic on its head. In 1997, it was carved out of the mountains and valleys of western Sichuan province, becoming China's first municipality in its west (which was important, because it placed it on an administrative par with Beijing and Shanghai, thereby giving it the autonomy to make policy and direct access to central funds).

It is an impressive sight today. As you sail up the Yangtze river in China's west, a towering skyline of lit skyscrapers and massive bridges emerges suddenly out of the mist. Local officials like to think of the municipality of 32 million people as the biggest city that much of the world's never seen. This boast is a somewhat exaggerated one, as less than a third of that number actually live in the city, the rest spread out over a semi-urban and rural agglomeration. Twenty years later, it is a bustling metropolis that is an economic and technological hub in China's west – and incidentally produces one-third of the world's laptops.

When I visited, Tang Wen, a long-serving official in the local administration, told me – over a dinner of spicy local hotpot – that there were two lessons from Chongqing's experience. The first was a sustained and steady building of infrastructure, notably of low-income housing projects, where the city has led the rest of China, by building massive complexes that were open and ready before an influx of migrants even began. The other was finding innovative ways to manage migration; for instance, by reforming *hukou* laws, and allowing farmers to sell their land and acquire urban residencies – an example of how decentralized administration allowed cities to come up with policies to suit their specific needs.

China's governance structure has helped drive this process, starting with devolving greater administrative power to cities. For instance, mayors in China have untrammelled authority to order large-scale projects and transform policy, as long as they deliver the results. India, in comparison, grossly underinvests in its cities, spending $17 per capita on capital investments in urban infrastructure annually, compared to China's $116.[2]

Likewise, with decentralization, which allowed provinces and cities to make the best decisions to suit their local conditions. By some metrics, China is more decentralized than even a country like India, where states are vested with a great deal of authority. The best illustration is the role played by a city mayor in China. In contrast with India, where the city-level administration in most cases is largely powerless, underfunded and beholden to a state government, which has competing priorities, the mayor of a city in China is vested with near complete power in terms of disbursal of funds and in carrying out development projects. While the mayor would report to the city's Party boss – who in turn is answerable to the provincial Party Committee – he (it is rarely 'she' in male-dominated Chinese politics) is still far more empowered than his Indian counterpart.

This system enables rapid development, but not always the most well-considered planning. As much as the myth about how Chinese officials supposedly think long-term and plan in decades is now widely pervasive, it is, in truth, a misrepresentation of the everyday reality of Chinese politics. Just as in India, mayors in China too have fixed terms, and just as with politicians anywhere in the world, their decisions are driven by political considerations and furthering their own career prospects, rather than by some farsighted and enlightened philosophy of governance. Regardless, Chinese cities are plainly much more liveable than Indian ones on almost every indicator, from housing to public parks. The statistics bear out the degree of decentralization. In the period between 1972 and 2000, the average percentage of the share of government expenditure at the subnational level was 25 per cent for democracies and 18 per cent for non-democracies. For China, in the period from 1958 to 2002, the average figure was 54 per cent, and by 2014 it had risen to as high as 85 per cent, a level of decentralization consistent with that of a federal democracy.[3]

Winners and Losers

As many lessons as China's urbanization experience offers, it's important to understand not just the winners but also the losers from this process. Some of the same aspects of the governance structure that enabled rapid development – such as the power that local administrations wield – also imposed huge costs on citizens, who have been compelled to make extraordinary sacrifices in this unforgiving onward march. In 2010, I travelled to Guangzhou to report on the last stage of what was one of China's biggest urban renewal projects. Unlike Chongqing, Guangzhou – with its long history as a trading port – is a city that grew organically. One legacy of that history was a cluster of villages that lies incongruously scattered among the skyscrapers. When Yangji, one of the last standing villages, faced the demolition crews, a forty-year-old woman named Li Jie climbed to the top of her five-floor building and jumped.

Down the road from where she lived, I visited the home of Yao Rongzhen. It was a sight I'll never forget – one ramshackle home that stood out in a sea of rubble. It took me half an hour to get there, clambering over the stone and concrete – all that was left of where people once lived. Yao told me how shortly before Li's death, she was sitting in the living room when the walls of their home came crashing in. Yao was negotiating for higher compensation when the bulldozers converged on her home, without warning. 'Our home collapsed,' she said, pointing to a hole in the wall of her living room. Theirs was the last of around 100 urban villages sitting on 540 square kilometres of prime real estate.

Residents filed petitions to stop the plans, arguing that the compensation paid out by the Hong Kong–based developer was far too low. Men hired by the developer, residents alleged, threatened and assaulted Yangji's residents to sign contracts, also cutting off water and electricity supply. Many residents have since signed the contracts and left the village, leaving only a few 'nail houses' – as the Chinese media terms homes that resist development – that still stubbornly stick out amid an ocean of debris, like Yao's. Her family has lived and worked in Yangji for more than 500 years, and she said the government also saw the village's older ways of life as an anachronism in a modern Guangzhou. 'But where do we go?' she asked. 'We have been living here for generations, and with the money they are giving us, we cannot find a home in this city.'

China's system doesn't offer much recourse to those who fall by the wayside of this development march. That is perhaps true of the development experience of most countries – we are probably kidding ourselves if we think that India's own development experience hasn't imposed similar costs on the disenfranchised despite the recourse to justice that citizens have, in theory. The difference in China is that the model is systemically designed to mute all dissent. I often think of the story of Ma Yalian, whom I met in Shanghai. Hers was a story of what happens when a Chinese citizen openly challenges this system's arbitrariness, and it all began, as so many stories do, with a knock on the door.

On the morning of 4 August 1998, Ma found three officials from a local real estate firm outside her Shanghai home. Demolition papers in hand, they uttered the words Chinese homeowners dread hearing: her three-storey family home in downtown Shanghai was to be torn down to make way for an urban redevelopment project. Then came the second blow. She would be relocated to a cramped, dingy apartment in Shanghai's outskirts, and given little compensation. 'Fight the order at your own risk,' the men warned. In many ways, Ma Yalian's story was hardly unusual. But she fought the law. A decade-long struggle took her across every level of China's judicial system, from a local district in Shanghai to the Supreme People's Court in Beijing, the highest in the land. She faced threats to her life, suffered beatings and spent months in detention centres.

The Chinese Constitution guarantees human rights, the rule of law, and an independent judiciary, as in any liberal democracy. But, given the nature of China's one-party political system, the courts have always functioned within limits firmly set by the ruling Communist Party. It is true that the country's courts today, particularly when it comes to commercial disputes, are far more professional than what Ma encountered. Particularly after China's induction into the WTO in 2001, Beijing has had to professionalize its courts to make them more transparent. The last decade has seen a slew of significant judicial reforms. The Chinese enjoy more legal rights now than they have ever before in the country's history. However, there are limits to this reform. Despite progressive changes in central laws, their enforcement by local governments remains arbitrary at best.

China has a unique redressal system, a legacy from the Qing Dynasty (1644–1911). Citizens can appeal the verdicts of provincial courts – notorious for their willingness to bend central laws for local interests – by petitioning the central government. The petition system has in recent years come under strong criticism from lawyers and rights activists, who say it has grown into yet another mechanism that facilitates the silencing of dissenting voices. Ma told me of her experience navigating this system, which is far from unusual if you are a petitioner. She travelled to Beijing, petition in hand, to appeal the verdict. Her trip didn't last long. Before she reached the national petition office, she was intercepted by Shanghai police officials, who locked her up in a special kind of prison – a detention system run by provincial Party authorities, with the sole purpose of preventing petitioners from having their voices heard in Beijing.

Over the next two years, Ma would make at least half a dozen trips to Beijing. On each occasion, she was, along with other petitioners, detained by officials. On one Beijing visit, Ma managed to secure a meeting with a well-intentioned Supreme Court judge, who she said was alarmed by the facts of her case. He presented her with a court order calling on the Shanghai court to hear her case. But when she returned home, the court refused to heed the order. Finally, in September 2001, she was arrested in Shanghai on criminal charges for 'illegal petitioning activities' – a contradiction in terms, considering petitioning is what passes for legal recourse.

When I met Ma during my first visit to Shanghai in 2008, I was struck by two things: her willingness to tell her story, despite the many threats she continues to face, and her unwavering faith in the law, even after her many failed trips to Beijing and repeated detentions. She said she decided, early on, that the only way she could challenge the legal system was from within. So, at every opportunity she got, she began studying it. She wrote a series of widely read articles in online journals, criticizing the petitioning system and calling for judicial reforms. Slowly, her voice began to be heard in the legal community. Unfortunately for her, it was also heard by the authorities. Following the publishing of her articles, she was sentenced to eighteen months of 're-education through labour' in February 2004, on the serious charge of stirring social unrest.

Ma's case and a few similar ones from the 1990s have resulted in small but significant changes. In 2003, following protests from lawyers, Beijing began dismantling the controversial detention system, but only partially. In cities like Beijing and Shanghai, governments have vastly improved compensation payments, so much so that I've heard of many cases in Beijing where the residents actually wanted their houses to be torn down so they could live off the compensation from sky-high real estate prices.

The urbanization process has brought with it prosperity for many, but has also widened inequalities. Rural China, where the country's growth story first began, is being left behind. That was a story I heard on every trip to the countryside. I remember driving just two hours out of Beijing to one village in Hebei province, called Beixinxiao, which was at the centre of a land dispute. One farmer, Tao Qingyuan, told me how he lost his land to a big development project. When the developers swooped in, he was given no compensation but only a stern warning: protesting would land him in serious trouble. Like Ma, the forty-year-old corn farmer was left outraged, and over five years, he went across every level of local government, starting with the village committee. He filed petitions, hired lawyers and took to the courts. All to no avail.

I often found that these plans divided opinion, broadly on generational lines. In the village next to where Tao lived, older farmers told me how redevelopment projects were stripping people of their livelihood, part of a broader push to acquire small farms and create larger holdings to enable the mechanization of agriculture. In the process, landowners were being moved into residential blocks, paid little compensation and told to find work in the cities, where they discovered they were too old and unskilled to find jobs. The government framed the redevelopment plans as rendering a service – giving farmers, who sometimes lived in ramshackle homes, modern apartments with piped water and gas. As one farmer, Wang Huizhen, asked me, 'How can I grow vegetables in my apartment?' Her two young daughters saw things differently, telling me they saw no future in farming, even if they worried about what their parents would do for their livelihood.

Journey to the West

The inequality that is a legacy of China's urbanization process isn't just urban–rural but geographic as well. If you draw a vertical line right through the middle of the country, you will find, on either side, contrasting growth stories. Much of China's development since the economic reforms and opening up in 1978 has been driven by the booming factory towns along the eastern coast. Prosperity has since spread inward to the fertile river deltas of the east and the south, where poverty has all but disappeared. Western China, however, lags behind.

A vast, barren but mineral-rich region stretching across nine provinces and administrative regions, including Sichuan, Gansu, Qinghai, Tibet and Xinjiang, western China is home to more than one-fourth of the country's 1.3 billion population. It is also home to more than 70 per cent of China's poor, as well as most of the country's fifty-five ethnic minorities. The far west has historically lagged behind the rest of the country. After three decades of growth since reforms, the disparity has only widened. In 2000, the then president, Jiang Zemin, unveiled a massive 'Go West' industrialization drive, pledging to build 35,000 kilometres of roads, 4,000 kilometres of new railway lines, and dozens of factories in the west. His successor, Hu Jintao, earmarked more than $125 billion on infrastructure projects, part of a 'New Socialist Countryside' project.

I could see the benefits of this two-decade-long infrastructure push in Sichuan, where I spent two weeks. My idea was to travel across one of China's largest western provinces by road, driving up from the provincial capital Chengdu to the far northern areas on the Tibetan plateau. The first village I stopped in was Zitong, an easy drive from Chengdu. The first thing that struck me was the importance of connectivity. The four-lane expressway has helped shorten distances, bringing the markets of small towns and cities closer to once-remote villages. The national highway system went from less than 5,000 kilometres in 1997 to 1,12,000 kilometres in 2014.[4] Even more important are the country roads that connect small and hard-to-access villages like Zitong. 'If you want to get rich,' a local farmer Zhang Si Cui told me, quoting a popular Chinese saying, 'the first thing you need is a good road.'

I stood outside her home as we watched a steady stream of tractors and small trucks on the newly laid concrete road that runs right past her doorstep. Getting rich and good roads eluded Zitong for long. Farmers like Zhang, who was in her seventies, watched as the rest of the country, in the south and east, got rich. As Zitong shows, fixing this gap is still a work in progress. Tractors recently bought on government subsidies, with the paint still wet, stood parked in cowsheds that were still in use. An unfinished apartment block, painted yellow and grey, rose above green fields, where paddy grows. 'If you came here ten years ago, you wouldn't have recognized this place,' said Wang Jing Hua, a farmer in his seventies. 'There were no roads, no cars, no trucks. People were just sitting around with no work to do!'

The infrastructure, he said, has been the catalyst to change. It has brought connectivity with the sprawling provincial capital, Chengdu, and access to one of China's fastest-growing tier-two markets. This development has fundamentally changed the kind of agriculture being practised in Zitong. Farmers were earlier only growing paddy, which brought in little money and was largely only for subsistence. But the local government is now supporting farmers to grow different kinds of fruits and vegetables, and plant trees and flowers, all for the Chengdu market. Incomes are rising. Farmers in Zitong said they were earning almost threefold what they were a decade ago. From 2003 to 2015, the average gross income of farmers increased fourfold, from 2,622 yuan to 10,772 yuan, also helped by the abolition of agriculture tax in 2006.[5]

While it is obvious that infrastructure is playing a crucial role in bringing farms closer to cities, the fact that China's villages are broadly so much better off than those in India may be largely the legacy of the pre-1990s policies. The investments in health and education stand out as two key factors, as also the reforms of the 1980s. Besides the setting up of rural health clinics that played a key role in drastically bringing down infant and maternal mortality rates, free and compulsory education was the other major policy initiative. In Zitong, while there are local kindergartens, for primary and middle schools a preferred option is to send children to one of the larger county schools, some of which offer boarding as well. The logic is that having a school in each village would lead to variances in quality and teacher absenteeism, but the system in place now requires good roads and buses for connectivity.

The data shows the importance of education and investment in research in improving agricultural productivity in China. It came as a shock to me to learn India has more arable land than China, despite having only around one-third the land mass, and yet lags behind on almost every aspect of production. In 2011, China produced 40 per cent more wheat and rice, and three times India's fruit production. India has more land under paddy cultivation, yet produces far less. Fertilizer usage in China – and its over-usage – may be one factor, but doesn't entirely explain the higher yield. Better irrigation, more intensive cultivation of land, and investments in research are where China has fared better.[6]

The Railway to Prosperity

In Sichuan, one of the biggest changes unfolding across the province is the bullet train network. There's no better example of China's capacity for infrastructure construction. A decade after the first line came up in 2008, connecting Beijing with Tianjin, China had built an astonishing 29,000 kilometres of track by the end of 2018 – by far the world's longest network, accounting for two-thirds of the world's high-speed rail lines. What's all the more impressive is that bullet trains run on an entirely different track, so the network was essentially built from scratch.[7]

From Zitong I travelled to Dujiangyan, a small, leafy town two hours away from Chengdu by road. Its claim to fame in China is being the hometown of Li Bing who, more than 2,000 years ago, devised an irrigation system that revolutionized farming. Every morning, a train built with European technology and Chinese workmanship ferries the town's residents at 250 kilometres per hour to Chengdu in a little under thirty minutes.

The high-speed rail network is still a matter of debate because of the huge investment involved. Yet it is also changing the way millions of Chinese across the country live, work and travel, bringing people and markets closer. Dujiangyan was devastated by the Sichuan earthquake of May 2008, which left more than 70,000 people dead across the province and reduced dozens of cities to rubble. As part of Dujiangyan's reconstruction, the government sanctioned a 13 billion yuan ($1.96 billion) high-speed rail line. Announced only sixteen days after the earthquake, the project was billed by government officials as one that would mark the city's rebirth, as well as revive its crumpled economy by bringing it closer to the provincial capital.

The huge investment involved – each kilometre of the 65-kilometre railway line costs $30 million – triggered debate, with some arguing that the money could have gone elsewhere, to the task of rebuilding homes and schools, for instance. The project was, nevertheless, rushed through by the local government in eighteen months, in time to mark the earthquake's two-year anniversary. Local officials told me the high-speed network, which connects fifteen towns, would revitalize the local economy. 'More businesses from Chengdu are already coming to invest in land in small towns and villages,' said Yue Shaohua, a local official in Penzhou, a small town that lies along the railway line. Dujiangyan is now just a nine-hour train journey from China's capital, Beijing, which is some 2,000 kilometres away, around the distance from Delhi to Chennai.

Signs of new money were everywhere on the road from Chengdu to Dujiangyan. All along the railway's route are advertisements urging Chengdu's rich to invest in grand property developments. One advertised luxurious 'Greek villas' with access to a private lake and golf course, all for a couple of million yuan. Local officials told me that real estate prices had shot up in the past year, largely because of the high-speed rail project. The government was not complaining: real estate presents its biggest avenue for recouping its $1.96 billion investment in the project. Sichuan's farmers and migrant workers, however, were less enthusiastic about the project. Farmers in Penzhou and Zhongxin, towns which lie along the route, voiced concerns at being priced out by the property bubble and the inflation.

The railway is mainly targeting the business community and Chengdu's affluent. Yue, the local official, accepted that the huge investment had strained finances. But he defended the need for the project, arguing that it is part of the larger trend of an economic transformation and move towards urbanization that China cannot escape. 'Yes, there are concerns among farmers who are losing their livelihood, but the fact is agriculture is changing,' he said. 'Farms are becoming more mechanized, and younger people will have to move to cities.' He envisioned 'a future of interconnectivity' between small towns and big cities. Farmers in his county, he pointed out, are now growing specialized produce for the Chengdu market. In the village of Nongke, groups of farmers had pooled in their land and money to set up hotels, with some government support. They are all targeting Chengdu's residents, who can get away for the weekend, riding the high-speed rail for 'a countryside experience'.

If China's high-speed rail network has made a strong case for some in India on the merits of building such a system, there is one major difference. China had almost completely modernized its existing railway complex by 2008, before it began the more capital-intensive project of building an entirely new bullet train network on new tracks.

When the People's Republic of China was founded in 1949, the country's rail network was in a shambles. Stretching over only 20,000 kilometres – less than half the route length India possessed in 1947 – the tracks were in disrepair, destroyed by years of civil war. Sixty years on, China has added an astounding 55,000 kilometres to the network, which now extends for more than 75,000 kilometres, surpassing India's. The country boasts a modern and efficient railway system, powered by European-designed, China-made express trains and high-speed trains, connected by modern stations that often resemble airport terminals. As of 2020, China will have increased its network length to 1,20,000 kilometres and expanded its high-speed rail network track to 30,000 kilometres.

A big reason for the success of the network is what the World Bank calls a 'single-point responsibility model', buttressed by technical capacity. The Ministry of Railways holds complete control both over planning and executing projects, as well as building trains and running the system. As in India, and unlike in the West, there are no private companies that ply on the state-built system. The ministry also finances all projects, and has not pursued any public–private partnership models, which have led to longer execution periods in many countries, owing to financial and other constraints. China's strength in planning has also helped in facilitating rapid expansion. The government runs six railway design institutes, each employing around 4,000 people. This gives it the ability to churn out a feasibility study in a time frame of six to twelve months, compared to an average of two years elsewhere for major railway construction projects.[8]

The financing model, however, remains a matter of some debate in China. The high level of debt from the speed of expansion has led to questions about the long-term sustainability of the network, and China's ballooning debt crisis has been worsened by the huge outlay on the project.[9] One of China's leading advocates for the bullet train programme over the last two decades is Wang Mengshu, one of the foremost experts on tunnel engineering. Wang told me there was compelling logic for this spending, because railways were 'a public good and a public investment'. Debt, in his view, was unavoidable and tolerable. The benefits, he felt, firmly outweighed the costs, even if the actual gains from the transformative change in mobility weren't always easy to quantify. In Wang's view, in countries like China and India, where land is scarce, high-speed rail is a perfect solution because the lines can be built on elevated tracks (as is largely the case in China), minimizing the need for massive land acquisition.

Even advocates of the high-speed rail stress that the necessity and feasibility of the model will depend on local contexts and needs, and this has to be carefully assessed. They concede this hasn't always been the case in China. The full-throttle approach of some local governments, who have rushed to jump on the high-speed rail bandwagon and given short shrift to public concerns, is a case in point here. Some projects certainly make both financial and developmental sense, on routes where existing lines are congested and pose bottlenecks to development. For instance, a strong case could perhaps be made for a line between Beijing and Shanghai, or even between cities on China's crowded eastern coast, where high-speed travel could potentially boost development. For a smaller town like Dujiangyan, however, the case appears less convincing and more of a pride project.

The broader goal of the network has to be kept in mind. The idea is to bring towns and cities closer as part of China's urbanization push, particularly in the western regions, which have lagged behind the east and south. China's current emphasis on driving urbanization is part of a wider effort to transform its growth model and build a consumption-driven, innovation-led economy. And its leaders know its cities will have to drive the change.

The Pollution Problem

When I first moved to Beijing, the two things I disliked the most about the capital were the traffic and the pollution. The traffic problem was relatively easy to get around: Beijing has an excellent subway system, which has a stunningly broad reach, and until 2015, only charged a flat rate of 2 yuan (around $0.30) regardless of how far you were travelling. Not so the pollution, however, which wasn't easy to manage, no matter how many air filters you set up at home to give you a false sense of comfort.

On occasion, the traffic problem even made the news. For three days in the autumn of 2010, China's capital became one giant, smog-filled parking lot. What was meant to be routine road maintenance work ended up causing what has since become known as the world's longest-ever traffic jam: a 100-kilometre pile-up that stretched all the way from Beijing to towns in nearby Hebei province, with cars on some stretches covering just 2 kilometres in two days. It took ten days for the jam to ease. The travel chaos didn't end there: a burst of heavy rain three days later – which at least cleared out the smog and dust – further plunged Beijing's traffic into chaos, leaving 4,321 roads congested for more than half a day.

The two incidents prompted the city's traffic and environmental planners to undertake an emergency review of the traffic policy that had been in place since the 2008 Olympic Games. Shortly after the Olympics, during which Beijing put in place a short-term 'odd/even' vehicle restriction on alternate days to ensure blue skies, the city introduced its current road rationing policy that prevents residents from taking out their cars one day a week. The measures worked like a charm at first, Ping Qin, a professor of economics at Beijing's Renmin University, who has researched Beijing's traffic policy, told me. Pollution levels fell and the congestion index dropped significantly the first year. The city put in place a network of 2,000 cameras to monitor license plates. Most of the implementation was automated; leaving the enforcement to traffic police, the government felt, would disrupt traffic and leave room for corruption. For every sighting, drivers were charged 100 yuan (around $14) to their online accounts. Failure to pay meant a suspended license.

Within just three years, Ping said, traffic levels were right back to where they were before the restrictions began. 'It was similar to what happened in Mexico City. Ten years after they started limiting cars, the city became even more congested and polluted because people began buying secondary vehicles. There was similar evidence in Beijing also that the second-hand market became very active.' The government decided against further restricting traffic with an odd/even limit. For one, planners decided the move would have risked a backlash from China's middle class and inconvenienced commuters – an unwelcome prospect for the unrest-wary planners of the Communist Party. And two, it would have likely fuelled the purchase of second cars.

Instead, the government came up with another solution: capping the number of vehicle registrations issued every month. Shanghai was the first city to issue a monthly auction system, following Singapore's model. The measures had worked reasonably well in the Chinese city, decreasing congestion and also bringing in a cash windfall for the local government, with costs of registrations soaring to 100,000 yuan (around $14,000). Beijing decided on a more egalitarian approach, issuing 17,600 registrations every month in a lottery. 'Congestion has decreased,' said Ping, 'and the growth of vehicles has slowed.'

Traffic and pollution, the two banes of my existence, were closely interconnected. In Beijing, vehicles account for one-third of all polluting emissions, as the authorities were reminded in the winter of 2014, when what came to be known as an 'airpocalypse' descended on Beijing. That December was surreal. The entire city was blanketed under a suffocating smog, and no amount of air-purifying machines at home or face masks provided relief. This might not be all that unfamiliar for residents of Delhi, but what was different was how the airpocalypse had a transformative impact on China's war against pollution.

It kick-started a warning system that has now become the norm – not just in China, but in Delhi as well. That month, an unprecedented three-day 'red alert', the highest of a four-tier warning system, was issued, calling for the closure of schools, halting of all construction activity, and the reintroduction a temporary odd/even car restriction. And even beyond the short-term measures, a range of steps were put in place that made Beijing's winters demonstrably better by the time I packed my bags for India five years later.

There's much for us to learn from the transformation. It is true that every winter, Beijing does get some smog, but some of it is unavoidable. One reason is its geography, boxed in as the city is by surrounding mountains. The other reason is the spike in energy demand and coal burning to power Beijing's central heating systems in the cold winter. The state provides central heating for around four months every year. Despite the annual winter smog, Dong Liansai, the climate and energy campaigner for Greenpeace in Beijing, told me, there was undoubtedly long-term improvement in air quality. One key takeaway is a series of new emission standards for factories, a beefed-up new environmental and air pollution law that fines violators, and the closing of three out of four coal plants in Beijing.

In the year after these measures were enforced in 2015, the PM2.5 particulate pollution fell by 12 per cent, Dong told me. But just as in India, pollution from cars and factories is just one part of the puzzle. There is also the annual problem of crop burning and pollution from rural areas in surrounding Hebei province, which is harder to tackle.

I travelled to Miaoergang, a quiet village that is 50 kilometres away from Beijing's crowded ring roads, to see how this war was being waged – and the way the Chinese authorities were pursuing the matter, it did sometimes seem like a war. Smog, whether in Delhi or Beijing, doesn't respect city limits. So the realization early on was that without a coordinated campaign involving the city and villages in the four surrounding provinces, no amount of traffic restrictions would help. There was also the problem of some older neighbourhoods in Beijing that still used wood and coal stoves. And thus began a massive door-to-door campaign.

In Miaoergang, a CNG power station was built at the centre of the village in 2014. 'At first, this station was only serving this village, but we have since expanded it to serve six surrounding villages as well, which have all now stopped coal burning,' one of the workers manning it told me. This was followed by officials going door to door to replace older stoves, and setting up gas and electricity-powered units. In Beijing alone, the authorities estimated this campaign helped reduce coal burning by 1.6 million tons and sulphur dioxide by 16 million tons.

For years, the government dragged its feet on pollution, prioritizing economic growth over blue skies and clean water. The Beijing airpocalypse was one trigger. Another was the role played by the Chinese media, which, make no mistake, is under the thumb of the Party–state. But one powerful documentary that went viral played a huge role in generating public awareness. In 2015, popular television host Chai Jing released a film telling a powerful and personal story on how PM2.5 pollution affects the health of ordinary people, in particular the health of pregnant mothers. The film prompted a huge debate and discussion online, and finally pushed the authorities to act. Even in China public pressure can, on occasion, do that.

Cities of the Future

'People-centred urbanization' is the in-vogue phrase in China to refer to a more equitable urbanization process. When the new Party leadership took over in November 2012, the new premier and second-ranked leader Li Keqiang penned an article in the *People's Daily*, arguing that 'urbanization is not simply about increasing the number of residents, or expanding the areas of cities'. 'It is about a complete change,' he wrote, 'from the rural to the urban in industrial structure, employment, living conditions and social security.'[10] As a student, Li Keqiang's PhD thesis in economics at the elite Peking University researched urbanization. His adviser was a renowned economist called Li Yining, who is one of China's most prominent pro-market economists (and known by some as 'Mr Stock Market').

This is the idea: imagine an India with twenty Mumbais – or, at least, twenty well-planned Mumbais. Mega urban centres, each home to 20 million–plus people, and each major centres of migration, economic growth and innovation 'Twenty cities of 20 million each – twenty agglomeration economies that will become the centre of the Chinese economy,' in the words of Zhao Jian, a leading Chinese expert on urbanization, who advises the government on its policies. When I visited him at Beijing Jiaotong University where he teaches, he pointed me to a map on the wall of his office. On it were marked twenty cities across the length and breadth of China: from Chongqing in the west and Wuhan in the heart of China, to Beijing in the north and Shanghai, Shenzhen and Guangzhou in the south.

For years, urban-centred plans had few takers, Zhao said. One reason was the leadership's wariness at de-emphasizing rural China as the centre of economic growth. Under the previous Hu Jintao–Wen Jiabao administration, the centrepiece economic policy was the 'New Socialist Countryside', aimed at directing funds to rural infrastructure projects – in part to entice people to stay in the countryside or third-tier cities. 'The market power was pushing people in the opposite direction,' said Zhao. 'And ultimately, people only go where opportunities lie'.

'My basic argument,' he said, 'has been that megacities should be embraced as an idea, as they inherently have more efficient agglomeration economies and production efficiency. In every country this is the same. And in countries that are the size of China – or India – you need at least twenty such metropolitan areas if you are going to have a strong urban economy and a good standard of living for people. Integrated urban clusters with large and efficient public transportation networks, centres of innovation and learning, and greener economies. Small cities simply don't have the capacity to build large public transit networks, for example.'

Plans are all well and good on paper. But there are enormous challenges to be tackled. I travelled to one town that is in the midst of this shift. Yanjiao, a suburban town in Hebei province, was being subsumed as part of an expanded megapolis that will be China's biggest megacity within the next decade – a sprawling area called Jing-Jin-Ji, planned as an agglomeration of existing Beijing, nearby Tianjin and several cities in the province of Hebei (whose ancient name is Ji). 'The basic idea of Jing-Jin-Ji is to use Beijing's advantages – like human resources and capital – to develop surrounding areas in an integrated way,' explained Zhang Chunxiao, a professor of economics at Peking University. By the end of the decade, he said, this will be a massive single administrative area that is home to 100 million people.

Among them will be the residents of Yanjiao, a dusty town that was still very much a work in progress. Construction cranes dotted the city's main avenues, which were lined by giant billboards advertising luxurious villas and golf courses. At the centre of the city stood a gaudy new apartment complex, fronted by a giant golden statue of running bulls. It housed a school that ambitiously called itself 'Cambridge Kindergarten'; while there was no connection with the venerable English university, it rather confidently guaranteed that Chinese three-year-olds would be set on the right track for admission to UK's best universities.

I met Bai Fang, among Yanjiao's first new settlers, at Maan Coffee, the only cafe in town, part of a popular Chinese chain (known for its distinctively large mugs and free Apple computers for patrons to use). She told me she moved to Yanjiao from a village in the southern province of Hunan three years ago to work for an information technology company in Beijing. The capital city's rents were too high, so Bai and her husband found a small apartment in Yanjiao for one-third of the cost. The other barrier they faced in moving to Beijing was China's restrictive system of household registration permits. For instance, with her Hunan *hukou*, Bai will not have the same access to Beijing's social services, including subsidized healthcare and schools, as the city's residents do. Changing one's *hukou* identity is arduous. Usually, a migrant worker has to work for fifteen years in a city before she gains access to social services, and even that may not be enough. *Hukou* reform, long discussed, has barely been implemented. When Shanghai passed a law aimed at making this process easier, reducing the wait time to seven years, only 3,000 workers out of more than a million qualified because the requirements were so demanding – such as educational qualifications and the amount of tax they contributed to the city.

To attract migrants as part of its urbanization drive, Yanjiao offered them urban permits, although Bai says the schools are nowhere near as good as Beijing's. 'There is nothing left in our hometowns for us to go back to, and we want to build a new life here,' said Bai. Everyone from her small rural town, she said, had headed to the cities, leasing out their farmland. Their life, however, is hardly an urban dream. She faced a daily commute of two hours each way, in a shared van, from Yanjiao to Beijing's tech hub of Zhongguancun. It will take several years for the Beijing subway to reach Yanjiao as part of an ongoing plan to expand the city's public transport network.

Yu Hongzhou, another Yanjiao resident, is the son of farmers who tilled their cornfields in Yanjiao's suburbs for generations. He is the first of his family to earn a living in the city, getting a job with Yanjiao's newly set up television station. He has seen a city grow out of the villages, which were, one by one, subsumed into its ever-expanding boundaries. 'Our village is the only one that's left,' he said, and his parents are among the few who still work on the land. The government bought farmland in neighbouring villages and gave the residents free apartments in Yanjiao, along with what Yu said were sizeable compensations. But the transition, especially for Yu's parents' generation, had been difficult. The farmers have homes and cash, but they sit idle as they cannot find jobs in the new urban economy. For them, there is little promise in their new life in the city.

Just as it is important to keep in mind the winners and losers in China's growth story, it is also important to re-examine our conventional wisdom about its benefits and costs. Often, judgement tends to veer towards either of two extremes: romanticizing the China model, or damning it in entirety. The picture, however, is more complicated.

The country has embraced urbanization with far more vigour than India has. Even so, its planners have been caught between their long-held belief of controlling the movement of people, such as through the *hukou* system, which has only fuelled inequality, and an increasing realization of the need to embrace an equitable urbanization process, if China is to succeed in its ambitions of building cities of the future.

6

The Next Tech Giant

IT DOESN'T TAKE A VISITOR to any major Chinese city all that long to notice how technology is transforming day-to-day lives. I moved to China just as the WeChat revolution was taking off. Fast forward ten years, and what was a simple messaging app is now the beating heart of a massive tech ecosystem. WeChat is perhaps the most innovative social media platform in use anywhere in the world. It's often wrongly described as a Chinese WhatsApp, but it's actually WhatsApp on steroids. It is far more advanced, and had introduced voice and video calls years before WhatsApp did. It is to some degree an amalgam of WhatsApp, Facebook and Paytm – users can post photographs, messages and use its e-wallet, and, in the process, generate massive amounts of data – but it's even vaster, tied into a massive ecosystem that covers every aspect of life in China. WeChat is so pervasive that as an experiment, I found it was entirely possible to spend a day in Beijing relying entirely on this one app and leaving my wallet at home. It could help me do everything, from buying movie tickets and ordering taxis to paying electricity and gas bills, all with the touch of a fingerprint.

It is a world of convenience. It is also a world without privacy. My movements and behaviour, from dawn to dusk on 10 December 2017, are recorded for posterity in a server somewhere in China. If anyone were so inclined, they could find out that I used WeChat to book a car on Didi Chuxing, the Chinese Uber, to travel from my house to a subway station. They would know that on arrival, I used a WeChat 'mini-app' – an ingenious invention that embeds external apps into the WeChat programme – to log into Mobike, a dockless bike-sharing app that gets bookings for 25 million rides a day and has transformed transportation in China, to cycle to a nearby Starbucks. They would know I ordered a tall Americano, paid through another mini-app (Starbucks) on WeChat. More troubling, they would also know whom I met there – both from the messages we exchanged to confirm our meeting and from our geolocations. Welcome to the end of privacy.

Driverless cars that are close to 100 per cent accident-free on city streets. Face recognition software in hospitals and restaurants that can pull up your medical history, or order your favourite dish, in a split second. Artificial intelligence that guides a city's traffic management, predicting traffic and deploying shared bicycles, not every hour but every minute, exactly where you need them. Intelligent applications that approve bank loans in two seconds. And overseeing it all, an all-watching 'big brother' surveillance that uses big data to predict street crime, but also tracks citizens' every movement using some of the world's most powerful face recognition programs to 'predict' crime – and silence dissent. This isn't a fanciful glimpse into an Orwellian future. This is, in fact, already becoming China's present.

One only need look at how China harnessed technology after the coronavirus pandemic as life limped back, following the lockdowns, into a new tech-driven normal. Health is no longer a private matter. A health QR code in 2020 became the most important passport to get you anywhere in any Chinese city. An app that every citizen has to download marks you green (safe), while orange or red may mean you can't enter a shopping mall or restaurant. The colour depends on your travel history and whom you have been in contact with, among other things. During the pandemic, more than 300 million Chinese students in schools and universities were taking classes online every day, and all kinds of new e-learning platforms, teaching everything from classical music to Pilates, were booming.

No country is moving faster in investing in – and deploying – what most experts see as the next technological wave, harnessing big data and AI to power future industries. In September 2017, the government in Beijing outlined what has been seen by many experts as perhaps the most ambitious AI plan in history, aimed at paving the way towards deploying this technology in every industry, right from education in primary schools to healthcare and transport. AI, for China, is at the heart of the great technological leap forward, and Beijing is doing everything it can to be at the top of the next wave.

Despite all these changes unfolding in the country, a 'Made in China' caricature that comprises fakes, cheap toys and electronics is still widely pervasive in the imagination of many in India. In truth, Chinese manufacturing today is far removed from the 'world's factory' that drove its export-led growth two decades ago. In a Xi'an factory I visited, robots have replaced workers on assembly lines and on factory floors, and they are churning out not toys or cheap electronics but some of the world's most advanced laser diodes.

In southwest Guizhou, I saw how the government was building what is one of the world's biggest ever data facilities. And in Beijing's technological hub of Zhongguancun, which I visited regularly, internet companies that began as small start-ups were becoming global behemoths. Of the top 10 biggest internet companies in the world by revenue in 2017, four were Chinese: e-commerce giants JD and Alibaba; Tencent, which is behind WeChat; and Baidu, which started as a search engine but is now leading the AI push, including in autonomous cars. For all of India's software prowess, there is only one in the top 25, Flipkart.[1]

China's Google

In the summer of 2016, I headed to Baidu's sprawling campus, a modern space filled with glass buildings and manicured lawns in north Beijing. It was easy to see why it's often called China's Google – and it's not just about the search engine. The Baidu campus is quite unlike anything you'll see in the Chinese capital, more suited to Silicon Valley than central Beijing. On the morning I visited, groups of young Chinese students and visiting foreign MBA students waited in the reception area that sits at the heart of the company's massive glass headquarters. Covering the lobby is a giant bear paw print – the company's symbol, inspired by the idea of a hunter relentlessly searching for and tracking his prey.

Baidu rose to prominence as China's first popular search engine. The company was launched in 2000 by a little-known entrepreneur called Robin Li, who had just returned from the US after patenting a new kind of search algorithm called the hypertext document retrieval system. Today, the NASDAQ-listed company is a behemoth that casts a giant shadow not only over the strictly government-controlled internet, but also over the lives of millions of Chinese.

From a sole search engine, the company today operates a massive ecosystem that infiltrates every aspect of Chinese life – maps, food delivery, online wallets, an online personal secretary, healthcare, and now, AI. In 2016, when I visited, I was told Baidu search commanded a massive 657 million monthly active mobile users. China then had 700 million internet users; the number crossed 850 million by the middle of 2019.[2] Despite India's prowess in IT, no company has come close to developing such an ecosystem. The rise of Baidu has been in sync with the emergence of China as a global tech power, with companies like Huawei, Lenovo, Xiaomi and Tencent acquiring a global presence.

'People's attitudes to entrepreneurship and innovation in China have changed dramatically since around 2012,' Beijing-based Andy Mok, who invests in tech start-ups and appears as a tech commentator on Chinese television, told me. 'What we're seeing is a new wave of innovation, and companies like Tencent, Baidu and Xiaomi are all part of this change. The biggest change that I have seen is that young people are now seeking jobs not only in government or the state sector, but also in tech companies and start-ups, and that's also because of the government's emphasis on transitioning the economy away from exports to innovation and technology.'

The Big Tech Rivalry

For long, the popular belief was that a democratic and open society had natural advantages when it comes to innovation. That belief brought a certain complacency that China would never be able to compete when it came to technology with a country like India, let alone the US. China's tech story, however, warns of the dangers of such assumptions.

Kaiser Kuo is an American who has closely followed the evolution of China's technology sector (including through a stint at Baidu) and has lived in Beijing for two decades (where he also co-founded the popular rock band Tang Dynasty). He told me that China's digital story was single-handedly upending long-held views on innovation. 'Actually, even America's own story shows the importance of the government in creating the right conditions,' he said. 'The mythology of Silicon Valley forgets the extent to which defence department expenditures played a role. The internet is a primary example. Where the state has been smart in China is in knowing when to get out of the way, and also in setting tax policies, putting in place the infrastructure, and bringing back Chinese entrepreneurs. It's also gotten right its investment in R&D, which you are now seeing in AI as well.'

Today, the rise of digital China is changing conventional wisdom about what it takes to innovate. 'Indians, like Americans, have this idea that somehow freedom of expression is a necessary condition for innovation to happen,' said Kuo. 'I simply don't think that's true. It is maybe unfortunate that it's not true. What's dangerous is if you think it's a sufficient condition to make people innovate.'

The rise of China's tech giants has certainly been helped by the many restrictions on the entry of foreign companies, including the 'Great Firewall of China' that ensures a massive censorship mechanism. Google left the market in 2010 citing the restrictions, although it had struggled to expand its market share even prior to that. Today, Google, Facebook, YouTube and Twitter are all inaccessible in China. Search for Tiananmen Square on Baidu, and the first result you see is 'Tiananmen Square massacre a myth', an article from the official *China Daily*. At the same time, said Kuo, there is a misplaced perception that it was only China's blocking of foreign competition that enabled the rise of its own giants. 'Twitter was blocked in 2009, Google didn't pull out until March 2010, but even by then, these companies were far behind their Chinese competitors. I don't think anyone would have foreseen fifteen years ago that four of the ten biggest internet companies today would be Chinese,' he said, referring to Alibaba, Tencent, the e-commerce giant JD, and Baidu.

The US is still the leader by far, but China's tech push is already closing the gap rapidly in many areas. Alarmed by the country's strides, especially in AI, the Barack Obama administration in 2016 outlined a National Artificial Intelligence Research and Development Strategic Plan, which noted that trends of AI research 'reveal the increasingly global nature of research, with the United States no longer leading the world in publication numbers'. That mantle has now gone to China. The US plan said that the impact of AI on society 'will continue to increase, including on employment, education, public safety, and national security, as well as the impact on US economic growth.'[3] Since then, however, the new Donald Trump administration has cut funding, including in areas that support AI research.

Tu Zipei is a former president of Alibaba and a leading figure in the world of big data in China. 'Big data' refers to the use of complex data generated on massive scales, whether from telecommunications, transport or even e-commerce sales, to study trends and patterns that enable advancements in technology. 'In algorithms, the gap between China and America is becoming smaller and smaller,' he said. The use of big data is also enabling advancements in AI or machine learning, and allowing technology to predict human behaviour by discerning patterns.

'This is a big chance for China to become an AI leader,' Tu said, pointing to how China, more than any other country, is best situated to make the next big tech leap. As he puts it, 'data is the soil for AI to grow', and China has more than 850 million internet users, more than anywhere else in the world. Only India comes close, but it does not have the home-grown technology giants to tap into this number. It is the Googles and Facebooks that are growing on India's soil.

Perhaps the two biggest digital innovations in China that are at the centre of its data deluge have been Alibaba's Taobao and Tencent's WeChat, which has 1 billion users. Alibaba has transformed how business is done in China, and a huge portion of all private commercial transactions pass through its platforms, whether on Taobao, China's biggest e-commerce site, or its e-wallet Alipay. WeChat generates 100 million photos every day, which, as someone put it, places it in pole position to develop the best facial recognition technology in the world.

The AI Race

For China today, AI and big data are national priorities, so much so that even President Xi Jinping specifically mentioned them as such at the Party's once-in-five-years National Congress in 2017 – akin to the prime minister of a country mentioning AI and big data in a major annual address to the nation. 'We need to speed up building China into a strong country with advanced manufacturing, pushing for deep integration between the real economy and advanced technologies including internet, big data and artificial intelligence,' Xi said, unveiling plans to make China a centre for global AI by 2030.[4]

There is also the fact that for the Chinese government, building a digital state is seen as a crucial weapon for the one-party regime to exercise even stricter social control. One video that went viral in

China in 2019 showed how face recognition technology was being used by a local government: at a busy traffic intersection, every passer-by was immediately identified by their national ID number. The company, SenseFace, is deploying its technology in Beijing, Chongqing, Guangdong, Sichuan and Hainan, and, according to its CEO, caught sixty-nine criminal suspects in forty days in one city. SkyNet is a nationwide system of millions of AI-powered cameras that watch Chinese streets, tracking traffic violations and crime. It is being widely deployed in China, most notably in Xinjiang – a region that has, by most accounts, become perhaps the twenty-first century's first truly dystopian security mini-state.

Among the companies betting big on AI is Uisee in Beijing, which is developing autonomous cars. 'We want to use AI and big data to transform society,' says Wu Gansha, co-founder and CEO. 'From traffic jams to accidents to air pollution to city layout, we believe autonomous driving can do a lot to remove all of society's problems. Few months back, if you ran autonomous driving in Chinese roads you would get a ticket as it was not allowed here. Our driverless cars now operate in Hangzhou without one accident for three months.' Wu says the Chinese government is gung-ho about the prospects, and he is working with the government to take the Hangzhou experiment nationwide. He believes China is even more bullish than the US in this regard. 'I have been involved in several discussions with the Ministry of Industry and Information Technology, and they believe autonomous cars are an integral part of smart cities. China has planned 1,000 new towns by 2020. So we have the opportunity of having 1,000 new towns that are autonomous car-friendly.'

China is far ahead compared to its peers when it comes to AI policy as well. Kaifu Lee – the former head of Google China who runs Sinovation Ventures, an AI-focused investment firm, and has written a book on the China–US AI race – believes that the country's AI industry incentives are 'world leading'. 'If you are a credible venture capital fund setting up a fund in a region, the local government will be a leading investor in your fund up to a third.

If you do well, you can buy back shares from the government. If you don't, they subsidize your losses.'[5] Lee said if the first wave was the internet, the second wave is 'applying AI to businesses that already have digitized data', which China is pushing under its AI policy across every sector – from banking to healthcare and transport (where it's used in everything from bike sharing to law enforcement). The third wave, he says, is robotics and autonomous vehicles, which China is already positioning itself to dominate.[6]

I travelled to Xi'an, the old capital famous for its terracotta warriors, to see how technology is changing the way business is done. Robots have already replaced workers on the assembly lines of Focuslight. The ten-year-old company manufactures some of the world's most advanced laser products, used in industries ranging from space and IT to life sciences. The story of Focuslight underlines how China's success in manufacturing is underpinning its moves in AI and other fields, and how one could not have come without the other. The 'Made in China 2025' plan envisages a revolution in smart manufacturing, and Focuslight is a poster child of the plan, a company emblematic of Made in China 2.0 – high-tech manufacturing that Beijing hopes will replace the older export-driven Made in China of cheap goods.

It was this determination to move up the value chain that made the government reach out to Victor Liu, who was working in Silicon Valley. When he left the US in 2006, Liu was a reluctant returnee to his homeland. By then, China was a manufacturing behemoth, but was nowhere near the West when it came to innovation. Liu was part of the first batch of a government programme, backed at the highest levels, to bring back some of the waves of talent that China, like India, has lost to the West. Where the countries' experiences differ is Beijing's determination to bring back this talent, which it has demonstrated with action. Liu was told simply that he was wanted to innovate. He was offered a 10 million yuan ($1.5 million) research fund, and a 1 million yuan ($150,000) tax-free relocation package.

Supported by the influential Chinese Academy of Sciences, Liu launched Focuslight in Xi'an to make advanced laser diodes; it would, in less than five years, rival the American and European giants that Liu once worked for, and become the third-most advanced in the world in its field. 'What people don't understand is that manufacturing is key to innovation. R&D you can design, but manufacturing allows you to have a better idea of how to design and actually produce a product,' Liu explained to me one morning over coffee in Beijing's Zhongguancun. 'I cannot emphasize enough how important the ecosystem – policy and administration – is. It can make life difficult for you, whether taxes or something else, or it can be transformative.'

The Chinese are Coming[7]

With the Chinese markets reaching saturation, many of its companies are now going overseas. Baidu is a case in point. It started off by launching a search engine for Brazil, followed by apps for the Egypt market where the company is making inroads. One of its apps was called Muslim Touch, marketed as a one-stop prayer guide for the Muslim world, including reminders of praying times in texts. Then followed Japan, where a Japanese emoticon keyboard developed by a company owned by Baidu became a rage, with 20 million-plus downloads.

Richard Lee, the suave director of Baidu's global business unit, told me that one market, above all, remained the big prize for Chinese firms: India. In September 2017, Baidu opened a modest office in Gurgaon. It is now working on a number of apps tailored to the Indian market. What was promising, Lee said, was that three of the company's apps had already been big hits in India. The DU Battery Saver and Speedbooster apps each have 8 million monthly active users in India alone, while a file explorer app has 10 million users. Many of the users are unaware that these apps were developed in this corner of Beijing.

Baidu knows it cannot replicate what Google and Yahoo have achieved in India, so it has focused on niche utility apps rather than trying to compete directly with them. The next step is localization. The company has started rolling out a mobile marketplace app that is in Hindi, Tamil, Bengali, Marathi, Telugu and Urdu. Utilities and apps are phase one; next is strategic investments and mergers with Indian digital companies. Baidu is also thinking of launching content apps that have been successful in China, such as a popular newsreader app that aggregates headlines. 'We think India is going to be a very dynamic market for us and we plan to keep investing there for a few years,' Lee said. 'We are very interested in mergers and acquisitions, and strategic investments. We have had talks with quite a lot of potential partners.' Its plans have, however, taken a big hit with India's moves to curtail Chinese apps, with a ban on fifty-nine apps announced in June 2020. The popular DU Battery Saver app was one of six Baidu apps on the banned list.

Baidu is actually among the latecomers in engaging India, which is, as Lee puts it, the next big market for China's tech sector. Since 2017, Chinese companies have become the biggest investors in India's tech sector, closing the gap with the Americans and Japanese. China's 'big three' tech companies – Baidu, Alibaba and Tencent – as well as the e-commerce giant JD, led this outward surge of the country's tech investments globally. Following the e-commerce explosion starting in 2009, particularly led by Alibaba's Taobao and Tencent's WeChat, private companies amassed a war chest that enabled their moves overseas.

One objective in going overseas is to replicate their success at home in a similar market abroad, which is one big factor in their gravitating towards India – seen widely as a similar market to China's in terms of its stage of development, e-commerce requirements and consumer behaviour, and in terms of size. In the US, deals have included well-known American brands such as image-messaging app Snap, ride-sharing service Lyft, and virtual reality player Magic Leap. China's four largest internet companies have invested $5.6 billion in forty-eight US tech deals over the past two years.[8]

In India, the trend of major Chinese investments and acquisitions took off in 2016. Alibaba and Tencent have been the two biggest investors in the country by some distance, together accounting for more than $3 billion. Alibaba, in some sense, led the way with its entry in 2015 – the behemoth and its affiliate Ant Financial invested $680 million that year for a 40 per cent stake in One 97 communications, the parent company of the widely used online wallet Paytm, which has more than 300 million users in India. Another $177 million put in by Alibaba in 2017 further raised its stock in the company.

Make no mistake, the relationship between Paytm and Alibaba is more than just funding. It is strategic. To begin with, the Paytm app, from its design to even its colours, is a mirror image of Alipay, Alibaba's widely used payments app in China. Among the agreements between the two companies is an exclusive partnership for Paytm to use AliCloud, Alibaba's cloud computing platform, and to integrate the payment instruments of Paytm and Alipay to allow Indian users to access Alipay's merchant base and Chinese users to pay Indian merchants via Alipay. When questions were raised – including in the Indian parliament – as to whether Alipay or Alibaba would have access to Indian users' data, Paytm said that all users' data would be stored locally and no data would be shared with any of its investors.[9]

Alibaba's other big plays in India include a $500 million investment along with SoftBank and Foxconn in the e-commerce company Snapdeal, and the 2017 deal of $146 million that made it the biggest shareholder in the online grocery service BigBasket, which was followed by another investment of $50 million in the same company. Then came a $210 million investment in Zomato, a restaurant directory and food delivery app, and a reported $35 million put in the logistics firm Xpressbees. More recently, Alibaba has been eyeing the entertainment, news and media space, with Alibaba Pictures, a major investor in China, putting in $17.3

million in the online ticketing platform TicketNew. The group is also reportedly considering a bid for the news aggregator app Dailyhunt, that has received funding from another major Chinese tech firm, ByteDance.

If Alibaba was the trailblazer, it has to some degree been left behind by its competitor Tencent, which has made a string of mega investments in almost every sphere of the tech space, with stakes in the biggest Indian apps, from transport and food delivery to education and health. The first notable investment was $400 million in the ride-hailing app Ola, which interestingly came at a time when both Ola in India and Tencent-backed Didi Chuxing in China were in a heated competition with rival Uber. This was followed by a massive $700 million investment in the e-commerce platform Flipkart, then India's most valuable start-up, in a deal that made Tencent the biggest Chinese investor in India.

Tencent has acquired a diversified portfolio in India, targeting stakes in the biggest players in every vertical, from leading a $175 million fund-raising round into messaging app Hike Messenger to leading a $90 million injection into healthcare start-up Practo, which was followed by another $55 million round of funding. In the education space, it has invested $40 million in the learning app Byju's, followed by a further $11.4 million in a subsequent funding round. Tencent also made an entry into the food delivery space, joining its shareholder Naspers in a $1 billion funding round for Swiggy, a rival of the Alibaba-invested Zomato. It has also put $100 million in Dream11 Fantasy, part of reported plans to spend $200 million in the online gaming space in India, and led a $115 million funding round into music streaming service Gaana. Tencent, like ByteDance, has also entered the news space, leading a $50 million round into the aggregator app NewsDog.[10]

This influx of Chinese money is changing the nature of the India–China trade relationship. It is only in the past five years that Chinese enterprises have begun to emerge as major stakeholders in the relationship between the countries. Trade relations began to expand since the early 2000s, growing from under $2 billion in the year 2000 to $38 billion in 2008, when China became India's largest trading partner. It reached $93 billion in 2019.[11]

Despite this rapid growth, the nature of the trading relationship in the period 2000–14 largely did not create the incentives for Chinese enterprises to emerge as long-term stakeholders in the Indian market or help shape China's policies towards India. The relationship was broadly transactional, driven by Indian purchases of Chinese machinery and equipment, and India emerging as the biggest overseas market for China's companies for project contracting, with the cumulative value of projects in this period reaching $53.46 billion.[12]

In both equipment purchases and execution of contracts, Chinese cost-competitiveness was the determining factor. As a result of this largely transactional relationship, Chinese companies were neither required to establish a permanent presence nor invest in India, which remained low on the list of key destinations of Chinese outward investment. Second, the nature of trade has not led to the interdependencies and close linkages that closer commercial relations brought between China and some of its other major trading partners, such as the US, Japan and South Korea. Unlike its dynamics with those countries, Chinese companies were not deeply invested in India – other than viewing it as one of many key overseas markets for equipment sales and executing project contracts – nor dependent on their relations with Indian companies for technology.

This has now begun to change. If the first phase of the trading relationship was marked by a distant, transactional yet robust engagement, the post-2014 period has seen the start of a new kind of engagement marked by two changes. First, the post-2014 period has seen a surge in Chinese investment in India. Until 2014, the total Chinese investment in India, according to Chinese Ministry of Commerce figures, was $1.6 billion. By the end of 2017, it had increased to at least $8 billion according to official figures, which underestimate the total investment. This is part of the broader surge of Chinese investment abroad in the 2013–16 period, almost doubling from $107.8 billion in 2013 to $196.2 billion in 2016, following which overseas investment fell to $134 billion in the next year.[13]

For the first time, Chinese companies are not only investing to establish a long-term presence in India, but also acquiring controlling stakes and developing joint strategies with Indian companies, which gives them – also for the first time – a long-term stake in the Indian market. What is striking about this change is that it has largely happened without the involvement of both governments, and is led by the private sector in both countries. This has been especially evident in the spate of acquisitions in the tech sector, 2016 onwards. This presents both opportunities and challenges for India in pursuing its strategic and commercial goals with regard to China.

From payment apps that record every user's private transactions to India's most widely used mobile browser – the Chinese app UC Browser – safeguarding access to private data that could be potentially sensitive has emerged as a new challenge for Indian policymaking. Another issue is the expanding footprint of Chinese companies in new areas, such as news and entertainment apps. While there are limits on foreign ownership of print and television media, this is not the case for news apps, which have recently become a source of interest for Chinese investors. Tencent is an investor in NewsDog, but the company making the biggest waves in this field is ByteDance, which is behind both the most popular news aggregator in China, Jinri Toutiao, and its most popular video-sharing app, Douyin. The company, which plays a key role in ensuring the Party's censorship mandates are followed strictly in its offerings in China, has now entered the news aggregator space in India with a $25 million investment in Dailyhunt – a news aggregator available in seventeen languages.

But most stunning has been the success of Douyin's English version, TikTok, which as of 2019 grew to over 300 million users in India.[14] The success of Tiktok has been the clearest example of how Chinese apps have found a major market in India. Another is Alibaba-owned UC Browser, the most widely used mobile browser in India as we have noted, which has also entered the news aggregation space with its UC News offering. The success of Chinese apps in India has certainly been phenomenal; so much so that forty-four of the 100 most downloaded apps in India in 2018 were apps made by Chinese companies.[15]

No Longer Business as Usual

Following the border clash on 15 June 2020 that claimed the lives of twenty Indian soldiers and marked the worst India–China violence since 1967, there were growing calls to more strictly regulate Chinese investment, particularly in the telecom sector and in the tech space. Two weeks after the clash, India took the unprecedented step of banning fifty-nine Chinese apps, including some of the most popular, such as TikTok, UC Browser, SHAREit and WeChat. The Ministry of Electronics and Information Technology said it made the move 'upon receiving recent credible inputs that such apps pose [a] threat to [the] sovereignty and integrity of India'.[16]

There certainly are benefits in pursuing investment from China. At the same time, the challenges, which were broadly overlooked before the border clash of 2020, need to be considered as well. So far, the focus of capital-hungry Indian start-ups and a foreign investment–seeking government had squarely been on attracting investment. This has, however, led to inadequate attention on the specific challenges of regulating investments from China. Chinese companies in India had largely escaped the kind of scrutiny that their investments have come under in the West, despite several high-profile investments and acquisitions. Besides the current emphasis on investments, another likely reason is the assumption that money from the Chinese private sector is different from state investments. This is despite the fact that the private sector in China, more than in any other country, is a channel for the state to pursue its goals – certainly at home, and more than likely abroad.

This is especially true of the technology sector, which is widely seen as playing a key role in the Party's enforcing of a digital authoritarianism at home, from surveillance to censorship. In the West, there has recently been considerable debate on whether a clear distinction should be made between Chinese SOEs and the private sector. The private sector's relationship with the state is now under the lens in many Western countries over the decision to allow Huawei, a privately owned giant with close state ties, to participate in 5G networks. As of September 2019, the US, Australia and Japan were among countries that have blocked Huawei from their 5G plans. However, Huawei has already supplied equipment to build India's 3G and 4G networks.

'It cannot be business as it was earlier,' former ambassador to China, Gautam Bambawale, told me. 'I firmly believe that Chinese firms must be kept out of the 5G trials and roll-out in India as well. That is where it will hurt in the pocket. I am not advocating a complete break. Normal trade and investment can continue.' While the Government of India initially allowed all companies to participate in 5G trials, several officials subsequently expressed concerns about the inclusion of Chinese vendors in the trials.[17]

The investments and acquisitions by the Chinese private sector in India have largely been driven by market compulsions, and these companies are unlikely to take any action that adversely impacts either their market share or the hundreds of millions that comprise their user base. At the same time, the implications of having India's most valuable start-ups – including in potentially sensitive newly emerging sectors, such as fintech services – ceding controlling stakes to Chinese firms have emerged as a concern for Indian authorities. This is particularly so in an industry where notions of what may be sensitive to state interests are changing rapidly. Moreover, users of these apps need to be made aware of the context and implications of these acquisitions, which broadly has not been the case so far.

The influx of Chinese capital has certainly been beneficial to both countries, and to the broader relationship as well, emerging as a potential factor of stability. For Indian tech companies, the infusion of capital has allowed them to scale up, as well as benefit from the experience and technological know-how of Chinese companies that have achieved bigger scale and success in their home market in similar verticals. Chinese investment also holds the potential for rebalancing what has been an extremely lopsided trading relationship, which, as mentioned, has been driven by Indian dependence on Chinese goods in various sectors. In addition to their stakes in Indian companies, several Chinese industries now see the Indian market as among their most important overseas markets, with hundreds of millions of dollars in revenues at stake. Whether this can be better leveraged by India's trade strategy, which has so far failed to balance the trading relationship or secure market access for Indian firms in China, needs to be explored.

This flush of investment from China has only served to underline the need for a transparent, credible and predictable regulatory framework – aimed at *all* overseas investment, rather than singling out one country, which would be counter-productive. The framework should be such as to strike a much better balance between creating a friendly, open and predictable investment environment on the one hand, and safeguarding longer-term considerations of security and privacy on the other. Doing so would better harness the benefits of greater Chinese investment in India – this has already given some of China's biggest and most influential companies a long-term stake in the success of India's economy – which is certainly to be welcomed. After all, the billion dollar–plus portfolios acquired by companies such as Alibaba and Tencent are not only long-term bets on the Indian economy, but also the biggest bets that have been placed, despite all the political uncertainties, on the future of India's relations with China.

PART III

DIPLOMACY

7

Building a Chinese Order

I ONLY EVER MADE IT into Zhongnanhai – the high-security compound where the Communist Party's top leaders live and work – on perhaps ten occasions during my nine years in Beijing. Each of those visits occurred when I accompanied a visiting Indian official as part of the press contingent. Usually, only high-ranking visiting officials – for instance, foreign ministers and national security advisers – are given the honour of a visit to Zhongnanhai.

No matter how many times I visited, the choreography and ritual never failed to impress. The point of entry for visitors is usually the west gate – not the grand main entrance, called Xinhuamen (or 'New China Gate'), that tourists see a few kilometres from Tiananmen Square. The west gate is hidden out of sight on the busy and tree-lined Fuyou Street, a few yards from the Beijing No. 4 Middle School, one of the capital's most famous schools that educates the children of the Party elite. Among its alumni are the now disgraced princeling Bo Xilai, fellow princeling Chen Yuan, a former head of the China Development Bank, whose father Chen Yun was among the Party's 'Eight Immortal' revolutionary leaders, and Liu Yuan, a PLA general whose father was Liu Shaoqi, the former president.

After having your details verified, you are made to board a bus that runs only within the compound. It drops you off at a room where you are thoroughly searched. You then board the bus again, and are driven to the assigned villa where your country's representative will be met, far removed from the buildings where the leaders actually live and work. Meeting over, you are promptly taken back to the west gate. No strolling or stopping for photos.

Zhongnanhai lies to the west of the Forbidden City. It used to be a grand imperial garden with man-made lakes – its name literally means the middle and southern lakes, on whose banks the property sits – which was later taken over by Mao to become the Party's headquarters. Mao's battle-hardened communist revolutionaries needed surprisingly little time to make themselves at home in the luxurious imperial gardens. Visitors today are usually only taken to a small part of north Zhongnanhai, where the premier and the State Council have their offices. The exquisite Hall of Purple Light, also in the north, is used to receive foreign leaders. The Party's offices are in the south, where outsiders are rarely taken.

Secrecy is essential to the way the Party does business. No one even knows where exactly China's president resides: some say he lives in Zhongnanhai, others believe he is in another high-security compound near the Summer Palace. Often, the only glimpse Beijingers have of their leadership is when their fleet of black Audi cars is seen zipping from Zhongnanhai to the Great Hall of the People, on the opposite side of Chang'an Avenue. They emerge from behind high walls, and then immediately disappear behind another set of high walls.

New Emperors

There is some logic to all this ritual and secrecy. It is intended to shock and awe outsiders, drawing from a centuries-old tradition of Imperial China. Truth be told, I have seen it work effectively, with even the most seasoned visiting government officials left somewhat overwhelmed, waxing effusively about the 'unique' and 'special' treatment they were given, unaware this is all par for the course and part of a well-practised routine.

In Imperial China, the Forbidden City was built to amaze, laid out in great detail, with each section and hall imbued with deep symbolism. Every hall was aligned with the other gates of Beijing on the city's central axis. The message from the Forbidden City to visitors was to show 'the connectedness of things personified in this man the Chinese termed the Son of Heaven'. Just being in the emperor's presence was meant to overwhelm and subdue, and how far inside the complex you reached revealed your place in the scheme of things – something that often came to mind during our Zhongnanhai visits as we waited for our brief meeting with the top leaders, confined to a small corner of the compound.[1]

The communist leadership adopted, and adapted, this practice. The goal is the same – to shock and awe. Indeed, no one does ritual and grandeur on a larger scale than the Party. And it isn't only in the carefully choreographed audiences that foreign visitors are given with President Xi. It is especially evident in how China does summitry.

For a few days in the summer of 2017, the capital city of 20 million came to a complete standstill. The subway stations were closed, roads blocked, and, in some neighbourhoods, residents in apartment buildings were told to board up their windows if they wanted to avoid being in the sights of snipers, or better yet, just pack their bags and leave town. The only silver lining: picture-perfect blue skies and a break from the smog, thanks to a government order shutting down polluting factories in the city's vicinities.

If such extreme measures seem befuddling to outsiders, the logic is clear: when the Party's leader is involved, no detail is too small to be left to chance, and there can be no room for error. That explains why factories are shut down every March, just so Beijing can boast of blue skies, a weather phenomenon dubbed as 'Two Sessions Blue' by the city's residents, referring to the annual sitting of the two houses of parliament that month. (Two Sessions Blue was followed by 'APEC blue' in 2014, when China's hosting of the Asia-Pacific Economic Cooperation summit that year brought unseasonably clean air.) My strangest encounter was in Hangzhou, where I was covering the G20 summit in 2016. The security arrangements were so extreme that in some areas residents were given a small payment to leave the city. It resembled a ghost town during the summit. Hotels barely had supplies, and, curiously, the establishment where I was staying couldn't serve any dish with potatoes or tomatoes. 'Security reasons,' a waiter shrugged.

But even by China's exacting standards, 2017 was different. The city was even more on edge than usual, because this time it wasn't just the Chinese government hosting a summit, but one that was overseen personally by Xi Jinping. 'A project for the century' was how Xi had described his grand plan to remake the world, as he hosted twenty-nine foreign leaders that May in the beautiful surrounds of Yanqi lake, on Beijing's outskirts, to formally unveil his pet initiative, dubbed 'One Belt, One Road' (OBOR). The summit was the highest-profile event yet to push the plan, which was first unveiled in 2013. OBOR was very quietly rechristened the Belt and Road Initiative (BRI) in English before the summit, with Beijing belatedly realizing that the optics of touting 'one' project did not sync with what it claimed was a multilateral and consultative global initiative. Curiously enough, the name remained unchanged in Mandarin, in which it is still referred to as 'Yi Dai, Yi Lu', or 'One Belt, One Road'.

If 'One Belt, One Road blue' was the latest addition to the ever-growing meteorological vocabulary of Beijing's residents, the initiative had, since its 2013 launch, grabbed plenty of headlines overseas and found its way into the vocabulary of people all over the world. And one reason for that was the remarkably successful marketing campaign China used to push the plan. In spite of the very savvy propaganda blitz and the buzz around the plan, the curious thing was that when the summit was finally convened four years later, no one still quite knew what the plan actually entailed.

Beijing encouraged this ambiguity. Part of the genius of the BRI campaign was in allowing and encouraging everyone to frame it as they saw fit, even if, until that point, there was no blueprint, no list of projects, and no funding plan. So it was quite something to see the commentariat, including in India, try and outdo one another in attempting to explain to their readers and viewers how the BRI would change the world, even if Beijing itself didn't have an idea – yet.

By the time Xi convened the summit, China's most powerful leader since Deng decided he had to show that he meant business. Four years after the plan was first announced, the country finally came out with a dizzying spread of projects covering Africa and Eurasia, along with generous funding plans.[2]

The BRI may have been named with the hope of signalling to the world China's benign intentions, but in Beijing, the country's leading thinkers were aware that a lot more than building roads was at stake. Through the BRI, what China was doing was staking a claim, for the first time, to global leadership. At a time when America under its new President Donald Trump was speaking of building walls, many in Beijing saw the current period as one of what they like to call a window of strategic opportunity. This was China's moment. This was also Xi's moment.

Restoration and Renewal

The idea of restoration and renewal has been a powerful one throughout the history of China. As historian Jonathan Spence writes, even after the many disasters of the mid-nineteenth century, at one of the lowest points in Chinese history, 'invoking the idea of restoration which had historical resonance' was a theme the Qing rulers returned to, even if doing so 'only delayed the inevitable' (in most cases and most certainly for the Qing).[3]

Since Xi came to power as the Party general secretary in 2012, two of the core pillars of his mission were declared: building a better life for people at home – what the government calls the Chinese Dream – and raising the country's profile abroad – what Xi has dubbed the 'Great Rejuvenation of the Chinese nation'. These two campaigns aren't just empty words; they are crucial to Xi's broader goal of boosting the Party's legitimacy at home and ensuring its survival, which is his most critical task. The Chinese Dream is, first and foremost, a domestic mission, but it is also inextricably linked to establishing what China sees as its rightful place in the world.[4]

The idea of national rejuvenation was not Xi's. Indeed, every leader since Sun Yat-sen, who in 1912 became the first president of the Republic of China and had founded a 'Revive China Society' as early as in 1894, has spoken of the country's revival. But it is an idea that Xi has pushed more than any of his predecessors, not just in speeches but in action, for instance, by championing China's drive for a greater global role. As Xie Yanmei, a policy analyst who studies Chinese politics at Beijing's Gavekal Research puts it, 'We are looking at a situation where the country, nation, state and party rise and fall with Xi.' Having consolidated power at home and stamped his authority over the Party, Xi is now leaving his mark on how China deals with – and views its place in – the world.

In this regard, Xi has presided over a marked shift. For the past four decades, the focus was very much at home, and on China's reform and opening up. The guiding mantra was what China called its 'peaceful rise' – its doctrine for engaging with the world. Taking off from former leader Deng Xiaoping's maxim of '*tao guang yang hui*', which can be translated as 'biding time, hiding brightness', it framed China's engagement as being essentially cautious and as a follower, rather than shaper, of the US-led unipolar world order. Since 2012, it has become increasingly evident that this is not Xi's vision. China, for long subjugated through its hundred years of humiliation, has, in Xi's view, now stood up.

For Xi, the BRI is a vehicle to deepen China's global influence, while simultaneously carrying immense domestic value in showcasing his country's emergence. Kerry Brown, a former British diplomat who closely follows Chinese politics from his vantage point as director of the Lau China Institute at King's College, describes the BRI as 'a festival of validation' for the country. 'At home, it is offering an emotionally intoxicating message, of China on its own terms conquering modernity.' It is also the platform for Xi to position China as a rival to the US – both by presenting the alternative of a different kind of superpower, and in its championing of globalization as a contrast to 'America First'.

Exporting the China Model

Along with promoting the BRI, Xi is doing what no other Chinese leader since Mao has done – he is speaking of the 'China model' as a solution for countries abroad, a sharp contrast to the defensiveness shown in the past by China's leaders when talking about their political system. At the October 2017 Party Congress in Beijing, where Xi described China as 'moving to the centre stage of the world', he, for the first time, spoke of the country as having 'blazed a new trail for other developing countries to achieve modernization'. The China model, he said, provides 'a new option for other countries and nations who want to speed up their development' and 'offers Chinese wisdom and a Chinese approach to solving the problems facing mankind'.[5]

China's push for global influence by no means began with the Belt and Road Initiative. Indeed, even the genesis of the BRI goes back a decade. The underlying logic of the plan was articulated by Chinese thinkers more than a decade before the project was finally conceived. Zheng Bijian is a leading Chinese intellectual, who is seen by some in Beijing as one of the brains behind both the 'peaceful rise' mantra and now, the BRI. In the years after China's reforms and opening up process, he was among the most influential advisers to the leadership in making a case for China to embrace globalization.

In his 2018 book, *Economic Globalization and China's Future*, which is an insightful explainer of Beijing's thinking underpinning the BRI, Zheng elaborated that the journey of re-examining China's stakes in globalization and its engagement with the world began in 2004.[6] That year, he led a research team compiling a report for the government on the 'peaceful rise' doctrine. Zheng's job was to flesh out what this would entail, and in the report, which had 22,000 Chinese characters, he identified nineteen key strategic issues.

The first and most important, for him, was whether China would always be able to maintain the impetus for economic reform and ensure the continuous expansion of its economy. The next seven challenges concerned the country's ability to handle various domestic challenges as it continued down the path of economic globalization, while the following eleven challenges dealt with China's external environment, such as the Taiwan question, relations with major powers and its dealing with neighbours.

The last part was the most striking. Zheng's report to the government highlighted as a key long-term challenge the need to ensure 'a strategic resource passage network', pointing out that China was then the world's second-largest oil importer, with 50 per cent of its supply coming from the Middle East and 80 per cent through the Malacca Strait, which China termed its 'Malacca Dilemma'. What was needed, the report argued, was a web of channels to ensure the free flow of resources through strategic passages, making the case for a BRI-like project a good ten years before it was finally unveiled.[7]

What prompted Zheng's report in 2004 were the sweeping changes in China's own post-reforms economy, and its increasing economic integration with the rest of the world. In 1996, President Jiang Zemin pushed what was then called a 'going out' strategy for SOEs. In a decade, China's overseas investments surged from a paltry $3 billion to $100 billion. This was buttressed by the country's rising share of global trade following its 'opening up' and accession to the WTO in 2001. When China entered the WTO, it accounted for less than 5 per cent of global exports. Today, it is the world's largest exporter, with a 14 per cent share. It is the largest trading partner for more than 100 countries that are now firmly in its economic orbit, and has emerged as the biggest source of foreign investment for countries ranging from Venezuela and Angola to Nepal and Sri Lanka.

The China Development Bank (CDB) and Export-Import (EXIM) Bank are funding this investment spree, and are today lending more in Africa than the World Bank and International Monetary Fund (IMF) combined.[8] In Africa and Central Asia, an increasing number of countries fell into the country's economic orbit as Beijing's SOEs embarked on massive 'resources for infrastructure' deals. China, as an authoritarian one-party state, was offering to regimes from South America to Africa a different way (from the West) of doing business. As China gobbled up the resources of these countries – it is today the world's biggest producer and consumer of everything, from coal and iron ore to copper and rare earths – it built them roads, railways and dams, with no questions asked. The BRI is a logical evolution of 'going out'; only that China's needs are now different.

On the New Silk Road

The BRI may certainly have a global footprint, but what's often forgotten is that much of the driving motivations for it lie closer home. And there are few places where you can get a better sense of the economic transformation unleashed by the initiative within China than at Xi'an, which is a crucial point on the plan. Famed for its terracotta warriors, Xi'an – or Chang'an (meaning 'eternal peace') as the old Imperial capital was known – was the starting point for many of the trading routes that comprised the network that came to be known as the Silk Road (there was never just one 'road'). Beyond the symbolism, its location in north-central China along many rail routes has given it a key role in the new initiative.

In the autumn of 2016, I travelled to the end point of the Europe–China railway in the city's suburbs. Here, three days every week, freight trains loaded with forty-one containers carrying a range of 'Made in China' goods – from machinery, auto parts and construction material to toys and clothes – pulled out of the newly built platform at the Xi'an logistics park. The trains travel 9,048 kilometres over fourteen days, traversing China, Kazakhstan, Russia and Belarus, all the way to Warsaw and Hamburg.

The first China–Europe train to Warsaw left a few days before I arrived, on 8 August 2016, hailed as perhaps the first major concrete undertaking of President Xi's grand vision to revive the old Silk Road. It takes only six days for the Chang'an train to reach the Alataw pass that separates China's western Xinjiang region and Kazakhstan; the pass has been developed into a major land port to facilitate China's westward march.

The developments reshaping Xi'an today present a snapshot of the country's ambitions as it attempts to revive the Silk Road that propelled the old city into a major trade and cultural centre. Beijing is spending billions of yuan to build a sprawling trade and logistics zone, a commodity market and other infrastructure aimed at making the city the nerve centre for the Silk Road Economic Belt that will run to Central Asia and Europe. Other branches of the belt will run to Pakistan (the China–Pakistan Economic Corridor) and Southeast Asia (the Kunming–Thailand–Singapore railway link).

In the suburbs of Xi'an, I found a new wave of projects unleashed by the BRI, centred on the newly expanded trade and logistics park located in a suburb an hour away from the city. There were office buildings and apartment blocks, and the massive, newly constructed commodity market that China hopes will become a new centre for regional trade, albeit in an unlikely suburban but still semi-rural location. At this gleaming new commodity market, the stock tickers flashed non-stop, showing the rise and fall of commodity prices across Eurasia. There were, however, no traders occupying any of the pristine white desks yet.

'We are now at maybe 50 per cent occupancy,' one representative said hopefully, despite the negligible activity on what should have been a busy weekday morning. He acknowledged that it had been a challenge to attract people because the park was so far from the city, even though the government had offered apartments for a fraction of the cost to bring in tenants. A 'Silk Road shopping mall', offering sales of goods from across South and Southeast Asia, the Middle East and Europe, was similarly deserted, with few occupied shops and fewer customers.

At the customs clearance hall that abuts the China–Europe train platform, where the freight trains arrive and depart, there wasn't much action when I visited, but it was the calm before the storm, said Li Pingwei, an official of the committee that oversees the park. In all fairness, he did acknowledge that the timing of the launch of this mega project hadn't been ideal, with Europe being swept by a tide of anti-globalization and protectionism. Concerns about Chinese goods flooding the market were rising. The train from Xi'an leaves with full containers and returns almost empty, but for 200 tons of sunflower seed oil that a local company is now importing from Kazakhstan. 'The fact is,' lamented Li, 'they [the Europeans] do not have goods to offer that the China market needs. If they can produce something good enough, Chinese consumers will welcome them.' He shrugged as he said the last line.

There appear to be at least three principal motivations behind the BRI. The first is to secure China's access to natural resources and energy in the long term, through pipelines for oil and gas from Central Asia, as well as long-lasting energy deals with oil companies from Russia, Central Asia and the Middle East. The second is to address the internal challenge posed by the transformation of the country's economy from manufacturing dominance to services. This not only requires finding markets to absorb the excess capacity of older industries, such as steel and cement, which were on the wane, but also finding new markets for Chinese companies in the services sector. Lastly, there is the security issue, revolving around the need to bring development and jobs to western China, where areas such as Xinjiang and Tibet lag behind the rest of the country, and to address potential sources of instability from outside China that could spill over, most notably in Afghanistan and Pakistan.[9]

The Xi'an projects underline the search for new markets which China is trying to secure in different ways: through connectivity initiatives that will bring markets closer, and undertakings overseas – either by direct investments or massive lending – with the hope that these projects in partner countries will increase the capacity of those states to absorb Chinese exports. Under the BRI, the breadth and depth of China's involvement in South and Southeast Asia, Central Asia and Africa has deepened. It is true that many of the current projects predated the BRI, with the genesis of some in the earlier phase of the 'going out' strategy, starting in the early 2000s. What the BRI is doing is adding both investment and ambition to these projects. But its most important legacy is perhaps beyond money or infrastructure creation: by bringing these many disparate projects under one banner, the BRI is creating a powerful idea to sell to the world.

Chinese state-owned enterprises today are building railways in Africa, acquiring and operating mines all over the world, from Latin America to Afghanistan, constructing dams from Argentina to Myanmar, and building ports at every other littoral Indian Ocean state. It is building railways in Indonesia, Malaysia and Thailand, and working to extend its bullet train network, already the world's longest, from Yunnan province south into Laos, Thailand, Malaysia, all the way to Singapore. It has opened a pipeline connecting the Kyaukphyu port in Myanmar with Kunming in Yunnan, giving it access to the Bay of Bengal for energy shipments. On the other side of India, in the Arabian Sea, the Gwadar port in Pakistan –

planned as an alternative point of access to avoid the Malacca problem – has been revamped, although even Chinese economists concede that the suggested idea of a pipeline to Xinjiang, going right across the Himalayas, is uneconomical and risky.

The Debt Burden Problem

The China–Europe transcontinental rail network, aimed at linking the former's manufacturing hubs to the latter, was the first major BRI project to be launched. Under this plan, China has added routes and doubled the number of trains to 1,700. Besides Xi'an, there are trains from the world's biggest commodity market at Yiwu, in southern Zhejiang province, and from the western metropolis of Chongqing – laden with everything from electrical machinery and laptops to toys and clothes – travelling all the way to London, Hamburg and Duisburg.

The long-term feasibility of the network has become a matter of debate within China. As a result of the change in track from standard gauge to Russian gauge, containers have to be switched onto different trains in Kazakhstan, and back again to standard gauge cars in Poland, all adding to the already steep costs. While the trains halve the thirty-day shipping time, they cost twice as much, making little sense for most companies to switch from shipping.

Chinese economists have also flagged the financing risks – issues that have grown in the wake of the coronavirus pandemic, when many partner countries have expressed their inability to pay back loans or continue financing some joint projects. Debt-fuelled growth has been part and parcel of China's infrastructure building at home. The problem is that when this model is exported overseas, it creates friction with the host countries, particularly if a takeover of sensitive assets is involved.

What is clear is that through its model of lending, China is tearing up the rule book for international financing of infrastructure projects. The nation has surpassed the World Bank and IMF as the biggest lender for developing countries, accounting for a quarter of total bank lending for emerging markets. In the past, creditors such as Japan, which was the biggest overseas lender in much of Asia, lent to developing countries at concessionary, below-market rates to fund infrastructure projects that often bore low returns over a long period.

Chinese lending, by contrast, is typically at market rates, with shorter maturities, according to a study of 1,974 Chinese loans and 2,947 grants to 152 countries from 1949 to 2017 by the Kiel Institute for the World Economy in Germany. 'Chinese loans have helped to finance large-scale investments in infrastructure, energy and mining in more than 100 developing and emerging market countries, with potentially large positive effects for growth and prosperity,' the report noted.

> At the same time, however, the large lending flows resulted in the build-up of high debt servicing burdens. For the 50 main recipients of Chinese direct lending, the average stock of debt owed to China has increased from less than 1 per cent of GDP in 2005 to more than 15 per cent of debtor country GDP in 2017, at least according to our lower bound estimates. For these countries, debt to China now accounts for more than 40 per cent of total external debt, on average.

Moreover, the study found around 50 per cent of lending was 'hidden', or not recorded by the IMF, World Bank or credit rating agencies, and was particularly severe in Venezuela, Zimbabwe and Iran.[10]

In the forthcoming decade, the two main sources of Chinese lending, the CDB and EXIM Bank, will lend billions of dollars for projects overseas. In addition to a $50 billion Silk Road Fund, the CDB and EXIM Bank have said they will lend up to $100 billion annually in the next decade. The huge demand for infrastructure, coupled with the limited availability of lending from either the West or multilateral institutions, means that the demand for Chinese funds, regardless of the higher costs of repayment, will persist.

But the risk isn't only for the borrowing countries. Many top Chinese economists have expressed fears that China may be overextending itself. When debt burdens are becoming impossible to finance for partner countries, which are also facing criticism at home because Chinese companies are being given contracts without competitive bidding for projects, deals may have to be renegotiated. In Malaysia, the railway project was suspended after a change in government, and only resumed after China was forced to renegotiate, offering more favourable terms to the country.

The worry among some economists in Beijing is that the Malaysia example is just the start. Xu Chenggang, a leading economist who is professor at the Cheung Kong Graduate School of Business in Beijing, told me there was growing concern that many of the countries China is lending to might fail to pay back loans because they had incentives not to pay. 'Eventually, China will suffer from defaults,' he said, suggesting that even if Chinese companies took over assets or stakes in overseas projects, there was no guarantee of returns. While there are signs of greater due diligence, in the first few years after the launch of the BRI in 2013 there were clear indicators that political considerations, aimed at showcasing the project's success, were being given greater weight than economic ones.

The view of some economists in Beijing, including Xu, is that the BRI has taken China's economic reforms process, aimed at giving the market greater sway, in the wrong direction, particularly when it comes to the role played by bloated SOEs. 'Rather than carry out reforms to privatize the state sector, the BRI is designed to overcome the overcapacity problem by exporting machines, steel and cement to other countries, to let them borrow from China and purchase Chinese capacities,' Xu said. 'So we are not only facing this disease, but now exporting it to other countries.'

Sri Lanka has emerged as one of the debtors struggling to pay back loans. The government that took over in 2015 under Maithripala Sirisena had to ask China to renegotiate contracts approved by the previous Mahinda Rajapaksa regime, which was blamed for being too generous to Chinese firms. Despite the backlash in many countries, there are two powerful factors in China's favour. For one, the amorphous and ambiguous nature of the plan has lent the BRI flexibility that could allow the country to tweak and adjust the plan as it sees fit. And, more importantly, the lack of an alternative for many countries means that even if they do have grouses with Chinese projects, they ultimately come back because other options end up being costlier. And until that changes, the likelihood is that the BRI isn't going anywhere, despite the new wave of uncertainty unleashed by the pandemic.

Considering all the issues and risks, the consultancy firm Silk Road Associates outlined five possible scenarios for the BRI. Under the best-case scenario, total investment under the plan – which will come, it is important to note, from various Chinese sources, public and private – would reach $1.3 trillion by 2030, if China was able to show flexibility and learn the lessons from the less successful projects, such as those in Sri Lanka. The worst-case scenario, it suggested, would leave the BRI struggling to go beyond $560 billion in net investment, crippled by political opposition abroad.[11] What is striking is, even going by the report's worst-case option – although this assessment pre-dated the coronavirus pandemic – we are likely to see more than half a trillion dollars worth of Chinese investment, which would still mean a considerable deepening of the country's stakes abroad.

A Vision for the World

Will the BRI succeed? Whether or not it does economically, there is no denying that it has already made a deep geopolitical impact. And that has to do with the power of ideas, of creating a narrative about the inevitability of Chinese supremacy. The BRI is sometimes criticized for its ambiguity, for being a nebulous project without a blueprint. Yet, this ambiguity is also a strength. The BRI isn't really a multilateral or global initiative. And more than a project or initiative, it can perhaps best be thought of as 'a movement representing slow but ineluctable expansion of Chinese influence'.[12]

The BRI is only one element of a much broader picture of how China sees the world and its place in it. In his book, *Belt and Road: A Chinese World Order*, Bruno Macaes writes that this ambiguity is reminiscent of the older Chinese idea of *tianxia*, or 'all under heaven', where tributary states 'attracted by the splendour of Chinese civilization, voluntarily submitted to the Chinese order'. 'Legally and politically,' Macaes writes, 'states in the Belt and Road would remain fully sovereign and independent. In practice, economic power would bind the system together and prevent it from falling apart.'[13]

This informality distinguishes it from the Western liberal order, founded on institutions and law. 'The Belt and Road is not an entity with fixed rules; it is deliberately intended to be informal, unstructured and opaque.' Comparing it with the European Union, Macaes says it is 'less ambitious than the EU because no body of supranational institutions has been envisioned, but it is more ambitious because it touches the core of national sovereignty by propounding a model of state relations where every decision is in principle open to external influence'. National sovereignty, in other words, 'is never renounced, but neither is it affirmed or consecrated. Tianxia is neither national nor supranational.'[14]

China's strategic thinkers are, more than ever, looking to the past to etch out this vision for the future, drawing on its very long history of strategic thought. One prominent example is the work of Yan Xuetong at Tsinghua University, who has been pointing to pre-Qin era (221 BCE) strategic thought and making a case for how it still influences Chinese strategic thinking today. One idea that is finding currency is the concept of 'humane authority', which was popularized by pre-Qin thinkers. In Yan's view, current-day thinking doesn't make a distinction between what he calls power and authority. Power is based on the strength of enforcement and built on force. Authority is based on the strength of legitimacy and built on trust. The idea of *tianxia* is an example of what Yan calls 'humane authority'. And it's this idea, he believes, that will ultimately decide China's future. 'Only when the international community accepts that China is a more responsible state than the United States,' he writes, 'that China will be able to replace the United States as the world's leading state.'[15]

Yan acknowledges China has a long way to go on this count; the reputational loss it suffered from the COVID-19 pandemic has, perhaps, served a stark reminder of this fact, although Chinese strategic experts, including Yan, have been quick to point out that the US has suffered on that count too. The problem for China, as Yan puts it, is that 'whether a state is a responsible major power is not something the state itself can decide. It is a matter of judgement by other states.' And this presents a paradox. Should China increase its material power without at the same time increasing its political power, it will perhaps only create further anxieties in the international community, and thereby erode its own authority and legitimacy.

Yan believes the US successfully replaced Britain as the world's hegemon not only because of its economic and military strength, but also because of its role in liberating and rebuilding countries after the Second World War. He cautions that if China's foreign policy fails to improve the state's authority in the eyes of the world, it will follow Japan's example, and fail to emerge as a leading state in the world. One way China should distinguish itself from the US, he believes, is when it comes to promoting its values abroad. He says China should reverse the US approach and 'not impose a single standard on international society'. The traditional idea of 'all under heaven', in his view, should become the Chinese way.[16]

What China has been able to do effectively – and here India has much to learn – is offer its own vision to the world, regardless of whether you agree or disagree with it. India has its own incredibly rich history in this realm, but one very stark difference is the systematic and rigorous manner in which modern Chinese strategic thinkers are both educated in – and are actively tapping and moulding – this history to China's present context. They aren't studying only Western schools of thought of political science and international relations but Chinese ones as well.

It is too early to tell whether the BRI will succeed in remaking the world in China's vision. As we have seen, there are innumerable risks involved. But where it is succeeding is in creating a narrative that suggests the inevitability of Chinese ascendance. In truth, there is nothing inevitable about it. Ultimately, its success or failure will hinge as much on the role of the country's partners – especially in its neighbourhood – in this initiative, partners whose agency is often overlooked. One reason why many countries choose Chinese financing, as has been noted, is the lack of credible alternatives. This is where some other countries have a crucial role to play in shaping a world in flux. And none more so than India, which is among the few that can potentially offer the alternative that many are seeking – but only if it steps up to the plate.

For China, as is the case for any country, its global ambitions ultimately rest on developments at home. Nothing has illustrated that more clearly than the coronavirus pandemic. If China's continued economic growth is the basis for all of its global ambitions, the state of its politics is just as important. History tells us so. In 1793, Lord Macartney, a former governor of Madras, set sail on what was Britain's first diplomatic mission to China, sent as an emissary by King George III to the Qianlong emperor. He was spectacularly rebuffed – the emperor writing to the king that China did not have 'the slightest need of your country's manufactures'. Of the king's request to have a representative in Peking, the emperor noted it was 'not in harmony with the regulations of the Celestial Empire'. That would set the stage for a series of developments that would eventually culminate in the disasters of the Opium War and China's 'century of humiliation', a powerful memory that continues to underpin its nationalism and resurgence today. On his long journey back, Macartney wrote, 'The Empire of China is an old, crazy, first-rate man-of-war, which a fortunate succession of able-bodied and vigilant officers has contrived to keep afloat for these one hundred and fifty years past, and to overawe her neighbours merely by her bulk and appearance.' But without those men, he concluded, China would only drift, until 'dashed to pieces on the shore'.[17]

8

Competition and Collaboration

'SOME FOREIGNERS WITH FULL BELLIES and nothing better to do,' remarked the Chinese gentleman in a sharp suit, 'engage in finger-pointing at us. But China does not export revolution. Second, it does not export famine and poverty. And third, it does not mess around with you. So what else is there to say?'[1] In the decade since Xi, then China's vice president, summed up in those five sentences the country's view of the world – and his thinly veiled disdain for the US-led world order – he hasn't been as undiplomatic in his public speeches. But neither has he disguised his ambitions.

Xi's comments in 2009 would presage a new kind of diplomacy, of which the Belt and Road Initiative (BRI) is perhaps the clearest example. The Xi doctrine – once dubbed 'Xiplomacy' by the state media – is less shy about pushing China's goals and speaking up about its view of the world. As one Beijing international relations scholar put it to me, it is a mix of strong nationalism and assertiveness on China's core interests and territorial disputes, coupled with a more proactive diplomacy in the neighbourhood. And all this is riding on, by Chinese standards, an extraordinarily personalized role for the country's leader.[2]

Xi has implicitly taken ownership of China's overseas engagement – both the rewards and the risks – a responsibility shared in the past by the division of power between the president, premier and Politburo Standing Committee. Xi's predecessor, Hu Jintao, was a stickler for protocol. For instance, he rarely directly engaged with prime ministers from India and elsewhere as much as Xi has done, instead leaving the task to the premier. Hu only engaged with heads of state and presidents as per protocol.

This shift, of course, is about more than just protocol. Beijing appears willing to play a greater role in shaping global institutions, taking a lead in mediating in international disputes, and perhaps most importantly, demonstrating confidence in offering China's authoritarian capitalist model abroad as an alternative to the Western liberal order. For the past four decades, China's diplomacy has followed Deng Xiaoping's cautious maxim of '*tao guang yang hui*', or 'biding time, hiding brightness'. The new phrase of choice in Beijing is a more confident '*fen fa you wei*', 'strive for achievement', underlining its desire to 'proactively shape' (as its diplomats now like to say) its external environment.

India in a Chinese World

At the heart of the India–China strategic dilemma is a fundamental difference in how the two countries see each other, and their place in the world. India sees China as an equal. And Chinese strategic thinkers resent that notion. In fact, they see it as somewhat insulting that the Indian strategic elite dare to think of themselves as being at par with a five-times-larger economy and a country that spends at least four times more on its military. For many Chinese strategists, it is the Indian reluctance to acknowledge this power differential that is at the heart of the multiple problems confronting the relationship. For Indian strategists, in turn, it is the fear that the country will be forced to acquiesce to China's regional dominance which poses the greatest concern. The debate about the BRI, and India's role in it, was just one example of this worry.

This resentment in China about suggesting any sort of equivalence is not new. For all the talk from the two governments of being two old civilizations that share close cultural and historical links, the fact is that for more than a century, this resentment has been a prominent strand of Chinese thought. One manifestation of this was during Rabindranath Tagore's visit to China in 1924 for a lecture tour, at the invitation of the prominent Chinese intellectual Liang Qichao. Tagore remains beloved in China today for his poetry. He was certainly a star when he arrived, eleven years after he became Asia's first Nobel laureate in literature. He was greeted by throngs of fans, even worshipped by some as a sage-like figure, but he also faced a frosty reception from many of China's leading intellectuals of the time.

At a time when Chinese thinkers were looking to Western ideas as the antidote to all of China's ills, Tagore's preaching of Asian values and solidarity was not welcomed. 'The poet-saint of India has arrived at last, welcomed with thunderous applause,' the famous Chinese novelist Mao Dun complained. 'We are determined not to welcome the Tagore who loudly sings the praises of eastern civilisation. Oppressed as we are by militarists from within the country and by the imperialists from without, this is no time for dreaming.' Chen Duxiu, the towering Chinese intellectual who co-founded the Communist Party with Li Dazhao, wrote of the Chinese youth, 'We must warn them not to let themselves be Indianized. Unless, that is, they want their coffins to lie one day in a land under the heel of a colonial power.'[3]

A hundred years on after Tagore's visit, the idea of India as a weak, colonized power still persists within China's strategic community. The image of Indians who policed the streets of Shanghai and Hong Kong at the behest of their British masters remains deeply etched in public consciousness. The most commonly used racist insult towards Indians even today has its roots in a term directed at the widely reviled Indian policemen from colonial times. If it was the British Empire then, the view among many Chinese strategists today is that India cannot emerge as a challenger on its own merits. In their view, India is merely riding on the coattails of the US, happy to be used as a pawn in its rivalry with China. Hence, for many Chinese strategists, the relationship with India is not seen on its own merits, but viewed in the context of China's great rivalry with America.

This line of argument surfaces whenever there is a dispute in the India–China relationship. During one such instance, when ties were strained in 2009 after tensions along the border and ahead of the Dalai Lama's visit to Tawang, a rare commentary on India in the *People's Daily*, the Party's official newspaper, complained that although 'India is still a lesser power than China in terms of economy and military, both conventionally and unconventionally', it was 'evident that the U.S. has been tipping the balance between China and India, seeking to woo India away from Russia and China and, in the meantime, feeding India's ambition to match China force for force by its ever burgeoning arms sales to India.' 'Emboldened by the U.S., and fuelled by the media over the flare-up of nationalism in India and chauvinism among the Hindu public, the Indian government is somewhat eclipsed by the media-manipulated public opinions, and gets disoriented when making decisions,' it said.[4]

Disparaging India's global ambitions – and highlighting the power differential – is an argument often made by Hu Xijin, the firebrand editor of the *Global Times*, a nationalistic tabloid published both in Chinese and English by the *People's Daily*. The English edition devotes a lot of coverage to India, although many of its articles aren't published in the more influential Chinese edition. In the view of some diplomats, who don't take the English edition very seriously, many of the articles in it are just clickbait. But there is no denying the influence of Hu, a journalist who rose to fame for his coverage of the bombing of the Chinese Embassy in Belgrade in 1999 by the US, which stirred massive outrage and protests in China. Among Chinese social media users, Hu is both praised for his nationalistic views and also disparaged for being a paid shill of the Party. In the government, Hu is seen as both an asset – for articulating views that diplomats share but cannot voice – and sometimes as a headache – when the government is criticized by the readers of Hu's paper for being too 'weak'.

Following the border tensions and the clash in Galwan Valley in June 2020, Hu was among the most outspoken Chinese voices hitting out at India. 'I must warn Indian nationalists: If your soldiers cannot even defeat Chinese soldiers in unarmed clashes, then guns and other firearms will not help them. The reason: The military strength of China is much more advanced and stronger than that of India,' he wrote in one commentary. 'Some Indians arrogantly believe that the modernization of Indian troops will allow them to... take revenge on China for India's defeat in the 1962 border war. I'd love to tell them that there was not much difference between China and India in terms of economic strength in 1962, but today, China's GDP is about five times that of India and China's military expenditure is over three times that of India according to Western estimates. If India escalates the border dispute with China into skirmishes or even local wars, it would be like an egg dashing itself against a rock.'[5]

With China's growing global ambitions under Xi, these views are only deepening. In the three decades since the normalization of the India–China relationship, a bilateral relationship had assumed global importance, with India and China cooperating – and competing – on a global canvas on various issues. These range from climate change and global trade, where they see eye to eye, to the freedom of navigation and maritime security in the Indo-Pacific region – a new theatre where the two countries with expanding global footprints are increasingly rubbing up against each other.

Both countries have done remarkably well over three decades to carry on what has become an increasingly difficult dance of cooperating and competing. Much of this cooperation, particularly when it came to global issues, was predicated on a somewhat shared understanding of the world order, and a common desire for both multipolarity and a greater voice for developing nations in global institutions. As two large, emerging economies that benefited tremendously from globalization, both seek a larger voice and fairness in the running of global institutions historically dominated by the West. On climate change, for instance, India and China have found common cause in shaping the discussions on the role of developing countries and in pushing the West to extend financial support to the developing world. It is these shared interests, coupled with finding bilateral convergences, such as a growing trade relationship, that provided a strong logic to drive a cooperative relationship despite many bilateral points of discord, from the boundary to China's relations with Pakistan.

With China's changing view of the world and its place in it – as the lone challenger to the current global hegemon, and as the dominant power in Asia – this convergence appears to be fast eroding. As some had imagined over the past two decades, would China be content to merely be one of the world's many emerging new poles? India, for its part, has made clear that it has no intention of acquiescing to China's regional dominance.

Indeed, India was the only prominent country to boycott the first BRI forum in 2017, to which even the US and Japan sent delegations. Its initial objection to the BRI was informed by China's inclusion of the China–Pakistan Economic Corridor (CPEC) – which runs from Kashgar in Xinjiang to Gwadar in Pakistan, through Pakistan-occupied Kashmir (PoK) – as a flagship project. In one sense, the problem was one of Beijing's own making. While it is true that the CPEC plan predated the BRI, it was made clear to Chinese officials on many levels that if they included the CPEC under the project, it would leave India no option but to refuse to collaborate. One possible solution would have been for China to reframe the CPEC route so it would not run through the territory India claims as its own, instead linking Gwadar to the eastern edge of Khyber Pakhtunkhwa. This would have neatly solved the problem, but a narrow Chinese view that insisted on a definition of the corridor that ended in Xinjiang put an end to the alternative prospect.

For many in India, China's BRI approach only reinforced the perception of a country that was increasingly following one maxim in the way it dealt with the world: 'my way or the highway'. The CPEC has come to be seen as not a cause but merely a symptom of the broader Chinese unwillingness to address India's concerns, but to also increasingly prioritize Pakistani sensitivities in its dealing with India – in a break from a two-decade approach of carefully balancing the two relationships. The CPEC issue was, for many Indian officials, a reflection of a wider problem confronting the BRI: Beijing chose not to bring on board the views of India or any other country during the many months when the blueprint was being firmed up. Indeed, Indian officials in the embassy in Beijing were not approached even once for talks on the initiative in the four years that passed from Xi's unveiling of the project in 2013 and the first forum in 2017. This was a 'project for the world' that was presented to the world by one nation, as a fait accompli.

In 2017, when India decided to boycott the first BRI forum in Beijing, it did so in isolation. Moreover, its statement explaining its decision went beyond issues of sovereignty in PoK to also questioning China's modes of financing the BRI, the debt burdens foisted on partner countries, and issues over a lack of transparency in Chinese projects. By the time the second BRI forum was held in Beijing two years later, these same criticisms were echoed by a number of countries, and are now regularly voiced by the US and others.

Of course, pushing back against China's narrative is one thing. The more difficult challenge lies in fronting a concrete response to the rising Chinese influence in India's backyard, and offering a credible alternative. Here, India hasn't stepped up enough. For many of China's Asian neighbours, the pull of its economic orbit is too strong to resist, especially when the US, still the dominant military power in Asia, appears unwilling to offer an economic counter. The Trans Pacific Partnership (TPP) trade deal, that excludes China, was pushed by the Barack Obama administration, but one of President Donald Trump's first acts was to withdraw from it. Japan remains a major player in overseas financing but has a limited capacity. Regardless of these challenges, for India, the decision in 2017 was a bold step. It may also turn out to be one of the most consequential decisions in India's foreign policy for years to come.

When Modi Came Calling

The legacy of the border dispute and the 1962 war – which the next part of this book examines – still casts a long shadow on ties between the neighbours. Prime Minister Rajiv Gandhi's surprise visit to China in 1988, when he met with then paramount leader Deng Xiaoping, was path-breaking in many respects. Not only did it mark the start of a thaw in relations following the post-1962 freeze, it also set the framework for the relationship, which was essentially, as Deng suggested, to shelve differences and work on areas of common interest. To be sure, the 1988 model worked effectively, opening up the relationship in the decades since Rajiv Gandhi's visit in unprecedented ways. Bilateral trade surged from a few billion dollars at the turn of the millennium to $93 billion in 2019, when China remained India's biggest trading partner. There are close to 25,000 Indian students in China, most studying medicine. China is today the biggest overseas market for Bollywood by a mile.[6] Yet, despite all these changes, the boundary dispute always lingered, with tensions erupting with regular frequency, leaving a relationship stuck in an endless cycle of ups and downs.

When Narendra Modi was elected India's prime minister in 2014, officials in both Delhi and Beijing sensed an opportunity to break this cycle. In May 2015, Xi laid out the red carpet for Modi's first visit to China as prime minister. Breaking the country's carefully followed diplomatic protocol, Xi – for the first time for any foreign leader – travelled out of Beijing to host Modi.

Even the location, Xi'an, was chosen with much thought, and was laced with symbolism. This visit would mark the second leg of what was called 'hometown diplomacy'. In September 2014, barely four months after taking office as prime minister, Modi had taken a political gamble by going out of the way to host Xi, travelling with him to his home state of Gujarat. In fact, his election victory had sparked an unusual amount of optimism in China.

There were at least two reasons for this. For one, the wide perception among analysts I spoke to in Beijing was that China had, in the past, found it easier to deal with Bharatiya Janata Party (BJP) governments – a view that dates back to the favourable impression many Chinese have of the Atal Bihari Vajpayee government. It was the Vajpayee government that backed the setting up of the Special Representatives mechanism to resolve the border dispute in 2003. That there was a government in Delhi with a strong mandate had also raised hopes, drawing comparisons with Rajiv Gandhi's government in 1988 when his visit to China brought the relationship out of the post-1962 deep freeze.

The second reason for the renewed attention on India was Modi's own track record as Gujarat chief minister, when his state became a favourite among Chinese companies for investment. Modi, then persona non grata in the West following the 2002 riots, made regular visits to China – three, in fact – and Japan, and saw the economic success of both countries as a model for India to follow. Some Chinese newspapers even speculated that he could emerge as India's Deng Xiaoping, the country's architect of reform and opening up. Lan Jianxue, among the younger hands in the Beijing strategic community, who also served a stint in the Chinese embassy in Delhi, told me that Modi 'is believed to be a business-friendly politician'. 'And he had been engaging with Chinese entrepreneurs since he became Chief Minister of Gujarat. If he wins with a stable ruling coalition, we expect he can do something substantive to remove obstacles and barriers and discrimination imposed against Chinese investments in India. I expect the bilateral relationship will not suffer too many curves.'[7]

China certainly wasn't wasting any time after Modi's election victory. Less than two weeks after the new government took charge on 26 May 2014, President Xi dispatched his foreign minister, Wang Yi, to Delhi as a special envoy – something China had never done with such speed for any country. The suave Wang

Yi is among the finest products of China's well-oiled diplomatic machinery. He speaks Japanese but is also an India hand, having dealt with the country for many years when he was an official at the Asia Department of the Ministry of Foreign Affairs (MFA).

The MFA in Beijing granted me a rare interview with Wang before he left Beijing for Delhi – itself a sign of unusual outreach from China – although, unfortunately, it turned out to be a written interview. Wang waxed eloquent about the possibilities for the relationship under Modi and Xi. 'I was here in this beautiful country many times, but this trip is different. It is a trip to convey messages and to get to know more friends. It is also a trip to cement our existing friendship and explore further cooperation,' he said. 'My trip brings a most important message to the people of India – China stands by your side throughout your efforts of reform and development, and your pursuit of dreams.'

On the boundary question, he expressed the hope that although it was 'difficult', with 'strong will and resolve, we will eventually find a solution'. 'Even if we could not resolve it for the time being,' he suggested, 'we could at least manage it effectively, not allowing it to affect the normal development of our relations.' Wang used the favoured Chinese phrase for the dispute, describing it as being 'left over from history' – a reminder that its origins were not of India's or China's making, but an inheritance of the two newly created states in 1947 and 1949.

Despite the heady optimism of a fresh start, the first Modi–Xi meeting in India did not go as planned. The first leg of Xi's trip, in Gujarat, did make global headlines for the incredible optics. Photographs of China's most powerful leader in years sitting on a traditional Gujarati *jhula*, or swing, along with his glamorous singer wife, Peng Liyuan, went viral in China, at a time when there was enormous interest in the very private life of the president. 'Xi and Peng showed their love for each other abroad,' read one later article on the Qixi festival (known as China's Valentine's Day), published on the front page of the *People's Daily*. 'In India, after Peng sat down on a swing and played with it for a bit, she patted on the seat beside her, inviting Xi to play with her together,' it gushed, about what happened to be the first-ever image the Chinese public saw of the couple in a somewhat relaxed setting.[8]

Equally powerful were the images of Modi and Xi casually strolling in Sabarmati Ashram, appearing relaxed in each other's company, conversing only in the presence of their interpreters with no trailing aides. Modi was reasonably pleased with the first day of the visit, although he did most of the talking. But, by the time the two leaders were in Delhi the next day, news had broken on India's rambunctious television channels that a stand-off at the border in Chumar, in Ladakh, had escalated. This is one of the points where there are differing perceptions of the Line of Actual Control (LAC), where patrols regularly run into each other, the latest in a long series of stand-offs because of the lack of clarity on both sides of the LAC.

The trigger this time was the PLA extending a road into what India saw as territory on its side of the LAC. The previous year, a similar impasse in the Depsang plains in the run-up to the visit of the Chinese premier Li Keqiang had cast a shadow over the entire trip. Just a year later, history was repeating itself. Modi's political gamble hadn't worked. He was left facing criticism at home, both from the Opposition and, according to reports, from some within his own party, for indulging in '*jhula* diplomacy' (as it was disparagingly called) even as the PLA was sending in more forces to escalate an ongoing stand-off. The deadlock was, however, resolved reasonably quickly, a few days after Xi returned to Beijing.

By the time Modi landed in Xi'an the following summer, in May 2015, the reality check from the Chumar stand-off had somewhat dampened earlier expectations of a major breakthrough in relations. Even with the two new strong leaderships at the helm, India–China relations had reverted to type: back to the cycle of ups and downs, where border crises give way to rapprochements and hopes of new beginnings – until the next crisis sets in.

Despite the disappointment of the 2014 visit, Xi for his part made sure to go all out to receive his guest, just as Modi had done.

He flew to his native province of Shaanxi and the old imperial capital Xi'an and personally oversaw preparations for the Indian prime minister's visit. He ditched protocol in two major ways, which Chinese officials were keen to highlight to me. For one, Xi, as president and head of state, usually engaged with other heads of state. According to diplomatic protocol, it should have been second-ranked Premier Li Keqiang who hosted Modi. While it was presented as a signal of how seriously Xi was investing in Modi and India, it was equally revelatory of how he was taking a hands-on approach to diplomacy, in contrast to his predecessor who had shared the responsibility with the premier.

Second, this was the first time Xi was travelling outside of Beijing to host any foreign leader. This was certainly significant, and was seized on by Indian officials as well, who said that under Modi and Xi, India's relations with China had entered a new phase. The high point of the visit would be a 'walk and talk' between Modi and Xi at Xi'an's famous Great Wild Goose Pagoda, another location full of symbolism.

The pagoda was where the famed Chinese monk Xuan Zang translated the scriptures he brought back to China ruled by the Tang Dynasty (618–907), after his epic journey to India in the seventh century, when he stayed in Nalanda and travelled around the country. Xuan Zang is himself an interesting representation of India–China cultural contact: widely known in both countries and the ultimate ambassador of historical and cultural links, but somehow is still a source of confusion. Spelled Xuan Zang (pronounced shuwen zaa-ng), the monk is, for some reason, still referred to in Indian history textbooks as 'Hiuen Tsang' using a long outdated Wade–Giles romanization. This has led to unfortunate consequences, leading to not only tongue-twisting pronunciations that bear no resemblance to the old monk's name, but much confusion when the subject comes up in conversation between Indian visitors and their Chinese hosts. I've seen a visiting Indian dignitary or two invoke with much delight the story of this monk as a way to establish a connect with their Chinese counterparts, only to leave them with utterly confused expressions as they wondered who this fascinating 'Hew-en Sang' character was.

In Xi'an, the disappointments from Depsang and Chumar appeared long forgotten, and the Chinese side went to somewhat extreme lengths to demonstrate its hospitality. One of the more peculiar sights of Modi's first day in Xi'an was a clearly prearranged cheering squad (by the Chinese government), which greeted the Indian prime minister as he got down from his car at the Daxingshan temple, chanting 'Modi! Modi!' The spectacle harked back to the days when crowds lined the streets as Nehru and Zhou Enlai rode into Beijing in an open-top car. The Indian television channels that followed Modi in Xi'an fell for the bait, describing the prime minister as a rock star, who was beloved in Xi'an, even if the choreographed welcome was plainly evident to anyone familiar with the city. Most of its inhabitants were unaware of who Modi was, or even for that matter that China's own president was in town, as my conversations with a dozen or so locals in the Great Wild Goose Pagoda square showed.

As far as body language went, there appeared to be far more warmth between Modi and Xi this time – where perhaps, unlike in Gujarat, a reticent Xi had to open up to play host. It was fascinating to watch the two leaders stroll side by side at the pagoda, in the midst of a light drizzle, and I was lucky to be among the few journalists selected randomly to trail behind them, albeit just out of earshot. The most interesting exchange came at the end of the talks. Xi waited patiently as Modi wrote a long note, in his impeccable handwriting, in the visitors' book following his guided tour – with China's most powerful man playing guide – of the priceless Buddhist relics housed in the pagoda museum. As they prepared to leave, by which time the television crews had been shown the door, Modi grabbed Xi by his arm and ushered him, out of the view of the remaining cameras, behind one of the gingko trees in the pagoda's courtyard. There, only in the presence of the translators, both leaders had an animated conversation – the most animated they were during the entire visit. It lasted perhaps five minutes, but what was said remains a mystery.

After the 2014 visit, expectations had been tempered, and the focus was more on managing – rather than resolving – thorny issues, such as the boundary question. That was the one main outcome of Xi'an, with Modi and Xi declaring that while an early settlement of the boundary 'should be pursued as a strategic objective' and both sides need to resolve differences including the boundary 'in a proactive manner', the more immediate priority was ensuring peace and tranquillity on the border.[9] This would serve as a guarantor for continued development in the relationship.

In essence, they reaffirmed the 1988 model, saying that differences would not come in the way of other areas of development. One immediate takeaway was the confidence-building measure of opening up a new and shorter route through the Nathu La pass for pilgrims undertaking the Kailash Manasarovar yatra, for which Modi thanked Xi. I travelled to Yadong, on the Chinese side of Nathu La, the following month to report on the arrival of the first batch of the pilgrims. The political optics were certainly hard to miss. Top provincial officials from Tibet, including the vice governor, had travelled all the way from Lhasa to welcome the pilgrims, who were led by BJP Member of Parliament Tarun Vijay.

'This is a new beginning,' an excited Vijay told me. 'A place where there were negative vibes before, we are having coffee, such a welcome and such bonhomie. This is a great example to the world of how two nations can create a pilgrimage of friendship, and this would not have happened without the leadership of Prime Minister Modi and President Xi.' But rather than mark a new beginning, that day in the summer of 2015 would turn out to be yet another false dawn. Modi would find, like many before him, the cycle of ups and downs would prove hard to break.

9

Where China Meets India

YADONG, ON THE SOUTHERN EDGE of Tibet, is the point where China meets India. Getting there by road from Lhasa takes you right across the roof of the world. As I left Lhasa on a summer morning in 2015 and headed south, towards India, the long, winding road skirted pristine lakes. Many of these are sacred to the Tibetans, their banks dotted with dozens of prostrating worshippers, yaks in tow.

The immaculately paved G318 national expressway takes you all the way to Shigatse, and right past the stunning backdrop of the Tashilhunpo monastery, the old seat of the Panchen Lamas. Running close to 5,500 kilometres, G318 is the longest highway in China. Travel on it end to end and you will cover the entire breadth of the country. You will criss-cross seven provinces and take in some of the ultimate symbols of Chinese engineering. Your journey will begin amid the gleaming skyscrapers of Pudong – the centre of Chinese financial power in Shanghai – before you traverse the manufacturing heartland of Zhejiang, head west past the Three Gorges Dam and the megacity of Chongqing on the Yangtze, before you finally make the steep climb up the Tibetan plateau into China's western frontier.

Feats of Chinese engineering are easy to spot in Tibet, standing out amidst the barren landscape. En route to the India border, I spot the newly laid railway line that connects Lhasa with Shigatse, which was opened just a few months before we got there, in early 2015. It was completed less than four years after its construction began in 2010, ahead of schedule. Within the next five years, I was told in Shigatse, the railway will run all the way to Yadong and the border with Sikkim.

The smooth surface of G318 allows us to cover much of the 700-kilometre distance from Lhasa to the India border in half a day – a pointer to the enormous asymmetry in infrastructure, with crumbling border roads winding their way on the other side of the Himalayas in Sikkim. Chinese officials take pains to point out that the highways, railways and airports are all indications of how Beijing's rule has brought development to the Tibetan plateau. Yet, as we drove past sparsely populated villages on our way to the border, it was difficult to miss the strategic logic that underpins China's remarkable infrastructure building across the plateau.

The journey from Lhasa ended in the Chumbi valley town of Yadong, one of the more undignified end points for G318. A small, muddy and underwhelming frontier outpost, the town, in a sense, presents a perfect snapshot of the India–China relationship. Yadong, on the Tibet side of Nathu La pass across the border from Sikkim, is the gateway between two behemoth economies. Yet, this sleepy town is in sharp contrast to the booming border ports that dot China's other frontiers – with Central Asia, Russia and even, for that matter, Nepal.

A few hundred kilometres northwest from the potholed main street of Yadong, China is investing millions of dollars in revamping another small frontier town, Gyirong, which was designated a bilateral trade and transit land port with Nepal in 2014. In October 2018, an international goods trading market, built by China at the cost of $6 million, was opened in Gyirong, months after China and Nepal confirmed plans to go ahead with an $8 billion cross-border railway that will connect Lhasa with Gyirong, and extend all the way to Kathmandu.[1]

A Tale of Two Borders

Yadong is still awaiting such grand plans. Time seems to have stood still here, a legacy of an unresolved history that hangs heavily upon the relationship between the two countries. Elsewhere on China's frontiers, history is marching on, as it were, with new chapters being written. A few months before I set foot in Yadong, I had a glimpse of some of those changes unfolding on the far side of the country.

Manzhouli, on China's northeast border with Russia, was also once a sleepy town that sat astride a disputed border. Today, it is brimming with trading activity. The main attraction is on the town's outskirts: a sprawling trade and logistics zone, built by China at a cost of $500 million. A transcontinental railway line connects China's southern trading centres with Russia through this city, and runs all the way west to Poland. In the new trading zone, 70 million tonnes of cargo are processed annually, most of it travelling in the direction of Russia.

This was not the case seventy years ago, when the People's Republic of China, recovering from a bruising civil war, was reliant on its communist brethren in the Soviet Union for technological support and skilled labour. Then, largely agricultural and poverty-stricken northern Chinese villages, decades behind the towns across the border, were reliant on everything from food to industrial goods from the Soviet Union. Today, a bulk of the traffic is in the other direction, with Russia importing Chinese machinery and China buying timber from Siberia. And, as a symbol of the changing fortunes across the border, the old border gate erected by the Soviet Union is now dwarfed by an imposing concrete and glass edifice that greets those entering China.

Manzhouli is not just a trading gateway; it is also, for many Chinese, a gateway into Russian culture, and has become a popular tourism hub, giving inland travellers who can't quite make it to Russia a unique flavour of a Little Russia. Its stunning surroundings, in the grasslands of Inner Mongolia, are an added attraction, where tourists can stay in Mongolian yurts and learn horse riding. The town's main street is a China–Russia hybrid. Paved with cobbled stones, it has sitting on either side Russian-style churches and houses, nestled rather incongruously among Chinese restaurants and trading shops, most built only in the past few years with the influx of new money.

Just two decades ago, Manzhouli was not unlike Yadong. But after the two neighbours settled their long-running boundary dispute, and Russia pulled its troops out of Bezrechnaya on its side of the border, Manzhouli's transformation – from disputed border outpost to a trading gateway – began. Can Manzhouli offer lessons for India and China? I put the question to Li Xiguo, who heads what Manzhouli proudly calls its 'port affairs office' – a rather curious nomenclature for not just any inland town, but one that sits right in the heart of the Inner Mongolian grasslands – underlining how seriously it takes itself as a major trading centre.

'It is difficult to imagine what we are seeing today a few years ago,' he said, reminding me that it was in 1969 – seven years after the India–China war – that Chinese and Soviet soldiers had their own border conflict at the height of the Sino-Soviet split, resulting in violent clashes and hundreds of deaths. It was only in 1991 that negotiations began in earnest. But, unlike the meandering India–China border talks, both sides made quick progress, leading to an agreement in 2004. Some of the areas settled in 2004, such as the Abagaitu islet on the border of Argun river, are not far from Manzhouli. Li says the agreement transformed the town's future. Eight years after the deal, Manzhouli was designated an 'experimental' zone for opening up cross-border commerce. By then, soldiers from both sides had left the border areas.

Driving along the border through the grasslands, all you see in some stretches is a flimsy barbed fence marking where Russia ends and China begins, with holes big enough to allow grazing sheep to cross over and back. It's not quite as open for people, but Russians who land in Manzhouli are allowed to enter China without visas. If they make this city their first port of entry, they can travel anywhere in China visa-free for a month – a policy aimed at encouraging cross-border commerce.

Many Russians end up in Manzhouli for a night or two, before heading south to their favoured holiday destination of Hainan island on the South China Sea. In addition, they are allowed to repatriate the equivalent of 8,000 yuan per day without paying any taxes. The free flow of people, as Li put it, was the single most important factor in a once barren region's economic revival.

History's Shadow

In Yadong, Manzhouli felt like it was not just at the other end of the country, but from another century altogether. Little traffic traversed the main street of Yadong that ran through the city centre. Rains the previous night had left the road riddled with puddles of water, a sight I was more accustomed to seeing in India than in China. Dated posters of Aishwarya Rai were displayed outside small stores, most of which appeared to only sell Indian incense sticks. This seemed the only rather sad indicator that at the end of the road, beyond a towering, heavily fortified frontier gate, lay India.

Here, geography is as big a barrier as politics: the Himalayas are hardly as conducive to the movement of people as the flat plains of Inner Mongolia. Yet, one feels in Yadong a profound sense of what might be. This crumbling little town, instead, is a reflection of what is, and of the cards that history has dealt this town – the unlikely meeting point of two great, old civilizations.

It is only for a few months every year that Yadong bursts into life, to welcome the annual group of pilgrims from India who begin their journey to Mount Kailash and Lake Manasarovar here. It was only in June 2015, as we have seen, that the route through Nathu La pass and Yadong itself was opened. Both India and China had invested considerable energy – and political capital – in the initiative, which Beijing framed as a goodwill gesture from

President Xi Jinping to the new government in New Delhi under Prime Minister Narendra Modi.

I had travelled from Beijing with three other Indian journalists to report on the opening of the new route, on the invitation of the Chinese foreign ministry. This was a rare chance for us to see Tibet. For journalists, it is usually next to impossible to be able to travel to Tibet – foreign journalists are effectively barred from travelling alone, unless on government-arranged tours – and this trip in 2015 was my first and only one during an entire decade in China, all thanks to the new route.

The red carpet was truly being laid out for the first batch of pilgrims. Le Yucheng, the Chinese ambassador in Delhi, had driven all the way to Sikkim and crossed over the border at Nathu La into Tibet, for the event. The day before the arrival of the pilgrims, Le and his aides waited in the Shanghai Garden Hotel, an old Chinese-style hotel that had obviously seen better days. A tired-looking Le nevertheless appeared enthused, and told me he saw the opening as the beginning of a new chapter in relations. 'We can have lunch in Gangtok and dinner in Yadong,' he offered optimistically.

The account of his journey, offered by his aides, painted a more realistic appraisal of the situation. 'The roads in Sikkim were frightening; our car almost rolled off a couple of times!' said one young diplomat. The following morning, Le and some of the top officials from Tibet waited on the Chinese side of the imposing border gate at Nathu La. With much fanfare, the gates were opened, allowing forty Indian pilgrims, the first batch who would undertake the pilgrimage through the new route, to cross the border into China.

Contested Frontier

The disputed – and as yet un-demarcated – border that runs between India and China is the longest contested land frontier in the world. The India–China boundary dispute is so complex that even the length of the border itself is in dispute. Ask India, and it's a 3,488 kilometre-long border. China, however, says it's only around 2,000 kilometres. In the west, where India claims 38,000 square kilometres of land in Ladakh, that is now under China's control, Beijing doesn't appear to count the PoK border with China's Xinjiang region as part of the dispute, perhaps explaining the difference in length. This is the western sector of the boundary. China says the main dispute, in its view, is in the eastern sector over Arunachal Pradesh, where it has made claims to 90,000 square kilometres of Indian territory, covering essentially all of Arunachal. There are also disputes on a smaller scale in the middle sector, where Himachal Pradesh and Uttarakhand border Tibet, but it's in the west and east that the crux of the dispute lies.

The border dispute led to war in 1962, which plunged relations into a deep freeze for twenty-six years. India and China have signed four landmark agreements on the boundary since 1988, committing to settle the issue peacefully through negotiations. These include a 1993 agreement on maintaining peace and tranquillity, a 1996 agreement on confidence-building measures, a 2005 agreement on the political parameters and guiding principles to settle the dispute, and a border defence cooperation agreement in 2013.

If both sides agreed in 1988 to shelve differences and work on other areas of cooperation to revive their relationship, the long shadow cast by the unresolved boundary has certainly imposed limitations. The dispute rears its head every so often as if to remind both countries that it isn't going anywhere.

The LAC, the effective marker that separates territory that is under India's control from China's, is perhaps the single most important element that ensures the two countries across the Himalayas do not go to war. It underpins the four key agreements. Yet, the line remains a source of much confusion. When reporting on border incidents, newspapers often misleadingly talk of 'incursions across the line', as if it is a settled and demarcated boundary that is being violated. The LAC is neither an agreed upon line, nor is it a final border. It is, as the name suggests, a reflection of land that is, at present, under the control of each side, pending a resolution of the boundary dispute.

The problem of course is that India and China do not agree on the alignment of the LAC everywhere. Differences in perception, particularly around twenty-three spots in the western, middle and eastern sectors of the border, often lead to what are called 'face-offs', when patrols encounter each other. Some of these areas are Chumar, Demchok and the north bank of the Pangong lake in the western sector, Barahoti in the middle sector, and Sumdorong Chu in the east. Most incidents are resolved at the local commanders' level, at border personnel meeting points that have been set up in all sectors, including Chushul and Daulat Beg Oldi in the west, Nathu La in Sikkim, and Bum La and Kibithu in the east.

Face-offs aren't unusual, and in some sense are an entirely expected outcome of having an un-demarcated LAC, where both sides patrol up to where their claim lies. These are actually regular occurrences, as much as the Indian media often breathlessly reports on the annual number of Chinese 'transgressions' while remaining mum about the number of times India has similarly transgressed. In fact, the 2005 and 2013 agreements detail how patrols should handle such incidents, by displaying their banners and returning to their base, without engaging with one another. The modalities of the 1993 agreement held until the unprecedented events of June 2020, when tensions in the Galwan Valley erupted into the worst violence seen on the border since a clash at Nathu La in 1967. While 1975 remains the last time a bullet was fired, when an Assam Rifles patrol was ambushed by the Chinese at Tulung La, the shocking events in Galwan Valley effectively upended more than fifty years of relative calm.

A Question of Perception

The obvious solution is to clarify the LAC and ensure both sides know where the other's claim lies, particularly in the twenty-three sensitive spots. Given the ambiguity of the LAC, clarification is key to keeping the peace. That was the intent of the 1993 agreement, which was, in fact, the first-ever agreement between India and China on the boundary, signed more than three decades after 1962.

The 1993 agreement 'on maintenance of peace and tranquillity' acknowledged the differences in perception, declaring that 'when necessary, the two sides shall jointly check and determine the segments of the line of actual control where they have different views as to its alignment'.[2] The second boundary agreement in 1996, on confidence-building measures, went a step further, pledging that both sides recognized the need to arrive at 'a common understanding of the alignment of the LAC' and 'to exchange maps indicating their respective perceptions of the entire alignment of the LAC as soon as possible'.[3]

The exchange of maps began four years later, when both sides began working on the section that is least disputed: the middle segment of the LAC. The exchange of maps for the middle sector, which took place in September 2000, was helpful, Indian and Chinese officials say, even if there were differences in alignment, most significantly in the region near Barahoti in Uttarakhand. A year later, however, when both sides began to discuss the crucial western sector, where India sees China as occupying at least 38,000 square kilometres, things went wrong. China looked at India's claims in the west in the map presented to them, and quickly returned it. There ended the process.

China has been mum about why it was opposed to clarification. When Modi visited China in 2015 on his first trip as prime minister, he flagged the LAC issue front and centre, saying in a speech in Tsinghua University that 'a shadow of uncertainty always hangs over the sensitive areas of the border region'. 'It is because neither side knows where the Line of Actual Control is in these areas,' he said. 'That is why I have proposed resuming the process of clarifying it.' Modi invoked a key passage of the 1993 agreement that said this could be done 'without prejudice to our position on the boundary question'.[4]

Along with a few other Indian reporters, I met a top Chinese foreign ministry official, Huang Xilian, who is the deputy director general in the Asia Department and Beijing's point man on

India, after Modi's visit. Huang told us that Beijing was opposed to restarting the process. In fact, he said doing so would be 'a stumbling block' in resolving the boundary dispute, warning that the LAC clarification process had made the border issue even more complicated instead of narrowing differences. 'We tried to clarify some years ago but we encountered some difficulties which led to an even more complex situation,' he said. What went wrong? 'Those details,' Huang replied, 'are beyond my remit.'

Chinese officials have never publicly spoken about what stopped the process. But a former official involved in boundary negotiations told me China's opposition lay in India bringing in PoK into the discussions, although India sees PoK as an integral part of its own territory. 'In the beginning,' the official said, 'we had differences on the middle sector but we resolved it. But when we tried to negotiate on the western part, India said, "You have to confirm the China–Pakistan border first, then decide the China–India border." This is hard for China to do so we cannot continue.' Hu Shisheng, a strategic expert at the official China Institutes for Contemporary International Relations (CICIR) concurred with that assessment, telling me that it was claims 'in the extreme west' that were a stumbling block.

'In 2002, when both sides were ready to exchange the LAC maps of both western and eastern sections, it was said that the Indian side wanted to include the extreme western section, which is between Pakistan and China. This requirement has totally derailed the bilateral border talks. The Chinese side felt frustrated about this new development. It is India who strongly opposes the involvement of any third party in the Kashmir issue,' he said. That's an argument that doesn't hold water in Delhi. After all, the border agreement China signed with Pakistan to settle their territorial disputes in 1963 leaves open the question of Kashmir, and declares that after the resolution of the Kashmir dispute, 'the sovereign authority concerned' would reopen negotiations with China.

Officials in Delhi told me that China had come up with this PoK argument as a post-facto justification for abandoning the

LAC clarification process, which the People's Liberation Army had been opposed to from the start. As they pointed out, this didn't explain why Beijing didn't agree to clarify the rest of the frontier if they were only concerned about PoK. The more likely reason for Beijing stalling the process was that it preferred the ambiguity regarding its territorial claims, an approach also seen in how China deals with other territorial and maritime disputes. This way, Beijing isn't bound by its claims. It can keep its adversaries at bay, and expand its claims if doing so serves its strategic interests – as it did in the Galwan Valley in 2020. 'The Chinese are masters at this,' Nirupama Rao, former foreign secretary and also a former ambassador to China who has engaged with the country as a top diplomat for decades, told me. 'They don't stick to positions, and their actions on the ground constantly defy things they have done in the past. The Chinese line has kept shifting. There is always scope for redrawing, and we have never had the chance to look at their maps.'

China has since responded to India's call for clarification with a counter proposal of a 'Code of Conduct', which has been viewed warily by India, as it calls for freezing infrastructure along the LAC – thereby also freezing China's advantage.[5] The problem, however, isn't a lack of protocols, with four already in place; it is in following them.

With this unsettled question, the legacy of the boundary, more than any other issue, continues to imprison the relationship in a seemingly endless see-saw, where every apparent new dawn is very quickly extinguished by a harsh reality check, often triggered by some new incident on the border. Every new government that comes to power in Delhi has sought ways to break out of this cycle, but to no avail. China likes to say the dispute is one 'left over from history', referring to its colonial origins.[6] It may certainly be left over from history, but it has never left, as the events of the summer of 2020 reminded us in the worst possible way.

10

From Doklam to Galwan

IT WASN'T OFTEN, DURING MY time in Beijing, that I received an invitation from China's People's Liberation Army. My first one came in rather unusual circumstances. The PLA was getting ready to mark its ninetieth anniversary on 1 August 2017, and was to hold a rare meet-the-press event the week before. 'Are you interested?' asked a voice on the other end of the line.

I had spent some eight years trying unsuccessfully to get into the PLA's monthly press briefings. It allowed only a limited list of Chinese and foreign reporters to attend.

The PLA is unlike most militaries. This is evinced in the curious fact that it predates the founding of the People's Republic of China in 1949 by a good twenty-two years. It's often forgotten that the government is not its real master; the Communist Party of China is.

The PLA is the army of a political party, and its abiding objective, besides its stated ones of defending China's territorial integrity and sovereignty, is ensuring the continued survival of the Party. The ninetieth anniversary event was meant to be a grand celebration, but it was becoming increasingly awkward for both the Party and the PLA. And that had something to do with India.

Contested Plateau

Less than two months before the grand 1 August anniversary, a cryptic announcement from India's Ministry of External Affairs, on 23 June 2017, said that because of some 'difficulties being experienced' by Indian pilgrims, the annual Kailash Manasarovar pilgrimage to Tibet had been stopped. Seven batches of fifty pilgrims, each who had been given permission to undertake the yatra, would not be able to go through the Nathu La pass – the grand opening of which I had just reported two summers earlier – while eighteen batches of sixty would be allowed to travel through the older route at Lipulekh.

The announcement was puzzling, given all that had been invested in the new route. The reason emerged three days later, when a harshly worded statement from China's foreign ministry accused the Indian Army of crossing the border and 'obstructing normal Chinese activities' of road construction on the Doklam plateau, which abuts India, China and Bhutan.

This is a contested plateau that China claims is part of Yadong in Tibet, but India and Bhutan see as Bhutanese land. So, it turned out that China had essentially stopped the pilgrims as a punitive measure. This was in itself a worrying step that served as a reminder, if we needed one, of the limitations of the principle of 'shelving differences' that underpinned the 1988 model. A confidence-building measure both sides had invested in was so easily cast aside just to prove a point on the border.

In the weeks after the Doklam stand-off began in mid-June 2017, India–China relations fell off a cliff. Those two months were among the strangest I'd experienced in a decade in China. For seventy-two days, I would go to the Ministry of Foreign Affairs building every afternoon to listen to what became an almost daily rant aimed at India. I hadn't, in a decade, seen the atmosphere so vitiated, so much so that the non-stop anti-India propaganda began to make itself felt in everyday life. The 'Donglang incident', as China called it, using the Chinese name for Doklam, became a daily topic of conversation on Beijing taxi rides. Some Indian businessmen were hearing from Chinese partners that it was unofficially a time to not do business with India. Even the country's most beloved Indian film star, Aamir Khan, had to quietly put a film release in China on hold.

The PLA invite came one month into the stand-off, as the warnings began to reach fever pitch. I walked into the State Council Information Office, which was then located in a dull, grey Stalinist building across the Third Ring Road from the foreign ministry, to find a PLA major general flanked by three senior colonels, all ready to meet the press. The PLA senior colonel, Wu Qian, launched into what could only be called a stunning – and very well-rehearsed – diatribe, aimed perhaps as much at his domestic audience as at India.

'Our willingness and resolve to defend our sovereignty,' he thundered, 'is indomitable. We will do so whatever the cost. It may be difficult to shake a mountain, but it is even more difficult to shake the PLA.' Then he did the unthinkable, which was to mention what officials in India and China almost never bring up: the 1962 war.

Wu's speech that day went viral, and I would hear his comments played back on every website and television channel for a month. On my daily commute to the foreign ministry, I would see his face on the television screens on subways in the capital, followed by threatening images of Chinese aircraft and missiles. China's most hawkish voices were given a free rein. The retired firebrand PLA major general and strategist Luo Yuan called on the public to rally behind the army.

'The public should be confident about our soldiers,' he said in one widely circulated article. 'Do not trust the words of those who would condemn us for being too aggressive or for being too weak when we protect peace. Our army would never engage in a war without the full grasp of victory. Frankly speaking, India is truly different from the India of 1962. We really don't want to engage in a war against India. But if we did, India would lose again.'[1]

One reason for China's public posturing was that Doklam was different from the usual India–China bilateral disputes; both sides knew those occurred because of an un-demarcated LAC. Here, India had crossed an international boundary to enter into Bhutan – into land it certainly didn't have a claim to – which was seen by China as crossing a red line.

This posturing did, however, mark a new Chinese approach that we would see repeated in future boundary crises that followed. The *PLA Daily*, the army's official newspaper, termed the approach, during the Doklam crisis, an information warfare strategy, aimed 'to fully integrate the publicity forces of public opinion, radio, TV, newspapers and social media, and carry out a multi-wave and high-density centralised publicity in a fixed period of time to form favourable public opinion situation to allow for a final victory'. The PLA's Western Theatre Command said in a 2017 analysis of the Doklam media strategy that 'seizing the initiative was key in the struggle for public opinion'. It asserted that the aim was 'to make India succumb without a confrontation between the two armies,' adding that the approach served lessons 'for future struggles'.[2]

Xi's New Army

In Beijing, the view among people I spoke to was that the timing of China's muscle flexing over the Doklam incident, amid the most sweeping reforms of the armed forces, was no coincidence. The military's massive transformation that Xi had pushed for had created its own stresses and uncertainties. In the past too, PLA observers said, such circumstances had led the army to adopt a hard-line posture, driven both by domestic political considerations and the need to rally public support for the military. In the lead-up to the PLA's ninetieth anniversary, for instance, its officers publicly pledged their allegiance to Xi and showered praise on his reforms. Former PLA officers even used the Doklam incident to attack the army's critics and demand total support for the military.

Since Xi Jinping took over as the general secretary of the Communist Party of China and became president of the People's Republic of China in November 2012 and March 2013 respectively, perhaps the most marked difference from his predecessor, Hu Jintao, has been in his dealings with the military. Under the terms of his succession as head of the Party and as president, Xi was also given his third post – Chairman of the Central Military Commission (CMC), putting him in the unique position of commanding the Party, government and military all at once.

On 1 February 2016, Xi announced what the *PLA Daily* described as 'the largest scale military reform since the 1950s'.[3] The reforms cemented his direct control over every sphere of the vast military, which has, for decades, functioned as a state within a state, with untrammelled power and nil supervision. With four main components – the army, navy, air force and Second Artillery Corps that commands missiles and nuclear weapons – the PLA had been run by a vast bureaucracy, spread over four general departments – general staff, political, logistics and armament. These were largely autonomous fiefdoms: favoured generals promoted their own, lined their pockets, and ruled over vast bureaucracies and commercial interests worth billions.

In January 2016, Xi, in one swift stroke, disbanded the four departments and brought them under the direct control of the CMC. Cut to size, they were placed at par with fifteen smaller, specialized functional 'services' departments, including one devoted to anti-corruption and 'discipline inspection'. Xi described the move as 'a dramatic breakthrough made in the reform of the military leadership and command system'. So, for the first time in the PLA's history, the CMC took control of its entire administration.

A second major reform was consolidating what were earlier seven sprawling military area commands covering China's entire territory into five theatre commands, to be responsible for combat readiness and to report directly to the CMC. For the first time, the five theatres also had a joint command of integrated land, air and navy services, in addition to two new services that have been set up: a PLA Rocket Force that would be a scaled-up Second Artillery Corps and control China's missiles; and a PLA Strategic Support Force, which would, according to observers, include an expanded cyber warfare division.

The reforms were overdue. For all the impressions of the PLA – both in China and overseas – as a fearsome fighting unit, its recent history has been anything but glorious. Its last real experience of combat, against the Vietnamese in 1979 (which continued into sporadic clashes until the mid-1980s), was a wake-up call, leaving the Chinese with a bloodied nose. The PLA hasn't been in major combat since. But two recent episodes that tested its capabilities caused its top brass and military observers in Beijing consternation, cementing the perception that a once hardy revolutionary army – that fought the Americans in Korea, bested India and challenged the Russians – had become a bloated outfit, whose generals concentrated more on the army's vast commercial interests than in training troops.

The first episode came in May 2008, when a devastating earthquake struck western Sichuan province, claiming over 70,000 lives. The PLA was called in to lead the rescue effort. The quake struck remote areas, but it was not entirely out of reach of the PLA's sprawling headquarters in the provincial capital, Chengdu. The response, however, was slow and lumbering, so inept, in fact, that it prompted an internal inquest into overhauling training at all levels.

Barely a year later came the second test, when mobs of armed Uighurs went on a rampage in Urumqi, capital of the Muslim-majority Xinjiang province, setting buildings afire and slaughtering Han Chinese residents over two days. Again, the army's response was found wanting. One former official of the paramilitary unit, the People's Armed Police, who I happened to sit next to on a flight and who spoke with surprising candour, recalled the confusion in the chain of command and the chaos.

Initially, young officers, with barely any training and not armed with guns, were sent to confront armed mobs of several thousands.

According to protocol, permission was required to deploy more advanced units. It never came. So confused was the response that Hu Jintao, who by then had taken over the PLA as head of the CMC, had to leave the ongoing G20 summit in Italy and rush back.

Xi is taking no chances. Both Hu and Jiang Zemin, who came before him, had to cede control of the army to their predecessors in their first few years in power. In Hu's time, so influential was Jiang that even after retirement, he continued to hold an office in the PLA headquarters and receive files. No Chinese leader in a generation has had the kind of power Xi now has. And he, clearly, isn't afraid of using it.

The relationship between the Party and the PLA is complex. So concerned is the civilian Party leadership about control over the PLA that not a month goes by in Beijing without a high-profile announcement reiterating that the PLA's loyalty must be only to the Party. Troops are made to undergo political training, sitting through hours of study of Marxism and Mao Zedong Thought, and now, of course, what is called Xi Jinping Thought. In practice, however, the PLA has largely been left to its own devices. In a sense, its loyalty was bought: the army was given vast commercial interests, from real estate to valuable industries – much of which it lost following military reforms in the 1990s – and supported by a ballooning defence budget that has recorded annual double-digit growth this past decade, reaching $180 billion in 2020.[4]

Xi's reforms are aimed at improving the PLA's combat effectiveness and ability to project power – a challenge India will have to grapple with. Centralizing PLA decision-making in the hands of the CMC, Xi wants to transform what has historically been a land-dominated military into a nimble, integrated force. To that end, he announced a demobilization of 3,00,000 troops of the 2.3 million-strong PLA in September 2015.

By no means are these reforms an overnight transformation: the groundwork was, in fact, laid more than two decades ago. Through the reforms what is being finally implemented is a strategy adopted in 1993 after the Gulf War. At the time, alarmed by the demonstration of US firepower, the PLA updated its abiding mission to winning 'local wars under high-tech conditions'. Given the PLA's history as a 'revolutionary army', with its special historical role that cast a long shadow over other services, it has been difficult for the Party to turn it into an integrated force.

'From an organizational or institutional perspective, these reforms are unprecedented,' M. Taylor Fravel, an expert on the PLA, who is a political science professor at the Massachusetts Institute of Technology (MIT) and the author of *Strong Borders, Secure Nation: Cooperation and Conflict in China's Territorial Disputes*, told me.[5] 'They represent the abolition of the general staff system and military region structure the PLA had adopted in the 1950s. If successful – and it's a big if – they should improve its combat effectiveness.' The reforms will dramatically alter the PLA's projection of power beyond China's borders. As Fravel told me, the orientation of the five new theatres is 'created to align China's strategic directions with the command of troops'. The northern theatre will focus on the Korean peninsula, the central theatre on the defence of Beijing, the eastern theatre on Taiwan and to a lesser extent the Senkaku/Diaoyu dao Islands that are contested with Japan, the southern theatre on the South China Sea, and the western theatre on India.

For India, the reforms could widen the asymmetry along the disputed LAC. In the past decade, China has already built a huge infrastructure network of highways, railway lines and airports across the Tibetan plateau. The idea is to be able to mobilize, at short notice, a vast number of assets to win a 'high-tech local war'. The integration of commands, if successful, will further facilitate this mission. Xi's PLA reorganization may also answer the long-running question of whether the PLA has been an impediment to improving conditions on the border.

'For years, India's wrestled with the question of whether border incursions, which seem to occur at inopportune times, are the product of local commanders acting autonomously or whether they are directed and managed by the senior leadership in Beijing,' Jeff M. Smith, research fellow at the Heritage Foundation and author of *Cold Peace: China-India Rivalry in the Twenty-first Century*, told me.[6] 'For instance, after the three-week border incursion in Chumar that overshadowed President Xi's inaugural visit to India, he gave what appeared to be a relatively stern and public lecture to the PLA top brass within days of returning from his trip stressing the pre-eminence of Party loyalty. On the other hand, the commander of the military region responsible for that section of the China–India border was later promoted.'

Warning Signs

The Doklam crisis was in many ways unexpected. Most of the previous border incidents had taken place either in the western sector or the eastern sector of the India–China border. The 2013 stand-off in Depsang and the 2014 incident in Chumar occurred in the west. This time, the genesis was familiar – yet another PLA encroachment by carrying out a road construction into a disputed territory – but not the location, which was in so unexpected an area that it had even seasoned analysts scrambling for their maps.

What was unusual was that the 2017 stand-off took place not on territory disputed between India and China, but in one disputed by Bhutan and China. This was land to which India had no claim, hence the extraordinary Chinese response. The area, called the Doklam plateau – or Donglang, by China – extends out of the very same Chumbi valley where Yadong sits and where the Nathu La pilgrims had arrived. As far as China was concerned, it is an extension of Yadong. Bhutan and India, however, see it as a territory of the former.

It is at Doklam where India, China and Bhutan meet, although there is disagreement on where the tri-junction of the three borders actually sits. China's claim is south of where India and Bhutan see it. Both India and China have been aware of their differences on the tri-junction, even agreeing in 2012 to mutually negotiate the matter. The PLA's road building towards the tri-junction was, however, a fait accompli, unilaterally changing the status quo. This is what prompted India to intervene, even though this meant crossing a few hundred metres into Bhutanese land. Much across the rest of Doklam, the PLA had already made inroads, building roads deep into what Bhutan saw as its territory; but it faced little resistance from the ill-equipped Bhutanese army, which appeared to be more concerned with disputed territory to the north than to the west, towards India.

For India, however, the stakes were high. The PLA road, just a short distance from India's border post, was heading straight to a ridge that overlooks the Chicken's Neck, as the 27-kilometre-wide Siliguri corridor linking the rest of India with the northeast is called. A long-held fear has been that the PLA could move troops down this valley in a future conflict, severing India's link to its northeast. These fears aren't entirely unfounded, and have only been fuelled by the PLA's activities including, in recent years, a Class 40 road – referring to a military classification describing the load it can bear, in tonnes – right through the Chumbi valley. The road had penetrated deep into the plateau, and it was only when the PLA moved its road building further southward, only a few hundred metres from the India border and perilously close to the tri-junction, that India's military stepped in and stopped them on 16 June 2017.

Long after the dust settled and the stand-off was resolved, there remained many questions about how it all began in the first place – and what it would portend for the future. When news of the incident first broke, it was immediately seen in India as only the latest in a number of surreptitious Chinese military moves of stealthy 'salami slicing' – nibbling up bits of disputed territory by extending its infrastructure gradually into disputed areas, as had been the strategy in the South China Sea, and elsewhere on the border with India and Bhutan.

There was certainly some truth to this. Indeed, Beijing had already extended its roads elsewhere on the plateau. The timing, however, was a mystery. Barely days before the crisis, Modi and Xi had, by most accounts, an extremely fruitful meeting in Astana, Kazakhstan, on the sidelines of a Shanghai Cooperation Organisation summit. This was where Modi had first suggested to Xi 'an informal summit', an occasion for them to talk freely, only in the company of aides as they had done in Ahmedabad and Xi'an. The idea was to take the informal aspect even further. There would be no formal talks at all, or the pressure of delivering agreements or a joint statement. The entire focus of the two-day summit would be long, unscripted and informal discussions between the two, only in the company of their interpreters.

Xi readily agreed to the pitch, remarking that he had had so many meetings with Modi but had hardly gotten to know him. Moreover, the leaders reached two important points of agreement: they would not let differences fester into disputes, and they believed the relationship could be a force for stability in an increasingly unpredictable global environment. The second point was particularly significant. India, and especially China, by the summer of 2017, had begun to take stock of the unpredictability unleashed in Washington with the election victory of Donald Trump. By then, Trump was beginning to come good on his promise of taking a sledgehammer to the global trading system, the two biggest beneficiaries of which, over the past two decades, had been India and China.

There were other details about the Doklam flare-up that didn't make sense. For a salami-slicing mission of stealth, the PLA had been unusually communicative. I had it confirmed from both senior Indian and Chinese officials that the PLA had conveyed, on no less than three occasions, to the Indian border post that it would be carrying out construction work. The Chinese officials claimed they received no response from the Indian side. Indian officials told me this was true, to the extent that the matter was conveyed beforehand. But they strongly disputed the Chinese account, and said India had made clear its concerns on the road. China went ahead nonetheless.

The Doklam episode underlined a new challenge India faced from an assertive China – and the limited options at its disposal to counter it. In Doklam, the Chinese road put India in a difficult position. It faced two choices: do nothing, and let the road reach the ridge and compromise India's security, or intervene and cross the border, thereby risking a serious escalation. Delhi took the risk, and did succeed in stopping the road reaching a strategically vital ridge. Yet, China responded by fortifying its position pretty much everywhere else on the plateau, to an extent that it is today far better positioned in Doklam than it was before the crisis.

Bloodshed at Galwan

At the time, the thinking was that this period of seventy-two days of the Doklam crisis was as low as India–China relations could go. After all, at the end of the day, the protocols and mechanisms in place worked. And to underline how serious both sides were about fixing things, they went ahead with the 'informal summit' that Prime Minister Modi had suggested that summer, a few weeks before the crisis exploded. In April 2018, Modi travelled to Wuhan for the first summit, which was unprecedented on many levels. Only for the second time did Xi travel out of Beijing to host a foreign leader – the first, again, was for Modi in 2015 – and they would spend two days in extensive talks, one-on-one.

Following Wuhan, India declared that both countries had agreed to issue 'strategic guidance' to their militaries to keep the peace and learn the lessons from Doklam. A second summit would be held in Chennai in October 2019, in the old town of Mamallapuram on the city's outskirts. To be fair, 2018 and 2019 marked the two most peaceful years on the border in recent memory. It seemed there was a consensus at the highest levels to keep the peace. This, coupled with the optics from Wuhan and Chennai, perhaps lulled everyone into a false sense of security.

Indeed, there were warning signs on two levels. Firstly, to a degree, both sides had been lucky in untangling previous crises. In the case of Doklam, as happened in Depsang and Chumar, there were significant political events that pushed both sides towards a relatively quick resolution. In Doklam, what helped was a BRICS Summit (a grouping of Brazil, Russia, India, China and South Africa) that China was hosting in Xiamen in early September. This presented a huge headache for the country. It had knowingly unleashed a torrent of nationalism at home, but was then faced with the prospect of Xi Jinping having to play good host to Prime Minister Modi. So while almost all normal bilateral engagement ceased during the Doklam crisis, the BRICS engagement still stood, resulting in the unusual prospect of top Indian ministers coming to Beijing for meetings in the middle of the crisis, even as the PLA threatened war. Media in China and India began to speculate whether Modi would cancel his visit, but as I learnt from officials on both sides, that possibility was never on the cards. Unlike in 1986, both sides agreed they had a deadline to sort out the crisis. The problem was how, and that took some time to resolve.

The second warning sign was that despite the resolution of the stand-offs, a structural problem, spurred by changing dynamics along the LAC that was fuelling new tensions, was getting ever more acute. Starting in 2010, India had embarked on a major effort to bridge the asymmetry in infrastructure which had earlier given China free run in many areas along the LAC. By December 2022, India will complete sixty-one strategic roads along the border, running close to 3,500 kilometres in length. In many of the contested spots, India will have roads that run all the way up to the LAC, allowing it to patrol the border with greater depth and frequency than previously. China's presence is being challenged. And Beijing is pushing back and pressuring India to stop advancing.

This cat-and-mouse game will continue as long as the boundary remains unsettled and the LAC remains undefined. This presents a two-fold problem for both sides. In the age of 24/7 news and social media, the smallest stand-off can very quickly get magnified and vitiate the atmosphere of the broader relationship, thereby undermining the founding principle, from 1988, of insulating other aspects of the relationship from the boundary problem. The greater concern is the likelihood of any unexpected escalation in the heat of face-offs. And that was what would happen, with tragic consequences, in the summer of 2020.

Starting in April that year, India had for the first time begun extending tracks into the Galwan Valley, a sliver of land that sits between steep mountains that buffet the Galwan river. The river has its source in Aksai Chin, on China's side of the LAC, and it flows west to Ladakh, where it meets the Shyok river on India's side of the LAC. The valley is strategically located between Ladakh in the west and Aksai Chin in the east, which is currently controlled by China as part of its Xinjiang Uyghur Autonomous Region. At its western end is the Shyok river and the Darbuk–Shyok–Daulat Beg Oldi (DSDBO) road, a key artery to India's northernmost point in Ladakh that was opened in 2019.

Most Chinese maps show most of Galwan river on its side of the border, but short of the confluence of the Galwan and Shyok. China's official claimed border passes through a bend in the Galwan, where it turns to meet the Shyok, called the Y-nallah. The LAC runs a little east of the bend, and is broadly aligned with the coordinates given by China during border talks in 1960.

Starting in early May 2020, however, Chinese troops began crossing the LAC and objecting to any Indian activity east of the Y-nallah. In India's view, Beijing was moving to unilaterally shift the LAC to align it with its maps. Doing so was seen as violating a key founding principle of all previous agreements. After all, territorial claims and LAC claims are not the same, and the LAC that both the countries abided by until recently ran across the valley. The distinction between territorial claims and LAC claims is sometimes blurred. The LAC refers to territory under the effective control of each side, not to their entire territorial claim. For instance, India's territorial claims extend 38,000 square kilometres on the other side of the LAC – not just all over Galwan Valley but across all of Aksai Chin – but the LAC India observes runs across the valley.

All this made for a toxic mix that exploded exactly three years to the day the Doklam crisis began. A little after noon on 16 June 2020, disturbing news started filtering in from Indian Army sources that a violent confrontation had unfolded in the Galwan Valley. Ten days prior, in a rare meeting between Corps Commanders, they had agreed to a plan of disengagement. But when verifying that the Chinese had indeed disengaged, an Indian patrol found a Chinese tent still standing on India's side of the LAC, despite the commitment to take it down. A dispute over the tent erupted into a brawl, and the Chinese dispatched – in a pre-planned attack, according to Indian officials – a large number of troops to charge against a vastly outnumbered Indian patrol. Some of the Chinese soldiers were allegedly armed with iron rods and nail-studded batons – a very cynical workaround for the no firearms rule that has been observed since the Tulung La ambush of 1975. In the unprecedented violence that unfolded in darkness, twenty Indian soldiers would lose their lives along with an unknown number of Chinese soldiers.

This would mark the worst violence on the border since 1967, and shatter decades of hard-won peace. Gautam Bambawale, who was India's ambassador to China from November 2017 to December 2018 and had been deeply involved in the restoration of ties after Doklam and in organizing the Wuhan summit, told me he 'never expected such a thing to happen'. 'The reason why,' he said, 'is because ever since 1993, when India and China signed the border peace and tranquillity agreement – and there have been many agreements following that – we have put in place certain tenets, certain operating procedures, which were aimed at maintaining peace on the border. And obviously, all those have collapsed in this particular instance. Knowing that we do not have a defined boundary, we wanted to maintain peace and tranquillity, but unfortunately that entire [border] architecture has collapsed, and is now in the dustheap of history.'

M. Taylor Fravel, the MIT professor, told me the competition along the LAC underpinned these new tensions along the border. 'From China's standpoint, the reactivation of landing grounds and completion last year of the DSDBO road that runs more or less parallel to the LAC in this area significantly improve India's position in the local balance of forces and India's capabilities across the LAC,' he said. 'Even though this construction activity lies on the Indian side of the LAC, China likely views it as challenging their position on and perhaps the stability of the LAC.'

There were also strategic considerations that made for the perfect storm, following the coronavirus pandemic and the worsening US–China relationship that had led to increasing insecurities within the Party leadership. 'Given Xi Jinping's tough and public commitments to defend Chinese sovereignty,' Fravel told me, 'China may feel it has to take a hard line everywhere it sees its sovereignty being challenged – especially if Beijing fears others may view it as weak or distracted by the coronavirus and its economic aftershocks. This is true not only regarding the border with India today, but also Taiwan, Hong Kong and the South China Sea.'

And with the LAC remaining un-demarcated and contested, odds are that similar crises are bound to recur. Bambawale told me it would be a long road back for the relationship to recover after Galwan, which caused shock and anger in India, and prompted a campaign to boycott Chinese goods – as unfeasible as the prospect may be, considering Indian dependencies on Chinese manufacturing. The entire trade and investment relationship, which had emerged as a key positive pillar holding up the relationship in recent decades, might need to be reconfigured. As he put it, 'It can no longer be business as usual.'

Shadow of War

Neither India nor China desires conflict, and neither expects it. The problem is, war rarely happens by design. The events of May 2020 unfolded even though there were compelling reasons for both sides to keep the peace. The summits at Wuhan and Chennai led people to think that both Modi and Xi saw eye to eye on not holding the relationship hostage to the boundary question when economic ties were growing, particularly in terms of Chinese investments in India.

At the same time, the PLA's strategy of testing India across the LAC had only continued, as had India's infrastructure building in sensitive areas. If clarifying the LAC would be the obvious solution to all of these troubling trends, it seemed that Beijing was in no mood to do so, preferring the ambiguity that marked its approach to many territorial and maritime disputes – this gave it cover to change claims and keep its adversaries off balance. Modi's proposal to clarify the LAC in 2015 hadn't been received favourably, with Beijing viewing the process as an unnecessary and parallel diversion to the stalled boundary negotiations.

If skirmishes were to escalate, what would war look like? During the Doklam crisis, my colleague at *India Today*, Sandeep Unnithan – one of India's leading defence journalists – and I tried to analyse how it might unfold, speaking to a range of experts on both sides of the border.[7] On the face of it, the odds appeared to favour the PLA. Weak infrastructure and a stalled military modernization had hobbled India's armed forces. The army was also embarrassed by revelations in 2017 of its tank and howitzer ammunition being adequate for only ten days in case of intense war fighting, against the prescribed forty days. Of even greater concern was the tardy pace of adding border infrastructure, although that was beginning to change. The navy was underfunded, and short on both submarines and anti-submarine warfare helicopters, key capabilities needed to track Chinese submarines that are now routinely deployed in the Indian Ocean.

Yet, even if the balance may be tilted in China's favour, this is not the India of 1962 (although, of course, it isn't the China of 1962 either). If Beijing decides to go to war, it will be only after carefully weighing the benefits of getting into a full-scale conventional war where it cannot score a decisive victory. To initiate a conflict will mean tearing up multiple peace and tranquillity border agreements with India, not to mention entirely upending decades of its efforts to convince the world of what it likes to call its 'peaceful rise'.

In the event of the most plausible conflict scenario, a limited war involving only the army and air force seems likely – an advancing PLA will have to deal with over 250 of the Indian Air Force's (IAF) Su-30MKI air dominance fighters (it did not have to contend with the IAF in 1962). The IAF jets can take off from their bases on the plains of north India with a full payload of fuel and weapons as opposed to the PLA Air Force fighters operating off the exposed airfields on the Tibetan plateau with reduced combat loads and fuel, due to the rarefied air.

The PLA will have to break through heavily defended passes and valleys guarded by over a dozen Indian mountain divisions with 16,000 soldiers each, protected by artillery, BrahMos missile regiments and, in certain places like Ladakh and north Sikkim, pre-positioned armoured brigades with T-72 tanks.

'It's advantage India in terms of the army's training and professionalism, and advantage China in terms of infrastructure, logistics, supplies, firepower quantity and their rocket force,' Srikanth Kondapalli, an expert on the Chinese military at the Jawaharlal Nehru University (JNU) in Delhi, told me. China, he said, was changing the way it wanted to fight wars, abandoning the 'Napoleonic kind of warfare'. 'The thinking is, we have to be focused, reorganize with rapid response forces, and have an objective not to occupy territory, but to paralyse the adversary. For this, you need concentration of firepower – air force, artillery in one area – and mobilization. And you can't have divisions among the army, navy and air force. They're raising forty rapid response units, of which thirty are already done, and an airborne corps for transporting troops.'

Since China's tenth five-year plan (2001–05), Beijing had embarked on an ambitious push to build a road and rail network across Xinjiang and Tibet. A decade and a half later, it is almost complete, in stark contrast to India's slower border road building. Beijing, no doubt, enjoys the topographical advantage of the Tibetan plateau in both western and eastern sectors; it is only at the Sikkim border in the Chumbi valley that it faces a major disadvantage. In 2018, the last two towns in Medog county that borders Arunachal – Gyalasa and Gandeng – were connected to the highway network, which is now over 82,000 kilometres long. In all three sectors along the LAC – western, middle and eastern – motorable Chinese roads now reach right up to the Indian border.

In the Chumbi valley bordering Sikkim and in Nyingchi across the border from Arunachal, the Chinese railway network will reach the border in 2020. In the current five-year plan (2016–20), the Lhasa–Nyingchi railway to the Arunachal border, the Shigatse–Yadong railway to the Chumbi valley and the Sikkim border, and the Shigatse–Gyirong railway to the Nepal border will be completed. This allows China to rapidly mobilize divisions from not only the western theatre command, but also from the central, southern and eastern theatre commands to the Indian border in a matter of days. The PLA Air Force also operates around a dozen airfields along the Indian border, with five big airports in Tibet, from Ngari Gunsa in Shiquanhe, which borders Aksai Chin, to Nyingchi airport near Arunachal. The other big logistical advantage for China is its indigenous military–industrial complex that ensures independence of supplies.

Most Chinese analyses of the border with India highlight Beijing's artillery and missile units as its biggest advantage. One study on the Sina military portal, China's most widely read defence website, assessed during the Doklam stand-off how the country would handle a conflict with India. It noted that the PLA had made big strides in mobilization, and revealed that in 2014, during the Chumar standoff, China was able to rapidly mobilize its 54th group army (which had been involved in both the India and Vietnam wars) from Henan to Tibet to undertake a drill, while long-range rocket artilleries and J-10 fighters were also sent to border airports as a deterrent. 'Weapons, drills, logistics, and military tactics have improved to a large extent,' it said. 'Troop deployments at the western frontier have been strengthened, as also field artilleries in Tibet. There is serious deterrence towards

India,' it concluded, suggesting China's aim was to win the war without fighting.[8]

Recent crises had also driven home to India the reality of a two-front war. Indeed, Chinese analysts after the Galwan clash were ascribing India's abrogation of Article 370 and changing the status of Jammu and Kashmir – which saw the creation of a new union territory of Ladakh that included within its boundaries Aksai Chin – as 'a challenge to the sovereignty of both China and Pakistan', language that has never been used before and suggested that the countries could intervene on the other's behalf in the event of a conflict.[9] For India, the China–Pakistan nexus – and the prospect of a 'two-front war' – has firmly emerged as its single most pressing diplomatic and military challenge.

11

The China–Pakistan Nexus

IT IS SUNSET ON AN autumn day in 2011, and the Pakistan Café is bursting with life. Seman Road, on which it is located, runs right through the heart of Kashgar, coursing past the high walls that line the borders of the city's famed old town, once a thriving centre along the old Silk Road. Today, Kashgar is the last big town in China's western Xinjiang province before you hit the Karakoram pass and the border with PoK. It is also the end point of the China–Pakistan Economic Corridor (CPEC).

The café is where Pakistani traders from across this dusty trading town gather for tea, sharing stories of their day's work, all united by a common ambition to grab a slice of this region's growth. China, in 2011, unveiled plans to build its first Special Economic Zone (SEZ) of western China here, hoping to boost development in southern Xinjiang, which has lagged behind the rest of the region. A community of several hundred Pakistanis has made Kashgar its home, with some traders marrying local Uighur women and settling down here. They spend half the year in Kashgar, and move back home during winter when travel becomes difficult.

I drove down the road they follow when they go home, heading west on the Karakoram Highway to the border town of Tashkurgan, through a rocky desert buffeted by the most stunning mountains you'll see anywhere. Forces of nature are the biggest obstacle here. My driver, a Kashgar native, told me he regularly hears stories of how winds blow cars away. 'But I've always been lucky,' he reassured me. We pitch a tent and stop for the night on the banks of the beautiful Karakul lake, before hitting the road again for Tashkurgan. That is as far west as I could get as an Indian – it is the last stop before China's border with PoK.

It's hard to imagine Kashgar and Tashkurgan – towns where even today most of the business gets done in the Sunday markets where sheep are traded – as important nodes on a global trading network, but that's exactly what China has in mind. And in the years since the CPEC was formally launched in 2015, changes are rapidly unfolding. Billions of dollars are being pumped in, a far cry from when I visited in 2011, when the only sign of international trading activity I could find there was one small and dusty office of the Pakistan China Business and Investment Promotion Council, staffed at the time by one man.

New Old Friends

'*Chun chi xiang yi*', or 'as close as lips and teeth', was how Mao Zedong once described China's close relationship with North Korea. For decades, North Korea was China's only ally, but in Beijing today, there is a new epithet that is the flavour of the moment for strategic affairs experts: '*Ba tie*', or 'iron brother' Pakistan. When Mao's People's Liberation Army marched into the restive Muslim-majority region on China's western frontier in 1949, the Chairman decided to christen the People's Republic's newest province as Xinjiang, literally meaning 'new frontier' – a historical name used intermittently for China's borderlands. Today, for many in Beijing, Pakistan is the new 'new frontier'.

If the twenty-year-old blueprint envisioned by China and Pakistan comes to fruition, Beijing will soon have a say in many facets of the Pakistani economy. A leaked draft master plan that was published in June 2017 by Pakistan's *Dawn* newspaper underlined the extent to which China plans to involve itself in Pakistan's economy. Besides roads, power projects and dams, which make up most of the investment, Chinese firms will even take up agricultural land as well as build tourism and cultural projects.[1]

Today, Chinese companies are building and managing the country's key transport networks, from national highways to Lahore's metro rail. China has bought a stake in Pakistan's stock exchange. It is building Pakistan's power sector – coal plant by coal plant – and will eventually, many experts believe, determine how much Pakistani citizens pay their government for electricity.

Ties between China and Pakistan go back to the early 1960s, a relationship forged in their mutual animosity towards India in the wake of their respective wars – a relationship that, as one Indian official at the time put it, was 'united in a strange marriage of convenience'.[2] But the lofty rhetoric often used by China and Pakistan to describe their relations as 'higher than the Himalayas, deeper than the oceans, and sweeter than honey' has not often been matched by reality. This was a relationship forged in the heights of the Karakoram Highway in the 1960s – when the two countries battled a common enemy, India – and one that has historically had immense strategic value, with China offering Pakistan missiles and aircraft, and both illicitly helping the other's nuclear programmes.

Since then, both governments, and particularly their militaries, have developed close relations. China has bolstered up Pakistan as a counterweight to India in South Asia, most notably through its continuing support of the country's nuclear programme. Ties remained close, but somewhat faded to the background as the US began leaning heavily on Pakistan for its war in Afghanistan, emerging as its biggest financial donor after the 11 September 2001 attacks.

This also coincided with Beijing more carefully balancing its relations with India. As China's economy lifted off in the 1990s, caution and self-interest, rather than romanticism, began dictating its approach to a neighbour whose periodic descents into chaos were viewed warily across the Khunjerab pass. This was all the more evident after the normalization of ties with India following Rajiv Gandhi's 1988 visit, when Beijing understood it needed to improve relations with its biggest neighbour to the west – and that to do so, it had to be seen to effect what one official described to me as 'a better balance' in its relationships with India and Pakistan. For two decades, Beijing has attempted to carefully strike a balance between its historical ties with Islamabad on the one hand, and a sensitive but growing relationship with Delhi on the other.

The Master Plan

The CPEC, however, has dramatically altered that calculus, and since its launch, India has been alarmed by the extent to which China has once again begun deferring to Pakistan's interests on key bilateral issues. This could potentially reverse the two-decade balancing trend we have made note of earlier.

China has now replaced the US as Pakistan's biggest benefactor. The launch of the CPEC has further reinforced this position. FDI into Pakistan increased fourfold in the three-year period following 2015, growing to $3.7 billion with China accounting for 70 per cent.[3] The CPEC will usher in an even more sweeping takeover of the Pakistani economy. The plan says thousands of acres of land will be transferred to Chinese companies to grow crops, build meat-processing plants, and develop free trade zones. Garment factories will, en masse, be transferred to Pakistan, while China will manage and run tourism projects and SEZs along the southern coast, with rather ambitious plans for even yacht clubs and hot spring hotels to develop an unlikely tourism hub in the restive Balochistan province, of all places. S. Akbar Zaidi, a leading Pakistani political economist, has written that the CPEC would reduce Pakistan to 'a vassal state', describing it as 'a Chinese project, for Chinese interests, and Pakistan just happens to be part of the geographical terrain'.[4]

Gwadar, a dusty town of less than 1,00,000 people that sits on the Arabian Sea in Balochistan, is the hub of the CPEC. China has already built a port here that it is managing. Beyond the port, which gives Beijing access to the Indian Ocean, it envisages a free trade zone and a manufacturing hub that could serve as a launch pad for exports to West Asia and Africa. The country has already secured a twenty-three-year tax-free deal for its companies that will operate out of Gwadar.

China is acutely aware of the enormous risks involved. In 2017, Renmin University in Beijing quietly sent a team of researchers to assess those risks. The findings, that were shared with me, were sobering. Security is one major concern, highlighted by the kidnapping and reported killing of two young Chinese nationals in Quetta, Balochistan, in May 2013. The Renmin study cited a number of other incidents that had targeted its citizens in 2016. In May 2016, a Chinese engineer at the Kazmu project was targeted by a bomb attack claimed by an outfit called the Sindh Revolutionary Force. Two months later, in July 2016, a bombing in Quetta killed seventy-four people, while in November 2016, a team from a Chinese oil and natural gas exploration company was targeted in an attack by a group called the Baloch Revolutionary Army in which two Pakistani security personnel were killed.

The wider concern was that because of security, Chinese staff in Gwadar, for instance, would have to be 'cloistered within the Chinese zone as the situation around the city is not stable'. The report worried this would alienate the local population because 'Chinese personnel are carrying out work under the protection of armed forces and this inhibits improving relations with local people to the extent that it could lead to opposition and lack of people's support'. The Pakistan army has deployed a special security division of 15,000 troops to protect Chinese personnel and assets, but the report argued that 'a troop size of 15,000 can hardly guarantee the safety of projects around the country ... And considering that Pakistan needs to deploy a large number of troops in its eastern borders adjoining India and now needs to deploy troops on the Afghan border, allocating 15,000 is the largest capacity.'

The report, however, came to the final conclusion that the only way for China to guarantee success was to assume even more sweeping control. 'Neither China nor Pakistan can afford the consequences of the failure of constructing the corridor,' it advised. 'If the current uncertainty was to continue, it would not only delay the opening of the flagship project but CPEC would end up becoming a burden on China and have a great negative impact.'[5]

The Chinese study was still optimistic about the long-term scenario. For Gwadar, it forecast an ambitious annual cargo throughput of 300–400 million tonnes, more than ten times that of Pakistan's current biggest port, Karachi; the study pointedly adds that this was almost equivalent to India's total current throughput. In February 2013, China Overseas Port Holdings Limited acquired the rights to operate the port from the Singapore Port Authority; the port was apparently in a state of ruin, 'filled with rubbish and garbage' as the Renmin study put it, until the Chinese took over. Since then, a first shipping route was opened by the Chinese state-run Shipping Ocean Company (COSCO) in May 2015 to export local seafood to Dubai. In November, the first CPEC export was flagged, as a convoy carrying sixty containers of a range of Chinese goods – from machinery to appliances being exported to West Asia and Africa – arrived in Gwadar after travelling 3,000 kilometres from Xinjiang along the Karakoram Highway. The study even outlined a move to transport China's waning textile industry, currently grappling with rising wages, to Pakistan. As a start, a cotton processing plant with a 1,00,000 tonnes output has been planned. The longer-term plan is 'shifting China's garment industries directly to Pakistan'. Beyond the lower wages and availability of land, China sees the favourable export tariffs Pakistan enjoys as a motivation.[6]

Still, Chinese assessments suggest the $62 billion figure that Pakistani officials regularly cite may not materialize for a long time yet. China's exposure, so far, is much less than the advertised figure, with estimates that in the first four years, its total investments would be only in the $5 billion range, spent largely on coal power projects that are being built, and the widening of the Karakoram Highway and sections of the Karachi–Peshawar expressway. The CPEC draft master plan from China's planning agency noted that 'Pakistan's economy cannot absorb FDI much above $2 billion per year without giving rise to stresses in its economy', and recommended that China's maximum annual direct investment in Pakistan should be around $1 billion – a damning reality check to fanciful figures of over $60 billion being invested in the country.[7]

Confronting the Challenge

For India, the deepening China–Pakistan nexus is arguably its biggest military and strategic challenge. The CPEC has given an already close relationship a deeper bind, with China's stakes in the country having expanded manifold.

Hu Shisheng is a leading Chinese strategic expert on India and Pakistan. He speaks Hindi and Urdu fluently, regularly travels to both countries, and is a regular and charismatic presence on international affairs talk shows in China, where he's known for his sharp takes on the country's interests that aren't couched in the cautious 'diplomatese' favoured by foreign ministry mandarins. Hu works at the China Institutes of Contemporary International Relations (CICIR), one of China's most influential think tanks, which reports to the Ministry of State Security, China's intelligence agency.

When we met at the CICIR's large campus in west Beijing one afternoon in the summer of 2017, Hu told me that the CPEC had changed the China–Pakistan equation dramatically. It is effectively pushing both countries in a direction where they 'will become mutual stakeholders of each other', he said. 'This means any disturbance in Pakistan,' he pointed out, 'will disturb Chinese interests.' I thought of his words three years later in the summer of 2020, when Chinese analysts began referring to 'joint challenges' to China–Pakistan sovereignty posed by India's moves in Kashmir, which were being cited as one reason for the border clashes. It was hence unavoidable, in Hu's opinion, that Pakistan will become 'a bigger factor' in China–India relations. Hu probably reflected the popular sentiment in Beijing when he said that 'China–India relations will become very problematic' if the India–Pakistan ties worsen.

Some in Beijing believe the two-decade 'tactical shift' to better balance relations with India and Pakistan, following the normalization of relations in 1988, may now be at an inflection point, with China once again tilting towards its old all-weather ally. Signs of this change in China's approach predate the CPEC to some extent. Starting around 2009, the US, which had emerged as Pakistan's principal military and financial donor, began winding down its presence in Afghanistan. Pakistan was seen by Washington as a needed ally in its war on terror, but as the US started to drawdown its troop presence from an unpopular war, China began to rapidly scale up its engagement.

While Islamabad's military ties with the US were growing rapidly during the war on terror, Beijing's often outdated arms exports became less valuable. But with the US scaling back and even reviewing crucial exports, such as F-16 fighter jets, while announcing a freeze in security assistance to Pakistan starting early 2018, China's support became crucial. And Beijing was more than willing to fill the gap. The two countries are now jointly producing JF-17 Thunder light fighter aircraft, while China has signalled its willingness to export its new fifth-generation stealth fighter.

Privately, many Chinese officials see the Pakistani military as a more favourable interlocutor in pushing the CPEC, rather than historically weak civilian governments. One of the CPEC's most important projects is the upgradation of infrastructure in PoK, starting with the Karakoram Highway. In the event of a conflict between India and Pakistan, this link will allow China to rapidly transport materials and assistance, even if it is unlikely to involve its own troops directly. Some Indian officials believe it is only a matter of time before the PLA has boots on the ground in PoK, ostensibly to protect Chinese personnel. In 2016, China and Pakistan for the first time began joint patrols in areas bordering PoK and Xinjiang.

A Pakistan Dilemma

Recent history has shown that Beijing has had clear limits on how far it will go to push Pakistani interests. This is, after all, not the 1960s or 1970s; in an increasingly multipolar, post-Cold War world, there are no blocs or permanent alliances, but shifting relationships based on self-interest. China's overriding strategic concern is not India. It is more preoccupied with the growing challenge posed by the US and its partners on its periphery. Beijing's 'biggest fear is India becoming a Japan or South Korea' – a full-fledged American ally – says one Party academic candidly, suggesting it would not be careless enough to push India into that position.

China is hence facing what some insiders describe as the 'Pakistan dilemma', as it weighs its ambition to build a regional counterweight to India against its fears of an India–US alliance. The former agenda is especially pushed by its military and security agencies that view India unambiguously as a clear threat. This explains China's often schizophrenic approach to its neighbour. Beijing is keen to develop investment and trade ties, and is pushing companies to invest in India as they deal with a slowdown at home. By some measure, China actually has greater stakes in India than in Pakistan – including the acquisitions of investments in Indian companies; as noted above, there are doubts about how much of its stated commitments in Pakistan (which in contrast to India's are generally state-driven investments) have actually materialized.

China is courting India's support on issues such as reforming global financial institutions and trade talks where they have common ground. But on security matters, including terrorism, Beijing appears to be deferring to the interests of its security agencies, which see Pakistan as key in ensuring stability not only in the western Xinjiang region, where Beijing is dealing with a Jihadist threat, but also in Afghanistan. This explains why China is often prepared to tolerate Pakistan's fostering of anti-India terrorists. Its rationale is that as long as Islamabad demonstrates willingness to crack down on groups that target China, such as the East Turkestan Islamic Movement (which in China's view it has done), it has no reason to complain.

China's embracing of Pakistan – and its raised stakes in that country – have complicated the three-way balancing act. The irony is that China's policymakers are aware that in many respects, its long-term goals in the region align more closely with India's than Pakistan's. In Kashmir, China wants to see a resolution of the dispute and stability that would allow its projects to continue unimpeded. In China's view, the resolution of the Kashmir issue is in some sense a prerequisite for a final resolution of its boundary question with India. Beijing hasn't been prepared to discuss the status of the PoK–China border in the western sector as part of its boundary talks with India because of Pakistan's sensitivities. In Afghanistan too, China – like India – is wary of the Taliban's growing influence and wants a stable environment to push infrastructure and development projects, even if it has been on board with bringing the Taliban back to the negotiating table. Beijing has also reached out to Delhi to work on joint projects, which may present an opportunity for both countries to build, step by step, much needed trust in the neighbourhood. It isn't lost on China that Pakistan's interests, in both regions, lie not in ensuring stability but in fomenting trouble.

As much as both India and China like to say, at least officially, that their ties are independent of third parties – read Pakistan, whose alliance with China concerns India, or the US, whose growing defence and security relationship with India likewise worries Beijing – the fact is that the China–Pakistan equation certainly presents a challenge. 'China has a desire to strike a balance,' according to Ashok Kantha, who served in Beijing as India's ambassador until his retirement from the foreign service in January 2016; he subsequently took over as director of the Institute of Chinese Studies, Delhi's premier China-focused think tank. 'India is not expecting China to downgrade relations with Pakistan as a prerequisite for our enhancing relations. But what we really expect is that when we look at aspects of China's engagement with Pakistan that have a negative implication for us, they must understand our concerns.'

Kantha cited the example of Beijing's consistent blocking of India's attempts to designate Pakistani terrorists at the United Nations Security Council 1,267 sanctions committee, which he said had certainly 'vitiated' the broader atmosphere of India–China relations. 'This isn't desirable for either country,' he said, noting that on this issue, 'China's diplomatic protection' was essentially 'encouraging Pakistan to adopt a more irresponsible attitude, including on an issue of direct interest to us, which is terrorism'. 'We know China and Pakistan have a long-standing strategic investment, but what one can say with a degree of confidence is that their strategic relations are certainly not getting eroded, and if anything, they are getting stronger.'

A Global Footprint

For India, the China–Pakistan challenge is only part of a broader puzzle of dealing with a growing Chinese footprint abroad, and particularly in its neighbourhood – a footprint being expanded rapidly by the Belt and Road Initiative. How China will safeguard the security of both its growing overseas assets and the increasing number of Chinese working abroad, often in unstable regions, remains an open question. There isn't, however, a more important one in setting the future direction of China's rise and its engagement with the world.

As Beijing's economic stakes overseas grow, so will its political heft in the countries where it is now acquiring massive assets – assets it will need to protect. If, in the previous decade, China's engagement with many countries was driven by trade and economics, and a very cautious approach to involvement in the politics of countries where it was doing business, now, for better or for worse, its stakes are larger. This is one important driving force for the shift we are seeing from 'hiding brightness' to being 'proactive'.

In 2017, China opened its first military facility overseas in Djibouti, without so much as a word of acknowledgement that it was abandoning a decades-old policy of not operating foreign bases. The naval facility is in the Horn of Africa, near the Gulf of Aden. Chinese firms have been seeking port projects throughout the Indian Ocean region, where China has built or managed ports in Hambantota and Colombo in Sri Lanka, Kyaukphyu in Myanmar, Chittagong in Bangladesh, and Karachi and Gwadar in Pakistan. The projects, Beijing says, are purely commercial.

But it is no coincidence that its interest in overseas ports coincides with the expansion of its blue-water navy and the rapid development of its aircraft carrier programme. China's second aircraft carrier – its first domestically built one, joining the Liaoning, which was essentially a retrofitted version of a Soviet carrier, the Varyag – launched in April 2017. Construction on a third carrier began in Shanghai that same month. Chinese naval experts have said a likely objective is to have six aircraft carriers by 2030–35, with two deployed in the Indian Ocean, two in China's near seas, including the South China Sea, and two in the Western Pacific.[8]

As China's stakes rise, it is emerging as a new player in the domestic politics of many countries, unlike in the past when it was merely content to enter, build, extract and leave. Beijing's appetite for risk is growing, albeit slowly. In Afghanistan, Myanmar and South Sudan, China has stepped in to play the role of political mediator, underpinned by its deep economic interests in all three places. In countries like Nepal and Sri Lanka, it is already exerting an influence on domestic political outcomes, for long a monopoly of India's.

If China's plans succeed, Delhi will have to deal with a fundamentally changed neighbourhood, one that is already gravitating into China's economic orbit. 'It is bound to affect us because it is obviously changing the balance in our immediate neighbourhood,' Shyam Saran, a former foreign secretary, who is one of India's sharpest China watchers, told me. The key message from the BRI, in his view, was 'to create a psychology that there is an inevitability of China's hegemony, and the sooner countries, including India, adjust to it, the better for them.' He said the BRI is reinforcing this narrative at a time 'when the US is either in decline or preoccupied', so countries find that 'they have to either shut up or accept Chinese hegemony, as there appears to be no countervailing force'.

How can India respond? Saran believes Delhi's response should begin in the neighbourhood, where its core interests lie. 'Even though we say our focus is "Neighbourhood First", we have to go one step further,' he said, 'and focus on first consolidating our position in the neighbourhood, instead of spreading ourselves thin.'

So a changed attitude to the immediate neighbourhood would be a starting point. In many ways, India's approach to its smaller neighbours has actually driven them into Beijing's arms. Rather than demand reciprocity as it did in the past, India could instead leverage its market, and open up and integrate with the neighbourhood, even if that comes at some domestic cost.

India has no shortage of initiatives, from 'Neighbourhood First' and working with Iran on the Chabahar port, to the 'International North–South Transport Corridor' to Central Asia. But the fact is that on scale and speed, China is in another league altogether. 'We need to focus on delivery of existing commitments because that's where China scores over us all the time,' said Saran. One long-proposed solution was the setting up of an independent agency that would be empowered to deliver on projects – many of which are managed by the Development Partnership Administration in the Ministry of External Affairs – and circumvent the bureaucratic webs. It was stymied on account of turf battles between different ministries.

Ultimately, India's bold stand on the BRI will not count for much unless the country steps up as a credible alternative. Matching China's deep pockets is not a realistic option. As much as we like to hyphenate the two countries, one statistic that Saran drew my attention to should provide a reality check: if China's economy grows at 0 per cent, India would have to grow at 10 per cent annually for twenty years to catch up. At the very least, the gap should be narrowing if India is to emerge as a credible alternative. That gap, instead, is widening.

But India doesn't need to match China, rupee for renminbi. What it can, at the very least, do is take a leaf out of the BRI playbook. Just as China has done, India needs to offer its own vision for the world, in line with its unique values. It has just as rich a tradition in strategic thought to draw from as does China. What does India stand for? Trying to answer that question would give us a good place to start.

PART IV

HISTORY

12

Original Sins

MOST ORDINARY INDIANS AND CHINESE are aware of the boundary dispute between their countries, but less so about its genesis and history. Over time, in both countries, a simple narrative comprising half-truths and myths, with large doses of nationalist sentiment, has come to replace the complicated story.

The crux of the dispute is in the western and eastern sectors, involving India's claims to Aksai Chin and China's claims to Arunachal Pradesh, as a result of which neither side is willing to accept the status quo as a permanent solution. However, the reality is that only a solution along the lines of the current status quo, with minor adjustments, will be viable as it is highly unlikely either side will countenance giving up territory they control.

Both, it would seem, are in denial about this reality, and, barring an all-out war – the prospect of which would be devastating for both – they are not going to get the lands they lay claim to. This hasn't stopped India's politicians from declaring 'they will die for Aksai Chin', as the Indian home minister Amit Shah told Parliament in 2019, or Chinese social media users routinely calling for the return of 'South Tibet' to the fold (China's leaders, at least, are somewhat circumspect about making such claims in public).[1]

In India, the popular view is that Aksai Chin – the 38,000 square kilometres in China's control in Ladakh – was *always*

Indian territory. In China, the popular view is Arunachal Pradesh – which the Chinese call 'South Tibet' – and especially the Tawang region, birthplace of the sixth Dalai Lama, was *always* China's territory. This latter claim is based on the argument that Tibet itself always belonged to China – a claim that, as we will see, doesn't square with the history of Tibet.

'Always' is a funny word. It's also a convenient word that obscures, misrepresents and distorts historical fact. History, however, tells us that both countries' claims are more tenuous than either government would like its people to believe. Yet, they have been repeated so often by the ruling powers that they have come to be accepted as the sacred truth in their respective countries.

Aksai Chin

This is a tale that goes back to the nineteenth century. It was the colonial-era great games that bequeathed unsettled boundaries to the new states that were established in the 1940s: India in 1947 and China in 1949. When the two states began talking about the unresolved boundary they had inherited, India pressed its claims to the western sector, citing, among other agreements, the 1842 Ladakh–Tibet treaty. Under the treaty, both sides had agreed to accept old, established frontiers, to confine themselves within their boundaries, and to refrain from any acts of aggression.

Interpreting the 1842 treaty is one part of the dispute. In his talks with Chinese Premier Zhou Enlai in 1960, Nehru argued the treaty conclusively settled the western frontier. The basis of his claim is, however, less clear than he made it out to be. For one, this oft-cited 1842 treaty was actually a treaty of friendship, and not an agreement for demarcating boundaries. The text of the treaty doesn't even mention where the boundary runs.

This, in itself, isn't all that unusual, when you remember we are talking about a time that predated the modern conception of a linear boundary, and there existed traditional customary boundaries that caravans and nomads abided by. The treaty does, however, refer to 'old established frontiers', which suggests both sides were indeed aware of where those frontiers were.[2]

Even beyond the treaty's cartographic limitations, the truth was the British themselves didn't see the 1842 accord as one that settled the boundary of Ladakh. And Nehru, being a keen student of history, almost certainly knew that. For if 1842 did settle the boundary, the British wouldn't have repeatedly asked China to enter into negotiations to define the frontier no sooner had they added the princely state of Jammu and Kashmir, into which Ladakh was incorporated, to their empire in 1846.

The problem is that for much of history, this contested frontier was largely an inhospitable no man's land, with no settled population and no administration. It was only traversed by nomads and caravans. But if anyone could lay claim to it, it would have been British India, as Jammu and Kashmir could at least claim its writ ran over those who traversed the region. In contrast, there is no record of Chinese presence there.

The other problem for India is that contrary to Nehru's argument, the fate of this no man's land was never really settled, although it could have been in 1846. The Chinese, who were then concerned with bigger problems on their eastern coasts in the aftermath of the Opium War, did not respond to British requests, and had no desire to fix the boundary.[3] So unlike in the case of the McMahon Line in the east, there was never any agreement to fix the boundary in the west.

Further complicating the western frontier is that there wasn't agreement even within the British government for years after 1846 about where the boundary ran, with varying alignments shifting to suit their geopolitical concerns. Their primary objective at the time was to halt the advance of the Russians and not to fix the boundary; so much so that the British suggested border alignments that were more than generous to the Chinese in the hope of creating a viable buffer. The fact is the British did not want rigid boundaries that would limit their influence.

It was precisely because of this conception of boundaries that India, in 1947, had to largely discover its frontiers for itself, and did not have clearly demarcated colonial borders that it could easily inherit – as much as India would have to claim otherwise during its border negotiations with China. Indeed, China was in exactly the same boat, and the boundaries that it inherited in 1949 were similarly from a period where empires – the Qing in China's case – had a very different conception about how to define the limits of their influence. Ironically, both India and China, as two young republics – and 'two successor states to two expansionary empires' – would find themselves in a situation where they would be going to great lengths to defend the imperial boundaries they inherited.[4]

That the frontier in the west was not entirely clear in 1947 is plainly evident in the Indian government's own White Papers on Indian states in 1948 and 1950, where it is designated as 'undefined', a fact that is mostly forgotten today. So while the map of India of the time clearly marked a dotted McMahon Line in the east, it showed the boundary in the western sector as undefined.[5]

The seeds of the dispute with China were sown in 1954 when Nehru unilaterally decided to issue new maps; he adopted the position that the problem was settled and there was nothing to be discussed. The year he did so would eventually become a turning point in the boundary dispute.

In April 1954, an 'Agreement between India and China on Trade and Intercourse between the Tibet Region of China and India' was signed, which gave birth to the famous 'Panchsheel', or Five Principles of Peaceful Coexistence, following which India would give up many of the privileges in Tibet it had inherited from the British.

Two months later, Nehru decided to print new maps showing India's northern frontiers as defined. He also declared that the frontier would be a 'firm and definite one which is not open to discussion with anybody' and that India 'should have check posts in such places as might be considered disputed areas'. It was, in truth, a stroke of a pen in 1954 – and not a treaty in the nineteenth century – that actually 'settled' the frontier we now declare with some certainty has existed for centuries.[6]

If India's claims at least had a basis in history, China did not even have that. India could present detailed cartographic data and administrative records. China had nothing.[7] Even so, the fact remains that this was never settled – whether in 1842 or later – and this was, in truth, a no man's land for much of history. Indian officials knew this. 'The main point is that neither India nor China has any strong claim to Aksai Chin, though our claim may be somewhat stronger,' R.K. Nehru, who was India's ambassador to China from 1955 to 1958 and a foreign secretary prior to that, said in a July 1971 interview that was part of the Oral History Programme of the Nehru Memorial Museum and Library (NMML). 'Graziers from both sides and traders used to go there, maybe more from our side, but no one can live there and there was no established administration.' He noted that until 1954 the boundary there was shown as 'undefined' in Indian official maps, before Prime Minister Nehru decided to change that to an international boundary. The Chinese mistake, he said, was to not question that from the start. He suggested the Chinese 'were thinking in terms of a quiet exchange, in the sense that "you occupy NEFA [the North East Frontier Agency, which later became the union territory of Arunachal Pradesh in 1972 and a state in 1987], we will keep on making our claims on our maps, etc. We will occupy Aksai Chin, then sometime later we will settle it."'[8]

To put it simply, there are two things that are clear about Aksai Chin. One, India has a far better claim on it than China. Two, regardless of who has the better claim, this frontier was never *settled*. Through the unilateral declaration that it was, made by Nehru, an unsettled question became a thorny dispute.

The McMahon Line

If the origins of the dispute in the west tell us the boundary there was far from settled, the east is less contentious. It is true that the very mention of the McMahon Line continues to raise hackles in Beijing, which, even today, at every opportunity, reiterates its anger and opposition to the events of more than 100 years ago. This, of course, is partly posturing, as Beijing was, as we will see, quite comfortable about accepting the McMahon Line when it settled borders with Burma. When Indian leaders visit Arunachal Pradesh, the foreign office will, inevitably, bring out its time-tested statement raging at the 'British colonialists who secretly instigated the illegal "McMahon Line" in an attempt to incorporate into India the three areas of China's Tibet'.[9] Suffice it to say, the origins of the line remain a source of much disagreement and controversy.

Unlike in the western sector, there is far less debate about the genesis of the boundary here. What we know is that at the Simla Conference in 1913–14, officials from Britain, China and Tibet met to discuss the boundaries of Tibet. The representatives, Henry McMahon, Lonchen Shatra and Ivan Chen, all initialled a map showing the boundaries between Outer and Inner Tibet, and between Tibet and India. While the conference ultimately ended in failure, with the Chinese refusing to sign the convention, their recorded objections only referred to the Outer Tibet–Inner Tibet boundary, and not to the McMahon Line.[10]

If the proceedings cast doubt on China's later claims of where it believed the boundary ran in the east, its subsequent actions further undermined them. While China rages about the injustices of the line today, there was no record of any Chinese objections to the line until the mid-1930s, more than two decades after the Simla Conference.

Moreover, the entire basis of China's claims rests on the assumption that Tibet was always a part of China. Tibet *today* may be a part of the People's Republic of China, which India recognizes, but the degree of China's sovereignty over Tibet through history is hardly a settled question. Only consider the simple fact that at the Simla Conference in 1913–14, Tibet had its own representative.[11]

Even beyond China's debatable claim on the past status of Tibet, the historical links of Arunachal to Lhasa are not what Beijing now claims them to be. Indeed, Arunachal's languages, like

Monpa, are non-Tibetan, and much of western Tibet and Ladakh have historically been independent of Lhasa.

To be sure, the McMahon Line was not a definitive resolution to the boundary in the east. Although based on detailed surveys, all we have from the Simla Conference is one very imperfect map. And imperfect is an understatement here. There is no textual reference or agreement on where the line actually ran. Moreover, it was drawn with a thick-nibbed pen using red ink on a scale of eight miles to an inch. This, in itself, would leave room for plenty of confusion when applied to modern cartography.

Leaving aside the imperfections of the line, the plot thickens with a series of extraordinary events that followed the conference. If the Simla Conference and the drawing of the McMahon Line are now seen as pivotal moments in history, in truth, the line was all but forgotten for the next twenty-one years, during which there was no attempt to certify it in maps or enforce it on the ground. The official record, in the 1929 edition of Aitchison's Treaties, an official record of treaties pertaining to India, did not even consider the line important enough to mention in its account of the conference, only saying that the convention was 'drawn up and initialled in 1914'. It also acknowledged that the Chinese government 'refused to permit their Plenipotentiary to proceed to full signature'.[12]

It was only in 1935, a good twenty-one years after the conference, that the forgotten memory of the line was revived by Olaf Caroe, then a deputy secretary in New Delhi and later a foreign secretary. Realizing that the absence of the line in the 1929 accord could be used by China to make the claim that there was no agreement between India and Tibet in 1914, Caroe suggested the line now be shown on all maps. To his horror, he realized that even until 1935, the official survey of India was showing the boundary along the foot of the hills, far south of the line.

London agreed that henceforth all documents from the Simla Conference should be incorporated in new maps. Caroe then went a step further; he decided in 1937 to republish the 1929 edition of Aitchison's Treaties that had omitted the line, and recalled and destroyed every old copy he could lay his hands on. The new – and some would say forged – additions dating 1929 now had the Simla documents showing the line. History was literally rewritten.[13]

Yet, even after Caroe's discovery, the British hardly considered the line to be as sacred as we do today. In fact, they decided against enforcing it on the ground and did not move to occupy Tawang, which remained in the hands of the Monbas. Even in 1944, the British considered conceding Tawang to Lhasa, arguing, 'It might be useful to agree, as a bargain counter, to draw the boundary south of the Tawang area.'[14]

Correcting the Record

The bottom line is this: an ultimate resolution of the boundary dispute hinges on India's claims to Aksai Chin and China's claims to Arunachal Pradesh. And the one big obstacle to any settlement is the view, in both countries, that each has a clear-cut claim that they are being denied by the other.

As far as the eastern sector is concerned, the Chinese public has been fed the notion that 'South Tibet' was always an integral part of Tibet; it was thus, in their view, always a part of China, since the question of Tibet's historical status is now a sacred truth in China, regardless of the actual history. Questioning that is heresy. The McMahon Line is seen as a devious colonial instrument, no matter that in 1956 China accepted the approximate contours of the McMahon Line as it settled borders with Burma – even up until the 1980s, Beijing appeared willing to give up its claims in the east for a settlement in the west.

Indeed, China may have perhaps done the same for India as it did with Burma. That prospect was probably shattered when Nehru decided to issue new maps showing India's claims in the west, and declared in 1960 that these claims would be non-negotiable and that China would acquiesce to them, perhaps because of India's concessions on Tibet – a move that the historian

Parshotam Mehra describes as 'an act of supreme self-delusion and wishful thinking'.[15]

In the west, as we have seen, India's claims to Aksai Chin are certainly stronger than China's. India has both cartographic evidence and records of tax collection to make its case, which China doesn't. As true as that may be, the problem is this frontier was never settled and this claim never enforced on the ground, leaving it a no man's land, regardless of subsequent over-exaggerated claims about 1842.

This convoluted historical record matters, because it leaves us with the inescapable conclusion that maps, historical records and details of tax collections are not going to solve the dispute. For every map that one side may furnish from one moment in history, the other could find something else to undermine that claim. We can spend another 100 years debating the historical merits of each claim. But that will get us nowhere, as the fruitless negotiations have shown. We will only be back to where we started.

Border Negotiations

The irony in all of this is that this was a dispute that was 'pre-eminently susceptible to a fair solution, for each had its vital non-negotiable interest under its control'.[16] For India, the McMahon Line in the east protects India's foothills. For China, Aksai Chin gives it its crucial Xinjiang–Tibet link. This was thus a dispute that was immensely solvable, but whose resolution was finally rendered utterly impossible by a series of actions for which both sides bear their share of the blame.

India and China had a golden opportunity to resolve the dispute just two years before the 1962 war, when Chinese Premier Zhou Enlai came to India for talks with Prime Minister Jawaharlal Nehru. If his visit hadn't ended in abject failure, war would have been all but averted.

The full record of the Nehru–Zhou talks – which laid bare the countries' differing approaches and intent towards settling the dispute – should be essential reading for any student of this period of history. It's now easily accessible in the public domain in the compiled documentary history of India–China relations by Avtar Singh Bhasin, which runs into five lengthy volumes. These books are a treasure trove of information, most of which has since fallen out of public memory.[17] The exchanges between Zhou and Nehru leave you with the impression that only one side was serious about making concessions in the talks.

And that side wasn't India. If Nehru was correct in saying that India had the far stronger claim to Aksai Chin – which China couldn't match with a shred of evidence – his approach to discussing the boundary doomed any chance of settling the question from the start. His steadfast insistence since 1954 that 'there was nothing to discuss' left little room to make headway. No government in Beijing could accept his maximalist position. Approaching any negotiation from a starting point that declared there was nothing to discuss guarantees only one thing: it will never yield an agreement.

Zhou Enlai's basic position was this: China was willing to take what he called 'a realistic view' in the eastern sector, as it had done with Burma, as long as India recognized there was a dispute in the western sector. The two couldn't be seen in isolation. Nehru rejected that outright. Ironically, that is, in essence, the position that both India and China have adopted today, calling for a 'package solution'. That was, however, ruled out by Nehru, who insisted there was no dispute in the west to begin with. 'The one common feature in the boundary between China and Burma and India is the presence of the McMahon Line. We stated we do not recognise the line but that we were willing to take a realistic view with Burma and India,' Zhou said. 'When we talk about the western sector,' he added, 'we should discuss it in relation with other sectors.'[18]

Zhou was right in saying that the boundary hadn't been 'determined or delimited' in the west, even if there were traditional customary boundaries. The 1842 treaty certainly neither determined it nor delimited it, considering it was done at a time that predated modern cartography. Zhou also came up with the idea of a 'Line of Actual Control', suggesting that 'each should keep to this line [of actual control that existed] and make no territorial claims beyond this, besides individual adjustments later'. As he defined it, in the eastern sector it is the McMahon Line and in the western sector, the Karakoram and Kongka passes. Zhou essentially laid the framework for settlement, saying that 'neither side should put forward claims to an area which is no longer under its administrative control'. He said, 'We made no claims in the eastern sector to areas south of the line but India made such claims in the western sector. It is difficult to accept such claims.'[19]

In his now famous press conference in Delhi, Zhou made a six-point statement that, in many respects, laid the ground for a solution. He said: there exist disputes with regard to the boundary; there is a line of actual control up to which each side exercises administrative jurisdiction; in determining the boundary, geographical principles such as watersheds, river valleys and mountain passes should be applicable in all sectors; a settlement should take into account national feelings; pending a settlement, both should keep to the line and not put forward territorial claims as preconditions, but individual adjustments can be made; and in order to ensure tranquillity and facilitate discussions, both sides should continue to refrain from patrolling along all sectors. 'I came here with the hope of seeking avenues for a reasonable settlement of the boundary question,' Zhou told Nehru. He added that while there were 'still distances between us' on the six points, he felt 'it will not be difficult to narrow down and eliminate these differences' following which both 'will have taken a big stride forward towards the reasonable settlement of the boundary question'.[20]

That hope was ultimately dashed by Nehru's insistence that the eastern and western sectors couldn't be equated, and there was nothing to discuss in the western sector. In his statement to the Lok Sabha after Zhou's visit, Nehru all but closed the door for a negotiated settlement. 'The attempt was made,' as he put it, 'to equate the eastern sector with the western sector.'[21] What explains

Nehru's stand? Hindsight often provides an illusion of clarity that can be very misleading. It would be unfair – and ahistorical – to cast the blame entirely on Nehru for the breakdown in talks without understanding the context for his stand. And for this, China has its fair share of the blame.

By the time Zhou arrived in India in 1960, Indians were already outraged by developments in the western sector where China was unilaterally changing ground realities, most notably by building the Xinjiang–Tibet road through Aksai Chin. Beijing's attempt to change facts on the ground by stealth through the road construction jeopardized any prospect of meaningful negotiation by putting the Indian government in a corner. Public opinion was also inflamed by the killing of nine members of an Indian patrol in an ambush by China at Kongka pass in Ladakh, in October 1959. After those events, it certainly would have been difficult for any Indian government to negotiate.

At the same time, neither can Nehru be absolved of responsibility for a series of decisions that pushed a resolvable boundary dispute, which China appeared eminently willing to discuss, into an intractable one. His big decisions in 1954 was the starting point, as well as his assumption that China would happily accept India's new maps at the time. If China had pushed India into a corner, so did Nehru with the new maps. His taking this public stand on the boundary made it impossible for him to negotiate meaningfully for the western sector.

Ultimately, Zhou's offer of a swap in 1960 – that would see China give up claims in the east and India give up claims in the west – was rejected out of hand because India believed it had the better claim to Aksai Chin. As we have seen, that belief was certainly correct. In India's view, there was a traditional customary boundary line between India and Tibet, formalized by various agreements.

India was also of the view that China had acquiesced to these boundaries as it did not raise them for ten years after the PRC was founded, although that was a questionable interpretation as China was only beginning to negotiate boundaries with other countries in that period. Beijing's argument was that a traditional boundary was hardly the same as one that was delimited and delineated, which both sides needed to negotiate.[22]

Two States, Two Approaches

What perhaps doomed the pre-1962 negotiations from the start were two fundamentally different approaches to the talks. 'China saw the boundary negotiation as a bargaining process, and boundaries as reflecting the balance of power. We did not,' Shivshankar Menon, a former national security advisor, foreign secretary and ambassador to China, who was also the Special Representative (SR) on the boundary negotiations with China from 2010 to 2014, told me. Menon has spent four decades engaging with China, both as a diplomat and scholar, and to my mind, there is no one in India who understands China better.

'We didn't see territorial boundaries inherited from history as negotiable,' Menon said. 'That was a difference from the beginning.' India, in contrast, took 'a legal approach'. 'Part of it was the legal training,' Menon told me. 'We had a whole generation of leaders who were lawyers. If you look at the amount of evidence we gathered – about where we exercised jurisdiction and where we collected taxes, and so on – there is no way the Chinese can match any of this. It is in no way comparable. Which is why the Chinese say that settling the boundary is a political, strategic decision. By saying it is a dispute left over from history, they try to suggest that history cannot provide the solution. We even said we were ready to take the dispute to the International Court of Justice, since we are confident of our evidence. China was not willing because there was no comparison. When the officials of both sides started doing the exercise of comparing evidence in the official talks in the early 1960s, both started believing their own evidence and that they had an open and shut case. And the Chinese had not much of a legal case, frankly, in either [the] eastern or western sectors.'

In the west, Menon said, 'Everyone knew where the boundary was and it was respected in practice before 1949. For instance, the caravans knew just where it was. Nehru always drew a distinction, even in Parliament, between the western sector and eastern sector until after the war of 1962. This was so even after 1959, when the dispute was formalized and out in the open, and is clear in his letters to Zhou Enlai. Before 1842, the Chinese had no real conception of boundaries in a Westphalian sense. For them, the world was all under heaven, of varying shades of civilization from the centre out. And all the treaties setting boundaries with Russia and others they regarded as unequal, certainly post-1840 after the Opium War.

'When it came to the boundary talks with India and other countries in the late 1950s and early 1960s, the Chinese used whatever came to hand to justify what they thought they could get as a boundary. For the Chinese at that stage, the approach was that "we are a modern state, we have to have boundaries, so let us negotiate wherever we can." They initially even had trouble in agreeing on a boundary with North Korea and didn't settle that until much later. And this was a fraternal, communist state, dependent on them and for whom they had fought a war. This was a period when China was drawing boundaries with all her neighbours. With Myanmar, she accepted the McMahon Line. With Nepal, she was more than generous because of the dispute with India and the trouble in Tibet.

'I suspect that they genuinely thought that to start a negotiation you make an exaggerated bargaining bid, which has to be expansive. But they were possibly willing to give some of that up. Certainly, you would assume that from what Zhou Enlai said in 1960. Now they might be calling Arunachal Pradesh "South Tibet" and so on, but during Zhou's 1960 visit, I do not think that they had any real expectation of gaining territory south of the Himalayas. In the western sector, they had got what they wanted with the war of 1962. So they were willing to speak of the status quo, the line of actual control, and so on. But we were not. That's where the difference was.'

What complicated the issue for India were the developments in Tibet, starting with the uprising in 1956, the suppression of which by the PLA generated waves of anger in India, and then the Dalai Lama coming to India in 1959. 'The bottom was knocked out of the Chinese case once there was a guerrilla war in Tibet, broad Tibetan resistance to Chinese rule, and its suppression by the PLA after 1956,' Menon said. 'In the Indian public's mind, China's very presence in Tibet was illegitimate. It became very hard for an Indian political leader in that situation to agree to the Chinese demand that India cede 38,000 square kilometres of territory in the western sector.'

If the seeds of the dispute were well and truly sown by the time Zhou Enlai left India in 1960, both sides began hurtling towards war, which finally broke out in the October of 1962, when China launched a full-scale attack on India in all sectors. This would finally cement its occupation of Aksai Chin, which continues until today.

13

Ghosts of 1962

MAO ZEDONG, WHO WAS A keen student of history, was aware that the attack on India he was about to order was not the first by a Chinese leader. In the lead-up to 1962, Mao had been delving into books on Indian history, and was struck by the friendly interactions starting in the seventh century and the Tang dynasty, when the scholar Xuan Zang famously travelled to India and brought back Buddhist texts to China.

Before 1962, Mao observed, there had only been 'one and a half wars' in the entire history of the two civilizations. The first was in 648 CE, when barely a few years after Xuan Zang's heroic return, the Tang dynasty emperor sent troops into India after a Tang diplomatic mission came under attack. The mission had been sent by the emperor, and was led by Wang Xuance, to return the compliment after Harshavardhana sent emissaries to the imperial capital of Chang'an (now Xi'an). Wang Xuance, unlike Xuan Zang, did not receive a warm welcome in the wake of Harshavardhana's death, and his mission was attacked. He escaped to Tibet. A joint Sino-Tibetan force was sent the following year – travelling through the Chumbi valley and Nathu La pass – and 'inflicted a heavy defeat'.[1] The half war that Mao referred to was Tamerlane's capture of Delhi in 1398, only because, as he put it, Tamerlane's army was made up of Mongols, and Mongolia 'was then part of China, making this attack "half-Chinese"'.[2]

Was War Inevitable?

The debate about what led to war in 1962 – and who bears the responsibility for it – remains as unsettled today as the boundary dispute between India and China. The scholarship on 1962 reflects varying views. On one end of the spectrum is the still dominant view in Beijing that the cause of the war was Nehru's refusal to negotiate and his 'territorial aggression' through the implementation of the 'Forward Policy', which saw India setting up posts in disputed areas.

This argument is best captured in the late Neville Maxwell's *India's China War*, where he argued that the question 'who is to blame' could 'squarely be answered: India'. 'India created the dispute,' Maxwell wrote, 'made its resolution by diplomacy impossible, attempted to impose a settlement by force, and met defeat.'[3]

On the other end of the spectrum from Maxwell is the argument that China was entirely to blame for the massive onslaught unleashed on 10 October 1962. This is the dominant view for many in India, a view that lays the entire responsibility at the door of Mao. Bertil Lintner's *China's India War*, which, as the title suggests, was written as a direct response to the Maxwell thesis, is one example of this argument. It suggests the war had nothing to do with either Nehru or the Forward Policy, and was entirely because China wanted to teach India a lesson.[4]

Lintner, for example, suggests that the decision to go to war was not made by Mao in October 1962, but as early as three years before the war. To make his case, he points to China's upgradation of its military facilities in Tibet, the construction of new roads, and the mobilization of thousands of troops and supplies as suggestions of a Chinese plot that was hatched long before Nehru's Forward Policy was put in place in November 1961. The war, he concludes, 'had nothing to do with the establishment of an Indian Army post' and was an inevitability between what he believes are two fundamentally irreconcilable civilizations.[5]

What is common to both arguments is the assumption that war was always an inevitability. A close reading of the events that led to the October 1962 Chinese attack suggests that was far from the case. In fact, the record shows, there were many missed opportunities on the road to 1962. The 1960 talks are the clearest example.

If Lintner's argument is to be believed, the long and detailed negotiations of which we have a record – including Zhou Enlai's offer to settle – and Zhou's visits to India would have been perhaps the most elaborate political theatre concocted in modern history. The fact is that both sides had the opportunity to step back from the brink they were drifting towards. It was an opportunity missed.

Why China Went to War

Chinese perspectives of what led to 1962 remain largely absent from accounts of the time that we are familiar with in India. These are important perspectives to understand, even if they were, as we shall see, often based on questionable assumptions, particularly when it came to what the Chinese saw as Indian designs on Tibet.

I spent the summer of 2012 going through declassified Chinese documents from that period, which were briefly made available to the public at the Ministry of Foreign Affairs archives in Beijing. I was fortunate to be able to access them, and learnt that a year later some of the 1962 documents were removed from the archives, and those that were returned to it were heavily redacted. What really struck me from the documents, many of which were diplomatic cables sent to Beijing from Delhi, was that even in the months leading up to 1962, there were several opportunities to settle. There was nothing inevitable about the war.

An internal note dated 20 July 1962 recounted a meeting in Geneva between Zhang Hanfu, the Chinese vice foreign minister, and R.K. Nehru, a former ambassador to China and at the time a senior diplomat. Zhang emphasized that 'the border issue was serious, and if India did not withdraw troops, it should bear all the results', the note said.[6]

The failure of meetings in Geneva between Zhang and R.K. Nehru, and between Chinese Foreign Minister Chen Yi and Indian Defence Minister V.K. Krishna Menon, was seen by China as the turning point, the documents suggest. R.K. Nehru himself later reflected that the July meeting led him to conclude it would be incorrect to say China 'did not give us sufficient warning' of a military attack, questioning the deeply entrenched narrative of the 20 October aggression being a surprise or betrayal.

> [Zhang] said, in their notes they sent to us they had indicated, "It is bound to lead to a serious military conflict." May be the nature and scale and magnitude of the conflict was not anticipated, but I am not prepared to say that they did not give us sufficient warning that military encounters might follow. My own interpretation is that as in India, so also in China, there were various schools of thought. May be the military elements, coming on the top, wanted a clash.[7]

There were two sets of factors in the Chinese decision-making leading up to 1962. The first was what Beijing saw as continued provocations from Nehru's November 1961 Forward Policy, which led to China gradually losing bits of what it saw as its territory. Initially, the Chinese leadership seemed to believe it was posturing, and that Nehru would come to his senses. After a point, Mao appeared to realize that what he saw as Nehru's inexplicable faith that China would only 'bark and not bite' would lead the latter to pursue the policy through to its conclusion. This was unacceptable to Mao, leading to a need 'to punish India'.

The second factor involved China's misperceptions about Delhi's intentions in Tibet, fuelled by the unrest that was caused more by Beijing's own disastrous failings than any imagined

Indian designs. Tibet appeared to weigh more heavily in Mao's calculus than the question of territorial claims. Many of the Chinese writings on 1962 place far more emphasis on Tibet than on the dispute over territory. What did add to Chinese anxieties – and became a source of discord in relations with India – was the presence of Tibetan rebels in Kalimpong in West Bengal, and the involvement of the Central Intelligence Agency (CIA) in training them, which the Dalai Lama's older brother, Gyalo Thondup, later reflected, 'create[d] misunderstandings and discord between China and India', even if the whole project turned out to be ineffectual.[8]

The 1962 war was never only about land for China, as evinced by its unilateral withdrawal, despite its crushing victory, particularly in the eastern sector. The PLA history of the war said one reason for the attack was that India 'sought to turn Tibet into a buffer zone' – for long a British hope – and described Nehru as 'a complete successor' to the British imperialists.[9]

Why this belief – albeit a wrong one – was significant is that it came from Mao himself. As he put it in a meeting with the Party's top cadre in Shanghai on 25 March 1959, two weeks after the uprising began that led to the Dalai Lama fleeing to India in exile, 'India was doing bad things in Tibet', but China 'would not condemn India openly at the moment'. 'Rather,' Mao said, 'India would be given enough rope to hang itself.'[10] Mao was in complete denial about China's own failings in the region. When Soviet leader Nikita Khrushchev told him bluntly during a visit later that year that 'the events in Tibet are your fault', Mao replied that this was also what Nehru thought. 'No,' he then countered. 'This is Nehru's fault ... The Hindus acted in Tibet as if it belonged to them.'[11]

With Nehru's misplaced convictions, on the one hand, that there was no dispute to begin with on the boundary – coupled with a mistaken belief that the Chinese would never attack India, keeping in mind the broader relationship and a pan-Asian future – and on the other, Mao's deep paranoia about Tibet, it was the perfect cocktail for an epic disaster.

Myths of 1962

The popular narrative in India remembers the war as a betrayal by China of Nehru's hand of friendship. This was a narrative encouraged by Nehru himself and by his government, in part because they needed to hide the colossal failings – both political and military – that led to the debacle.

This narrative is so deeply embedded in public consciousness that the events that led to the war – from the failed negotiations to the Forward Policy – are but footnotes now. Leaving aside the absurdity of the idea of 'betrayal' providing a meaningful explanation in foreign affairs and war – you cannot be betrayed unless you leave yourself open to betrayal – one explanation for why this narrative remains so deeply entrenched in India's national consciousness is that there never really has been a full public accounting of what went wrong.[12]

The great irony, of course, is that we do have an accounting of some of the failures in India's decision-making that led to 1962. Only it has remained hidden from public view. The Henderson Brooks–Bhagat Report (HBR), commissioned to assess the military failings of 1962, is still classified in India. The report doesn't carry any great secrets. It is the reluctance to release it that has bestowed on it an almost mythical status. But what the report does do very clearly is shatter the myth that 1962 was in any way an entirely unexpected surprise, or, as Nehru would have it, a betrayal.

The report – or at least the 190 pages from Part One of the HBR that the late journalist Neville Maxwell temporarily made available by uploading it on his website in 2014 – presents a damning failure of military leadership, both in the Indian Army headquarters as well as in the defence ministry headed by V.K. Krishna Menon. It does not delve into political leadership or Nehru's decision-making, as its mandate was on matters military.[13]

The HBR tells us that even as far back as 1960, the Western Command was sending to army HQ dire on-the-ground reports on the state of military preparedness. It notes that a reappraisal through a war game in October 1960 revealed that 'a minimum of one division was required to meet the Chinese threat in Ladakh'. Recommendations were forwarded to HQ, but 'no decision on this was given'.

Perhaps most alarming of all was the clear intelligence from the military that warned of the likely repercussions from China if the Forward Policy was to be implemented. This was contrary to the view held by the Prime Minister's Office (PMO), as is evident from a meeting held on 2 November 1961 at the PMO, attended by the defence minister, the foreign secretary, the army chief and the director of the Intelligence Bureau (IB). The IB director expressed the view then that 'the Chinese would not react to our establishing new posts and that they were NOT LIKELY TO USE FORCE AGAINST ANY OF OUR POSTS EVEN IF THEY WERE IN A POSITION TO DO SO' (emphasis as in the original).

The HBR notes 'this was contrary to the military intelligence appreciation', which in the annual 1959–60 review 'clearly indicated that the Chinese would resist by force any attempts to take back territory held by them'. From the outset, the military commands on the ground were, to put it simply, opposed to the way in which the Forward Policy was being implemented by the HQ, which remarkably remained unresponsive to their grim on-the-ground appraisals dating back three years. The report is scathing about the HQ which, it suggests, both misled the government about the situation on the ground and also dictated a policy that was 'clearly militarily unsound'. It is less critical about the political leadership, assessing the actions of which was, in any case, beyond its mandate. 'The Government [which] ... politically must have been keen to recover territory, advocated a cautious policy,' the HBR notes. The report says the government's original decision was itself only partially conveyed down the chain of command.

The order had three elements in the western sector: to patrol as far forward as possible in Ladakh; to occupy the whole frontier in other northern areas, which were more accessible than Ladakh; and to position a 'major concentration of forces' along the borders so that they could address the operational difficulties and be situated close to the forward posts. The third decision was perhaps the most crucial, as the first two objectives would be impossible to achieve without enabling a 'major concentration of forces', considering the deficiencies in troop strength as had been pointed out in 1960. Yet, the report suggests that the third decision was not conveyed by army HQ to the commands, and their final directive to the commands carried 'a major deviation' from the original Forward Policy decision as it 'did not reflect the prerequisite ... laid down in the third operative decision'.

'Fire a Few Rounds, They Would Run Away'

The report tells us that this omission was catastrophic. It was also peculiar, as 'there was no question of headquarters not knowing that such bases did not exist at that time'. In short, the report tells us, 'The Army headquarters dictated a policy that was clearly militarily unsound.' This laid the foundation for failure, as it 'literally meant the commands had to take Army headquarters' directive at its face value'. It concludes, 'Had the whole of the directive been conveyed to the commands, it is almost certain that the Western command would have brought out its inability to implement the Forward Policy till an infantry division as asked for by them had been inducted into Ladakh.' The report notes that 'with [the Forward Policy's] introduction, the chances of a conflict certainly increased'.

What really comes through from the report was the extent to which 1962 was a disaster of India's own making. It was not that the country was somehow caught off-guard by a 'surprise' attack. Indeed, both army commands on the ground and military intelligence saw that the dangerous combination of an aggressive posture coupled with ill-preparedness would lead to disaster. These warnings, that go back to 1960, were neither heeded by army HQ nor by the rest of the leadership.

These warnings continued right until a few months before the outbreak of war in 1962, with senior figures warning Delhi of 'the fatal consequences of pursuing a provocative policy without the accompanying conventional capabilities'. One memo, written by Lt. Gen. Daulat Singh, the then General Officer Commanding-in-Chief (GOC-in-C) of the Western Command, noted that since the inception of the Forward Policy, the Chinese reaction had been 'sharp and significant', and 'led them to build up to a full division in Ladakh'. 'Our forward posts in Ladakh are nowhere tactically sighted, whereas the Chinese everywhere are,' the memo warned. 'Our forward posts ... are tactically dominated by Chinese posts on higher ground ... The Chinese build-up shows clear evidence of a tactically sound military plan, in support of a declared objective. We do not as yet appear to have a clear cut aim in Ladakh.'[14]

Why were such warnings ignored? The HBR argues there was a sense of complacency in the military leadership that completely misread Chinese reactions. 'General Staff Branch Army Headquarters not taking note of the warning of Western Command could only be attributed to an incorrect assessment of Chinese reactions together with a sense of complacency that nothing would happen,' the report surmises, noting this extraordinary comment of 'the Deputy Chief of General Staff to Lt Gen L.P. Sen in September 1962 that "experience in Ladakh had shown that a few rounds fired at the Chinese would cause them to run away."'

The commands on the ground were left with unrealistic orders while the HQ had 'abandoned' all 'prerequisites of proper military functioning'. The report laments that, 'Militarily, it is unthinkable that the General Staff did not advise the Government on our weakness and inability to implement the Forward Policy.' The orders were given to the commands after brushing aside the prerequisite of first having in place the bases and logistics.

The army's Chief of General Staff, General B.M. Kaul, had 'time and again ordered in furtherance of the Forward Policy the establishment of individual posts' and was 'overruling protests made by the Western Command'. 'There might have been pressure put on by the Defence Ministry,' the report says, 'but it was the duty of the General Staff to have pointed out its unsoundness.'

The situation in the eastern sector was no different. Here again, military intelligence had conveyed to army HQ that they were under-strength and mismatched, and that the Chinese could muster the strength of three divisions – rather than just one division, as HQ believed – in the east. Army HQ did not respond to those concerns either.

This led to a bizarre situation wherein 'the planning at all levels continued, to be against a threat of a division, as against three divisions the Chinese could easily bring against NEFA'. This finally led to a calamitous rout in the east, which was overrun even more easily than the west, where the Chinese faced some resistance. The report came to the conclusion that 'as in Ladakh, so in NEFA, we were hardly in a position to adopt the Forward Policy with all its aggressive purport ... and it was based more on preconceived notions of a lack of reactions by Chinese than on sound military judgement'.

The straw that broke the camel's back, according to both the report and Chinese documents, was the establishment of a post at Dhola, in the Namka Chu valley on the southern slopes of the Thag La ridge. The report goes into detail about the situation at Dhola, as it was 'the focus of the start of hostilities'. Originally, the plan was to establish a post west of Khinzemane, which was the only area in the east where the Chinese were patrolling beyond the McMahon Line, at the Bhutan–India–Tibet tri-junction.

One key reveleation from the HBR is that there was some debate on where the boundary line as India saw it actually ran, and there were 'discrepancies' in Indian maps. What was significant is that the final location where the Dhola post came up was 'actually NORTH [as emphasized in the report] of the McMahon line'.

The report concludes that what ended up as the final trigger for the war was a post 'established North of the McMahon Line as shown on maps prior to the October/November 1962 edition'. These older maps had also been given to the Chinese but India 'tried to clarify the error ... but the Chinese did not accept our contention'. 'The General Staff must have been well aware of this,' the report concludes, 'and it was their duty to have warned lower formations regarding the dispute. This was not done, and the seriousness of the establishment of the Dhola Post was not fully known to lower formations.' This move gave Mao enough ammunition to launch his war.

Ordering the Attack

Mao made the final decision to go to war in early October, when the deputy chair of the Central Military Commission Lin Biao briefed the Party leadership on continuing advancements made by Indian troops and firing in both sectors. The PLA intelligence reported to Lin that India planned an attack on Thag La ridge, to fulfil, as Nehru publicly promised, an eviction of all Chinese forces.

Mao summoned a meeting of the top Party and PLA leadership in the western hills outside Beijing – still a sprawling base for the PLA – where he announced the decision to go to war. In making his case, Mao drew from history, both from the PRC's recent history as well as from China's Imperial past.

> We fought a war with old Chiang [Kai-shek]. We fought a war with Japan, and with America [in Korea]. None of these did we fear. Once we give ground [to Nehru], it would be tantamount to letting the Indians seize a big piece of land equivalent to Fujian province. Since Nehru sticks his head out and insists on us fighting him, for us not to fight with him would not be friendly enough. Courtesy emphasizes reciprocity.[15]

A case can be made, as the American sinologist John Garver argues, that Mao would never have taken the decision to go to war with India over just the Forward Policy and territory if he had been disabused of his almost paranoid view that Nehru – despite the 1954 agreement and all his efforts in 1956 to convince the

Dalai Lama to return to China rather than seek Western help – was hell-bent on 'overthrowing China's status' and 'returning Tibet to its pre-1949 status'.[16]

The irony was that Nehru was, on the contrary, accommodating China to a great extent on Tibet – which itself caused disquiet in India – in the hope that supporting its sovereignty over Tibet would in return lead Beijing to guarantee genuine autonomy for Tibetans, as well as make possible a partnership between India and China. He hoped China would repay his accommodation by both ensuring autonomy in Tibet (which Mao had guaranteed to the Dalai Lama only to renege on it in 1959) and preserving China's friendship with India, Mao's desire for which Nehru had greatly overestimated.

All the same, the war was by no means inevitable. Mao's own comments to the Party leadership underline that even until a few months before the war, the CPC was leaving a window to possible de-escalation. That was, however, contingent on Nehru changing course. While Mao responded to the Forward Policy by telling the PLA to resume patrols within 20 kilometres of the McMahon Line (these had been suspended since 1959), he did also tell Chief of Staff Lou Ruiqing not to fire first. Firing of the first shot had to be approved by Mao himself. As he put it, 'Their continually pushing forward is like crossing the Han-Chu boundary. What should we do? If they do cross, we'll eat them up. Of course, we cannot blindly eat them.' By the spring of 1962, Mao was convinced Nehru would not budge. 'A person sleeping in a comfortable bed is not easily roused by someone else's snoring,' he famously said of Nehru. Yet, that position began to change. 'You wave a gun,' he later said, 'and I'll wave a gun. We'll stand face to face and can each practice our courage.'[17]

Chinese patrolling stepped up, and when facing new Indian posts, rather than withdraw, they began standing their ground. Nehru ignored the warning signs, convinced of his long-held view that China wouldn't oppose his Forward Policy. Possibly on account of domestic compulsions, he chose to not revisit the policy, although China's new strategy was a clear indicator that his fundamental assumption had been proven wrong. Even an official Indian history of the war notes, 'This reappraisal ... never took place and the situation was allowed to drift.' Towards war.[18]

When, in September, the Nehru government announced the army had been told to drive Chinese forces from the Thag La ridge, the die had been cast. The tense confrontation at Thag La 'forced Mao and other Chinese leaders to reconsider in late September the earlier policy of armed coexistence'. Nehru's Forward Policy, despite the numerous warnings of Chinese repercussions, continued unabated, convincing Mao that Nehru believed that no matter what the cost, China wouldn't attack.

Mao came to believe Nehru mistook 'China's policy of restraint for weakness' on account of a number of factors, such as China's internal problems during the Great Leap Forward, Sino-Soviet tensions and what Nehru saw as India's standing in the world. Each of these convictions turned out to be mistaken. The Chinese leadership received assurances not only from the Soviet Union but also from the US that they would stay out of any India–China conflict.

Mao concluded that Nehru needed to be taught a lesson – one that would be remembered. 'If we strike, we must strike big ... resolutely hit the wolf and make it hurt,' he said. 'We can guarantee that for a long time to come they will not dare to come again to conduct aggression against China's borders.'[19]

Was Mao proven right? Sixty years later, the war remains an unhealed wound in India, still casting a long shadow on how we view our neighbours on the other side of the Himalayas. Mao won his war. But he lost China the peace.

14

The Case for Settling

AN UNRESOLVED HISTORY – OF both the boundary and the war – presents a daunting obstacle to any eventual resolution of the India–China boundary dispute. It is an obstacle that is difficult, but not impossible, to overcome.

One only need look to 1980, when Deng Xiaoping, twenty years after Zhou Enlai's fateful visit, hinted at a solution along lines proposed by the former premier. In a 21 June 1980 interview, Deng noted, 'In the eastern sector we can reconsider the existing status quo – I mean the so-called McMahon Line – but in the western sector the Indian government should also recognize the existing status quo. I think you can pass this message to Mrs Gandhi.'[1]

Could such a solution still be on the table? Evidence suggests that as far as China is concerned, the ship may have sailed. In 1985, the country specified that the concession it was seeking in the east was Tawang, and that the McMahon Line was no longer acceptable. For any government in India, that is an impossible proposition. Not only is this a settled area that had 'sent representatives to every Indian parliament since 1950', the Supreme Court in the Berubari case of 1956 declared that no government can cede territory without a constitutional amendment, although it could make adjustments and rectifications in the boundaries of India.[2]

Missed Opportunities

Long-time negotiator Dai Bingguo, who served as the Chinese SR for over fifteen rounds of talks from 2003 until his retirement in 2013, suggested in a 2016 book that India and China had moved tantalizingly close to resolving the dispute when Atal Bihari Vajpayee was prime minister, only for the BJP's unexpected 2004 electoral defeat to thwart a final resolution.

Dai, who was appointed SR by Premier Wen Jiabao in 2003, credits Vajpayee for breathing life into talks that had meandered for years with little purpose. At a dinner with Wen during his 2003 China visit, Vajpayee suggested the setting up of the SRs mechanism, where the representatives would be empowered 'to detach themselves from the current boundary negotiations', 'directly report to their prime ministers', and find a solution 'from a political level'.[3]

Vajpayee's 2003 visit, no doubt, helped make serious headway in the stalled talks. China finally recognized Sikkim as an Indian state, while India, in the 'Declaration on Principles for Relations and Comprehensive Cooperation' signed by both sides during the visit, said it 'recognizes that the Tibet Autonomous Region is part of the territory of the People's Republic of China'.[4] In a major confidence-building measure, both sides signed a memorandum on expanding border trade, agreeing to use Nathu La pass 'for entry and exit' and designating 'Changgu of Sikkim state' and 'Renqinggang of the Tibet Autonomous Region' as venues for border markets.[5]

As the Chinese saw it, Vajpayee was 'the first Indian prime minister who publicly showed that some adjustments need to be made' by both sides, which, Dai says, 'led to a new hope emerging in the dull boundary talks'. India's first national security adviser and SR, Brajesh Mishra, who passed away in 2012, left an impression on the Chinese SR. When Dai suggested at the first SR meeting that both sides could aim to make headway 'in three to five years', Mishra, seventy-five years old at the time, retorted, 'If it takes so many years as you say, I won't be around to see it!'

After the second round of talks ended, Mishra quietly took Dai aside and told him to convey a message to the Chinese leadership. Dai recalls, 'He said, Prime Minister Vajpayee is 79 years old, and very concerned about the boundary question. Mishra was himself 75 years old, and said he hopes to settle it as early as possible.' As the BJP headed into elections in mid-2004, which Vajpayee expected to win, Mishra told Dai that the plan was 'to speed up the progress of the SRs meetings' after what they expected to be a successful re-election, and to push for an early settlement. For his part, Dai believed that these were not mere words and that an early settlement was indeed possible. 'I had hopes [at the time] that the SRs meeting would achieve results as early as possible,' he writes.

But it was not to be. The 2004 elections were a turning point, says Dai. The Chinese felt that the Congress-led United Progressive Alliance (UPA) was 'a weak government with coalition partners'; it was 'restrained by many factors and had a limited capability to make decisions'. Mishra stepped down as SR, and the focus shifted away from finding a solution. The Indian government, the Chinese felt, was concentrating on domestic issues and 'trying to maintain stability at the Centre'. 'It lacked the sense of urgency in solving the boundary question,' Dai says, leaving undone the process pushed by Mishra.

Hopes were briefly revived when the UPA was re-elected in 2009 in a stronger position, by which time M.K. Narayanan succeeded J.N. Dixit as SR. Dai says Narayanan 'conveyed a message to me from the Indian government saying that India hopes to solve all problems between India and China in three to four years'. Dai told Narayanan, with whom he had eight meetings, that he 'hoped we would not continue negotiating till the 99th meeting'.

Dai carried on the talks with Shivshankar Menon, who succeeded Narayanan, with their last round in 2012, before Dai stepped down as a new leadership took charge in Beijing. In December 2014, Dai and Menon – who had stepped down as NSA and SR following the May elections that year when the National

Democratic Alliance (NDA) government under Narendra Modi came to power in India – shared a platform at a rare event, interacting with students from Peking University. Six months into the new government in Delhi, and a year and a half into Xi Jinping's new rule in Beijing, both the former SRs expressed confidence that a solution was possible with 'governments in both countries who have strong mandates'.[6]

Following his last round as SR, Dai recalled a last informal meeting he had with Menon, where both sides summed up the progress made over fifteen rounds. By 2012, says Dai, both sides had 'created a good condition for finally solving the boundary question' and taken forward the three-stage plan, of which the first, which involved agreeing to political parameters, was completed in 2005. While the second stage of negotiating a framework was the most difficult (the last involves delineating and demarcating the border in maps and on the ground), Dai says both sides agreed that 'meaningful and mutually acceptable adjustments' would be required. Dai believes that both countries 'need to have a sense of urgency' and that solving the boundary question today faced 'advantageous timing'. The biggest barrier, Dai suggests in his book, is creating the right public opinion, with the idea of ceding any territory still an extremely sensitive issue in India and China. Can that hurdle be crossed?

The Tawang Puzzle

The momentum infused by Vajpayee's 2003 visit, and the landmark agreement two years later on 'Political Parameters and Guiding Principles' for settling the boundary dispute, created real hope that both sides were pushing for a final resolution. Indeed, the 2005 agreement was in many ways path-breaking, and created the broad contours for a fair settlement. The most significant takeaway from the 11 April 2005 agreement was, as described in Article VII, a consensus that 'in reaching a boundary settlement, the two sides shall safeguard due interests of their settled populations in the border areas.'[7] Reading between the lines, this agreement formalized what remains the obvious framework for a settlement – one that broadly recognizes the current LAC but with minor adjustments in the west and east, since both sides have ruled out accepting the status quo. In the months that followed the agreement, proposals were considered to resolve what remains the biggest sticking point – China's insistence that the status of Tawang in Arunachal Pradesh, the birthplace of the sixth Dalai Lama, was non-negotiable. One reported proposal was the creation of a 'soft border' in Tawang, that 'would allow the Chinese, especially Tibetans, to cross over and pray at the Tibetan monastery in Tawang'. This idea, at the time, was seen by some as 'the instrument that cracks the dispute'.[8] Whether such a proposal is still on the table – and whether it would be acceptable to China – remains to be seen, although at least in public statements, both by officials and strategic experts, Beijing has appeared to harden its stand.

From India's point of view, the biggest hurdle lies in China's claims to Tawang. In a 2017 article, Dai suggested that a resolution would be possible only if India made some concessions in the eastern sector, with both sides having ruled out a status quo solution. Tawang, he wrote, was an 'inalienable' part of Tibet and that a boundary settlement would not be possible unless India agreed to make concessions over here. But if India did so, China would also make concessions in Aksai Chin, according to Dai.

'The major reason the boundary question persists is that China's reasonable requests [in the east] have not been met. If the Indian side takes care of China's concerns in the eastern sector of their border,' he said, 'the Chinese side will respond accordingly and address India's concerns elsewhere.' Dai suggested that the fifteen rounds of talks he participated in had moved both sides closer to 'a political settlement', suggesting this would probably involve minor mutual adjustments or concessions, both in the west and in the east. 'China and India are now standing in front of the gate towards a final settlement,' he said. 'The gate is a framework solution based on meaningful and mutually accepted adjustments. Now, the Indian side holds the key to the gate.'[9]

Ma Jiali is one of China's most respected scholars on India. For two decades, he has been the leading authority in Beijing on relations between the two countries. One story goes that when relations with India had fallen into a tailspin in 2009, amid rows over the border and a visit by the Dalai Lama to Arunachal Pradesh, which unleashed a torrent of nationalism in China, Premier Wen Jiabao called Ma and told him to write a piece calling for a toning down of the anti-India rhetoric. The piece was duly published in the *People's Daily*. Ma has followed the vicissitudes of the relationship for years, and today holds a position at the China Reform Forum, which is affiliated with the influential Party School in west Beijing that trains future leaders.

I asked Ma Jiali where he saw the boundary dispute going. Were there prospects of a settlement at a time when many in China were emphasizing on the presence of strong leaders at the helm of the two countries – following Modi's 2019 re-election and Xi firmly in charge in China – but also when tensions along the border were growing?

Ma was cautious in his assessment. 'This is not like the border settlements that China did in the 1950s or 1960s,' he said. 'You can no longer do it in secret. People will criticize Xi Jinping for *mai guo* [selling the country] if he gives up claims. The key question is how to educate people and handle national sentiment.' Ma, who has studied the China–Russia settlement process, thinks it can offer a guide. 'With Russia, we started with joint research with Chinese and Russian scholars. I think that's one possible way to start. You need, on both sides, scholars with enough authority to come out and say something. Maybe Indian and Chinese scholars need to take the lead to work towards the basis of a final settlement. Why can't they work on a joint study, and at least at the academic level, exchange views and try and find the way to resolve the boundary issue?' What of China's claims on Arunachal? 'Mutual accommodation is the key principle,' he continued. 'In many cases,

China lost more from settlements. For example, the settlement on the island with Russia – it was ours but occupied and controlled by Russia. Finally, now, it is half-half. So what there has to be is give and take.'

The lack of political will on both sides, Ma says, is the biggest obstacle. 'Honestly, it is not a top objective for the Chinese leadership. Same for Mr Modi – it is not a top priority. But we need to make it a very important issue. Otherwise we lose time, we lose time, we lose time. We lose opportunities. This leaves me concerned. After some years, many things can change, and it will only become harder. We have had three historical opportunities, in 1960, the 1980s package resolution from Deng Xiaoping, and 2003.

'In 2015, I wrote an article saying China and India are facing an important historic opportunity. Both have strong leaders now. Both governments have their own big dreams to be realized domestically. This is an opportunity to resolve issues, including the boundary issue. Both countries agree that the final decision will be a political settlement. If you solve the boundary dispute, the relationship will be much improved. I believe that. Our relationship without the boundary dispute will be an entirely different relationship. It opens the door for more economic cooperation. Trade. Road building. International affairs. Everything. If the boundary is solved, there will be fewer doubts about China's intentions. Look at China and Russia. At one point, the dispute was very difficult. Now we have a strategic partnership.'

Ma is of the view that a settlement is possible if both India and China make minor concessions. He doesn't spell out what that would mean: discussing specifics of boundary settlements, particularly when it comes to what China could concede, is a no-go area for scholars of the country, given the sensitivities about matters of national sovereignty. But in essence, that would mean India giving up most of its claims in the west and China giving up its claims in the east, including its claims to Tawang.

The Russia example that Ma cited offers both encouragement and warnings to the Chinese leadership, said Han Hua, another leading India hand in Beijing, who is a professor of international relations at Peking University. 'The lessons we have drawn are good and bad,' she told me. 'What is good is the approach of negotiating. We had talks and we both compromised. The bad is the compromise we did provoked domestic pressure. And in the post-Deng Xiaoping era, nationalism is growing in China. Even in 2005, when China and India signed the agreement on political parameters and guiding principles, I remember there was nationalist backlash in China. Two articles in the agreement were debated, one on settled populations and the other about natural boundaries. Both those brought some problems inside China.'

India took the 'settled population' reference in the 2005 agreement to mean areas like Tawang would not be part of any exchange. China subsequently appeared to renege. Han Hua offered an explanation. She said she noticed an uptick in online references to 'South Tibet' after the 2005 agreement. 'Now, public opinion is a challenge. We have never had such a challenge and in the 1960s it was no problem. In the 1960s, Mao and Zhou Enlai said we both mutually accommodate each other – you take Arunachal and accept the McMahon Line as the border. Now, Zang Nan [South Tibet] has become a term to replace the McMahon Line. In the 1990s, we used to say McMahon Line, now it's Zang Nan.'

The widespread use of 'Zang Nan' today – including by China's state media – shows how over two decades, the country has quietly solidified in the public sphere an expanded notion of its territorial claims in the eastern sector. This propaganda has consequences. Today, such is the sentiment that the offers by Zhou Enlai and Deng Xiaoping would be condemned as traitorous. 'Zang Nan is a complicated term,' Han Hua said. 'When the netizens started to use Zang Nan is interesting. I think it started with the 2005 parameters. Zang Nan is a relatively new term and means all of Arunachal. Nan Zang, on the other hand, means a south part of Tibet.' Ma Jiali told me he refrains from using 'Zang Nan' as much as he can – within the straitjacket that Chinese scholars work. 'My opinion is Zang Nan is not Nan Zang. Zang Nan means all the disputed land [in Arunachal] belongs to China. Nan Zang means a southern part of Tibet.'

Voices such as his and Han Hua's, who believe a settlement where each side makes concessions is in the interest of both countries, appear to be increasingly in a minority in China's strategic community. There seems to be a growing divide along generational lines too. The new generation of Chinese scholars is broadly more hawkish, and often takes hard-line positions that bring one fame and popularity in the age of social media. It's no surprise that the most followed Chinese journalist or expert on Twitter is the hard-line editor of the *Global Times*, a tabloid run by the *People's Daily*.

Han Hua said she still thinks a solution with India could be possible, if only because national sentiment may be less of an issue than the media may think. 'The media doesn't really reflect the feeling of the people, in either country, I think. I suspect you will find rational and reasonable sentiment among the people, not what you get in the newspapers. And in China, this is not something you will see if you ask Chinese people about Japan. With India, it is different. For China now, it has become more difficult to push mutual accommodation. At the same time, we never felt that the Indian side has been prepared either for mutual accommodation. In 2005, we did see a softening stand from India and a shift from a legal approach to a political settlement. India has never, never accepted the status quo. China did, in the 1960s and 1980s. China wanted to show the way for the status quo to be the final solution. But it did not succeed. Now, the chance for that is gone.'

Like a festering wound, Han Hua believes the longer both sides wait, the harder a resolution will become. 'The official line in China is that the border with India is the most tranquil. Yes, there are intrusions on both sides, but the two governments have generally managed them well. At the government level, relations are good. Maybe not at the media level! Compared to the maritime disputes on the east coasts of China, this is much less volatile. The only two land border issues left over for China, with India and Bhutan, are both quite peaceful when you compare with the maritime borders, or even with the North Korean border where we have seen incidents. During Mao's time, we saw the use of force or military resolutions to disputes. After Deng Xiaoping, we have followed the "shelving disputes" approach. Maybe now it is time for a "settling disputes" approach. We should settle the border, before it becomes like the South China Sea.'

The Long Road to a Settlement

'The fundamental reason a boundary settlement is taking so long,' Shivshankar Menon told me, 'is that both sides think time is on their side.' Both, of course, can't be right. 'Why should any political leader in India or China take the responsibility of changing the way we all learnt to draw our map of our country in school,' Menon asked, 'unless there is considerable political gain? Either a settlement has to be part of something much bigger, or it has to be attractive to the Indian people in some way.'

If one obvious solution is to make the de facto situation into a de jure boundary, as China and Russia broadly did, both India and China have said a status quo cannot be the basis of a solution. 'For India,' Menon said, 'the present status quo is the outcome of the humiliation of 1962, so the thinking so far has been, how can we accept it? For a nationalist party leadership – and that includes both the BJP and Congress – that is very hard. In China, there is an increasing reliance on nationalism, almost xenophobia, for legitimacy by the Communist Party. With the changed nature of its society and political power, it is that much harder for a Chinese leader to agree to the status quo today. The last real chance for the status quo as a solution was probably between Indira Gandhi and Deng Xiaoping in the early 1980s. They had the authority. If they had said let's do it, people would have accepted it.'

Both Menon and Dai Bingguo, his long-time counterpart, have said publicly that all the technical work has been done – there is only so far negotiators can go until the lack of political will to make concessions and settle becomes a roadblock. 'Ultimately a boundary settlement has to be political, we have to do a deal,' Menon said. 'The Political Parameters and Guiding Principles agreed in 2005 accept the fact that a settlement has to be a package settlement that covers all sectors together. Both sides have said so. Both have said that the status quo is not acceptable, so there will have to be adjustments. Some adjustments will come anyway, because the present maps used by both sides to show our boundaries do not reflect reality. So there will be notional gains or losses of territory.'

Menon does not believe that public opinion will necessarily be a huge obstacle. 'I think the problem of public opinion is overrated,' he told me. 'Before we did the BPTA [the Border Peace and Tranquillity Agreement in 1993], everyone said that people would react negatively. But instead, everyone was happy. If you explain to people that this makes their life easier, no one objects. Why did the India–US civil nuclear deal have 93 per cent approval ratings among the Indian public when the political leadership was busy arguing? Because for most people the deal was more about our power situation improving and load-shedding stopping. It is often the chattering class that makes noise on foreign policy issues. We over-emphasize their importance because we assume that the media reflects public opinion.

'On these issues, such as the Land Boundary Agreement with Bangladesh, or the civil nuclear deal with the US, or the Teesta agreement with Bangladesh, political parties take a stand depending on whether they are in [the] government or out of it. When they are in [the] government, they support these initiatives, if not they oppose even if it is their own idea, as with the civil nuclear deal which was a BJP idea to start with. The moment they were out of [the] government they opposed it. I actually believe that the public has a much saner attitude to foreign policy than our hothouse in Delhi. I do talks in cities such as Cuttack, Tiruchi and in universities around the country, and find that the people have a much more straightforward and rational attitude. I don't think public opinion is what stops a boundary settlement or working out a new modus vivendi with China. The real limiting factor is our own imagination.'

What would a potential settlement look like, and what would it bring? Most officials in India and China will privately tell you neither side expects their full claims to be realized, regardless of home ministers making statements in Parliament saying they would 'die' for Aksai Chin, which is, at the end of the day, only posturing and playing to the gallery. Both have also ruled out maintaining status quo. So the only reasonable solution would be to use the status quo as a basis, and make minor adjustments in the western and eastern sectors. These adjustments would reflect on a map the current reality of what each side holds, and would have no bearing on settled populations, as both India and China agreed in 2005. The losses for India and China would be largely notional.

And what of the Tawang puzzle? Even if China has, with growing frequency, publicly reiterated its claims to Arunachal Pradesh, and especially Tawang – every visit by an Indian leader to the state prompts an official statement of protest from China's foreign ministry – the claims are the symptom, not the root, of the problem. Chinese officials know that no Indian government can contemplate parting with Tawang. Their very insistence on its status being non-negotiable only reflects their unwillingness to settle the boundary dispute, for it is, in short, a demand they know can never be met.

In my view, more than public opinion, the biggest obstacle to settling is how China now views the boundary dispute. Zhang Jiadong, a scholar in Fudan University, summed up this view in a 2018 article, writing that 'China's experience indicates that resolving border disputes is usually the result rather than the cause of improvement in relations.' He argued, 'But India insists that its relations with China won't improve fundamentally until the border dispute is resolved. The two countries' different understanding of the order between trust and misgivings demonstrates their strategic divergence, which will keep lingering.'[10]

In other words, China doesn't see the solution of the boundary question as an endeavour that holds value in itself. As long as relations with India remain troubled, Beijing sees the boundary as leverage it can use to keep Delhi unsettled and pinned down. It can turn up the temperature when it sees fit. The irony in this thinking, of course, is that the primary reason for the troubled relationship is the boundary itself.

Recent trends in China's foreign policy have only reinforced this impression. Its deepening relations with Pakistan and the manner in which it has pursued projects like the CPEC have underlined an increasingly adversarial outlook in dealing with India. So until this strategic calculus, that of using the boundary as leverage, changes, the prospects of settlement remain bleak.

At the same time, recent history has shown China's strategic thinking is by no means ossified. In fact, Beijing has been more amenable to breaking the mould and pushing for a settlement in the past, when the wider geopolitical situation suited a settlement. It is tempting to ask, if such a moment arrived again, as it did in 1960 and the early 1980s (and perhaps even in the early 2000s if Dai Bingguo is to be believed), how would India respond? If China was to agree to give up its claims in the eastern sector – as Zhou Enlai and Deng Xiaoping did – would India be able to do the same in the west, in Aksai Chin, given the challenges of negotiating domestic politics in a democracy?

Even if nationalist sentiment is indeed a problem in China, the fact is that the might of the Party–state, with all institutions under its control, could force public acceptance if it chose to. That is much harder in India. After all, the territory that China sits on was occupied by force in a humiliating war. Giving that up would be seen, quite understandably, as legitimizing Chinese aggression. For any government, the perceived political cost – the cost of giving up Aksai Chin, a territory that in public imagination has been an 'integral' part of India for centuries, and was snatched away in a war we haven't come to terms with – would be too high to bear.

The disputes that are hardest to solve are those where one party gains and the other loses. The irony of the India–China boundary dispute – which is routinely described in news reports with the adjectives 'vexed', 'intractable' and 'complex' – is that it is one that was 'pre-eminently susceptible to a fair solution, for each had its vital non-negotiable interest under its control', with the McMahon Line for India in the east protecting India's foothills, and Aksai Chin granting China its crucial Xinjiang–Tibet link.[11]

History, however, had other ideas. And it still stands in the way of a solution. As I see it, a resolution would only be possible if there is a public reckoning in India of both the history of the boundary dispute and the events that led to war, including an introspection of its own actions that led to 1962, beyond the simplistic narrative that continues to maintain a tight grip over public imagination.

If the boundary dispute lends itself to what appears to be a reasonably fair solution, the irony is that so does this contested history and memory of the war, as I have discussed. The scholar John Garver sets out clearly the reasoning behind his conclusion that both sides shared responsibility for the war: 'India's policies along the border' could be seen as 'constituting incremental Indian seizure of Chinese controlled territory', and 'Chinese perceptions of Indian policies toward Tibet were fundamentally erroneous'. Hence, he argues convincingly, '*both sides* [emphasis as in the original text] bear onus for the 1962 war, China for misconstruing India's Tibetan policies, and India for pursuing a confrontational policy on the border'.[12]

Why India and China Should Settle

Regardless of China viewing the unsettled boundary as leverage – which, in my view, remains the biggest obstacle to settlement – is there merit in India taking the lead and pushing for a settlement along the status quo, and leaving the ball in Beijing's court? By doing so, Chinese officials, at the very least, would no longer be able to hide behind the reasoning that it is India's inability to make concessions that is the stumbling block in negotiations. To me, the question of whether India should accept a settlement on the lines of the current status quo is one that should be assessed with cold, hard logic, reviewing the costs and benefits. It is also one that needs to be debated publicly.

The answer seems obvious. Stripping away all the sentiment – as valid as it is – and all the historical baggage, and all the myth-making, India would be giving up a claim to territory it has never had direct control over, certainly since the 1950s. A solution would see both conceding what are, at the end of the day, notional claims. If describing 'integral' territory that we do not control as 'notional' sounds like heresy, it is also a plain fact.

I asked Shivshankar Menon what benefits a settlement would bring. 'Objectively,' he said, 'it is not as if with a boundary settlement border trade will suddenly boom, tourism will increase dramatically, the border areas will suddenly develop and flourish. Once you have a settled boundary, you can theoretically open up with Tibet and you can start normal business. But remember, this is not a boundary in the plains between two large neighbours. The actual mass of our economic activity, society, population is miles away from this boundary. In that sense it is not going to make a huge immediate difference to people in the border lands.

'But it would be transformative politically in the sense that India and China would have put that issue behind us – as we did with the India–US civil nuclear deal. It will be transformative in the sense that it would show the determination of both sides and leaders to put aside an issue that is complicated, very difficult to settle, and which involves changing policies, laws and attitudes. Just as in the case of the nuclear deal, which did not result in US reactor sales, but as George W. Bush himself said, that was not the point. The point was it would remove the whole weight of the past from the relationship. You are then free to make what you will of the relationship.

'A similar phenomenon might occur with India and China as well, because we do have other issues. We rub up in the periphery, we have to come up with some understanding about how we will behave on each other's core interests. In our case, those other issues include the Indian Ocean, maritime security, the neighbourhood, China's commitments to Pakistan in Pakistan-occupied Kashmir, all of which are issues today. We cannot predict that all these will be settled, but they should be easier to deal with and settle in an atmosphere that is much calmer. And we would have the confidence after having proved our ability to handle much harder and larger issues. So you can start a very different conversation with China.'

As Menon puts it, 'there isn't a single boundary on earth between two countries which is where it was two hundred years ago'. Even the US–Canada boundary has changed. 'The nineteenth-century European nationalist idea that somehow we have sacrosanct boundaries, firmly fixed lines which always had great legal validity,' Menon reflected, 'is ahistorical rubbish.'

As important as it is for us to come to terms with this contested history, this long and complicated story tells us that the past will not solve this dispute. For me, one of the most striking elements of the Doklam crisis was the weaponization of history, and how often during those seventy-two days this contested history was still being invoked by both sides. To support its claim about India's 'trespassing' at the Sikkim border, I would hear the Chinese foreign ministry regularly cite a letter written on 22 March 1959 by Jawaharlal Nehru, where he referred to an 1890 convention between Tibet and Sikkim that China claims settled the issue. I would then hear Indian officials rebut this claim by pointing to the very same letter, where Nehru reminded China of an 1842 treaty on Ladakh and the drawing of the McMahon Line in Simla in 1914, which China doesn't recognize. So, if Beijing was citing one treaty that helped make its case, it was, at the same time, rejecting two others that undermined it.

Whether we like it or not, that is the reality of history. Contrary to what we are taught in school textbooks, it isn't about certainty and definitive answers – all the more so when it comes to lands that passed in and out of competing influences for centuries, when modern notions of states and boundaries didn't exist. We can endlessly debate nineteenth-century maps and tax records, but that will get us nowhere. If one map tells us the frontiers of Aksai Chin were always a part of Ladakh, another can just as easily show it was no man's land. We will still be debating historical claims for another 100 years.

History won't solve the boundary dispute. What will solve it is a political decision taken by governments that conclude that the benefits of settlement will outweigh the costs. If the recent boundary incidents have taught us anything, it is that the costs are only escalating. And with devastating consequences. Depsang in 2013. Chumar in 2014. Doklam in 2017. Galwan in 2020. The list is growing. And the stand-offs are progressively getting harder to resolve. It sometimes feels like pressure is building. To what end though, neither side knows.

The clash on the border in June 2020, marking the worst violence since 1967, in my view, only reinforced the case for a settlement. Writing in the aftermath of the tragic loss of life of twenty Indian soldiers in Galwan Valley, Admiral Arun Prakash (retd), a former chief of naval staff, eloquently argued why the nation required settled boundaries if it wanted to grow and successfully carry out its domestic transformations. He noted that 'in 1962, India's Parliament had expressed "the firm resolve of the Indian people to drive out the aggressor from the sacred soil of India", a resolution interpreted as a pledge for the restoration of Aksai Chin'.

> As a nation, we need to be pragmatic enough to realise that neither conquest nor re-conquest of territory is possible in the 21st century. Parliament should, now, resolve to ask the government, 'to establish with utmost urgency, stable, viable and peaceful national boundaries, all around, so that India can proceed, unhindered, with the vital tasks of nation-building and socio-economic development.[13]

I often think of a settlement as akin to letting the air out of an inflated tyre that's forever on the verge of exploding. Even coming to terms with this contested history won't suffice until both governments, with the support of their publics, conclude that the benefits of settling would indeed outweigh the costs – of giving up territorial claims that neither has a realistic prospect of reacquiring without war. We can only hope it will not take an explosion for India and China to realize why they should settle. But for them to see that – and for their publics to see that – we would also need to unlearn and relearn the politicized histories that we have inherited – histories that tell us that the lines on a map are sacred truths that are beyond questioning.

PART V

FRONTIERS

15

Tibet: Past and Present

THE DEYANG SHAR COURTYARD, OR the 'eastern courtyard of happiness', sits right at the heart of the Potala Palace. It served as the home of Tibet's Dalai Lamas – from the fifth to the current fourteenth – for more than 300 years, until the failed uprising of 1959 and the Dalai Lama's exile to India.

On the clear morning I visited it in the summer of 2015, the courtyard was teeming with people. Groups of Chinese tourists – there were no foreigners in sight – posed for photographs under the looming tower of the White Palace, the former residential section of the Dalai Lamas. Dressed in bright orange uniforms, firefighters patrolled the square, while standing watch from a corner in the shadows was a People's Armed Police officer in uniform.

The firefighters were a fixture everywhere I went in Lhasa. In the main square that the Potala overlooks, there was another fire truck, while in the streets of Barkhor, the old neighbourhood that fans out around the Jokhang temple – the city's beating heart – there they were again, strolling among the worshippers. They were not there by accident. In the summer of 2012, two Tibetans had set themselves on fire in front of the Jokhang Temple. They were among more than 150 who carried out self-immolation protests across China in 2011 and 2012. Their protests made headlines around the world before fading from attention, but, even three years on, their legacy made itself felt in the Potala where fire extinguishers were forever at the ready.

That tourists – and firefighters – outnumber worshippers in the halls of the Potala today is a result of China's grand project in Tibet: a project of remaking it in Beijing's image. The country says it is investing billions to uplift one of its most underdeveloped regions. This investment is certainly evident in the newly paved expressways that sprout from Lhasa in every direction. Lhasa is connected to the Chinese hinterland with a geography-defying multibillion-dollar railway that cuts through 'the roof of the world' – all unthinkable two decades ago.

What the world generally thinks of as Tibet is actually a sprawling region that stretches across five Chinese provinces or regions today. But when news reports refer to 'Tibet', they usually mean China's Tibet Autonomous Region (TAR), of which Lhasa is the capital. Only around half of China's 6 million Tibetans are in the TAR. The rest are spread across contiguous autonomous prefectures in the neighbouring provinces of Sichuan, Qinghai and Yunnan, and in Gansu that is north of Qinghai. Tibetans in exile sometimes refer to the overall region as Greater Tibet.

The area is also often seen in terms of three traditional Tibetan regions, U-Tsang, Amdo and Kham. The TAR largely overlaps with the region of U-Tsang, seen as the cultural heartland for Tibetans, and home to some of its most important monasteries and temples, like the Jokhang in Lhasa and Tashilhunpo in Shigatse. Amdo, where the fourteenth Dalai Lama is from, runs across northern Gansu and Qinghai, while Kham extends into Sichuan and northern Yunnan. The three regions have historically had distinct regional, linguistic and cultural identities and practices.

Old Becoming New

As a journalist, I could travel freely to the four provinces, but not to the TAR, which required a permit. Journalists can only travel to the TAR on government-arranged tours, and the only time I joined one was in the summer of 2015, when two other Indian journalists and I were invited to cover the opening of a new route for Indian Kailash Manasarovar pilgrims at Nathu La, where Tibet meets Sikkim.

The trip was arranged at the last minute. We had only a few days to prepare ourselves for the flight to Lhasa. We would then set off by road to Nathu La, all the way south to the border with India. Chinese tourists usually spend a week taking medicines to prepare themselves to acclimatize to the high altitude and to avoid altitude sickness. We had no such luxury. On landing, we were advised to rest, to slowly get used to air at 4,000 metres. But who in their right minds would spend their first evening in Lhasa in a hotel?

I took a taxi to the heart of the city, the Jokhang and Barkhor (and, to my surprise, wasn't followed). Dusk was falling, and worshippers milled about the square in front of the old temple, which was a centre of protest during the agitations and riots of 2008, which began in Lhasa on the forty-ninth anniversary of the failed 1959 uprising and spread across many Tibetan areas in China, and again in 2012, when the self-immolations swept across Tibet. When I visited, there was still police presence: two large black buses for security personnel were parked beside the square. But gone were the snipers that locals said were, until a few years ago, a permanent presence on overlooking rooftops. That the government even invited us to visit that year reflected its confidence that normalcy had been restored.

Lhasa is being transformed. From the lofty balconies of the Potala, relentless sounds of hammering and drilling fill the valley below. Outside the palace, the streets are not unlike any tier-two Chinese city. Beyond the ever-shrinking old city of Lhasa, wide avenues carry street signs written in large Mandarin Chinese characters; signage in Tibetan, written in much smaller script, hints at the government's priorities.

'There is not much of the old city,' says Zong Kyi, a Tibetan who makes a living as a tour guide taking Han Chinese tourists around the Potala.[1] Barkhor, a maze of narrow streets that spreads out around the Jokhang monastery in all directions, is an ever-decreasing speck in a fast-expanding Lhasa; a sprawling 'new development zone' of factories is the priority project that is today being built on the city's suburbs.

There is no doubt that the infrastructure China has built in Tibet is stunning. The Chinese government's White Papers note that Tibet sees double-digit GDP growth year on year; 99.59 per cent enrolment in primary schools; life expectancy reaching 68.2 years, double of what it was in the early 1950s; illiteracy, widely prevalent in the 1950s, completely eliminated among the young and the middle-aged; and completely free education and healthcare is provided to all. China says that since 1952 – two years after the PLA occupied Tibet – it has pumped in around 544 billion yuan (close to $90 billion) into the region. That is one part of the story.

The boom, coupled with huge improvements in living standards, has also brought in other changes that have been less welcome. Chinese census data shows that 90 per cent of Tibet's 3 million population of permanent residents are Tibetans. It does not, however, reflect the growing floating population of Han Chinese migrants in cities such as Lhasa. The number of Han permanent residents is also growing: between 1990 and 2000, while the total Tibetan population increased by half a million, in percentage terms the population fell by 2.7 per cent. Han Chinese, China's majority ethnic group, today account for 8 per cent, or a quarter of a million, of the population. The floating population in Tibet is also increasing, up from 1,51,000 to 2,62,000 between 2000 and 2010 according to census figures.[2]

Tibetans are still very much in the majority, but changing demographics have brought in tensions, as also the influx of tourists. Notwithstanding the statistics, two people told me that Tibetans were a minority in Lhasa – such is public perception. Beijing's development efforts should have ordinarily brought it goodwill, but one reason it hasn't convinced everyone is the unresolved question of the Dalai Lama. While many Tibetans continue to revere the Dalai Lama as their spiritual leader, the Chinese government continues to vilify him as 'a splittist' in public statements, banning images of the popular figure. By doing so, Beijing appears to be undermining the goodwill it may have otherwise engendered through its ambitious development plans for the region.

Chinese officials dismiss the Dalai Lama's following as a vestige of Tibet's old 'feudal' past. That is not how most Tibetans see it. Underlining the Dalai Lama's continued prominence, in the days before I visited Lhasa, there were numerous reports of Tibetans having defied restrictions and threats of jail to hold quiet celebrations to mark his eightieth birthday in many places in Tibet, and nearby Gansu and Sichuan. As one Lhasa resident told me, 'For us, the Dalai Lama is most important.'

One Tibetan tour guide told a group of tourists one morning, 'The greatest Dalai Lamas were the fifth, who made the Potala as it stands today, and the thirteenth.'

'What of his successor, the fourteenth?'

'We think he is just as great,' the guide later told me quietly with a smile, 'but we cannot talk about him.'

Raging Fire

In the summer of 2012, I travelled to Gansu and Qinghai to try and make sense of the rapid spread of self-immolation protests by Tibetans. By the time I visited, around thirty Tibetans had set themselves on fire since the protests began the previous year. Many had called for the return of the exiled Dalai Lama as they did so. Most of the protests had taken place in Sichuan, Gansu and Qinghai, starting from the Kirti monastery in the region of Aba in Sichuan, bordering Tibet.

Unlike for the TAR, I didn't need a special permit to travel to these provinces, but this was in theory. Most Tibetan areas in the three provinces had been put in complete lockdown. Aba, the heart of the protests, had become 'a warzone', Kanyag Tsering, a monk at Kirti, who left for India in 1999, told me. He believed the highly securitized environment in Aba was one reason for the continuing agitations. He pointed out that in neighbouring Qinghai, for instance, monks were allowed to perform ceremonial last rites for the bodies of the ones who had self-immolated. In Aba, however, in several instances, they were not even allowed to see the bodies. 'The security forces in Aba are more aggressive,' he said. 'Aba is a small area and it looks like a warzone. The security forces are disrupting daily life.'

Kanyag Tsering joined the famed Kirti monastery when he was nine. He spoke of a daily routine lost in education, with early morning sessions of scripture study and afternoon lectures. The oldest of four brothers, Tsering said his parents were proud when he joined the monastery. 'Things were getting better after the late 1980s, after the regional law on autonomy was passed,' he said. 'Things were worse before. The tenth Panchen Lama [Choekyi Galtsen, 1938–89] fought a lot to make things better, but after he died, conditions worsened.' Tsering left for Nepal in 1998 after, according to him, fourteen monks were taken away one night and accused of separatism. More than 100 Kirti monks have left Aba, setting up a monastery in exile near Dharamsala, in Himachal Pradesh, which has been the home of the Dalai Lama since 1959.

More than half of the thirty self-immolation protests had occurred near the Kirti monastery in Aba, but the movement was beginning to get traction beyond the monastery. Besides Tsering, Sonam Dargye, a farmer in neighbouring Qinghai province, and Kalkyi, a widowed mother of four in Aba, had also self-immolated for the cause. Aba was completely out of bounds, so I thought I would try my luck in Gansu and Qinghai to get a sense of the situation on the ground. My first stop was the Labrang monastery, which is a four-hour drive from Lanzhou, the bustling provincial capital that sits on the Yellow River. Labrang has historically been the most influential monastery outside the areas now demarcated as the TAR. A few weeks before I arrived, a twenty-year-old student named Tsering Kyi had set herself on fire and died in Maqu, a small town close to the monastery. Her death had shown how a protest movement started by monks had begun to spread into the broader community.

Maqu is a small town of a few hundred once-nomadic families like Tsering's. With short hair and deep-red cheeks, Tsering Kyi was described by her relatives as an eager student. The first in her family to go to high school and speak fluent Chinese, she took her lessons seriously, never failing to finish outside the top three ranks. She was so attached to her textbooks that in the winter holidays, she would take the family's sheep out to graze, books in hand, recounted her relatives. Her favourite subject was the Tibetan language, which she saw as a rare window into her culture.

Days before she died, Tsering told relatives she was distressed by developments in her high school. In 2009, students at the school got together to protest moves to expand the use of Chinese language in the curriculum. After a popular Tibetan teacher, Kyabchen, and a writer named Do Re, were expelled, with the former sent to work in a water supply authority, Tsering was disheartened, her relatives said.

When news of protests in nearby Aba filtered through to Maqu, Tsering told a relative, 'We must do something too.' None of them, however, expected her to do what she did. 'Her parents are in grief and in shock,' a relative told me over the phone. 'She was the family's big hope, the only one with education. They wanted her to go to college.'

Tsering's death brought an outpouring of public sympathy in Maqu and in surrounding monastery towns, where prayer meetings were held for her. After she died, her body was kept at a local police station. Authorities were reluctant to release it, relatives said, fearing that a funeral would trigger protests. After dozens of relatives demanded the handover of the body, the police agreed on the condition that no public memorial was held. Monks at the nearby Tsedrak monastery, where Tsering's brother was studying, were allowed to quietly perform her last rites.

In the weeks following her death, Gansu's Tibetan areas saw a number of protests by monks. In the Bora monastery near Xiahe, at least sixty monks marched 'before being persuaded by local authorities to return to their monastery', state media reported. Labrang, I was told, was in lockdown.[3]

We had an uneventful three-hour drive south from Lanzhou, down to Gannan Tibetan Autonomous Prefecture, which lies on the eastern edge of the Tibetan plateau where it meets the Yellow River's plains. As we entered Gannan, the highway was mostly deserted, but as we were approaching Xiahe, the town where the monastery is located, we saw a stream of more than forty police and paramilitary vehicles in a convoy, heading into the town. When we approached the town, we saw someone waving us down. Two police cars had been parked to block the road at a makeshift checkpoint. We had company.

'You can't go further,' a policeman told me. 'This is a special time.' He knew I was a journalist, and we were clearly expected. The cop told me I needed a permit, which was plainly untrue. According to China's press regulations, as an accredited correspondent I could travel wherever I wanted, barring the TAR. But as I often found on the road, the writ of the Ministry of Foreign Affairs and Beijing didn't extend very far outside the capital. If I was in a village even in neighbouring Hebei province, the local village Party chief mattered far more than even China's foreign minister, and it would have meant little to him or to the local police if I called any contact in Beijing to plead my right to be there.

My experience on the ground was, to be sure, varied. I've met welcoming local officials, who were more than happy to share their stories, particularly if I was there to report on development issues. I've often been struck by how frank some of them were, and at times, I had to be careful in my reporting to ensure their remarks didn't get them into trouble. But there had also been others who had me chased out of town by goons, which tended to happen if something sensitive – such as a land acquisition protest – was brewing.

The police in Xiahe was clearly in the latter camp. I knew my reporting trip had gone up in smoke, but I was more worried about my driver. I had met him at Lanzhou airport, and had told him upfront about where I wanted to go, my work and the risks. He had called a local contact, and was told there would be no issues. When we were stopped, the cop demanded to see my driver's ID, but I pleaded his case, assuring him we would leave immediately and that my driver had no idea why we were going to Labrang.

'They knew you were coming,' he told me on our quiet drive back. 'It must be your phone. If you don't remove the battery, they can track you.' We had a police car behind us for company all the way, and were told to drive straight to a hotel next to a police station. We had to spend the night there; we would be driven straight to the airport the next morning and put on a flight to Beijing.

The entire reporting trip was now in doubt, and I was set to go back having learnt little about the situation besides the extraordinary security clampdown at Xiahe. One cop in plain clothes was stationed at the lobby of the hotel. I was told to leave for the airport by eight the next morning, but taking a chance I packed my bags, rose at five and quietly slipped out of the lobby that was fortunately empty. Lesson learnt, batteries were taken out from phones before I jumped into a taxi straight for the train station, and hopped onto a train for Xining, the capital of the neighbouring province of Qinghai.

Inside Rongwo Monastery

The Rongwo monastery in Rebkong has to be one of the most exquisite places on earth. Light snowfall greeted me on arrival, though it was already early April, falling gently over the monastery's golden roofs. Jetsun Dolma, a Bodhisattva and female deity known for her compassion, is said to watch over the square at the entrance of the sprawling 700-year-old monastery. A golden statue of Dolma stands at the square's centre, drawing the gaze of pilgrims and passers-by who mill around the edges of the plaza, which overlooks a valley surrounded by the snow-capped peaks of the Tibetan plateau. The gushing waters of the Rongwo river, which gives the monastery its name, puncture the silence of the mountains.

It felt surreal to be standing in Dolma's shadow. Just weeks before, at the same spot, Jamyang Palden, a thirty-eight-year-old Tibetan monk, had walked out of the monastery's old wooden gates and stood at Dolma's feet. There, witnesses said, he doused himself in kerosene and set himself on fire. Three days later, his friend Sonam Dargye, a poor farmer employed at the monastery, followed in his footsteps. These two acts shook Tongren – as Rebkong is called in Chinese (all Tibetan towns in China are officially referred to only by their Chinese names) – a quiet monastery town. Black vehicles, marked SWAT, were parked near the monastery gates, while paramilitary policemen, guns in hand, patrolled the town's crowded streets, walking among monks, pilgrims and students returning home from school.

Rongwo is among the most influential monasteries for the Gelugpa, or Yellow Hat sect, which is headed by the Dalai Lama. Tibetans, old and young, prayer beads in hand and prayers on their lips, travel from far and wide to Rongwo. On the drive from Xining, we spotted paramilitary vehicles at regular intervals on the narrow mountain road that runs to the town, through deep valleys and along the upper reaches of the Yellow River. Checkpoints had been set up outside the town and the monastery, but in a stroke of luck, the checkpoint outside the town had been unmanned when we crossed it.

The monastery was deserted, with many of its 600 monks who had gone back home for the Tibetan new year holiday yet to return. Those present were at first reluctant to talk about Jamyang Palden's protest. 'We have been warned not to speak,' said one monk in his early twenties. 'There is a lot of tension here,' he added in hushed tones, avoiding eye contact. A video shot on a mobile phone by one monk showed dozens gathering to protest at Dolma Square the day after Jamyang's self-immolation, as they chanted for the return of the Dalai Lama. In another grainy video, the body of forty-four-year-old Sonam Dargye could be seen lying on a street outside Rongwo, covered in flames, as passers-by looked on in horror. Some at the monastery said he was in financial distress, and left behind four children and an ailing wife.

While there was widespread sympathy for Jamyang and Sonam, their actions had divided opinion. Some worried that the self-immolations would be counterproductive, ushering in a harsh response from the government. 'After 2008 [when the riots that broke out in Lhasa spread across the region], things were improving,' said one monk. He led me to one of the monastery's main halls, where a huge portrait of the Dalai Lama occupied the centre of the room – unthinkable in most monasteries in the TAR, where the image is banned.

At the monastery, the Dalai Lama's images were in every hall, part of new measures introduced after 2008, when there was a general easing of restrictions aimed at winning the support of monks and restoring stability after the unrest. Other measures included moves to release some detained monks and improve facilities in Rongwo, where modern living quarters had recently been opened. With the self-immolations, there was once again tightening, including a greater deployment of police, new management rules for monasteries, and enforced 'patriotic education', calling on monks to put the country first, above all else.

The monks I spoke to appeared to be divided on the questions of whether the self-immolations were the right way to express grievances and whether they would improve the situation. 'If the situation is bad, we must do something to change it,' said one monk, who like others declined to be named. 'But our teachings tell us to respect life. We must not give it away.'

Stability at all Cost

From Rongwo, we drove to Kumbum, another old monastery that is close to Xining, the provincial capital. As in Rongwo, I heard a similar story of a push and pull with the authorities, periods of relaxation that had been followed by tightening, as the Chinese government alternated between carrots and sticks to ensure stability. As monks began setting themselves on fire a few hundred kilometres across the provincial border in Sichuan, local officials in the monastery quickly jumped into action. A meeting of the temple management authority, a body comprising provincial Communist Party representatives, senior monks and government officials, came up with a plan of action. 'The message was simple,' said one monk, who was told about the meeting. 'Do whatever it takes to maintain stability.'

The sixteenth-century Kumbum monastery carries special significance for Tibetans. It is one of the most influential centres for Tibetans affiliated with the Gelug sect outside the TAR. Kumbum's history dates back to the thirteenth century, when Tsongkhapa, the scholar who founded the Gelug sect, set up a prayer site here. The monastery is particularly popular with followers of the Dalai Lama. The current Dalai Lama was born in a village called Taktser, which lies only half an hour away from the monastery.

Kumbum had remained relatively stable through the troubles starting from 2008 to the more recent self-immolation protests. One possible reason, I heard, was the slew of welfare measures introduced 2008 onwards, from the renovation of prayer halls and increase in stipends to improved living conditions. Signs of change are easy to spot at Kumbum. Construction cranes hover over a main prayer hall as workers add touches of paint. The ceaseless sounds of construction reverberate through the monastery's narrow passageways. As I walked through the grounds, groups of migrant workers from Sichuan laboured through light snowfall to lay new roads over the muddy by-lanes that run through the sprawling monastery, which sits on a hilltop.

As in Rongwo, there were renovated living quarters and pictures of the Dalai Lama displayed in the halls. More controversial were measures to introduce patriotic education. 'We are now continuously administering patriotic education,' one of the head monks at Kumbum told me. Asked if the steps had been welcomed, he said, 'That question, I cannot reply to.' Other monks said while they welcomed moves to improve living conditions, the newly imposed security restrictions were unpopular.

'We cannot talk freely. Even our cell phones are monitored,' said one monk. 'We are also barred from travelling outside the monastery.' Authorities have set up a nationwide 'blacklist' for monks found engaging in any political activity; this could even include posting an 'objectionable' message online. They would be expelled and barred from joining any monastery in China.

At Kumbum, which the Chinese call Ta'ersi, one monk said policies were more relaxed because the number of ethnic Tibetan monks was lower than in places such as Rongwo or Labrang in Gansu, where there had been protests. Here, only half of the 700 residents were Tibetans, he said, with other students from Inner Mongolia and elsewhere in China.

'The atmosphere is better here,' said one student from Lhasa, who moved to Kumbum after the 2008 riots, following which many monks in the TAR were sent to other provinces. The young monk was waiting outside a teaching hall as his friends prepared for an afternoon debate, dressed only in their maroon robes even as the snow fell on their shoulders. Down the road, policemen stood watch at a makeshift station, while paramilitary cars slowly patrolled the by-lanes. As the class began in a snow-covered courtyard, the young monks began debating in the distinctively Tibetan style – stamping their feet on the ground, slapping their forearms to drive home a point – and forgetting briefly the world outside their classroom.

As I left the dream-like world of Ta'ersi for the airport, my beeping phone, which I finally turned on after days on the road, brought me back to reality with a thud. I found a text message from my policeman friend, who had stopped me in Gansu. I felt quite pleased about evading him. 'I hope you are having a good trip in Qinghai,' the message read. 'How was Ta'ersi?'

'A Moral Issue'

On 31 March 1959, the fourteenth Dalai Lama, who was born a stone's throw away from Kumbum, arrived in India following the failed Tibetan uprising of 10 March. Three days earlier, the Communist Party had dissolved the Tibetan local government and launched what it described as democratic reforms in the region.[4] On the fiftieth anniversary of his arrival in India, I travelled to Delhi to speak to the Dalai Lama about the unresolved political question of Tibet. That meeting in 2009 was the first of two interviews I had the pleasure of conducting with His Holiness. The second would come three years later, in Dharamsala, on his seventy-seventh birthday.

In 2009, there was still some hope – albeit very limited – of a political settlement. The Dalai Lama's representatives, Lodi Gyari and Kelsang Gyaltsen, had by then had eight rounds of talks with the Communist Party to work out some sort of reconciliation over the question of the Dalai Lama and his return to Tibet. The talks had stalled over two sticking points. The first was on the question of history. China wanted an acknowledgement that Tibet had historically always been a part of the country. That was impossible to accept for the Dalai Lama's camp, because in the view of the Dalai Lama – and most historians – the historical record suggested otherwise.[5] The second was the Dalai Lama's demand for a unified central Tibetan administration in China that would look after the rights of the Tibetans not only in the TAR, but in Gansu, Qinghai, Sichuan and Yunnan as well. China called this demand 'disguised independence'.

'We have had direct contact since 1979,' the Dalai Lama told me. 'In the early 1980s, there was real hope with Hu Yaobang [the liberal Communist Party leader whose death triggered the Tiananmen protests]. He publicly acknowledged past mistakes and publicly apologized. At that time, we were very hopeful. Since the democratization movement started, he was disgraced. This is when the Chinese government's attitude hardened, including its attitude towards minorities and Tibetans. In 2002, we renewed direct contact. They asked us to put our demands on paper and we submitted the memorandum. Then they totally rejected the proposal as a proposal of disguised independence.'

The Dalai Lama insisted he 'was not asking for separation'. 'We are happy to be a part of China. We just want dignity and respect. They have to leave the past. Or, the best thing would be to have some kind of international discussion, research or investigation objectively about the past history. That is the best way. On many occasions, I have expressed that it is up to historians and legal experts. Let them decide. The Chinese government should also allow international media in Tibet, to go there and see for themselves. That is the real answer. Let the world know. If things are really good for Tibetan people, why then don't they let people go see for themselves? If things are as good as they say they are, then I will admit my mistake. "You say things are good, they say things are bad" – this is not the argument we should be having. Let unbiased objective international media go and look objectively.'

I asked him about the need for a unified administration for all Tibetans in China, which would be difficult for China to accept considering it would violate the provincial divisions. The Dalai Lama said it was the only way to ensure the rights of all Tibetans were protected. 'The [then] foreign minister [Chen Yi] himself mentioned the whole Tibetan area is one-fourth of Chinese land. But we are not seeking separation – we are just seeking a guarantee for the preservation of Tibetan culture, language and spirituality. This is a right every Tibetan must have. For instance, I come from Amdo. How can I forget their rights? Six million Tibetans put a lot of trust in me. If I speak for one small portion, what will the rest of the 4 million feel? And you must remember, these areas have not invaded into Chinese land. For more than 1,000 years, this area was Tibetan land.

'In 1956, Chen Yi came to Lhasa and actually expressed to a group of high officials that eventually all Tibetan territories should be looked after from Lhasa. He actually expressed that. This is a practical view. The late Panchen Lama has also strongly expressed this. This demand is not our creation. I am always telling the world I am just acting as a spokesman for the Tibetan people. I have to express myself according to the wishes of the Tibetan people. They have this strong desire, and I have to speak, whether the Chinese listen or not.'

Despite the two hurdles, it was still possible to imagine a settlement in 2009. After all, the two sides were talking, and both issues appeared solvable if the negotiations continued. I asked the Dalai Lama if he thought it possible to ever return to Tibet. 'If you carry on a certain struggle with the possibility of it materializing in your lifetime, it means you are selfish,' he said. 'It is a moral issue, it is not a question of whether it is possible or not. It is a just cause and it is worthwhile to fight. You have to carry on and it's not a question of it being possible. This obstacle is due to ignorance and short-sightedness and political miscalculation. If the problem is due to civil war or ideology, then it is more difficult. Our problem is nothing like that. A few individuals have a distorted view. When we can clearly achieve a beneficial solution for both parties, then there is no problem.'

If the Dalai Lama believed in 2009 that a 'beneficial solution' for both was possible, those prospects had receded by the time we met for a second interview in 2012. I drove up the winding mountain road to his residence in McLeod Ganj, Dharamsala. The evening I arrived, the little town was decked out in fine colours, ready for the celebration of the Dalai Lama's seventy-seventh birthday. The next morning, I joined a long line of Tibetans patiently waiting to enter the residence for a morning prayer meeting that His Holiness was leading. Schoolchildren from around Dharamsala read out prayers and birthday wishes. After the event, we retreated into the inner quarters.

It was a time of uncertainty for the Tibetan movement. The previous year, the spiritual leader had announced that he would relinquish his political roles, a position the Dalai Lamas have enjoyed since the time of the fifth Dalai Lama, Lobsang Gyatso

(1617–82). The decision came at a time of new challenges facing the movement. Self-immolation protests had rocked Tibet, while negotiations with China had completely stalled. Only two rounds of talks had taken place since we had last met, and citing what they saw as a hardening Chinese stand, both envoys of the Dalai Lama had resigned.

His Holiness was still upbeat. I asked him how the adjustment had been both for him and the Tibetans, following his decision to upend what had been a 400-year-old responsibility for the Dalai Lamas. 'I am very happy,' he told me. 'In fact, one of my secrets is that the day I formally announced or handed over all my political responsibility, that night I had very unusual sound sleep. No dreams. Just very sound sleep. I really feel, in any case, I am getting older. Our struggle is for the rights of a nation. That responsibility should be carried on by Tibetan people themselves, and should not rely on one person.'

Elections were held to choose the next Sikyong, who would lead the government-in-exile and shoulder the responsibility of political leadership. 'During our election, I noticed that in the Tibetan community, they are really showing genuine interest and a sense of responsibility ... This is not only my own retirement but also that of a four-century-old Tibetan tradition. Now that has ended. Proudly, voluntarily, happily.'

The Dalai Lama was worried about the self-immolations. Beijing had ascribed them to a plot instigated by Dharamsala, but didn't provide any evidence to back up its claims. 'After the 2008 crisis,' His Holiness said, 'even Chinese Premier Wen Jiabao, who is usually considered more moderate, blamed all these crises as being instigated from Dharamsala. Then I immediately responded, saying please send some Chinese officials and check all of our records. But there was no response. When the first self-immolation happened, again I expressed that. The Chinese still blame everything on us. If the Chinese have the confidence, they must allow the international community to see the truth. That is very important. If they do not allow, it is an indication that they have the feeling of guilt, that they have something to hide. Since 2008, local conditions are much worse ... On the other hand, I met a number of Chinese who told me that after the 2008 crisis, they paid more attention about the crisis and feel genuine sympathy. In that respect, there is some benefit. The Chinese propaganda always says the Tibetan people are very happy, that they were liberated from the feudal system under the Dalai Lama. So now their propaganda is on shaky ground.'

The protests had presented the Dalai Lama with a dilemma. He was deeply saddened by the number of Tibetans who were giving up their lives. 'Now, the reality is that if I say something positive, then [the] Chinese immediately blame me. If I say something negative, then the family members of those people feel very sad. They sacrificed their own life. It is not easy. I do not want to create some kind of impression that this is wrong. So the best thing is to remain neutral. Right from the beginning, when this sort of event happened, what I said, and still I am insisting, is this is not happening due to alcohol or family quarrels [as the Chinese government was claiming, to discredit the protests]. Now the Chinese government must carry [out] thorough research – what is the cause of this – and not pretend that nothing is wrong. Like Hu Yaobang said in the early 1980s, when he came to Lhasa, he publicly apologized about what they had done, the past mistakes. He promised they would follow a more realistic policy. Now for that kind of courage, that kind of spirit, the time has come.'

The Future

That morning of his seventy-seventh birthday, it was remarkable to see the reverence the Dalai Lama elicited from the Tibetan community. There were Tibetans from not just all over India but around the world, and of all ages. The Dalai Lama has almost single-handedly kept alive the flame of the movement against all odds, and against the might of the world's second-largest economy. Yet, the inescapable fact is that international attention on Tibet has been dwindling, and the future appears bleak considering the uncertainty that awaits the next Dalai Lama.

Where will the movement go from here? The Dalai Lama's approach has been to call for a 'Middle Way', which seeks 'genuine autonomy' for Tibetans, but within the framework of the Chinese Constitution. Some younger Tibetans in Dharamsala see this approach as too moderate, but the Dalai Lama is convinced that this is the best way to fight for Tibetans' rights in China. 'That is the only way, the only realistic way,' the Dalai Lama told me. 'Number one, many Tibetans inside Tibet want independence, but according to the circumstance, the Dalai Lama supports the Middle Way approach, which is the best, realistic way. I have met personally quite a number of Tibetan intellectuals, some old, some young, and they all express to me they fully realize that our approach is the best approach.

'Second, in order to find the solution to the Tibetan problem, Chinese support is very important. The solution must be found between Chinese and Tibetans. And most important, [Tibet is] materially backward. Tibetans also want to modernize Tibet. In order to modernize Tibet, remaining within the People's Republic of China is in our own interest, provided they give us meaningful autonomy so that we can carry [out] any activity regarding preservation of our culture, we can promote our language, and carry out full protection of environment. So that is a mutual benefit.

'Realistically speaking, separate Tibet, at this moment – I don't think it is really a benefit to us. Our approach for meaningful autonomy is not only for the Tibet Autonomous Region but for the entire area where Tibetan population exists [in Sichuan, Gansu, Qinghai and Yunnan provinces]. The Chinese Constitution itself recognizes Tibetan areas – Tibetan autonomous regions, prefectures or counties. So we are asking the Chinese government that all the areas that the Constitution recognizes as a Tibetan area should have the same right of meaningful autonomy.'

There are at least two reasons why the Dalai Lama continues to be optimistic. The first is that he sees a growing unity in what has often been a fragmented Tibetan community. The second is his view that increasing Chinese pressure on countries, including India, to stamp out any and all voices of support for the Tibetan movement will backfire. 'We have never had the experience of democracy,' the Dalai Lama told me. 'Even in the refugee community, the Khampas, Amdos, U-Tsang people sometimes have unnecessary competition. Tibet is a huge area, and a majority of Tibetans are uneducated and have never experienced democracy. I also told the Tibetans now we, whether Amdo or Khampa, have a very remarkable unity. That is due to Chinese suppression, so we must thank the Chinese government.

'I think maybe in the late twentieth century and beginning of twenty-first century [India] has had an over-cautious and a reconciliatory attitude. For example, for my visit to Tawang [in 2009], in a Cabinet meeting, they had a discussion on whether I should go, but ultimately I was able to go. Now the Government of India has a more realistic position than in the past. For some period, there were no significant people supporting Tibet or expressing consideration for Tibet. Now, more and more people express support. I told [a meeting of groups] that this is due to Chinese pressure, so we should thank the Chinese!'

The Next Generation

The biggest question facing the Tibet movement is: what will happen after the fourteenth Dalai Lama? The Dalai Lama has previously said his successor could be chosen outside of China, and has even suggested that the institution may no longer continue – an unthinkable prospect for many Tibetans. On his seventy-seventh birthday in 2012, the Dalai Lama told me, 'After a meeting with Tibetan religious leaders, we had a consensus and I made a formal statement where I made very clear that when my age reaches around ninety, then I will convene a bigger meeting. Then I will decide.'

China will, in all probability, appoint its own Dalai Lama, as it did with the Panchen Lama. In 1995, Gendun Choekyi Nyima, who was announced as the eleventh reincarnation by the Dalai Lama, was disappeared by Chinese authorities. In his stead, Gyancain Norbu was announced as the reincarnation. China has subsequently said that all reincarnations must follow Chinese laws, in a bizarre twist for an officially atheist Communist Party, which has even passed laws to determine which of the incarnations are legal.

'In order for the Chinese government to take responsibility for the Dalai Lama's reincarnation, the Chinese Communists should first accept religion and particularly Buddhism, and they should accept the theory of rebirth!' the Dalai Lama said. 'If the Dalai Lama becomes 100 per cent pro-Chinese, then Tibetans will not respect the Dalai Lama. Like what happened with the Panchen Lama.'

That's not how Beijing sees it. Lian Xiangmin, an official at the government-run Tibetology Research Centre in Beijing, which advises the government, told me that the problem for China is essentially twofold. One is the Dalai Lama 'internationalizing' the Tibet issue and calling for changes that violated China's Constitution. 'If the Dalai Lama wants to come back,' Lian said, 'he can talk directly with the central government. History has proven that things will get worse if he attempts to involve those foreign forces in finding a solution to this problem.'

The other problem is the Dalai Lama's call for creating an administration that ensures genuine autonomy in language and religion for all Tibetans, including the 3 million who live outside the TAR in neighbouring Sichuan, Gansu, Qinghai and Yunnan provinces. This, Lian said, essentially meant redrawing China's provincial map. 'No Chinese will agree to this as it runs counter to China's Constitution. So I always tell people, do not only focus on what the Dalai says he does not want [independence]. Focus on what he wants.'

The result is an enduring stalemate. And as long as it persists, Beijing will find it difficult to bring about a lasting resolution to the question of Tibet's future. As much as China's government points out the development and welfare efforts it has undertaken in the region – which no one is denying – the fact is that it is undermining any goodwill it would have generated by its stance on the Dalai Lama issue and the tight leash it exercises on Tibet where there is little room for protest. Beijing's default reaction to any protest, whether against a development project or a mine, is to crack down on 'separatists', supposedly instigated by the 'Dalai Lama clique'. Beijing's officials appear to hold a worryingly simplistic view of Tibet's problems: any and all dissenters are seen as 'separatists' or members of the 'Dalai clique', whether they are students protesting against language policies or villagers opposed to mining.

Tsering Woeser, a one-time Lhasa resident, is a writer, who now lives in Beijing and has been critical of many of China's policies in Tibet. She has intermittently been placed under unofficial house arrest. Woeser told me that China's consistent goal has been to marginalize Tibetan identity, whether it is language or religion. In 2010, China pushed a new language policy to introduce 'a common language' in schools, which would further prioritize Mandarin over other languages. The country has been following what it calls a 'bilingual education' policy in minority areas. In theory, this means Mandarin Chinese and one ethnic minority language are taught, but in practice, it has meant a gradual erosion of minority languages, as most classes are taught in Mandarin in many schools barring one language class.[6]

When Qiang Wei, the Communist Party chief of Qinghai, proposed reinforcement of this system, protests broke out among students. In Rebkong, more than 1,000 university and high school students marched, calling for 'equality of ethnicities' and 'freedom of language', while even in Beijing, 400 students in Minzu University, which specializes in education related to minorities, carried out a rare protest. The government subsequently backtracked.[7]

'The government's objective is to unify the country,' Woeser told me. 'The second objective is their political intention. The government is trying to weaken Tibetans' identity as an ethnic minority.' In my travels in Tibet and Xinjiang, I found language to be one of the most serious concerns of the next generation. Mandarin is often a prerequisite for high-paying jobs, so they consistently lose out to Han Chinese migrants from other provinces.

In the 1980s, when Beijing passed what is in theory a progressive law on autonomy for minority areas, the moderate leader Hu Yaobang decreed that all government officials in minority areas must learn the local language. Today, that is a far cry from reality. While Tibetans who work for the government or state companies are expected to speak Mandarin, few officials from Beijing who work for the local government make the effort to learn Tibetan. And the climate has changed so much – with the perpetuation of the 'separatism' narrative – that even demanding what China's own ethnic autonomy law guarantees in theory can get someone thrown in prison.

Inspired by the Past

Every summer, young Chinese from the country's far corners gather at the foothills of the Taibai mountain in eastern China. The gathering includes doctors, lawyers, college graduates, and on occasion, even a couple of nuclear scientists. These young Chinese aren't at Taibai on holiday; they are there in search of answers. The Taibai mountain is home to the Tiantong monastery, a few hours' drive from the eastern port city of Ningbo. Tiantong Si is a 1,700-year-old centre of Chinese Buddhist learning, and it has influenced the thought and culture of much of China's east.

Even while Tibetans are facing a battle to hold on to their identity and culture on their own terms, their culture – and more broadly Buddhism – is finding a growing appeal among non-Tibetans in China. Even surveys by official Chinese think tanks have noted how millions of young people are turning to

Buddhism. Given the uniqueness of Buddhist thought and practice, and the incredible diversity of its many communities in China, from its south to Tibet, it makes little sense to talk of the religion as a monolith. There are an estimated 100 million followers of Buddhist faith in officially atheist China. Some estimates say there are more than 300 million, but in the absence of a government-sanctioned census, as well as the ambiguity of its practice, no one really knows for sure. I had many friends in Beijing who turned to Buddhism to deal with the alienation and stress that came with urban life in modern China.

One summer, Jiang Julang, a graduate in his mid-twenties from Beijing's elite Peking University, was an unlikely addition to the Tiantong crowd. Jiang was born in the eastern city of Hangzhou, now a sprawling industrial centre and emerging IT hub. Like most Chinese of his generation, Jiang had had a public school education, going to the government-run kindergarten around the corner from his home, then the primary school down the road, and finally, the country's most prestigious institution in its capital. And like most of his generation, he was brought up on a strict diet of Marxism and science.

His parents, grandparents and great-grandparents, who all used to frequent Tiantong Si, were Buddhists. For Jiang, however, their beliefs were 'backward superstition'. Or so he used to think. 'In China, we are brought up to not believe in faith,' he tells me one evening, when we meet at the lush, sprawling campus of Peking University in Beijing's northern Wudaokou university district, a bubble of calm and quiet in the chaos and dust of the capital city. 'As a person, we all want to know where we came from and where we are going. You can be taught perfect logic. But, at some point, you will have questions that logic cannot answer.'

Those questions brought him to Tiantong, where he found 'hundreds of other people with similar questions'. He told me, 'In the sutras, I found deep thoughts that spoke of the questions I had in my mind. In China, the only logic we're driven by now is that "You should get more money". We are taught that the answer to life's problems is to make more money. But the thing is, it's not solving the problems. It's only creating new ones.'

There is a strange irony to this. As young, urban Chinese like Jiang look to the past for answers, in many of China's Tibetan areas, older ways of life are being eroded by a narrow vision of modernity pushed by the state. Monasteries like Tiantong are thriving in the east, but community schools are struggling in the west.

I travelled one summer to Gyalthang, a small mountain town in China's far southwestern Yunnan province, near its border with Tibet. At the school run by Dakpa Kelden, young Tibetan monks sat cross-legged in front of small wooden desks as they pored over textbooks, written in the elegant and intricate Tibetan script. Most of them were from nearby villages. They had had little opportunity to learn to read or write their traditional script, let alone know more about their faith. But in this small two-storey house in Gyalthang's old city, under the watchful eyes of Lobsang Khedup, a monk from Qinghai province, they were being given a chance to study the scriptures.

Gyalthang's Chinese name is Xianggelila, or Shangri La in English. The name is a crude attempt to leverage the small town's incredible beauty to promote tourism. Its cobbled streets and wooden homes have made it a popular destination for Chinese and foreign tourists. Dakpa Kelden moved to Gyalthang in 1978. In 1959, the year the Dalai Lama went into exile in India, Dakpa's family – who have lived in Gyalthang for generations – too left for India. He was born in an exiled Tibetan community in Madhya Pradesh. He studied in monasteries in Karnataka and Dharamsala to become a monk. After China's opening up in 1978, Dakpa's family decided to return to Gyalthang, primarily to reunite with long-lost relatives.

After his return, Dakpa decided to open a school for young Tibetans. The school is hard to find, nestled in the maze of the town's narrow cobbled streets, hidden away between rows of handicraft shops. 'The main focus is for young Tibetans to learn about their heritage, to learn about traditional knowledge that they will not learn elsewhere,' he told me. 'This is important for their identity, and also for the community. Growing up in an exiled community, you are always taught that preserving your identity, your culture, is the most important thing, no matter what you do.'

When many Tibetan areas in China were under siege during the 2008 protests, Gyalthang remained calm. He attributes this to what he called the Yunnan model, which hasn't securitized its minority policies as much as neighbouring provinces – and the TAR in particular – have. In Yunnan, Dakpa told me he found a local government surprisingly relaxed in its approach to religious policies. One reason, he suggested, is the demographics: Yunnan is China's most diverse province and home to the highest number of the country's fifty-five officially recognized minority groups.

Dakpa told me he works with the government to find ways to promote culture through tourism. The challenge has been finding a balance, so one does not outweigh the other. He opened his school in Gyalthang, after the tourism boom hit the town in the late 1990s, fuelled by the new affluence in China's cities coupled with a rising interest in Buddhist thought and practice. He uses what is earned from the lessons offered to Chinese and foreign students to fund the education of young Tibetans.

Gyalthang sits at the foot of the Foping mountains, and under the shadow of the towering copper roofs of the 300-year-old Ganden Sumtseling monastery, also known as Songzanlin. Built in 1679, it is one of the most important centres of Tibetan Buddhism outside of Tibet. In 1959, the monastery was damaged by the People's Liberation Army as it moved in to take control of Tibet and surrounding regions. The upheaval during the Cultural Revolution (1966–76), when older values and traditions were under assault, left the monastery in ruins. Its monks left for India, and few ever returned.

Visitors to Songzanlin are usually surprised to find a giant portrait of the Dalai Lama adorning the main hall, and the curious sight of Han Chinese, China's majority ethnic group, lighting incense sticks and kneeling in front of the Tibetan religious leader. No SWAT teams here, like the ones I saw outside the Jokhang in Lhasa and in Rebkong.

Strength in Tradition

In Beijing, I spent one morning with Aj Namo, who in 2017 became the first Tibetan fashion designer selected to present her collection at China Fashion Week, the country's biggest fashion show. As she prepared for it, she told me that the organizers had offered the first-timer their models, including some of China's most well-known faces, to showcase her designs. She declined, instead choosing to display her striking Tibetan-style collections using young Tibetans she knew from her hometown of Kangba, a small grassland town in western Sichuan near Tibet.

That wasn't all she turned down: she also eschewed the customary grand fashion show opening that the Chinese prefer, with lights, music and dance; instead, she simply had her older sister, Kelsang, sing a Buddhist prayer. Aj Namo invited me to watch the show, in a glitzy hall in the heart of Beijing's shopping district, and it was quite unlike any other I'd ever seen. It began with Kelsang singing – simply and beautifully – as some of the Chinese fashion industry's most influential faces looked on. It was a powerful moment.

I waited for her at a trendy café one morning near her studio, and when she entered, heads turned, if only because Tibetan faces aren't all that common in the upmarket dining establishments of the Chinese capital. Aj Namo moved to Beijing in 2004, the first of her family – who have been herders for many generations – to leave the Tibetan plateau. When she moved to Beijing, there was no Tibetan community in the Chinese capital. The only Tibetans there were students on government scholarships, or displaced herders who made a living selling handicrafts on city streets.

Aj Namo headed to Beijing without a plan. 'The only clear idea I had was I needed to get out of my hometown,' she told me. 'I had no idea where to go or what to do.' She was always fond of music, and began singing Tibetan songs for small entertainment shows. She quickly made a name for herself as a singer, appearing on television at a time when Chinese audiences were beginning to pay attention to the arts and culture of ethnic minority groups.

Even as many Tibetans in China chafe at what they see as the state's attempts to dilute their sense of identity, for instance by forcing schools to teach Mandarin at the expense of Tibetan, Aj Namo sees a greater yearning among young Tibetans to rediscover their culture. 'Many young Tibetan people have also realized that many parts of our culture are missing, and they are trying to rediscover them,' she told me. 'More and more, I see younger Tibetans inheriting their traditions and culture, and having the sense to combine this with modernity.'

Today, as an established singer and a fast-rising fashion designer, Namo sees herself as an ambassador of Tibetan culture in Beijing. She wants to change pervasive Chinese perceptions of Tibetans and their culture as 'backward', in part because of state propaganda that ceaselessly emphasizes how the Communist Party brought 'development' and 'civilization' to the country's fifty-five minority groups. 'Tibetan culture actually has a long history and is advanced,' she reflected. She is optimistic about the increasing interest among young Chinese in Tibet, evinced by her selection for the fashion week. 'Tibetan culture is becoming a cool trend here; so many people are wearing Buddha beads now, even if maybe they have no knowledge of Buddhism. But it's a beginning.'

Her next step is to expand her studio in Beijing so that it becomes a platform to spread Tibetan culture; for instance, by bringing in musicians and holding events. She then wants to go global, and hopes to showcase her Tibetan designs in Paris and New York. She also hopes to one day reach out to the large, displaced community in India.

Many younger Tibetans are caught between holding on to their identity and needing to assimilate to survive. Those who have made it have had to embrace the narrow vision of modernity that is entirely premised on Beijing's terms. At the same time, my conversations with younger Tibetans have left me with no doubt that despite the policies aimed at assimilating them, they continue to be very proud of their religious and cultural history.

Aj Namo believes younger Tibetans are finding their own ways to balance tradition and modernity. 'Outwardly, it might seem we are just wearing Tibetan clothes, or doing *thangka* painting [Tibetan paintings] to be fashionable,' she told me. 'But we also still follow strict rules, reciting scriptures and praying for our lamas every day. It's not that young Tibetans are just fashion lovers. What we know is that our tradition brings us great strength.'

16

Restless in Xinjiang

XINJIANG – OFFICIALLY THE XINJIANG Uyghur Autonomous Region – is India's most overlooked neighbour. I was utterly ignorant about its history when I first visited in 2008, so I was left awestruck by an extraordinarily rich account of close cultural contact between the two. Another of China's 'autonomous regions', Tibet, is of course firmly entrenched in India's consciousness with the exiled spiritual leader, the Dalai Lama, and a vibrant Tibetan community now in residence in India for over six decades.

If you look at a map of China, you will see how close one of Xinjiang's important cities, Kashgar, is to Ladakh. One still finds clues to this connected history – Daulat Beg Oldi near the China border in Ladakh is often in the headlines. In 2020, it was once again the site of a stand-off between Indian and Chinese troops. The headlines didn't, however, mention that Daulat Beg Oldi is – as I was told in Kashgar – named after a sixteenth-century aristocrat who lived in the city and reportedly died there, along the road to Ladakh that was once a thriving trade route.

There were times in history when the once-prosperous independent kingdom of Kashgar extended its borders into Ladakh and what is today's India. Walk through Kashgar's streets, and you'll find that the people defy easy description: you will see Chinese eyes, Afghan noses, Russian cheekbones and even some

Indian faces, all testament to a place that has been a cultural melting pot for centuries.

Bridge to the West

My first visit to Xinjiang had me hooked. I would return to it three times, before the suffocating security of the Chinese state made it next to impossible to travel freely. By the time of my second visit, three years later in 2011, the landscape had demonstrably changed. The 2009 riots in Urumqi, the provincial capital, between Uighurs and Han Chinese had left at least 197 people dead. I found a city divided, and the long arm of the Chinese security state tightening its grip. The gradual securitization of Xinjiang would, by the time I left China in 2018, finally result in the unprecedented internment of close to 1 million Uighurs in a series of 're-education' camps – all while India and the rest of the world looked on, silently.

Xinjiang, a land of black deserts nestled between towering mountain ranges of the Karakoram and the Tibetan plateau, sits uneasily at the confluence of different civilizations, passing in and out of their competing influences through its long and complicated history. Before the newly set up People's Republic of China established control over Xinjiang in 1949, an independent republic briefly existed in the northern parts of the region, backed by Soviet support. Various Chinese kingdoms, dating back to the Han Dynasty in the second century BCE to the later Tang and Qing rulers, sought to bring this frontier land under their control; they met with varying degrees of success. Xinjiang has historically been China's cultural and commercial bridge to the west. Today, its significance also extends to the realm of the strategic: it links China with India, Afghanistan, Tajikistan, Kyrgyzstan, Kazakhstan, Russia and Mongolia. It also shares a border with Pakistan-occupied Kashmir, providing China with an important strategic link to Pakistan.[1]

This history has bestowed the land's culture with a unique duality: it is deeply resilient, accustomed to withstanding myriad competing onslaughts; yet, it also bears the marks of a long-standing syncretic engagement, absorbing elements of many cultures that have passed through this part on the Silk Road.

Since 1949, Xinjiang has been transformed. Downtown Urumqi feels like any second-tier Chinese city – with skyscrapers and shopping malls, highways and power plants. Indeed, prosperity is easy to find on Urumqi's wide boulevards, in the neon lights of Renmin Lu – 'the people's street', that bears the labels of international brands – and the flashy cars driven by the city's Chinese elite.

When meeting with journalists, Communist Party officials proudly reel off statistics describing Xinjiang's breakneck growth: double-digit GDP figures every year, soaring investments in fixed assets and infrastructure, more schools and hospitals. At the same time, the tensions fuelled by these changes are plainly evident. These were laid bare by the 2009 Uighur–Han riots and the subsequent sweeping security clampdown that remains in place even in 2020.

The government's strategy has been clear: bringing in fast-paced development led by Chinese companies, many of which rely as much on migrant labour as on local employment. Migration is a key element of this model, and a major factor in fuelling ethnic tensions. As early as the 1950s, Mao Zedong exhorted Chinese people to migrate to Xinjiang to seek their fortune and help serve their motherland by developing this backward but vital frontier territory. Mao looked upon the strengthening of China's grip on the region as an important and urgent matter.

In 1949, Han Chinese made up roughly 6 per cent of the population. According to the 2010 census, this number had risen to just under 40 per cent of Xinjiang's population – more than other ethnic groups, like the Kazakhs and the Huis, and second only to the Uighurs, who number 11 million.[2] The numbers do not account for the substantial floating Han population in major cities, where they constitute much of the migrant workforce. The Chinese presence is most evident in Xinjiang's prosperous centres (like Urumqi), where, for the first time in Xinjiang's history, Uighurs no longer find themselves in the majority.

A common gripe I heard in every town that I went to was the systemic discrimination imposed by this system. For Uighur graduates who do not read or write Chinese, there are few well-paying jobs on offer. They are faced with three choices: attend bilingual government schools where Chinese is the main language of instruction, barring an Uighur language class; settle for a low-paying job that doesn't require language skills; or leave Xinjiang to find work in another Chinese province. The last is increasingly the trend, and one the government appears to encourage.

Ramzan in Kashgar

I landed in Kashgar in the summer of 2011, just as the holy month of Ramzan was coming to an end. The city was bustling. The muddy alleyways of the beautiful and distinctive old quarter, where traditional mud-brick houses line cobbled streets, were buzzing, as hawkers wheeled around their carts of dried fruits and bread. One could barely move through the crowded streets around the Id Kah mosque that sits at the heart of the city and is one of Xinjiang's most prominent places of worship.

Festivities that year were still somewhat muted in Kashgar, which was reeling from violence that left at least twenty people dead in two separate attacks in the days before I got there. Two weeks earlier, explosions were set off in minivans in a crowded street of food stalls at the heart of the city. At the same time, two attackers hijacked a van and rammed it into a crowd of pedestrians, leaving at least eight people dead. Then, the following afternoon, attackers targeted a restaurant on a commercial food street in downtown Kashgar that is popular with Han Chinese tourists, killing its owner and at least four others. Four attackers were reportedly shot dead by the police.

Authorities responded to the attacks by deploying a heavy security presence across the city. When I visited, two dozen soldiers of the paramilitary force, the People's Armed Police, equipped with rifles and baton shields, kept watch over the Id Kah mosque. The expansive square in front of the mosque, a 1,000-year-old place of worship, usually buzzes with activity as the sun sets on the Taklamakan desert. The Id Kah hosts an estimated 10,000 worshippers every day. Every evening, worshippers, young and old, gather outside its distinctive yellow walls. The street nearby doubles as a bustling market, selling naan, dried fruits and lamb.

The square in front of the mosque was thinly populated when I visited, while local police conducted identity checks on the few that had gathered. Most were elderly. I heard older worshippers complain that religious practice was on the wane among young Uighurs.

At the nearby home of seventy-four-year-old Tunsahan Umer in the old town, three generations were about to break bread – generations that had lived through the tumult of the 1950s and 1960s, when thousands of Uighurs were persecuted for their faith by the Party and made to denounce Islam. The reforms of the 1980s brought relief, when thousands of mosques were reopened after the Cultural Revolution and ordinary Uighurs were allowed to practise their faith again. In the Umer household too, Tunsahan's middle-aged children did not fast during Ramzan; only the elders did. The state has actively discouraged fasting among government employees and in universities, where there have been numerous accounts of students being forced to eat. Today, the act of fasting can get you thrown into a re-education centre.

Securitization of Xinjiang

The violence in Kashgar in 2011 turned out to be the start of a string of similar incidents that unfolded across Xinjiang, especially in the Uighur-dominated south where Kashgar and Hotan are located. In April 2013, twenty-one people were killed, including fifteen police personnel and community workers, in a clash with six people in a town in Bachu county, also in Kashgar prefecture. The six were later identified by state media as members of a group that was 'planning to launch terrorist activities', similar to the one in 2011 on the pedestrian street.[3] A number of similar small-scale incidents followed, occurring intermittently in Hotan and other cities, garnering only brief mentions in the Chinese state media.

The events of 1 March 2014 would change all that. Kunming, the capital of southwestern Yunnan province, is a popular tourist destination for Chinese, known as 'the city of eternal spring'. On the morning of 1 March, as travellers milled about the lobby of the grand station, a group of masked assailants, armed with knives, went on a rampage. Eight masked men and women, all dressed in black, moved quickly and quietly, stabbing at will, leaving a trail of blood, panic and horror.

Carrying long swords and knives, they appeared to be highly trained, inflicting deadly cuts and often attacking their victims in similar, precise ways. The attackers appeared unfazed when armed police was deployed: one marched straight into a shower of bullets unleashed by the police, a witness said. Four attackers were killed, and one injured woman assailant was captured. Three others suspected of involvement in the attack were detained. The attack left thirty-one people dead, while around 150 were injured.

The Kunming attack came as a shock to Chinese authorities, being the first of its kind to take place outside Xinjiang. Qin Guangrong, the Communist Party chief of Yunnan, told local media that the eight attackers had previously planned to go 'for jihad' overseas, but were unable to do so. They had attempted to leave from southern Guangdong, but were tracked back to Kunming when they found no way to leave the country. The state media referred to the incident as 'China's 9/11', and when President Xi visited Xinjiang the following month, the groundwork was laid for an unprecedented crackdown that would culminate in the interning of close to 1 million Uighurs in a network of camps by 2018.

A series of secret speeches given by Xi during the visit was obtained by the *New York Times* as part of an extraordinary leak of internal Party documents on Xinjiang that suggested there were some in the establishment who were more than uncomfortable about the direction of policy. Xi called on Xinjiang officials to emulate America's 'War on Terror', launched after the 11 September 2001 attacks. 'The methods that our comrades have at hand are too primitive,' he said after visiting a counterterrorism unit. 'None of these weapons is any answer for their big machete blades, axe heads and cold steel weapons. We must be as harsh as them, and show absolutely no mercy.' The plans took off after 2016, when Xi appointed the Tibet Party Chief Chen Quanguo as the new boss in Xinjiang. The province's Party chiefs are almost always Han Chinese, while the less powerful governors are Uighur. Chen had made a name for himself in Tibet with a grid-based security system, where every city is divided into small grids, each of which is tasked to maintain security within its jurisdiction. The strategy required an enormous expansion of the police force, as well as flooding every city with surveillance. On arrival in Xinjiang, Chen used Xi's speeches as a foundation to launch a security crackdown, culminating in the building of a network of internment camps.

The Communist Party has rejected criticism of the camps, claiming they are 'job training' centres and entirely voluntary. The Party's own crude propaganda has belied these claims. Videos on state media show classrooms where 'students' sit in exact rows, all sporting the exact same haircuts, while each classroom has several security cameras. Testimonies of those who have left the camps, and of relatives of inmates who are abroad, paint a picture of prison-like conditions, where Uighurs are made to denounce their religion and ethnic identity. The Party's own internal documents list out criteria on the basis of which authorities are to select people for internment. These include 'wearing long beards, giving up smoking or drinking, studying Arabic and praying outside mosques'.[4]

Alim's Journey

I often thought of Alim when I read about the horrors of the camps, and wondered what fate had befallen him.[5] A brilliant student who left his small town near Kashgar for Beijing, Alim had sacrificed everything in search of a better life – leaving behind his family, learning Mandarin and doing everything it took to be 'a good citizen' as the Party saw it. But even that wasn't enough to save many Uighurs, and the extraordinary number of internments suggested that if you were a young male, in all likelihood you'd end up in a camp. Alim had spent his entire life fulfilling whatever unfair demands the state had thrown at him. It would be a cruel joke if he were to be sent for 're-education', like tens of thousands of others, and treated as a criminal until proven otherwise, for no fault of his.

Alim's journey had begun in a small village of mud houses and cornfields in the county of Kizilsu, in Xinjiang's poor rural south. He was the only one among his seven siblings who finished high school. For his aged parents, he was their great hope. His dusty village was home to fewer than a hundred families, most of whom scraped together a living by growing cotton and corn on their small plots of land. It had no elementary school. Families who were determined to give their children a good education had to walk their young ones to a town 5 kilometres away every morning. There were no buses, or even paved roads for that matter. Alim's two older brothers worked with their old father on the family's 3-acre plot of land, which barely provided enough to feed the family. His sisters married young and moved to other towns.

Alim's father shifted to the village in the early 1980s to start a new life, after the turmoil unleashed by Mao Zedong's Cultural Revolution began to ebb, which had also made its presence felt in this far corner of China. Alim's grandfather had worked for the Kuomintang (KMT) during the civil war in the 1940s; he switched his allegiance to the Communist Party shortly after 1949, when Xinjiang fell under its control. He could not, however, bury his past: during the Cultural Revolution, he was made to suffer for his KMT background. His family lost their property, and he was imprisoned for five years. They moved to the village after he was freed. He would strangely remain a staunch follower of Mao for the rest of his life: he even brought up his two sons in this largely Muslim region as atheists, teaching them to support the Party. Alim's father joined the police force after graduating from high school. Upon retirement, he tended to his farmland, with help from his children.

The journey from his village to Urumqi, the regional capital, takes three days: a bus ride to Kashgar and then a gruelling day-long train ride across the northern boundaries of the Taklamakan desert. Alim's village and Urumqi are two faces of Xinjiang: far removed from the dusty roads and sparse fields of the southern Uighur heartland, Urumqi is the grand centre – and symbol – of the government's ambition to develop the region. At the heart of the Urumqi oasis, Chinese construction cranes busily hover, day and night, adding an impressive new skyscraper to the skyline every other month. Sprawling shopping malls, selling the wares of high-end Chinese designers, line the city's downtown streets. On one main street stands a five-star Sheraton hotel, frequented by foreign tourists and government officials. Right opposite it sits Xinjiang's only Pizza Hut outlet.

Growing up in the countryside, Alim's family was largely insulated from these changes sweeping across Xinjiang's cities. Life here was simple. The days were spent in the elementary school, the evenings on the farm. While Alim's father was not religious, his mother was deeply so. The children were sent to the local mosque for lessons from the imam every weekend. They never missed their daily prayers. There were only few footprints of growing Chinese influence in the countryside: the only indications were Mandarin lessons that the students were made to learn in elementary school, starting when they were twelve or fourteen years old.

Despite the early start, schools in smaller counties like Kizilsu offered minimal language training. This left their graduates with little chance of either finding a job or joining a Chinese university.

Uighur high school graduates who wanted to go to university were, consequently, dispatched to far corners of China to undergo intense language training courses to prepare them for life at university, where they would be expected to take classes in Chinese, and compete with Chinese students for grades and then jobs. After graduating from high school in Kizilsu, Alim and his classmates were sent to Lanzhou, the provincial capital of the neighbouring Gansu province, for two years.

Alim's journey from the fields of his village to Lanzhou, and eventually to Beijing's hallowed university district, sheds light on the challenges faced by ordinary Uighurs as they struggle to find a role in China's blueprint for their homeland's future. Their journey away from home, and the process of assimilation that has been imposed by Chinese rule, have left many with a hard choice: securing a better life may mean leaving behind home, family, and, for many, their identity as well.

Away from home, Alim and his Uighur classmates led isolated lives: they were all housed in the same dormitory. Other residents in the dorm were Tibetans and Huis from neighbouring Ningxia, who were also sent to the university to learn Chinese, and were wrestling with the same challenges of this process of integration. Leaving home also meant leaving behind religious habits. In small towns in Xinjiang, Islam is, in some sense, at the centre of everyday life. Every village has a mosque, whose imam is a towering presence. His importance extends beyond the realm of religion: he provides moral advice, educates young children, and, in some instances, is even the arbiter of disputes. In schools in Xinjiang's small towns, religious studies are a central part of the curriculum, as are daily prayers. In Beijing, the Uighur students were shocked to find that their classes did not stop for daily prayers; many universities did not even have a mosque.

The Politics of Assimilation

'Language,' Alim told me one evening when we met on the campus of his graduate school in Beijing, 'is at the heart of all our problems.'

He speaks slowly in Chinese, a language he has mastered after a decade of immense effort. His tones are flawless, although heavily accented. The odd awkward pause hints that even after all these years, he still isn't completely at ease with it.

Accented Mandarin isn't, however, out of place in the hallways of Minzu University (in English, it is called the University of Nationalities, as China's fifty-five minority ethnic groups are often referred here). Nestled in Beijing's northwestern university district, it is the country's premier institution for the study of social science and languages related to China's ethnic groups. The university is a unique – and anomalous – bubble of diversity at the heart of Beijing.

Just a walk through its quiet campus presents a fascinating snapshot of China's remarkable diversity. Students from across the country's provinces, from every ethnic group, live and study together. Minzu University is at the forefront of many of the debates about ethnic harmony that today's China is grappling with. But given the sensitivity with which minority issues are viewed by the government, the university's programmes – and staff – are carefully and strictly monitored.

Over five decades and three generations, the government has clearly defined the limits of autonomy that Xinjiang and other ethnic areas would be entitled to as minority 'autonomous' regions and prefectures. In theory, the protection of ethnic groups' language, culture and religion is guaranteed under the Chinese Constitution, which, in fact, reads as a very progressive document. In practice, however, things are very different. Xinjiang's mosques and schools are closely controlled by the Communist Party. Xinjiang officially has 20,000 mosques and 800 imams, although far more operate unofficially and are not registered with the government's religious affairs bureau. Those that aren't registered can be shut down at any given moment.

Since 2010, the government has put in place new policies calling for all religious texts, even those used in local schools, to be submitted for approval. It has also expanded regular inspections of religious sites. 'Religious teachers are strictly prohibited from using non-approved texts, and no person may conduct religious activities outside of pre-approved religious sites, or face investigation as an unapproved Imam,' reads one regulation.

The Party's moves to regulate the role of religion, whether within the confines of mosques or in religious schools, have been unpopular. The government has also cracked down on informal schools and Quran study groups – for long an important forum for religious education.

Communist Party members, who dominate higher positions in the government, universities and state-run companies, are strongly discouraged from practising religion. Those who are found attending mosques are warned they will likely lose their jobs. Advertisements for job positions in the government openly declare they favour candidates without religious backgrounds; one classified for the education department said it sought a candidate 'who did not believe in religion' and 'did not participate in religious activities'. Students in state-run schools are routinely encouraged, from an early age, to follow the Party's official atheist line, although the state minority policy says otherwise.

The central role of Islam in Uighur life has been a persistent source of tension under the rule of the Communist Party. It particularly appears to view the influence wielded by imams with much anxiety, increasingly seeking to regulate their appointments and shape the messages they deliver in sermons. Government schools in Xinjiang, for their part, are phasing out religious education. Classes do not stop for prayers – a reason behind the unpopularity of official bilingual programmes, and why local schools are still the preferred option for many. Jobs in the government, or in government-run companies and universities, often bar daily prayers and discourage employees from attending mosques. Uighurs are, in essence, often forced to choose between their faith and their professions – a choice, they say, they should not have to make.

Xinjiang's 11 million Uighurs account for only around half of China's total Muslim population. Many of the rest are Hui, who are in the province of Ningxia. There are similar limitations there, but a far more relaxed environment pervades. The Hui have lived in China for more than ten centuries; they are the descendants of the first Arab traders the Silk Road brought to China. Over a millennium, they assimilated into Chinese culture, marrying with the local Han and setting up their own communities. The dynamic is very different from Xinjiang, where for many Uighurs, their homeland has a long history and cultural identity separate from the Chinese hinterland.[6]

In Ningxia's provincial capital, Yinchuan, the differences from Xinjiang are easily discernible. I walked through an old neighbourhood around the Xiguan mosque on a Friday evening. A call to prayer wafted through the neighbourhood, unlike in Xinjiang where they are banned. The faithful silently and patiently gathered outside the mosque.

Among them was Hai Ming Tang, seventy-eight. He hasn't missed a prayer at Xiguan in three decades. The last time, he says for the record, was during the Cultural Revolution, when Mao Zedong's Red Guards were running amok, decrying the 'four olds': customs, culture, habits and ideas. The mosque then had to close its doors to save itself from the rampaging mobs.

Hai Ming looked 'Chinese'; he even dressed in the dull, blue workman's uniform that is a common sight in small-town China, a legacy from the days of Mao. The only clues to his faith were his grey, square hat, and a small, white beard that protruded from his wrinkled chin. The call to prayer arrived as the light dimmed, diffusing through the stillness of the hot desert evening. Hai Ming briskly jogged up the steps of the grand mosque and disappeared into the darkness of the prayer hall.

The Turning Point

Looking back on Xinjiang's journey over the past decade, culminating in the tragedy of mass internment, the events of 5 July 2009 stand out as a sad watershed. That evening, hundreds of students from Xinjiang University had gathered at the heart of

Urumqi, in its grand and imposing People's Square. Their gathering alone would be unthinkable in today's security state.

The students were protesting the recent deaths of two Uighurs in a factory brawl in southern China. The soaring unemployment rate in Xinjiang, a legacy of its economic model, has pushed thousands of Uighurs to find work in factories in China's prosperous south. The government has encouraged this process of migration, viewing it as an easy way to address the rising unemployment problem without having to tinker with its development model.

In factories, Uighurs often work side by side with Han Chinese; their presence isn't always welcomed, particularly with work increasingly difficult to come by after the financial crisis left thousands of factories closed in China's southern manufacturing heartland. In one such factory in Dongguan in Guangdong province, rumours that a Han Chinese female employee had been raped by Uighur workers sparked a massive brawl. The rumours, police officials said later, were found to be untrue, spread by a disgruntled Han employee who had been recently laid off. That was, at least, the official version. As always with such incidents, it is difficult to know what really had transpired.

What did happen was that gruesome images of the attack by a Han mob on a dormitory of Uighur workers spread quickly on the internet, as calls for an inquiry into the deaths grew louder. The Chinese government's slow response, compounded by its clear lack of credibility and trust among many in Xinjiang, led to the protest that afternoon. Hours later, Urumqi was up in flames.

Those events would have numerous consequences. Among them would be the banning of Twitter, YouTube and Facebook in China – bans that last till today. Little is known about what unfolded that afternoon on Urumqi's People's Square. By the evening of 5 July, armed Uighur mobs were seen going on a rampage on the streets, setting fire to Han Chinese–owned businesses and brutally attacking Chinese residents of the city, including women and children.

The Chinese government said the mob violence was premeditated, organized by exiled groups with links to terrorist organizations. Many Uighurs have questioned that narrative, blaming the heavy-handed policing of the protests for sparking the violence. It had all the markings, to my eyes, of a communal riot that spiralled out of control.

Some Uighur students who were present at the initial protest, which they said had been organized by local universities, later said that rumours of a female student being shot by police firing had enraged the gathering. This could not be verified, but the news was enough to trigger an angry reaction. The scale of the violence – official reports said 197 people, mostly Han, were killed and more than 1700 people injured – indicated that the government was grossly unprepared. For three days, the city was torn apart by mob violence. On 6 July, organized mobs of Han Chinese attacked the city's Uighur neighbourhoods in revenge for the killings of the previous evening.

When I returned two years later, the city was divided. Han Chinese residents, long settled in old Uighur neighbourhoods surrounding the famous Erdaoqiao market where the riots began, were moving out. The violence had left deep scars on both communities, fuelling distrust between different ethnic groups and anger towards the government. This anger wasn't only from the Uighur community. Han migrants, many of whom had been encouraged by the government to leave their homes and families in poorer provinces like Sichuan and Gansu to seek their fortune in Xinjiang, had instead found a land where they weren't welcome.

Ilham Tohti told me the riots were a turning point, an event that pushed any hope for Xinjiang past the point of no return. An Uighur economist and scholar, Tohti has been a towering figure in the community, the one voice many Uighurs turned to when all the information they had to go by was an ocean of propaganda. The first time I met Tohti was around a year after the riots, when he was still teaching at Minzu University. He had just heard the news that his close friend Gehret Niyaz, who ran the widely popular

Uighur Online website that Tohti founded, had been sentenced to fifteen years in prison for endangering national security. His crime was providing unvarnished accounts of the riots.

Tohti's influence extended beyond the university, where empty seats were hard to find in his lectures. This was hardly surprising, considering they often ventured into areas that sterile textbooks don't dare touch. Brave and fearless, he was a mentor to his Uighur students. For years, Tohti had called for reforming the system of bilingual education in Xinjiang, and questioned the government's emphasis on promoting Mandarin at the expense of the Uighur language. He had also strongly criticized the government's energy-focused, heavy industry–led development model, arguing that it has led to widening disparities between Han Chinese and Uighurs, and allowed big industry to strip the land of its resources.

Xinjiang had vast resources of oil and mineral wealth; yet, Tohti would marvel, the queues at petrol bunks in most Xinjiang cities were almost always endless. He would often tell me of the joblessness among Uighur youth. 'Why can't your country take my students and help them?' he would ask. He was often scathing in his condemnation of the failure of the international community, including India, to speak out. 'It's because we are Muslims!' he would say. 'Look at how India has treated Tibetans. But I cannot send my students to study in your country. They wouldn't give them visas.' He blamed geopolitics too. With India trying to get China to crack down on terrorism from Pakistan, it was tacitly accepting all of its claims on Xinjiang being a 'terrorism problem'. 'Uighurs love Indians, I am sure you found that when you travelled,' he told me. 'Pakistanis, less so. They follow their masters in Beijing. They don't care about Muslims in Xinjiang.'

One afternoon, after lunch in his apartment, which was just off campus, he told me he was being increasingly called in for 'cups of tea' with the university's resident Communist Party representatives as well as security officials. His wife worriedly listened in. When we met on one occasion, Tohti told me he had just returned from a forced 'weekend vacation' with his wife and young child in the popular island holiday destination of Hainan. This would become a feature before important 'political events' in Beijing.

When we last met, Tohti was himself surprised that he was still teaching after a decade of pushing the boundaries. But, by 2013, his classes would be cancelled. The warnings and threats would become worse. That November, while he was in a car with his wife and children, plainclothes police rammed into them, staging an accident. He was told to not speak to foreign reporters.[7] In January 2014, the police raided his apartment and took him away.

After five months in detention, Tohti appeared in court looking frail and haggard – unrecognizable from the man I knew. He never had the chance of a fair hearing. He was sentenced to life in prison. In one last statement he prepared before he was taken away, he made a final plea.

> ... I have never associated myself with a terrorist organization or a foreign-based group. The path I have pursued all along is an honorable and a peaceful path. I have relied only on pen and paper to diplomatically request the human rights, legal rights, and autonomous regional rights for the Uighurs.
>
> I have relentlessly appealed for equality for Uighurs in regards to their individuality, religion, and culture. I have persistently demanded justice from the Chinese government. However, I have never pursued a violent route and I have never joined a group that utilized violence.
>
> I have never started an organization, but I have attracted a number of friends and supporters, both Uighur and Han Chinese, who share my vision. It would be absolutely unreasonable of the People's Republic of China government to use this fact against me. The only things I have ever wanted and requested are human rights, legal rights, autonomous regional rights, and equality. Uighurs should be able to receive the same respect given to the Chinese and they should also have the ability to preserve their dignity.[8]

The news of his detention came as a blow to his many fans in Xinjiang. On every trip there, I came across people who were aware of his work. Ilham Tohti was, for many, the only remaining beacon of hope, a flickering light in all the darkness, a voice of reason between the government on the one hand and the fringe extremists on the other, who claimed to be speaking for them. And then, just like that, the light went out.

17

The Fight for Hong Kong

MY THREE MONTHS IN HONG Kong in 2019 began and ended in the most unusual circumstances. Four days before I was scheduled to fly out for a three-month fellowship at the University of Hong Kong, my trip was in jeopardy. On the morning of 12 August 2019, thousands of black-clad protesters had occupied the island's Chek Lap Kok airport, one of the world's busiest, handling 70 million passengers annually. All flights were cancelled. International travellers, many in transit, were stuck indefinitely at the terminal. One of the world's most efficient airports was now in a state of complete chaos.

The previous day, a protest at Hong Kong's famous Victoria Park had turned violent, as police fired rubber bullets at the agitators. One young woman was shot in the eye. Many had shown up at the airport that day covering one eye with a patch of cloth as a mark of protest.

The city had been on the boil since June. Hundreds of thousands were out in the streets every weekend that summer, in what even Beijing was describing as the biggest challenge to its rule since 1997, when the former British colony returned to China. The immediate trigger for the protests, which first began in spring, was an ill-conceived extradition bill that would allow Hong Kong to repatriate fugitives to countries and territories with which it did not have an extradition treaty, including mainland China.

For many in Hong Kong who have worried about a gradual erosion of the 'one country, two systems' model that gives Hong Kong a high degree of autonomy, this was the straw that broke the camel's back. The fear was that this would give Beijing an entry past the firewall that had insulated the Hong Kong Special Administrative Region (SAR) for the past twenty-two years.

Water Canons and Molotov Cocktails

During my three months at the University of Hong Kong, or Hong Kong U to its students, I watched, week after week, the slow and sad descent of a city into despair. Many of those taking to the streets were teenagers or people in their early twenties. Some were Hong Kong U students who became friends of mine. Monday to Friday, they would be earnestly taking notes in class. Come Sunday, they would be out on the streets, dodging rubber bullets and water cannons, and hurling home-made Molotov cocktails in return.

The protests made headlines around the world for months, but life in Hong Kong was strangely insulated from them. The violent clashes – and images of streets set on fire – didn't really capture the quiet reality of day-to-day life, on campus and elsewhere. Even though they were denounced as 'rioters' by the authorities, most of the protesters' actions were anything but mindless. Most targets were carefully chosen, symbols of the government they had come to distrust, from the efficient Mass Transit Railway (MTR) to police stations and the Bank of China building.

There was no random violence. Hong Kong felt as safe as it always has been. It was also largely functioning as efficiently as it always has – even showing many countries the way in its quietly systematic response to the coronavirus pandemic amid all the political unrest, even if international media was breathlessly describing it as 'a failed state' in their headlines.[1] (If this was a failed state, I thought to myself, I wouldn't mind seeing one like this in India.)

As much as the weekend protests roiled the city, they still remained largely well-organized and hadn't really spiralled out of control. Remarkably, throughout 2019, there had been no deaths as a direct result of police action, despite the escalating violence. And after every Sunday evening's chaos, the city would miraculously return to its avatar as a financial centre on Monday mornings, the suits replacing the black shirts on busy streets, and the protesters back in their classes, in an extraordinary overnight transformation that perhaps only Hong Kong could have pulled off.

By November, however, the protests had spilled over into university campuses. Hong Kong U has the reputation of being the most conservative of the five big universities, the alma mater of many top government officials, including the embattled and unpopular Chief Executive Carrie Lam. The venerable institution was founded in 1911, with the generous help of Sir Hormusjee Naorojee Mody, a prominent Parsi businessman, whose bust I walked past on most days to work. Mody Road, one of Kowloon's busiest streets, stands testament to his influence on this city.

If Hong Kong U remained calm, barring the occasional and immaculately observed protest marches through campus, other universities, known for a more rebellious bent, were becoming sites of struggle. Across town, an extraordinary siege was unfolding at Hong Kong Polytechnic University. This was after clashes at the City University of Hong Kong, apparently triggered by police moves to enter the campus and arrest students – a move seen as an unprecedented violation of what has traditionally been a sacred space for free expression. Students at Poly U decided enough was enough, and began barricading themselves in and sealing off all entrances. Riot police tried to force their way in, only to be met by a barrage of bricks and bottles. The campus was on fire – an unlikely warzone in the middle of Hong Kong.

Within days, students all over Hong Kong rallied together. Overnight, barriers came up at Hong Kong U, including one right outside my door. Robert Black College, where I lived, was at the western gate of the campus. Day and night, black-clad students with their distinctive tear-gas masks stood watch behind a makeshift barricade, while the only road in was littered with pieces of glass and iron rods. No cars could go in or out, which meant long walks up the steep hill that Hong Kong U sits on, every time one returned from the city.

It would be two weeks before the siege ended. By then, the university had been forced to close a few weeks early for the winter break. Many mainland students, who account for the greatest proportion of non-Hong Kong students, had fled home by then. On my last day, the campus was a ghost town when I headed over to my office at the Asia Global Institute, a beautiful colonial-era building that sits right in the middle of the campus. I had to climb over makeshift barriers of desks and chairs, placed by students to ensure classes couldn't resume, to get in and clear my desk.

On my way in, I found what can only be described as an arsenal – boxes of Molotov cocktails and bricks – kept in readiness for the riot police. I feared the worst as I left, but, fortunately, a few weeks later, the situation on campus would be peacefully defused. Suitcases in hand, I slowly climbed up the hill one last time as I bade goodbye to Hong Kong U, stepping over nails and shards of glass. 'I'm sorry for the inconvenience,' offered one black-clad student politely, who was on watch at the barricades that morning, as he gave me a hand with my bags. 'I hope you can understand!'

After three months in Hong Kong, I was beginning to.

The Hong Kong Experiment

On 1 July 2019, the twenty-second anniversary of Hong Kong's handover to China, half a million Hongkongers marched through the streets of Asia's financial capital calling for democracy. The protest was peaceful for much of the day, but, by evening, it began descending into chaos. Two weeks earlier, on 16 June, more than 1 million Hongkongers had taken to the streets. Protest organizers said that an astonishing 2 million people had turned out in a city of 7 million residents, while the police claimed, somewhat improbably, that the number was less than half a million.

By the time evening descended on 1 July, the agitations, triggered by the anti-extradition bill, had snowballed into something larger. The protesters chanted for five demands: besides the complete withdrawal of the bill, they wanted a retraction of the government declaration terming the protests a riot; exoneration of the 1,400-plus people arrested since the protests began; an independent inquiry into police actions and the use of excessive force; and most importantly, universal suffrage and direct elections to choose the Hong Kong chief executive and the seventy members of the Legislative Council (LegCo).

Under the current system, only half of the seventy LegCo members are chosen directly through geographical constituencies; the rest are chosen by what are called functional constituencies which generally represent trade and commercial interest groups. Only 1,200 people vote to choose the chief executive, members of a nomination committee that is, again, largely dominated by representatives from commercial bodies and other professionals. In short, the system is rigged heavily in favour of the establishment.

'Five demands, not one less' was the chant on 1 July. Having made their point, most of the peaceful demonstrators began to return home, barring a restless few who felt unsatisfied. These hundred or so who remained were all young, mostly dressed in black, their faces either masked or covered in outsize teargas masks. As night fell, the group, armed with stones and poles, powered its way past a vastly outnumbered police force right into the heart of Hong Kong's political power: the LegCo complex. The remaining riot police within the complex fled, leaving this group improbably in charge over Hong Kong's seat of power.

Storming into the chamber, they defaced the People's Republic of China national emblem, and tore down the portraits of the current and past presidents of LegCo. Portraits of those who had served before 1997, however, were left untouched. The storming of LegCo brought the Hong Kong protests to world attention, and it was certainly an unprecedented event. Of the many images of that night – from the vandalized central chamber to the Chinese national emblem covered in black paint – one particularly stood out, a message spray-painted on to a pillar that would later go viral. 'It was you who taught me,' read the message to Hong Kong's leaders, 'that peaceful marches are useless.'

A few weeks later, I sat across the table from the young black-clad man who had written that message. By the time I met Levi, as he wished to be called, the protests had carried on for more than ten straight weekends and the several thousand 'radicals' had become the global face of the agitations with their distinctive appearance – all clad in black, faces covered with tear-gas masks, topped by helmets in yellow, the colour of their revolution. Every weekend, they fought the police, dodged tear gas and rubber bullets, and hurled Molotov cocktails at the forces in response. They trashed the metro stations of Hong Kong's famous MTR, blockaded roads and lit fires on the streets.

Levi hardly seemed like one of the black Ninjas I saw on television, wielding Molotov cocktails and pipes. He was a soft-spoken young man in his early twenties. Born to underprivileged parents, he had worked hard through high school and, thanks to good grades, made it into one of Hong Kong's most prestigious universities. A promising career awaited him, but he appeared uninterested in his career prospects when I met him. That could wait. He had one thing, he said, on his mind right now, which was: 'Fighting for Hong Kong.'

Levi was among the first who suggested, on 1 July, that the group storm LegCo. 'We had protested peacefully so many times,' he told me. 'And it got us absolutely nothing in our fight. So we decided we needed to do something different.' I asked Levi what exactly he was fighting for. The answer came immediately: 'Hong Kong independence.'

Since 1997, many of China's fiercest critics in Hong Kong and the pan-democratic parties had never uttered the 'I' word, only calling for the guarantee of universal suffrage and rights under the country's Basic Law. For the young protesters, however, their slogan was: 'Liberate Hong Kong, revolution of our times!' Levi said, 'In my opinion, and for most of the young protesters I know, liberate means one thing only: independence.' But this, in reality, is a complete non-starter for many reasons. But that even a minority – and an overwhelmingly young one at that – is now uttering the 'I' word should alarm Beijing.

How did it come to this? The general feeling in Hong Kong is that for the first ten years after the 1997 handover, the 'one country, two systems' model worked far better than most expected. The Basic Law guarantees most democratic rights to Hongkongers that are denied on the mainland, such as a free press and the right to protest. Article 2 of the law gives Hong Kong 'a high degree of autonomy' and 'executive, legislative and independent judicial power, including that of final adjudication'. Article 5 states that the 'socialist system and policies' of the PRC shall not be practised, and that 'the previous capitalist system and way of life shall remain unchanged for 50 years'.

There are, however, firm limits, starting with Article 1, which says Hong Kong is 'an inalienable part of the People's Republic of China'. The territory's external affairs and defence are handled by China, which stations a PLA garrison on the island.

A City Divided

The protests were the clearest signs yet that the two systems model was coming under increasing stress. Martin Lee is perhaps Hong Kong's most well-known pro-democracy politician. A barrister by training, Lee, eighty-one, helped draft the Basic Law in the early 1980s. His office is in one of the skyscrapers in Admiralty, at the heart of the business district on Hong Kong Island. That day, the streets outside bore signs of the carnage of the previous evening's protest. As we met in his chambers, Lee told me that the fundamental reason for the recent events was 'because Beijing has changed its basic policies'.

'Now,' he said, 'they have changed the whole concept of "one country, two systems", from trusting the Hong Kong people, allowing us to be masters of our house, and enjoying a high degree of autonomy which they promised to give us in the Sino-British Joint Declaration.' The extradition bill would have, in Lee's opinion, 'demolished the firewall and opened the door'. It isn't, however, just about the bill. 'The Basic Law says the ultimate aim is to have universal suffrage, but not in the first ten years from 1997. The idea was during that period, Hong Kong must develop gradually towards that ultimate goal. Now, we are in the twenty-third year. Where is that goal today?'

That was not how Hong Kong's pro-Beijing politicians saw it. Choy So Yuk is the island's representative to the National People's Congress (Beijing's parliament) from the pro-Beijing Democratic Alliance for the Betterment and Progress of Hong Kong party. She told me that if the democrats like Martin Lee hadn't stood in the way, 'there would be universal suffrage today'. Choy was referring to the NPC's 2014 decision to allow direct elections, but with a catch: all candidates would first have to be approved by more than half of the pro-establishment dominated nominating committee. It was this decision – rejected as fake democracy by many young Hongkongers – that led to the 2014 Occupy Central, or Umbrella Movement, which eventually turned out to be the political awakening for many young Hongkongers marching in the summer of 2019, including Levi.[2]

Choy wanted to draw a distinction between 'protesters' – 'maybe 700,000 or a million, and their concerns we certainly have to address' – and 'rioters', who she said were in the few thousands (including, presumably, Levi). 'The first priority is to stop rioters. Until their violence stops, it is difficult to take things forward.'

'The problem is a substantial number of people support the rioters,' she added. 'And they have succeeded in dividing society, families, couples, close friends, into yellow (pro-democracy) and blue (pro-Beijing). I listen to these stories from people I knew as a district councillor. One man told me he's stopped talking to his daughter. A second says his sons are now fighting, one yellow and one blue. A third said his entire company staff of 130 people went to protest. We are completely divided.'

What is worrying is that with two camps veering to extremes, the space for the middle ground is vanishing. Christine Loh, a former LegCo member and under-secretary for the environment in the previous government, told me both sides needed to re-examine their positions if the city was to be saved. 'The key point is that people need to reconcile that Hong Kong is a part of China and make "one country, two systems" work even better. The chief executive and her ministerial team have to come out and show that they are governing Hong Kong. They need much better communication with the public, but it seems this is an area where the government is seriously deficient. We need new Hong Kong leadership to be more effective in communicating with Beijing that Hong Kong's liberal soul needs nurturing too but it is not "anti-China". The government needs to respond to policy concerns, such as housing; and it cannot avoid people's desire for electoral reform.'

Hong Kong has its share of economic problems too, and is one of the world's most unequal cities. However, these issues do not seem to be driving the protests – and throwing money at them will not fix the political aspirations of the youth. Indeed, I barely heard any mention of economic issues in conversations with dozens of young protesters, many of whom come from middle-class families.

But there is little doubt that economic problems, especially housing, are feeding into the perception of a system that doesn't work for its people, said the economist Richard Wong, who is also the vice chairperson of Hong Kong U. He drew a contrast with Singapore, where 90 per cent of residents own homes – many through a public housing programme – compared to half in Hong

Kong. In the latter, one-third of housing is subsidized rentals, one-sixth is ownership-subsidized, and half is private in a territory where land is scarce and private real estate developers have historically enjoyed enormous influence. Ownership would solve many of the problems, Wong says, suggesting all public rental housing should be sold at a discount, following the Singapore model, with a waiver of all debt.

Then there are broader economic concerns about the city's future. In 2018, nearby Shenzhen's GDP surpassed Hong Kong's for the first time, leaving some to wonder if Shenzhen and Shanghai could replace Hong Kong as Asia's financial centre. That isn't going to happen, economist Chen Zhiwu told me, and the reason is 'one country, two systems'.

'Why is Hong Kong so important? Domestic and foreign investors believe that Hong Kong's judicial procedures are fair, so all parties can accept it as a dispute arbitration place when signing contracts and trade contracts.' As Chen pointed out, in 2018, 75 per cent of China's $120 billion FDI entered through Hong Kong.

Where does Hong Kong go from here? Martin Lee told me he saw two possibilities. Beijing may want to 'squeeze Hong Kong and turn it into a Macau'. They would play the long game, wait out the protests, allow the anger to dissipate, continue gradually pushing the limits of two systems, all the while not crossing a line that would hurt its financial prospects. This would include pushing in new legislation to tighten its grip, such as the national security law.

This approach, Lee told me, would continue to meet resistance. 'I am hoping it will be another way: they wake up and say, if I want this goose to lay golden eggs, I cannot kill it. Universal suffrage is the only way of resolving the contradiction of having a chief executive who is, under the Basic Law, answerable to Hong Kong and Beijing. How is that possible though, when she is not chosen by Hong Kong people?' I asked him, even if Beijing's worst-case scenario candidate was elected – 'You mean someone like me?' he joked – wouldn't their power be restrained by Article 1 in any case?

'The Basic Law is clear and Beijing has nothing to worry about,' he said. 'But their answer is simple. They want 100 per cent control.'

A Fight for Identity

It is this perception that drove many young Hongkongers to the streets. It was widely shared among many of the students I met at Hong Kong U. This was a fight for their identity. Among those who took to the streets every weekend was Gloria, who had just turned twenty. She was born in the mainland, and moved to Hong Kong to finish high school. She told me it was her schooling that entirely changed her notions of democracy and the role of a citizen.

'I've spent most of my life in the mainland, but if you ask me, I am a Hongkonger first, not Chinese,' she said. 'You don't know what freedom is until you feel it. Once you do, you cannot go back.' Speaking Cantonese like most native Hongkongers, she said, made her feel accepted in a way that many Mandarin-speaking mainland immigrants, who feel discriminated against in Hong Kong, do not.

Gloria described herself as a person who is easily scared. She now finds herself in a situation where she is not only facing riot police and tear gas every Sunday, but, in a strange sense, is happy to do so. 'Being there is the highest form of happiness I have ever experienced,' she told me. 'This sense of unity is different from the small forms of happiness you get from daily life. The sense of linking together and becoming something larger. I felt it deeply and cannot forget it. You don't know the name of the person who is standing next to you on the street, but you know we are friends, just by being there, by sharing the same values.'

Gloria said she wholeheartedly supported the 'frontline' like Levi, and understood why they had to resort to violence. 'They are fighting for me. They bear the consequences, they risk losing everything.' The sentiment that inspired young Hongkongers felt deep and pervasive, and it didn't seem as if it would go anywhere.

But what the protests achieved is more difficult to answer. As much as journalists like easy narratives – black versus white, David versus Goliath, yellow versus blue – assessing where the protests would go was far from easy. I asked Levi where he thought the agitations would end up. They may die down, he acknowledged, and fatigue, both of protesters and of a weary city, was possible. But he was convinced that the sentiments he was fighting for would not leave, and preserving that was a worthwhile cause in itself.

The protesters saw the leaderlessness of their movement as a strength. There were no chiefs who could be jailed or arrested, to begin with. Levi told me the idea of being leaderless was so that no one could negotiate on their behalf, ensuring there was no chance of a compromise. 'It is compromise that got us here in the first place,' he said. Levi was critical of most of Hong Kong's politicians, including pro-democracy leaders such as the older Martin Lee or the younger Joshua Wong, who emerged as the face of the Umbrella Movement. 'They have been giving us false hopes in "one country, two systems",' he told me. The only political figures that appeal are the radical ones, such as Edward Leung of Hong Kong Indigenous, a pro-independence and anti-immigrant party. There seemed to be a darker element to what was inspiring some of the protesters, which was an openly anti-immigrant sentiment. That was rising, and with it, the danger that it could spiral into communal violence.

The protesters saw compromise as anathema to what they stood for. And with a recent history of reneged promises, they could hardly be faulted. But Beijing was in no mood to compromise either. If anything, the more radical the protests became, the likelier it was that Beijing would harden its stand, especially as there appeared little sympathy in the mainland for what many saw as 'spoilt' Hongkongers.

As I left the island, I wondered if the protests could end up, in some sense, undermining what they set out to achieve, and only accelerate the very changes that the movement was resisting.

And that was exactly how it turned out. Beijing's move towards a hardened stand became clear in May 2020, when China unveiled a sweeping national security law that would for the first time allow its national security agencies to operate in Hong Kong, a move seen as undermining the latter's judicial independence.[3] The new law, Martin Lee said, contravened a fundamental principle of 'one country, two systems', which was that the territory would make its own laws. 'The Basic Law makes it quite clear that only LegCo can make and repeal laws,' he said. 'Beijing is afraid that the Hong Kong legislature may be controlled by democrats [after the next LegCo elections, going by the trend of recent electoral victories for pro-democracy parties], so they want to set a dangerous precedent of allowing Beijing to legislate for Hong Kong. When they lose control of the legislature, they can still pass laws. This is against the Basic Law, no doubt about it. Under Xi Jinping's "one country, two systems", the Communist Party will have complete administrative power over Hong Kong. This is the exact opposite of what was promised.'[4]

With Beijing's tightening grip and the new law, could the protests subside? They certainly could. Will the sentiment behind them dissipate? That is extremely unlikely. So, the stalemate will likely endure. One party in Beijing in no mood to listen, one movement in Hong Kong in no mood to compromise, one country with two systems that appear increasingly irreconcilable, and one city deeply divided.

The Taiwan Question

The developments in Hong Kong in 2019 and 2020 would have wide ramifications, for the SAR and beyond. Pro-democracy parties were gaining ground, despite the systemic disadvantage they faced by virtue of how the Legislative Council is structured. Pro-dems swept the local district council elections in late November 2019, which were widely seen as a referendum on the protests. The new national security legislation Beijing put forward in May 2020 –

that gives it powers to enact laws on national security in Hong Kong and bypass the LegCo, an insurance policy should it lose control over the house – was considered yet another nail in the coffin of 'one country, two systems'.

The impact was felt beyond Hong Kong. At a time when China was offering its model to the world, it was facing a stinging rebuke in its own backyard. The protests in Hong Kong had also reverberated in Taiwan where they were seen as helping the Democratic Progressive Party's (DPP) Tsai Ing-wen achieve a landslide win in January 2020.

One of the DPP's most evocative campaign advertisements, which aired on television three days before the polls, drew a contrast between the daily life of a young Taiwanese and that of a young Hongkonger. As one slept peacefully on their train ride home from work, the other was on the streets, evading tear gas and riot police. Protect democracy, it urged voters, or Hong Kong's future awaits you.

Throughout 2019, Tsai was trailing in the polls and looked set for defeat, but the events in Hong Kong revitalized her campaign. She has been outspoken in her support for the protesters. No surprise that since coming to power in 2016, Beijing has gone after Tsai, accusing her of pursuing a pro-independence agenda and making no secret of its preference for a KMT return. The KMT had pushed for closer economic relations with Beijing. It backed an economic cooperation agreement in 2010 that was the first of its kind, and the then leader Ma Ying-jeou – whose term ended in 2016 – held a landmark meeting with Chinese President Xi Jinping in 2015.

On the surface, Taiwan and Hong Kong may seem to have little in common. Unlike Hong Kong, which returned to China's fold in 1997, Taiwan has been entirely self-ruled since the end of the Chinese civil war in 1949, when Chiang Kai-shek fled to the island to set up the 'Republic of China'. Also, unlike Hong Kong, Taiwan has a thriving democracy and has held direct elections to choose its leaders since 1996 – incidentally, one of the five demands voiced by the tens of thousands who took to Hong Kong's streets in protest.

The few weeks I spent travelling around Taiwan in the summer of 2014 came as an eye-opener to me. The island of 23 million may have a population smaller than that of Beijing. Yet, it is remarkable how it has preserved its distinct identity in the shadow of the world's second-largest economy. Year after year, Taiwan's international friends are depleting. By the end of 2019, only fifteen of the 194 United Nations members maintained diplomatic relations with Taiwan. It has been losing two or three per year, with countries unable to resist the economic promise China offered. Taiwan, however, has been resisting relentlessly. The vision the KMT offered was one of economic prosperity riding on China's soaring economy. Yet, here it was, facing two stinging electoral defeats.

One summer evening in Taipei, I walked over to the Chiang Kai-shek memorial hall. The big square in front of it was buzzing with people. It was 4 June 2014 – the twenty-fifth anniversary of the Tiananmen Square massacre. The date would pass in complete silence in China. But the memory of it was being kept alive across the strait in Taiwan. A giant inflatable tank greeted me on arrival. On its other side, I found a small, inflatable 'Tank Man' standing up to it. Makeshift stalls had been set up, each espousing a different cause. There were Tibetans, Uighurs and Falun Gong activists, all handing out fliers.

The main event was a commemoration led by Wu'er Kaixi, a Tiananmen student leader who had spent the last twenty-five years in exile. As we have seen earlier, he had made four attempts to return to China. I asked him what he thought of Taiwan and its future. 'Look at this,' he said, pointing to the sea of people around him, some holding candles. 'Yes, life in exile has been difficult, but Taiwan has made it possible for me. That Chinese people cannot have democracy is a myth. This is a living example of that.'

In her election campaign, Tsai Ing-wen made sure that elections in Taiwan became a referendum on China – specifically, on the 'one country, two systems' model that is at the centre of the debate in Hong Kong, and is seen by Beijing as an eventual solution to the 'Taiwan question'.

All of Beijing's pressure on Tsai's government over the past four years, in some ways, worked to her advantage. It reinforced her campaign's message, as she swept home with 57 per cent of the votes. In her victory speech, she said this election's results 'carry an added significance, because they have shown that when our sovereignty and democracy are threatened, the Taiwanese people will shout our determination even more loudly back.' She said that through Beijing's 'increasing pressure and proposal of a "one country, two systems" model for Taiwan, China has hoped to force us to accept conditions that are entirely unacceptable'.[5]

Where does this leave the future of 'one country, two systems'? While Tsai sees the election as a resounding rejection of the model, Beijing sees things differently. Indeed, during a December 2019 visit to Macau to mark the twentieth anniversary of its return to China, President Xi Jinping said, 'Macau's successful experience speaks volumes about the viability and strength of one country, two systems, as long as we are committed to it and act on it.'

His remarks were seen as being directed at Hong Kong, but carried relevance for Taiwan as well. Xi outlined what he viewed as the core of the model, which was 'recognizing that "one country" was the premise and precondition for "two systems"'. Apparently drawing a contrast with Hong Kong, Xi praised the people of Macau for 'standing by the red line of the "One China" principle' and having a 'tradition of loving the motherland, as well as a strong sense of national identity, belonging and pride'.[6]

The problem for Beijing is that progressively fewer people, both in Taiwan and Hong Kong, appear to share this view that elevates 'one country' over the 'two systems' part of the formula. The protests in Hong Kong and Tsai's re-election make that clear, as does polling data that shows delicate shifts in how the Taiwanese and Hongkongers view their relationship with the mainland.

Polls conducted in Taiwan by the National Chengchi University in June 2019 showed that 56.9 per cent identify as being only

'Taiwanese', up from 54.5 per cent a year earlier – the first time that the number had increased since a 60.6 per cent peak in 2014. While 36.5 per cent identify as being Taiwanese and Chinese, 3.6 per cent identify as only Chinese. On the choice between independence and reunification, 86.1 per cent favoured maintaining the status quo. Within this group, 26.9 per cent preferred to maintain the status quo indefinitely, 19.9 per cent preferred to maintain the status quo and move towards independence (up from 15.1 per cent in 2018), while 8.7 per cent wanted eventual unification (down from 12.8 per cent).[7]

A poll conducted at the same time by Hong Kong University found that the number of people who identified only as 'Hongkongers' was the highest since the 1997 handover, at 53 per cent. While 23 per cent identified as 'Hongkongers in China', 11 per cent identified as Chinese and 12 per cent as 'Chinese in Hong Kong'. These may seem to be subtle differences, but they have consequences. A record 71 per cent said they were not proud of being a national citizen of China, a number that went up to 90 per cent among the 18–29 age group.[8]

China's leaders believe that the country's 'great rejuvenation', which President Xi has declared the 'Chinese Dream', will not be complete without Taiwan's return, for long the holy grail for the Communist Party. They believe the tide of history is on their side, and that the island of 23 million people will inevitably return to the fold of the mainland.

They may be right, and perceptions can, no doubt, change. Yet, if Beijing wants them to move in a favourable direction, it will probably need to offer more than the stability, security and economic growth that the China model promises, when issues of identity and values are involved. At a time when Beijing's leaders have spoken confidently of offering 'the China model' as a solution to the world, it is facing searching questions much closer to home.

PART VI

PORTRAITS

18

Renewing Links

HOW DO YOU CAPTURE THE diversity of more than a billion voices?

'The problem with making big statements about China is that you can immediately think of an example that suggests the opposite,' observed the writer Alec Ash in his 2016 book *Wish Lanterns*, where he traced the lives of six young Chinese. 'To generalize is to be an idiot,' he said, invoking William Blake. 'But single dots can form an image and six notes can make a melody.'[1]

Generalization, unfortunately, is something we are guilty of all too often, particularly when the subject is something we aren't familiar with. It is sometimes said about India that you spend a week, a month, in the country and you know enough to write a book. You spend a year, and you know enough to hesitate. You spend a decade, and the complexity overwhelms you so much that you realize it would be a fool's errand to try to make any sense of the place.

This summed up my China experience too. Of all the stereotypes about 'the Chinese' I encountered in India, one I heard most often – and one that particularly annoyed me – was the notion that 'all Chinese think alike'. In contrast to diverse, complex India – so the generalization goes – China is a monochromatic monolith. Sometimes I wonder if the mention of China still evokes in people's minds the bygone image of a population all dressed in grey Mao suits!

There is no question that China's one-party authoritarian system stifles free expression. But just because there is a suffocating censorship apparatus doesn't mean that all those bound by it believe everything they are told. As surprising as this may sound, I can say with certainty that I encountered as much diversity of views and beliefs in the many friends in China I was fortunate to make as I did in my friends in the US (where I lived for more than five years) – or in those in India for that matter.

It is, of course, another thing that the things said in confidence over dinner or a drink can't be written about. That doesn't mean those views don't exist. On topics that don't cross the red lines of Chinese social media – such as discussing the central leadership – I would often be surprised by the heated debates that rage every day, on everything from working hours and the state of hospitals to the difficulties of school admissions and inequities of the real estate market.

How do you capture the diversity of more than a billion voices?

Understanding China today requires far more than the Kremlinology-inspired methods of the past, where which Politburo member stood where in the front-page photograph of the *People's Daily* was what mattered most. If India is to have a better grasp of its neighbour, there's no doubt we – in the media, and the academic and the business communities – need to place far more attention and investment in China than we currently devote.

If normalization of relations starting in the late 1980s has allowed for three decades of expanding political and economic engagement between the two countries, one area that has acutely lagged behind is social and cultural engagement. In a sense, it is entirely understandable. You can't have cultural exchanges when there's only a limited number of people travelling between two countries. And that is a function of the reality that the first instinct of young Indians and Chinese dreaming of a career abroad is to head to the West.

Language is another barrier. Unlike in the West, where there is considerable investment in scholarship on China, in India it is meagre. And don't get me started on the media. As I have mentioned, when I left Beijing in 2018, there were only four permanent Indian correspondents in China. And there were none for any of India's private television channels that spend substantial airtime blasting a country they haven't even bothered to send a reporter to. So most of the news you consume is second- or third-hand. Also, unlike in the West, there is no large Chinese community that acts as a bridge in India. The once thriving Chinese community of Kolkata has all but vanished, with many leaving for better prospects in Canada, the US and Australia.

In the absence of familiarity, stereotypes proliferate, and, of course, generalizations. The COVID-19 pandemic perhaps brought out the worst of this trend. Social media in India was filled with blatantly racist portrayals of Chinese people and their 'weird' eating habits. The stereotyping, of course, works both ways. You'll find Chinese social media, too, full of condescending and racist portrayals of India as dirty and backward.

If the caricatures that dominate media and social media can leave you feeling dismayed at the competitive mutual ignorance, there is some reason to be optimistic about the broader picture. As more Indians and Chinese travel across the border to visit and work, the distances are narrowing. I've met so many young Indians and Chinese who, unburdened by the past, look at the other country as an opportunity, waiting to be discovered. There are 20,000 Indians studying medicine in China. And probably just as many Chinese, who are working in Bengaluru and Gurgaon, many of them young entrepreneurs in the tech sector, who look at India as the next big opportunity.

During my time in Beijing and my travels across China, I was fortunate to meet many people who inspired me with their stories that defied convention and shattered the stereotypes I carried with me when I first moved across the border. If six notes, as Ash wrote, can make a melody, I wish I had the ability to compose a sonata that captured the diversity of the people I met in China, and their hopes and fears about their lives and where their country was heading.

In the absence of that, here is my own melody of six people whose stories touched me in different ways. A discoverer of temples. A treasure hunter of scriptures. An interpreter of poetry. A cultural ambassador building bridges. A soldier turned green warrior. And a dreamer who chased her unlikely passion fearlessly. If the six notes appear disconnected, uniting them in an unexpected melody is a shared connection with India, a country with which old links have faded but are being renewed in surprising ways.

19

The Discoverer

WHEN I FIRST MET WANG Liming, in the summer of 2013, she was waging a lone battle. We met by chance. I was on holiday in southeastern Fujian, visiting Wuyi mountain and its beautiful tea estates. On my last day in Xiamen, the booming coastal town across the strait from Taiwan – on clear nights, you can see the glistening lights across the waters – a friend suggested I visit Quanzhou, once a thriving port city that was for centuries the busiest port in the world. The only tip I had was to visit the city's maritime museum. It didn't sound particularly exciting, but since I had a day to spare, I thought why not. I called in advance, and they told me to drop in.

I was surprised to find no less than its vice director welcoming me at the door, where a huge replica of the ship of China's most famous explorer, Zheng He, greets visitors. With closely cropped hair and a soft-spoken demeanour, Wang Liming is in charge of the museum's international contacts. Reporters are usually left to tour guides, but when she heard I was from India, Wang told me, she dropped everything to meet me. 'We've had visitors from around the world, but perhaps you're the first from India,' she told me. The surprise in her voice made sense once we walked in.

Ancient Connection

The Quanzhou Maritime Museum first opened in 1959, ten years after the People's Republic was founded. In the 1930s, a local archaeologist and historian named Wu Wenliang found a trove of artefacts that provided the biggest clues about Quanzhou's glorious past. During the Song Dynasty (960–1279) and Yuan Dynasty (1279–1368), Quanzhou was the centre of the world, a thriving hub of maritime commerce.

At the time, the discovery hardly made news. China was just recovering from Japanese occupation and the Second World War, and was then thrown into its own civil war. After the Communist Party came to power in 1949, it took another full decade for the stones, which were lying forgotten in Quanzhou warehouses, to come to the local government's attention.

The artefacts – bearing signs of engagement with Europe, the Middle East and Southeast Asia – underline Quanzhou's status as a centre of global maritime commerce. And one relationship above all others makes its presence felt in the collection: the history between Quanzhou and India going back more than 1,000 years.[1] The first record of an Indian residing in Quanzhou was as long ago as the sixth century CE, when the monk Gunaratna travelled there and helped in the translation of Sanskrit sutras. Inscriptions about the monk are still on display in the Yanfu temple, a sprawling shrine on the outskirts of Quanzhou on Jiuri mountain.

I trekked up the mountain, which, a local saying goes, 'charms visitors as a fairyland would'. Built in the third century, it is the oldest temple in Fujian. An inscription at the temple, written during the Song Dynasty by a local named Zeng Hui, says a monk from India called Liang Putong, as Gunaratna came to be known in China, travelled here by sea and lived in Yanfu, where he translated sutras from Sanskrit. A rock on the mountain still marks the spot where Gunaratna reportedly translated the Diamond Sutra, and it is called Fanjingshi, or 'sutra-translating rock'.

Quanzhou's most famous temple is the Kaiyuan temple, which sits at the centre of the old town. On the morning I visited, it was packed with worshippers. Smoke from their incense sticks covered the courtyard, where I waited for Huang Yishan. For centuries, Huang's family have been the caretakers of the temple. Built in the year 686 during the Tang Dynasty (618–907), the Kaiyuan temple, which was earlier known as the Lotus temple, is the oldest and largest Buddhist temple in Fujian.

The 78,000 square-metre site, legend has it, was once a mulberry grove. A Buddhist monk appeared in the dream of the man who owned the grove, and asked him to build a grand temple there. 'I will,' the man told the monk, 'but only if the mulberry trees in my garden bear lotus flowers.' Sure enough, a few days later, lotuses began to bloom on his trees. In the courtyard of the temple, a mulberry tree still occupies pride of place.

Huang took me behind the main hall. In a corner, behind the temple, there were at least half a dozen pillars, all displaying an extraordinary variety of inscriptions that were more than a little familiar to my eye, from Narasimha to Vishnu. Huang told me these old inscriptions were the most unique part of the temple, although, he lamented, that most of his compatriots were completely unaware of what they meant.

Forgotten History

The historical connections between Quanzhou and south India were largely forgotten until the 1930s, when dozens of stones showing perfectly rendered images of Narasimha – the man-lion avatar of Vishnu – were unearthed by Wu Wenliang. Elephant statues and images depicting mythological stories relating to Vishnu and Shiva were also found, bearing a style and pattern almost identical to temples of Tamil Nadu and Andhra Pradesh from a similar period.

Wang Liming's museum has done a remarkable job in piecing together this history. It carries a copy of an account written by a visiting Italian merchant, who wrote in the year 1271 that the Indian traders 'were recognized easily'. These rich Indian men and women,' he said, 'mainly live on vegetables, milk and rice, and the Chinese eat meat and fish.' Not much is known about Quanzhou's Indian community, but the maritime museum has on display some fascinating titbits. We know the traders were likely wealthy. And what they left behind is a remarkable legacy of grand temples they built throughout Quanzhou and its suburbs.

Wang told me there is no clear record of how many temples there may have been. Findings have been made across a rather vast spread in Quanzhou and the nearby town of Jinjiang, suggesting there may have been several temples that later fell to ruin. It is also unclear whether the statues of deities were brought from south India or made by local artisans based on Indian designs. It is a curious irony that several centuries later, statues and paintings of Indian gods and goddesses are still being made in China and are shipped in the other direction, as I discovered during my visits to the trading town of Yiwu, a few hundred kilometres north of Quanzhou. The pattern of distribution of the stones is remarkable. In an area stretching across Quanzhou and neighbouring villages, ruins have been found in at least three dozen sites, including of what Wang and others believe to be two grand temples.

'We have found them spread across so many different sites that we are very possibly talking about many, many temples that were here,' Wang said. 'This period of history is worthwhile for us to research more, and there are many mysteries about these sculptures. We want to find the secrets behind these stones. We really hope Indian scholars can cooperate with us to do this research together about the Indians who came to Quanzhou, what happened here, what the stones represent, and how the temples they built were. All this is waiting to be discovered.'

I asked her if everything had fallen to ruin, and if the pillars at Kaiyuan were the only standing remains. 'All but one,' she told me. In one small village in Jinjiang, a Hindu deity had remarkably survived – a simple shrine that lasted hundreds of years, through wars, the rise and fall of empires, a Japanese occupation, a Chinese civil war and the Cultural Revolution. 'You must see it,' Wang said. Alas, I had a plane to catch. 'Come back to Quanzhou,' she said, 'and I will take you there.'

The Road to Chidian

I returned a year later, in the autumn of 2014. Quanzhou is today a booming city, flush with funds thanks to the Chinese government's plan to launch a 'Maritime Silk Road' that harks back to the city's old history as a thriving port. A well-paved highway links the city to the village of Chidian, a poor suburb sandwiched between Quanzhou and Jinjiang, a manufacturing town famous as the shoe-making factory of the world. If your internationally branded sports shoe has a 'Made in China' label, there's a good chance it passed through Jinjiang.

Chidian village, like many in south China, is home to mainly the elderly and young children. The families here, for generations, made their living off the sea, but most people of working age are now employed in factories elsewhere. Several of the traditional wooden courtyards, built in the unique Fujianese style, have been replaced with brick homes. One corner of Chidian has, however, remained unchanged: the small temple that has occupied the centre of the village for centuries.

Every morning, residents light incense sticks and offer prayers at the shrine, which is perhaps the only one of its kind in all of China. The four-armed deity has unmistakably Indian features, bearing a striking resemblance to those found in the Vishnu and Shiva temples of Tamil Nadu and Andhra Pradesh. She sits upright, flanked by two attendants. At her feet is a vanquished demon. The golden deity that the shrine houses is clearly neither Buddhist nor Taoist, but a Hindu goddess.

'It was only around ten or fifteen years ago that we discovered this goddess was something different,' says Chen Jingtu, a school teacher in Chidian. 'The village had always thought this shrine was a local version of Guanyin [a popular Bodhisattva], but local scholars told us this goddess is from India.'

'This is possibly the only temple in China where we are still praying to a Hindu god,' chuckled Li Sanlong, another resident who joined in the conversation.

The shrine is just one of more than a dozen similar temples that were once spread across Quanzhou and surrounding villages, but is the only one still standing. It is a significant living monument to a forgotten 800-year-old history. While the story of the Chidian shrine is known only to residents and a few local historians, what is even more remarkable is that Chidian's treasures have never been documented entirely.

Strolling through the village, I found what are possibly invaluable Hindu stone statues still adorning old homes. These have never been studied. A particularly remarkable specimen lies in a corner of the Li family shrine – an ancient courtyard home that pays tribute to Chidian's most famous resident, a wealthy sugar baron named Li Wu. It appears to be a beautifully rendered Nandi bull, the mount of Lord Shiva and a common feature in south Indian temples. This Nandi lies out of sight, propped up against the walls of the home. Covered in dust are stone panels, possibly dating back more than eight centuries, that appear to show images of Hindu gods and goddess. These are valuable surviving testaments to a part of India's cultural history. Today, they lie forgotten in a village home in a corner of southeastern China.

A small museum set up in the village's local Communist Party headquarters chronicles the life of sugar baron Li Wu, who is six centuries on, still the most famous person to come out of Chidian. When historians told locals about the story of the deity, this goddess has become, after Li Wu, Chidian's most famous resident. Newspaper clippings from the local media about the deity have been preserved in the small Chidian museum, which documents proudly this village's role in 'the cultural links between China and India'.

Li Sanlong, who like many others here sports the Li family surname – they are all descendants of Li Wu – says the villagers are proud of the part they have played in protecting the deity. One story claims that 500 years ago, the shrine housing the deity collapsed, but villagers combed through the rubble to recover the statue and built a new shrine to house it.

'The belief is that this was a statue of Guanyin who brought good luck and good fortune,' Li said. 'Although we now know this is a goddess from India, this belief hasn't changed. At the start of every month, we all gather here and pray to her for our good fortune.'

Solving a Mystery

Back in Quanzhou, Wang told me much about the shrine is still an enigma. She dug up records showing that Li Wu's wife built a pavilion to protect the shrine in the fourteenth century. But, as she said, 'We don't know when this deity was first installed. That this was something different was discovered only in 1988, when people were already praying to what they called a Guanyin deity. People in Quanzhou are very religious, and the fact that they were praying to a Buddhist goddess that was actually a Hindu deity is fascinating.'

One reason for the mystery, she said, is that the solution to parts of the puzzle lie buried in India. 'There is so much in-depth research we need to do on this history, but there are still some problems we are facing. For example, in decoding the messages on the statues in Tamil, which will give us a lot more information about the communication between China and India in that period.'

Quanzhou wasn't home only to Tamil traders during this thriving period of history; there were Christian and Islamic shrines too. But it is the Hindu past of the city that remains the biggest puzzle. 'We are now clearer about the Christian and Islamic statues than the Hindu statues,' Wang said. 'The messages still remain a mystery, and there are many, many questions. We want to build a team with Indian scholars to try and answer these questions. Are these statues from one big temple? Or were there several temples? Who made them? Was it local artisans or were they brought from India? What do they represent?'

Five years after I last spoke to Wang, I was back home in Chennai, which the Chinese president was about to visit for what was being called the second 'informal summit' with India's prime minister. India had chosen Chennai for the summit because of the old trading links between Tamil Nadu and Fujian. Ever since President Xi Jinping launched his 'Maritime Silk Road' plan, there was renewed interest in Quanzhou. The Indian ambassador to China had even visited the museum, and pledged the country's support for Wang's work.

I sent Wang a copy of the statement that the Indian government issued after the Chennai summit. The statement said Xi and Modi 'both referred to [the] port city called Quanzhou in Fujian where recently Tamil inscriptions and fragments of architecture reflecting a possible temple build by Tamil traders in the 12th century have been discovered. President Xi Jinping also said that he was aware of this.'[2]

It may have just been two sentences, but Wang was thrilled beyond measure. Finally, the forgotten story of the shrines may yet get the attention it deserves. That it was buried for so long is perhaps the greatest mystery of all, considering the wealth of information that still survives, even if forgotten, in a small village in a corner of China.

20

The Treasure Hunter

WHEN YE SHAOYONG, A CHINESE scholar of Sanskrit, first came across the old yellowed palm leaves from Drepung, one of Tibet's most important monasteries, he was intrigued by the letters on the page. The fourteen palm leaves bore ancient writing, older than anything that the Sanskrit professor from Peking University had ever seen. What Ye stumbled upon that day in 2003 was one of the oldest Sanskrit texts from India: a second-century palm leaf that carried the entire *Mulamadhyamakakarika* ('The Fundamentals of the Middle Way') by Nagarjuna, one of the founding texts of Mahayana Buddhism.

Most of the old texts of Tibet have only come to light recently, thanks to the fact that many were smuggled out of the region in the 1950s. In 1970, the Library of Tibetan Works and Archives was set up in Dharamsala. Over the decades, it has translated many of these texts and brought them to public attention. These are, however, a fraction of the trove that remains undiscovered in many of Tibet's monasteries, according to Chinese scholars.[1]

I first heard of Ye's work during a visit to the China Tibetology Research Centre, a massive complex in north Beijing that is the Chinese government's most important official think tank on all matters Tibet. There, I found a copy of Ye's book: a translation of the *Mulamadhyamakakarika*, published after a decade spent painstakingly translating it. This was the first from the Tibet palm leaves treasure trove to be published in China. I was stunned to read there were thousands more of these ancient texts from India, which contained valuable information – not just about some of the earliest and foundational teachings of Buddhism but even about India's history. 'Tibet,' Ye wrote, 'might be the last treasure of Sanskrit manuscripts which has not yet been fully investigated. Nonetheless, they are still gathering dust on the public shelves of monasteries or in the drawers of museums.'

I reached out to Ye, who invited me to Peking University, where he is an associate professor in the Sanskrit and Pali section of the Department of South Asian Studies. I confess I was surprised to learn the university still had a thriving Sanskrit studies department, although I was aware of its rich history in Indology. It goes back to 1921 when Alexander von Staël-Holstein, a German scholar of Sanskrit, was invited to teach by the university's president Hu Shih. Holstein would help set up the first Sino-Indian institute at Peking University in 1927.

The German–Sanskrit connection continued when the scholar Ji Xianlin returned to Beijing in 1946 from Göttingen, and set up the Department of Oriental Languages. Along with Jin Kemu, who had spent five years in India in the early 1940s, Ji built up Sanskrit studies in Peking University into a formidable department. In 1960, the first undergraduates in Sanskrit and Pali were enrolled. This batch included Jiang Zhongxin, the first Chinese scholar to work on Sanskrit manuscripts from Tibet, who also translated the *Manusmriti* into Mandarin, and Huang Baosheng, whose translation of the Mahabharata into Mandarin would become widely popular, bringing the story to the Chinese masses. The experiment, however, was short-lived. Six years later, during the Cultural Revolution, many of these scholars were sent to the countryside to do hard labour, part of a broader persecution of scholars and intellectuals.

When normalcy was restored following the death of Mao, Ji Xianlin was among the intellectuals who were rehabilitated, and the respected scholar was promoted to the post of the vice president of Peking University. He set up an Institute of South Asian Studies jointly with the Chinese Academy of Social Sciences. This would become a leading centre for Sanskrit studies: it has trained some two dozen PhDs, some of whom went on to start Sanskrit studies programmes elsewhere in China. It is fitting then that a student of Ji's, the scholar Duan Qing, one of the world's leading experts in Sanskrit, Pali and Khotanese, is now carrying on his legacy at Peking University. Translating the Sanskrit palm leaves of Tibet is, today, one of the institute's high-priority initiatives.

Lost Treasures

When we met one morning at a terrace café in Peking University's leafy campus, overlooking the busy Zhongguancun tech district of northwest Beijing, Ye told me that not many people, either in China or in India, are aware of the huge significance of the work they are doing. The texts span a broad period, from the second to the fourteenth centuries, and are of immense religious, historical and literary value.

For Buddhists, some of the texts contain the founding precepts of their religion's thought, such as the *Mulamadhyamakakarika*, that Ye found in Drepung, and the *Lankavatara Sutra*, found in the Potala Palace in Lhasa. For historians, the manuscripts hold a wealth of information. 'These texts could change how we think of our history and philosophy,' said Ye, pointing to how a similar trove in Nepal brought out new elements of the country's early modern history. Most of the texts are of a philosophical nature, but, as Ye observed, they also hold a great deal of information about society and politics from that period – from the lineage of dynasties to their governance and administration.

The collection is of particular relevance to India, especially as, in some instances, they are the only surviving records. Thousands of texts in India from a similar period fell to ruin. In the high altitudes of Tibet, many manuscripts have remained untouched over hundreds of years. Some of the texts are in Tibetan, as the original Sanskrit texts they were copied from have been lost. More than 500 palm leaves have been discovered, each containing hundreds of lines of text. Most of them were brought to Tibet hundreds of years ago by monks who had travelled to India and Nepal. So far, Peking University has published five volumes since 2011, but, Ye told me, the texts that have so far been translated are just the tip of the iceberg. Hundreds of palm leaves still lie undiscovered in Tibet's monasteries, and the scope of the trove is as yet unknown, which is surprising considering the effort to retrieve the texts dates back to at least the early 1930s.

The Indian scholar and traveller Rahul Sankrityayan, who made several trips to Tibet to translate old Tibetan texts back to the original Sanskrit, first heard about the collection during his travels in the early 1930s. He later wrote that he first dismissed the stories of a vast Sanskrit palm-leaf collection as a myth, but, intrigued by the accounts, he returned to Tibet in 1934 to investigate. Sankrityayan was welcomed in Tibet, and even taken to see the Kalon Lama, one of the top ministers of the Tibet government, who was then the most powerful man in the region following the death of the thirteenth Dalai Lama in December 1933. Sankrityayan was taken to the Kundeling monastery, where he was presented with two rare manuscripts. Thanks to him, photographs of some of the texts were brought back to India and stored in the Patna Museum.

Caught in the political turmoil of the 1940s and 1950s, the Japanese occupation followed by the Chinese civil war, few scholars in China paid attention to the texts until the 1960s. Then, around 250 bundles of the leaves were brought to Beijing and catalogued, and returned to the Tibet Museum in Lhasa, where they are still kept. The decade-long Cultural Revolution halted the effort, but after Ji Xianlin's institute at Peking University took off in the 1970s, it resumed. Ye told me that the manuscripts brought back from India by the famous Tang Dynasty monk Xuan Zhang (or Hiuen Tsang, as we know him in India) have not been found. 'Not even a single leaf,' he said sadly.

Herculean Task

Ye is doing what he can to translate more leaves, and is working on several new texts. But, he lamented, China doesn't have the number of scholars or resources to systematically unravel the entire trove.

He explained to me how difficult the process is. The first and the most fundamental step for the study of these manuscripts is not translation but 'edition', or, to provide a critical edition of the text in its original language. It includes transliteration, collation with different versions, deciding how to choose the best of various possible readings, and reconstructing missing parts. 'Each of these tasks,' he told me, 'needs professional knowledge and special training, not only in Sanskrit, Tibetan and Chinese languages, but also on manuscriptology. For example, these manuscripts were written not in the uniform Devanagari script, but in various local scripts with different conventions. To read them, one has to understand Indian palaeography [the study of ancient writing systems].

'In addition, in order to provide a reliable edition of a certain text, one needs background knowledge of its content, such as the historical information, the philological matrix and the philosophical system. And, on top of all that, we to preserve the thought in an ancient text – nothing is more important than to preserve what was said in the original language.'

The work of Peking University's scholars, such as Ye, has been getting attention from intellectuals around the world. Everywhere, but India. Privately, the Chinese scholars I spoke to told me that their attempts to reach out to Indian scholars and institutions have received little response. Sanskrit students in China have struggled to find fellowships in Indian universities, which are often reluctant to host them unless they enrol in full-time courses, which makes little sense as Indian degrees are not recognized in the country. European and American institutions, by contrast, have shown greater interest and flexibility in working on the project, and are hence taking the palm leaves translation forward.

Ye believes this is an area where India and China should work together, and that his students would benefit immensely from studying under Indian scholars 'who have the best traditional teaching methods' in Sanskrit. This, he thinks, could also be an ideal project for the revived Nalanda University, which, however, has been slow to take off. The great irony, of course, is that this rich trove – which could fill vital gaps in understanding the history of both Sanskrit literature and philosophical thought – holds no greater significance for any country than it does for India.

21

The Interpreter

DURING MY FIRST FEW MONTHS in China, I was often puzzled by the reactions I got from people when I said I was from India. 'I love tiger!' was one of the most common phrases I heard. Strange, I thought, this Chinese fascination for tigers. It took me a while to figure out it wasn't a striped, four-legged animal they were talking about, but a bearded poet.

The scale of the popularity of Rabindranath Tagore – or 'Tai Ge Er', as his name is rendered in Mandarin – in China isn't often understood in India. Reading Tagore is part of the official curriculum in Chinese schools. He has been, by far, the most popular foreign poet in China for close to a century, revered as a saintly 'poet sage' figure, starting with his 1920s visit to Shanghai , which, as we have seen, also attracted its fair share of controversy. Ask someone who their favourite foreign writer is, and you'll inevitably hear Tagore's name.

Among his legion of Chinese fans is Feng Tang. So when Feng, who is one of China's most popular writers, decided to begin, in the summer of 2014, a three-month-long project translating Tagore's poems, it was a deeply personal exercise. 'For fifteen years,' he told me, 'I was running. I needed to stop and find peace. Which was why I turned to Tagore. To find peace.'

Voice of the Young

For fifteen years, Feng Tang has been one of China's most prolific writers. His six novels, three essay collections and one work of poetry have been read by millions. For Chinese born in the 1980s, the medical student-turned-writer has become a cult favourite, in part because of his widely successful novel *Beijing, Beijing* that presented a no-holds-barred account of growing up in a changing metropolis.

Beijing, Beijing established Feng as a voice for the youth, and as an irreverent, almost subversive writer, who told it like it was – who spoke in the language of the people, writing of youth discovering sex and poking fun at communist dogmas, and not dressing up his language in the formalities beloved the political and literary establishment. For an author familiar with controversy, Tagore would provide a welcome escape. Or so he thought.

Little did Feng expect that his translation of *Stray Birds*, a collection of 300-odd short verses penned by Tagore in 1916, would turn out to be perhaps his most controversial work yet. In the first week of December 2015, soon after Feng's translation was published, a number of commentaries appeared in the Chinese state-run press, taking aim at Feng, accusing him of 'vulgarity' and of blaspheming the revered Indian poet. The English-language government mouthpiece, *China Daily*, published an extraordinary commentary by its well-known film critic, Raymond Zhou, describing Feng's translation as a 'vulgar selfie'. Zhou's criticism went beyond the translation and attacked Feng personally, calling him a 'hormone-obsessed' writer with 'colossal insecurity'.[1] When the *People's Daily*, the Communist Party's official newspaper, penned a similar commentary, Feng's publishers were rattled. On 28 December, they took the unprecedented step of removing his translation from bookstores across China.

A few days later, on a cold January morning, I waited for Feng in an upmarket café in Beijing's Guomao business district. Dressed in a crisp white shirt and grey blazer, he walked in briskly, but not quickly enough to evade curious glances from almost everyone around us. I knew he was famous, but didn't realize he was well-known enough to be instantly recognized by every single person at a Beijing coffee shop.

Feng Tang never thought he would become a writer. He studied medicine, and was set for a career as a successful gynaecologist (a reason why, he told me, he wasn't squeamish about writing about sex and sensuality, even if it outraged some of his compatriots). He ended up at McKinsey, where he worked as a partner for nine years ('You may know Mr Rajat Gupta, he was our global managing director then.'). He then moved to a major Chinese firm that invests in hospitals and is one of the biggest operators of hospitals in the country. 'I was running, running, running, all the time,' he told me. 'I decided I wanted to stop.' And that's where writing began.

The day we met, Feng was downbeat. He told me that the storm of anger over the Tagore translation had left him puzzled and disappointed, and he wanted to explain his side of the story. In part, he also wanted to let people in India know that contrary to the portrayal in Chinese state media – which had been picked up and reported by several Indian newspapers – he bore no malice to Tagore. And that he was deeply pained by what was being reported about his views on one of his favourite writers.

What saddened him the most though was the charge of vulgarity – 'all based on five words out of 10,000', as he put it. The reaction in India particularly disappointed him. When the English-language *China Daily* published the article, the Indian media faithfully reproduced the accusation that his translation was 'vulgar', without either reading it or speaking to him, Feng noted. He has since received death threats online from Indian internet users angered by reports that claimed he had insulted Tagore. The irony is that one of his motivations was to bring Tagore to a wider audience in China.

A Modern Interpretation

Feng told me that his experience of translating Tagore and the reaction to his work have been illuminating. One reason for the anger, he suspected, was that people in China tended to worship writers and philosophers, whether Confucius or Tagore. They wanted to see Tagore as a saintly figure.

For Feng, the uproar also reflected the unease in China about anyone who dares to swim against the current. 'I feel uncomfortable with the Chinese way of worshipping. Confucius, his works were masters, but also human beings. Tagore himself was irreverent, and not someone who liked worship. What makes me uncomfortable is: how can they decide what it is that Tagore meant? People hate to have something that challenges their historical view of things. "The tree should be green. The flower should be red." If I write about a yellow flower: "Wrong! Change the colour back to red!" It surprises me after so many years in this modern economy, of opening up, so little has changed. A culture that can tolerate is a more advanced culture, not one that says, "A is A, and anything else is wrong."'

Feng told me that he loved Tagore when he was younger, reading him like many schoolchildren do. But when re-reading Tagore when he was much older, he realized there were many layers and depth to the poet's writing. The most popular Chinese translation of Tagore, Feng told me, was by Zheng Zhenduo in the 1920s. Zheng had been in his twenties when he had worked on the translation. His rendering, Feng felt, reflected both his youth and the stiltedness of the language at the time. 'While Zheng's translation is solid,' he said, 'he translated Tagore at a time when the modern Chinese language he was using was at an early stage. So it actually feels awkward in many places.' Feng thought it was time for an update.

'It was a meditative experience and I realized some things. One, Tagore is not soft. The early version is sometimes misleading. They believe it is soft, gentle, very mild – a kids' book. Sometimes he is very mild and gentle. But when he wrote *Stray Birds*, he was already in his fifties. There are some poems that are powerful and deep, dealing with relationships, difficulties and very adult problems.' Of all the verses, Feng told me, one really stayed with him: 'I thank thee that I am none of the wheels of power but I am one with the living creatures that are crushed by it.' Feng asked me, 'Do you think children can easily understand this? This is powerful and deep. I saw this not as a mother talking to children, but a man to another. The second thing about Tagore I realized is that he is so subtle when talking about love. Another of my favourite verses is this: "I cannot tell why this heart languishes in silence. It is for small needs it never asks, or knows or remembers."'

Feng was so keen to explain his case that he walked me through every one of the 326 poems he translated, and explained how he chose his words. 'Even choosing a simple word can take a long, long time. Translation is like sculpting. You can spend hours focusing on one word. For three months, I locked myself up in the Bay Area in the summer of 2014. I had a small house with a garden. I did 100 words a day, not more. So it took me ninety days. For me, this was also a personal exercise – to stop and think, and look back on the past fifteen years.'

The entire controversy was based on three verses. In the first instance, where Tagore writes 'The great earth makes herself hospitable with the help of the grass', Feng used a more suggestive word in Chinese for 'hospitable', meaning 'coquettish' or 'flirtatious'. In the second instance, where Tagore writes of the world removing its 'mask of vastness to its lover' and becoming 'one kiss of the eternal', Feng interpreted this verse sexually, speaking of a world removing its 'underwear of vastness' and a 'French kiss of the eternal'. The third 'offence' was Feng's use of a colloquial Chinese character, used by young internet users, instead of a formal article.

Tagore himself, Feng wryly told me, was a sensual writer and artist, who had no problems speaking of love and sex in his poems. As he walked me through his other verses, I came to love how he had interpreted – and reinterpreted – Tagore. In fact, in many ways, Feng's translations are more elegant – and truer to Tagore's original haiku-like verse – than Zheng Zhenduo's.

Feng said he wanted to closely reflect Tagore's own brevity and economical choice of words, which was very different from the 'flowery' language familiar to Chinese poets. Many of Feng's translations seem more in sync with Tagore's original verses than other Chinese renditions. For instance, where Tagore writes, 'O Beauty, find thyself in love, not in the flattery of thy mirror', Feng uses only eight Chinese characters to very neatly capture the verse: '*Mei, Zai Ai Zhong, Bu Zai Jing Zhong*.' Zheng had used a flowery twenty-three, interspersing Tagore's words with 'ahs' and other exclamations: '*Ah, Mei Ah, Zai Ai Zhong Zhao Ni Zizhi Ba, Bu Yao Dao Ni Jing Zi De Chan Yu Zhong Qu Zhao Ya!*'

Feng's reinterpretation adapted Tagore for modern sensibilities. Lost in the outrage in China and India is that the poet, who was rarely bound by convention and strictures, would have very likely approved.

The one silver lining in all the controversy, Feng told me, was that thanks to the attention, more young Chinese were reading Tagore – and not just reading him as they did in the classroom, as a saint whose words were to be memorized, but reinterpreting him and discussing him. Feng's translation went on to sell 50,000 copies – and many more online – which was the largest for any poem collection in China that year. That is, until it was pulled off the bookshelves.

22

The Fan

WHEN JING JING, WHO IS thirty years old and works as a manager in a state-owned Chinese company, heard that the Indian film star Aamir Khan was about to land in Beijing, she dropped everything to frantically look up flight schedules. She called a cab and dashed to the airport in the middle of a workday.

This was the summer of 2015, and Khan was about to make his first visit to China, to promote the release of his film *PK*. He was, at the time, not a household name in China by any means, but had begun to acquire a dedicated following among a small and passionate crowd of young Chinese who followed Indian cinema. The release of *PK* was to be a modest event – little expense was spent on promoting the film – and given the niche following of Indian movies, it was somewhat of a trial balloon.

For the generation of Jing's parents, Raj Kapoor and Indian films from the 1950s and 1960s were huge hits. Until the 1970s, Indian films were wildly popular in China – Raj Kapoor still remains a household name – but faded subsequently. Few Indian films have since made a mark, let alone managed to secure a release in China, which reserves its thirty-odd annual quota of foreign films for Hollywood blockbusters.

'Uncle Aamir'

That changed with *3 Idiots* in 2009, which became a cult hit, resonating to such a degree with China's stressed-out students that Peking University, the country's most elite institution, began prescribing it as a means of stress relief. That was the film that prompted Jing to start China's first Aamir Khan Fan Club – and to dash to the airport that day in 2015.

Both moves paid off. Her modest club now has more than 1,00,000 fans all across China, and 500 active members who regular post articles and organize events. And at the airport that day? The memory still leaves Jing giddy with joy. 'I spent all morning going through the flight information from Mumbai to Beijing, and guessed Aamir would take the shortest flight because of his busy schedule. I was right!' The crew meeting Khan was late, so she ended up speaking to him for a few minutes as he waited. 'I will never forget that day,' she told me, 'for the rest of my life.'

When it comes to the movies they watch, Jing's generation, born in the 1980s, is not limited to the choices that led their parents to embrace Indian and Russian films in the Cultural Revolution era. For their children, the stars of Hollywood, Hong Kong and South Korea – not India – were the ones that caught their imagination as China began to open up to the world.

Tastes are changing, however. Aamir's success comes at a time when increasingly sophisticated Chinese audiences are craving something different. The *PK* experiment in 2015 was an unqualified success: it would become the first Indian film to earn 100 million yuan (around Rs 100 crore) in any foreign market. This was followed by the runaway success of *Dangal* two years later; it became China's highest grossing non-Hollywood foreign film in history, earning more than 1 billion yuan (around Rs 1,000 crore), and underlining the rise of Aamir Khan as an unlikely Chinese phenomenon.

'Uncle Aamir', as he is widely known in the country, has in the years since become a household name in China – perhaps the most famous Indian actor since Raj Kapoor. *Dangal* became such a nationwide phenomenon that screenings were even arranged for the top Chinese leadership in their Zhongnanhai leadership compound.

Jing's friend Jian Bin works with her at the fan club. By day, he works for a Chinese company acquiring copyrights for foreign media content mainly from South Korea and the US. Jian told me that *PK* was a turning point 'when Aamir's following here went from niche, those who had loved *3 Idiots*, to really a mass following. I see the biggest reason for this connect as the emotion in his films, whether *Dangal* or *3 Idiots*,' he said. 'The lack of this intense emotion is a big problem for the Chinese film industry, as are simply good stories, and we found that in *Dangal* or *Secret Superstar* (2017).'

Buddies in India

On the morning of *PK*'s release in Beijing, a long queue snaked outside a banquet hall at the Grand Hyatt, a massive hotel that sits on Chang'an Avenue, a stone's throw from Tiananmen Square. There were young Chinese from all over the country for a 'meet and greet' with the star. In the queue were three college students, who introduced themselves, telling me they had spent three days on a train to get there, all the way from Xinjiang. For most Uighurs in Xinjiang, they told me, Indian films had become a raging passion, full of themes of hope – and, in the case of Aamir's movies, realism – that they couldn't find in the propaganda that assaulted them daily.

Shortly after *PK*'s stunning release, I travelled to Shanghai to meet Wang Baoqiang, a popular Chinese actor and kung fu star, currently the biggest action star in the mainland, who had contributed to the film's success in China by lending his voice for the main character in the dubbed version. I waited in a plush hotel lounge off Xintiandi, or 'new heaven and earth', an upmarket shopping district.

Wang trooped in, as film stars do, with a retinue of a dozen or so people. He told me he had surprised his team by agreeing to do *PK*, which was a contrast from the blockbusters he had done previously. 'No one expected it do so well,' he said, 'but I had a personal reason.' His mother was Buddhist, so when he watched the film, the themes instantly struck a chord.

'My sense of belief was shaped by my mother, and since I was a kid, I had this interest in India's gods, especially Hanuman. I believe it was destiny this film came to me, and when the part came to me I decided that I would direct my first movie in India and take my parents with me.' He did, and for his mother, he fulfilled a life-long dream. The film, called *Buddies in India*, was an action adventure. One of the first Chinese movies to be filmed almost entirely in India, it was a commercial success in China when it was released in 2017.

By the time Aamir made his second visit to China in 2018, Jing's fan club had mushroomed, with branches all over the country. For the movie star's birthday, Jing filmed a video of fans sending him their wishes. He wrote back, personally thanking them. When Aamir visited pandas in Chengdu and then held a yoga event in the mountains of Sichuan (where t'ai chi originated), his entire fan club, Jing included, accompanied him.

Her club now plays the role of a bridge to India for many young Chinese. Interest in Indian culture – with films and yoga leading the way – is today perhaps coming full circle, notwithstanding the difficult political relationship the two countries share. A cultural fascination for India has appeared strangely immune to tough political ties. This was especially evident in the 1970s, where a few years after 1962, a national obsession for Indian films grew against the incongruous backdrop of the Cultural Revolution.

'All is Well'

Does Aamir Khan's success mean Bollywood will succeed in China, the world's biggest film market? His Chinese fans don't think so.

They think it's more about Aamir than Bollywood itself. 'Most people who chose to watch *Dangal* are fond of Aamir and his acting, not because of the brand of Indian films,' said Jing.

'For instance, because I'm an Andy Lau fan, it doesn't mean I like all Hong Kong films. From my understanding and speaking with his fans, it's because of what Aamir as an individual represents, that he is always willing to concern himself with problems within society, [he] loves his country and wants to make it a better place. That is what appeals to us.'

As Jing put it, Chinese directors, many confined by the limits of censorship, don't pursue the kinds of themes that Aamir does. 'Aamir wants the audience to not only watch the movie, but also get inspired by the movie,' she told me. 'He concerns himself about the problems within society, especially the problems within the lower class.'

That has become an increasingly difficult proposition for Chinese directors, particularly in the Xi era. The films that make it to the movie theatres, more often than not, are ones that carry a message that the Communist Party is the most comfortable with. And that message is, to borrow a phrase from an Aamir movie: all is well.

23

The Green Warrior

THE LAST TIME I MET Wu Dengming was in October 2012, on a grey autumn day. We spent an afternoon in conversation in his Beijing hotel room, which overlooked an old neighbourhood of courtyard houses that lay in the shadow of the Forbidden City. Wu didn't look anywhere close to his seventy-three years. His broad shoulders and confident demeanour betrayed his past life as a PLA soldier. He spoke with a passion that burned as bright as ever, in defiance of his weakening health.

Wu had made the long journey to the capital from his native Chongqing at the invitation of the Chinese government. His relationship with the authorities had been awkward. The non-governmental organization (NGO) he founded in 1997, the Chongqing Green Volunteers League, had garnered a reputation for its muckraking. Wu revelled in taking on local factories guilty of polluting the rivers and fields of Chongqing and the surrounding Sichuan province.

He took great personal risks as he encouraged farmers to stand up to polluters, and went after the rampant ravaging of the environment unleashed by a growth-at-all-costs approach. From PLA soldier he had turned into a green warrior. And on occasion, the adversaries he confronted were from the very system he had once served.

'Less Talk, More Action'

Once, to the consternation of his family, he went undercover, posing as a businessman to gain the trust of illegal loggers. After infiltrating their network, he managed to get compelling evidence that forced even China's lumbering courts to take action and arrest them. The Green Volunteers League, founded in 1996, was Chongqing's first NGO. The story of how it was founded captures the relationship between the government and NGOs, which are sometimes known as GONGOs (Government Organized Non-Governmental Organizations), a concept only China could have come up with.

When Wu and Tian Dasheng, a Chongqing University professor, went to register their NGO with the government in Chongqing, as is required by the law, they were told that the city already had an NGO, so it didn't need another one. Tian and Wu worked around this by taking over a defunct organization called Green Volunteers League of Chongqing and breathing new life into it.[1]

'Less talk and more action' was the motto that Wu gave his NGO. It was, in some sense, the maxim that had governed his life. Born in 1940 in a working class family, Wu grew up amidst the heady enthusiasm that accompanied the founding of the People's Republic of China in 1949. This excitement soon gave way to the grim reality of economic hardship, compounded by Mao Zedong's excesses.

Wu, like most in his generation, worshipped Mao. He was eighteen when Mao launched his brutal anti-rightist campaign and the disastrous Great Leap Forward in 1958. Still in high school, Wu discarded his textbooks and plunged into the frenzy of steel making that would leave the countryside facing a desperate famine. He joined the PLA after he turned twenty.

At twenty-two, he was sent to Tibet in 1962, as China prepared for war with India. When I first met Wu for an interview about his work as an environmentalist at a friend's apartment near Peking University, we ended up talking not about the war against polluters but another war, that of 1962. He hadn't realized I was from India, and he told me I was probably the first Indian he had met since the war. Before that, he was sent to the front in Mêdog county, which today sits right across the border from Arunachal Pradesh.

When the war began, Wu told me he was assigned to an early morning offensive somewhere in the eastern sector on 22 October 1962. His company, he said, faced little resistance as they crossed the border into India. He spoke of how indoctrinated the young PLA soldiers at the frontier were, despite the terrible hardships, including famine, ravaging China at the time. 'We all wanted to be Chairman Mao's good soldiers,' he said.

Rather than the battle, his abiding memory of 1962 was of the friendships he struck with Indian prisoners of war. 'The biggest impression they left on me was their faith,' he told me. They spent the days sharing stories about the families they had left behind. He made it a point to stress that in his unit, the Indian soldiers were treated with respect. When the war was over and they returned to India, tears were shed.

Ecological Trailblazer

The battlefield was never Wu's calling. In fact, much of the rest of his life, in some sense, was a penance for some of his deeds as a soldier, as he later recalled. One of his tasks as a soldier was to join a hunting team of the PLA. One reason he turned to green activism, he later reflected, was to repay a debt to all the wildlife he had been ordered to kill.[2]

He left the PLA and took up a job in Chongqing University, where he began his green activism at a time when China had no significant environmental movement. As Deng Xiaoping took forward economic reforms and the country looked to get rich, growth was the abiding objective. Wu's first mission was to protect the forests of Sichuan through which the Yangtze river flowed. His green volunteers went into the villages, helping farmers and bringing awareness of the growing pollution that had begun to permeate the fields and rivers.

Wu's great quality was that he was able to immediately strike a bond with whomever he met. He was a born leader, but also a listener. As *The Economist* magazine wrote of him once, '... he would listen to the environmental horror-stories of ordinary working people, and teach them how to cope. No one else would. The party had placed itself too far above the woes, and rights, of common folk. As a farmer who had moved to the city himself, he spoke the language of the peasants ...'[3]

Wu saw education as his biggest mission. 'Our society's future depends on this,' he told me during one Beijing visit. 'In the past, Chongqing farmers suffered pollution, but did not know where it came from, and who they could hold responsible. Our movement was about giving them the tools to realize their rights. That is where rights protection begins.'

Wu was adept at using the media to draw attention to his causes. In 2011, his NGO was involved in a pioneering lawsuit when it filed a case against a chemical company in a Yunnan court. The case was one of the first ever filed by an NGO that was accepted by a Chinese court. As always, when a trail was to be blazed, there was Wu, leading the way.

Our conversation that October would be our last. The following summer, Wu, unused to losing the battles he plunged himself into, succumbed to illness. He passed away on 19 July 2013, aged seventy-three. His family members said he continued pursuing his green causes until the very end, disregarding their pleas. More than 1,000 people turned up at their humble 50-square-metre home to pay their respects to Wu. Among them were five officials who had worked for factories that Wu had taken on.

To be clear, Lao Wu, or Old Wu, as he was called, was no dissident. To be effective in China, he reasoned, it made little sense to openly antagonize the central government. In fact, to get anything done, he knew, their support was crucial. Wu occupied the often uncertain grey zone traversed today by a growing number of Chinese NGOs, journalists and activists, who believe that working for realistic change within the system – amid its many authoritarian limitations – can bring greater rewards, however painfully slow the process, than attempting to overturn it altogether.

Considering the fate that often befalls China's many dissidents who are pursuing more radical change, Wu's was a persuasive argument. Beijing, for its part, had begun to grasp, albeit belatedly, the value of people like Wu, who were far ahead of the curve in flagging the environmental problem; through their activism, they had also helped hold local governments, far away from Beijing, accountable. In the autumn of 2012, when the Communist Party was in the throes of preparing for its once-in-ten-years leadership change, officials in Beijing had called Wu and asked for his ideas on how the government should change its environmental policies.

'Not in My Backyard'

When we met, Wu appeared optimistic about the direction in which China was heading. The increasingly worse air pollution that had enveloped Beijing – and left Wu with an uncomfortable cough that day – didn't seem to have dampened his confidence. In the weeks before we met, China had witnessed an unprecedented series of NIMBY ('not in my backyard') protests across half a dozen cities in 2012 and 2013, as citizens took to the streets to oppose local governments who were setting up chemical factories or waste incinerators in their communities without following due process.

The protests against P/X chemical plants in Dalian and Kunming, a copper plant in Shifang in Sichuan, and a refinery in Ningbo had been unique in the way a cross-section of society – from college students and white-collar workers to retirees and migrant workers – had been mobilized to demand transparency from their local governments. 'The biggest challenge we've faced, since we started this work three decades ago, has been getting people to understand environmental issues and to raise their awareness,' Wu told me. 'That's now beginning to change.'

The mass street protests in Dalian and Kunming against chemical plants would have been difficult to even imagine two decades ago. That the protests appeared to be tolerated, rather than suppressed, underscored the government's realization of how deeply important the issue had become for ordinary citizens. Demands for greater accountability and transparency were growing, aided by a slowly burgeoning civil society movement and the unprecedented spread of social media. WeChat and Weibo, even if under the thumb of the suffocating censorship regime, were, for the first time, allowing wider discussion and conversation not mediated by the state.

I travelled to Kunming shortly after the protests there and dined with a group of youngsters who had taken to the streets. Over dinner, I heard from them about the pride they had in their city and its lakes, a city of spring they had grown up in, only to see it gradually fall into the grip of pollution. I heard how they organized and marched, regardless of the consequences they knew would follow from their universities and workplaces.

The space for activism has certainly shrunk in Xi's China, which has passed a stringent law on how foreign NGOs should operate. Many Chinese NGOs have benefited and grown from their engagement with their overseas counterparts. That process is now being limited. NGOs in some areas, such as legal advocacy, have been all but silenced, following the unprecedented '709' crackdown on lawyers that began with a wave of detentions on 9 July 2015. The years that have followed have brought a tightening grip on legal activism.[4]

At the same time, even the crackdown under Xi hasn't been able to dent the emergence of Chinese civil society. If it began in the late 1990s, with groups such as Wu's, the movement really took off after the Sichuan earthquake of 2008, when civil society played a huge role in fundraising and relief work. Environmental activism remains the one space where civil society is still able to play a role, and it is possible to push the boundaries, in part because the government knows how widespread public concern about this issue is in China. In fact, the next generation of activists, who are taking forward the work of people like Wu, are even more aggressive in doing so. As one activist put it, 'Environmental work may lead to greater democracy in China. Environmentalism and democracy are related. Many NGO leaders are hesitant to say we are related, but I believe the NGO movements are creating democracy.'[5]

Shortly after Wu's passing, Wang Yongchen, a prominent environmentalist who founded Beijing's Green Earth Volunteers, captured in a poignant tribute the challenges faced by the movement Wu helped propel. 'Lao Wu,' she wrote, 'we have so many things to do, and we want to work on so many things together ... But Heaven is ruthless, the disease is merciless, and the reality is ruthless ... Lao Wu, we believe you have not gone very far away, you might be able to hear us, so please listen to us and take it easy: we will continue what you have not completed.'[6]

24

The Dreamer

IN JULY 2014, A GROUP of twenty young women from China arrived in London. Dressed in red tracksuits and sporting near identical close-cropped hairstyles, the group quickly became an object of much curiosity. Emblazoned on their tracksuits was the logo of the Chinese National Women's Cricket Team. Before their arrival in the United Kingdom, some of their hosts were unaware that a Chinese National Women's Cricket Team even existed.

Part of the group was Huang Zhuo, twenty-nine, the captain and their most accomplished player. Born in Changchun, in China's far northeast, Huang first picked up a cricket bat when in university, eight years to the day she first set foot in London. During university, she familiarized herself with the game by watching videos of Sachin Tendulkar on YouTube. As she started playing, she copied his stance and style.

The team also included university students, who had touched a cricket bat for the first time in their lives less than a year before they came to England. For their first match, the group travelled to the green Berkshire county. Their first game attracted much attention, if only because for the English crowd, watching a Chinese team play cricket was, to put it mildly, a novelty. Against Berkshire County Ladies' XI, which did not field its strongest team, the Chinese struggled to adjust to alien conditions. They had prepared for the tour on artificial turf grounds in hot, dry northeastern China. For many, this was a first-ever experience, playing on lush grass and manicured pitches.

The team posted a creditable 110 runs, losing 5 wickets, in 20 overs. When Berkshire came out to bat, they found it much harder than the cakewalk they had expected. Their visitors bowled with discipline, and threw themselves around the Berkshire grass with passion. The home team limped to 109 runs, losing by 1 to their underrated Chinese guests.

During their month in England, the young team travelled across the country, playing matches at Lord's, the home of cricket, against the famed Marylebone Cricket Club (MCC) Ladies, and other first-division teams. In the match against a team from the Channel island of Jersey, Huang smashed 145, hitting one six and thirteen fours. The Chinese played nine games on their UK visit. They won eight.

An Unknown Game

Cricket is a sport with no history in China. Most Chinese have never heard of 'banqiu' – pronounced ban-chiyo, literally meaning bat-ball, not to be confused with 'bangqiu', or baseball, which is relatively better known. Yet, for a small group of Chinese athletes, it has become not only a passion but a way of life.

In the summer of 2014, I took a train to Shenyang, in China's far northeast, and headed for the campus of Shenyang Sports University (SSU). SSU is the home of cricket in China, and where the women's and men's teams are based and train for competitions. Terry Zhang, a quiet but determined administrator, who is in his late thirties, invited me over to meet the team.

It was only in 2005 that China was formally introduced to the game. That year, the first-ever coaching course was held in Beijing, under the aegis of a newly set up Chinese Cricket Association (CCA). The International Cricket Council's (ICC) Asia development wing, the Asian Cricket Council (ACC), helped bring trainers, who taught the basics of the game to a few dozen Physical Education teachers.

'At that time, no one I knew in China even knew what cricket was,' Zhang told me one morning at the CCA's spartan office, which sits in a government complex next to the Temple of Heaven, which hosts several sports administrative bodies. These bodies had been given this prime real estate when China started infusing billions of dollars into sports in the lead-up to the Beijing Olympics. The money flowed pretty much everywhere but to the CCA, as its office evinced; it seems to have missed out thanks to cricket not being an Olympic sport.

After that first session in 2005, the PE teachers went back to their schools and introduced the game there. A first national tournament was held the following year, which allowed the CCA to select a first men's national team, at the under-fifteen level. With this burst of support from the ICC, administrators quickly proclaimed they would bring China to a World Cup by 2020 – a claim that was perhaps made in haste.

The men's team has since struggled to compete, suffering humiliating losses, with the nadir coming at a 2009 ACC tournament. The men's team played three matches, losing all – to Iran, Thailand, and the Maldives, hardly cricketing giants. The team lost by 307 runs to Iran in their first match; were bowled out for 37 against Thailand, losing by 8 wickets; and suffered a 315-run defeat to the Maldives.

Perhaps the biggest challenge facing the game is official policy that overwhelmingly favours Olympic sports. Since the PRC's founding in 1949, Chinese leaders made it a priority for the sports programme to win as many medals at the Olympics as possible. The road to the Beijing Olympics in 2008 intensified this medal mania, when it became a national project to ensure that China secured more gold medals than the US. A consequence of this is that non-Olympic sports are not given adequate support.

When I arrived at SSU, the first thing I noticed was this Olympics-based caste system. The cricket team was practising on artificial turf, while just across the road from them, the rugby players trained on perfectly maintained grass fields. Thanks to rugby making it to the Olympics in 2016, they were plucked out of the second-tier status that their cricket colleagues were still stuck in.

Given all these hurdles, the success of the women's team has been spectacular. The team, which only made its debut in 2007, has taken to the game rapidly. Rashid Khan, the Pakistani coach of the Chinese men's and women's teams, told me their progress had been 'nothing less than remarkable'. 'Seven years ago, no one knew how to hold a bat or grip the ball,' he told me one morning before training. 'When we first played Hong Kong some six years ago, we lost by a big margin. We played the same Hong Kong team recently, and we now beat them by an even bigger margin.'

The week I visited, the team was training for the Asian Games in South Korea. At the tournament, the women's team came close to making history and becoming the first Chinese cricket team to win a medal. The team reached the semi-finals, but lost the bronze medal match to Sri Lanka. 'The biggest obstacle for us is that we can't train on grass,' said former Bangladesh cricketer Monjurul Islam, who coaches the youth team. 'If we're allowed to do that, we will be even better.'

Steep Learning Curve

Cricket will never replace the sports that Chinese follow with a passion – from table tennis and badminton to football and now basketball. The challenges before China's cricket project are indeed many, but perhaps the biggest positive has been the story of Huang and her team.

One day after training, I sat with Huang in the SSU canteen. 'I didn't know what cricket was,' she told me, when a teacher at the university where she was an undergraduate asked her to enrol for try-outs. 'I wanted to play volleyball, but I went anyway. The first training session I had was so special – learning how to bat, learning to lift my elbow to play a shot. It was a real challenge! But

I immediately fell in love with cricket, and I have been playing the game ever since that day.'

By the time Huang graduated, four years later, she was showing such talent for the game that the university went out of its way to keep her on as a student, enrolling her in a postgraduate sports course. She repaid their trust by leading the team to two consecutive ACC tournament finals, the pinnacle for Asian cricket.

Huang told me it had been a steep learning curve. 'The first time I competed with foreigners, there was a very big gap, and it was disheartening,' she said. 'We had one big disadvantage. We only started playing in university, but the foreigners usually start at a young age. The gap was huge at first, but after our England tour, I feel we have really closed it.'

The next generation of Chinese cricketers is starting much younger. One afternoon, I drove out to Beijing's suburbs near the airport to the sprawling campus of Aidi, a private school. What I heard as I entered wasn't the sound of dribbling basketballs that one usually hears on Chinese playgrounds, but the familiar sound of leather hitting willow.

Aidi is one of seventy schools in half a dozen Chinese provinces where the sport is now being taught (it is also played in thirty-one universities). With 140 active coaches, the game is being played by around 12,000 people and growing. At Aidi, kids as young as nine are now playing cricket. 'At first, students were very curious about this sport. They didn't know what cricket is, and even I thought I was teaching them baseball!' Yu Hai, the Aidi coach, told me.

'Kids at this age easily get curious about new things, so they found it very interesting to learn cricket. Now they love the game, and want to play and train even if it is raining or windy in Beijing. Cricket is a good sport – it is a good way to train their hands and brains. By teaching them we will also help promote the game in China because they are now starting training at such a young age. When we had our national tournament this year, so many parents came out to support their children. I think there is a lot of hope for the game to grow here.'

Huang and her teammates are their inspiration. They found cricket by chance, but have devoted their lives to a sport that few in their country have heard of.

Playing against All Odds

As Huang and I were chatting at SSU, Liu Xiaonan, their diminutive twenty-two-year-old wicketkeeper, joined us. 'I'm happiest when I'm playing cricket,' she told me. 'It's a gentleman's sport. I like the teamwork, and the way we support each other.'

Through cricket, Liu told me, she has found her best friends. In the sport, Huang and Liu have also found an escape from the pressures of university life in China – a liberation from one of the world's most stressful academic environments. Both, however, face difficult choices when they graduate, between finding a job and continuing with the sport. Cricket as a career is not an option. Players receive around 600 yuan (around $90) a month for representing their country. Huang told me she can't put a price on the game. 'When I told my parents this was my priority as a career, they were so anxious,' she said. 'At the beginning, they were not happy.'

There was little financial reward but enormous sacrifice, training day after day in the SSU campus, with all the limited facilities and countless other obstacles of playing a sport that no one in your country had heard of. 'Of course, it has been difficult. Balancing my life and cricket has been very difficult,' Huang told me. 'But I have no regrets. Cricket is a social experience for me. The game taught me better values.'

If she had doubts about her path and her passion, all that changed one day in 2010, when it was China's turn to host the Asian Games, in the southern city of Guangzhou. For the first time, an international cricket tournament would be played on Chinese soil. A stadium was set up in Guangzhou, and a pitch, laid by a curator from Bangladesh.

Huang flew her parents down from the far northeast, and they quietly took their place in the stands among a curious Chinese crowd. 'I will never forget that day,' Huang told me. 'When I walked out to bat for the Chinese national team, in front of my family, representing my country, my cricket bat in hand, that was the proudest moment of my life.'

Epilogue

China After the Pandemic

WHERE IS CHINA HEADED? THE question I get asked more often than any other is the one that is the hardest to answer. Predictions, particularly when it comes to China, have often proven to be spectacularly wrong. One only needs to look at confident forecasts of a collapse every time a mini crisis emerges in China; these are so frequent that they have spawned an entire genre of books that continues to thrive, unfettered by any limitations of accuracy. At the same time, thirty years after the events at Tiananmen Square, the Party has proved far more resilient than most had expected. 'The land that failed to fail,' pithily summed up one essay, reflecting China's ability to defy all predictions of its impending collapse.[1]

If it is foolhardy to predict where China is headed, then perhaps it is more instructive to look back. When I left China in 2018, the country was reflecting on forty years of its 'reform and opening up'. In 1978, China's GDP was $149 billion, just 1.75 per cent of the global GDP. That year, the country's economy was about the same size as India's $140 billion. China's per capita GDP was $156, even less than India's $203. Fast forward forty years to 2018, and China's economy is $12.2 trillion, accounting for 15 per cent of the global GDP, and nearly five times that of India's. Its per capita income is $8,825, over four times India's $1,939. China is the world's second-largest economy, and is forecast to surpass the US by 2030. From an isolated communist state, China is now a lynchpin in the globalized world.[2]

The past four decades haven't been without challenges, which have cropped up, curiously enough, every ten years since Deng Xiaoping's reforms. In 1989, the Communist Party faced an existential challenge as the country was roiled by pro-democracy student protests, ultimately crushed brutally by Deng. The Party adapted and evolved, and Deng sidelined conservatives to usher in the economic opening up of the early 1990s. In 1998, China weathered the Asian financial crisis, and, a decade later, China, in the wake of the 2008 Olympics and the global financial crisis, emerged even stronger, increasingly convinced of the inevitability of its own rise and the decline of the West.

Safe to say, another crisis was due. The Chinese leadership knew it too. The phrase of choice in Beijing in 2019 was to watch out not only for 'black swans' – referring to an unexpected crisis – but also for 'grey rhinos', which lurked in plain sight. When Xi Jinping addressed Party officials in September 2019, at the Party School in Beijing, the rhinos were on his mind – from the slowing economy and the trade war with America – as he warned of 'complicated struggles' facing the country. He specifically mentioned, as major risks, the economy, China's diplomatic environment, Hong Kong's unprecedented protests, and Taiwan, where the prospect of reunification seemed slimmer than ever.

Xi was speaking on the eve of what the Party was billing as the first of four key anniversaries. In October 2019, China marked seventy years of the People's Republic with a grand military parade. In 2020, the country is celebrating the landmark of eliminating absolute poverty. In 2021, the Party turns 100, while the following year, the twentieth Party Congress will mark ten years of Xi's rule. For China, these are landmarks on what Xi likes to call the country's 'Road to Rejuvenation' and towards achieving the 'Chinese Dream'.

Yet, three months after his speech, little could Xi have imagined that the biggest test of his rule would come not from faraway America but from the mother of all black swans – a tiny microbe that would surface in Wuhan, a beautiful town of lakes and parks that is famous in Chinese history for launching the uprising that brought down the country's last imperial dynasty in 1911.

* * *

I write this halfway through 2020, a year where I have lost count of the number of weeks I have spent in lockdown – both in China and in India. At this point, the chaos of the first few weeks of the pandemic in China already appears a distant memory; the country seems to have dealt with the crisis, and its economy is already limping back to life (albeit facing innumerable challenges), while the rest of the world, from India to the US, is still grappling with the consequences.

The coronavirus pandemic exposed in stark relief both the weaknesses and the strengths of the Chinese system. When I landed in Beijing in early January 2020, no one there had any inkling of the horrors that were unfolding halfway across the country in Wuhan. In mid-January, the only thing on everyone's mind was getting their shopping done before the lunar new year holiday. News of a 'pneumonia outbreak' in Wuhan had received passing mention in newspapers, but, even in the middle of January, officials were telling the media that it didn't travel between people, that it was some kind of strange infection from a seafood market.

When Xi addressed the country on 20 January, warning of a 'grim' situation, things in Beijing changed overnight. I saw upfront the power of the state being unleashed in the Chinese capital for the two weeks that I was there, before I had to fly back to India with an expiring visa and airports closing. Overnight, the streets in the capital emptied, everyone wore masks and neighbourhood committees in every residential block began organizing themselves for a 'people's war' against the coronavirus. There was a sense of both alarm and determination that I didn't see in many other countries, even when they were reporting thousands of daily cases.

For three months, the city was in complete lockdown. The suffocating measures worked: even if the low numbers in Beijing were met with a sense of disbelief outside China, there was no question that they had quashed the outbreak, as I heard from numerous credible sources there, from journalists to doctors. By April, Beijing was coming back to life, even though it had to deal with a second spurt of infections in May, tied to a meat market.

Yet, this very same all-powerful state failed spectacularly in its initial response to the outbreak, no matter that the subsequent rewriting of events trumpeted China's unqualified success. It was rewriting made possible by the mass outbreak and slow response in America, which the state media in China gleefully highlighted. But, in those first few weeks, the Party came under such enormous pressure as I had never before seen in over a decade in China. People asked searching questions about where the leadership had been for weeks as horrors unfolded in Wuhan. In February, Xi admitted the pandemic posed 'a major test of China's system and capacity for governance', as he chaired a special meeting of the Party's top Politburo Standing Committee.[3] This followed an extraordinary 25 January meeting of the Standing Committee, proceedings of which were televised for the first time ever, as the leadership scrambled to respond to growing public anger and to make up for days of inaction.

It was only on 31 December 2019 that the Wuhan government announced an outbreak of viral pneumonia, although hospitals were seeing an uptick of cases since early December. Until 20 January, Wuhan authorities would maintain there was no proof of human-to-human transmission of the virus. Decisions taken by authorities during those vital twenty-one days would come to affect the lives of millions , not just in China, but around the world. On 3 February, *Caixin*, a Chinese magazine known for its independent reporting – at least as independent as a media outlet can be in Xi's China – published the first of a four-part investigation. The article, headlined 'How Wuhan lost the fight to contain the coronavirus', laid bare a month-long cover-up that had allowed the novel coronavirus outbreak to spread, while the Chinese public remained completely unaware.[4] That very same day, the lead story on the front page of the *People's Daily* reported breathlessly on how a visit by President Xi Jinping to a village in Qinghai province had transformed its fortunes. That visit, incidentally, had taken place in August 2016.

For me, the two contrasting stories in two very different media outlets summed up the two sides of the China model. The Wuhan outbreak served as a reminder that when given the space to work, Chinese journalists can play a much-needed watchdog role. We now know, thanks to the reporting of *Caixin*, *Caijing*, *Beijing News* and a few other outlets, that the crisis was unfolding in Wuhan's hospitals throughout December, even as the city and provincial leadership hid the scale of the outbreak. As a doctor at the Wuhan Union Hospital told *Caixin*, clinics were being flooded since late December, with as many as 900 patients a day showing pneumonia-like symptoms.

On 30 December, eight doctors sent warnings about the outbreak on chat groups. Among the whistle-blowers was Li Wenliang, an ophthalmologist. The eight were hauled up by the police for 'spreading rumours' and were forced to sign statements withdrawing their claims. It is now clear that the Wuhan government lied about the number of infections until at least 16 January, which was, incidentally, when the city and province's annual political congress ended. While the congress was being convened, the official number of infections remained constant. On 11 January, the government said the number had actually declined to forty-one. By that point, there were likely tens of thousands of cases in Wuhan alone. 'All doctors in our hospital knew it was not correct as it was so different from what we'd seen,' one doctor told *Caixin*, which reported that the number of infections had grown so vast that CT scan machines in hospitals had started breaking down.

Moreover, a number of doctors and medical workers began falling ill, although hospitals that employed the doctors barred them from disclosing this. As mentioned, the provincial government would maintain until 20 January that this viral pneumonia was under control and there was no clear evidence of human-to-human transmission – a premature and ill-considered statement that helped magnify the crisis. Indeed, on 19 January, the local government even held an annual community dinner for 40,000 families. It was only the following day, when respected Chinese epidemiologist Zhong Nanshan revealed the scale of the crisis, did Wuhan realize it was in the middle of an unprecedented outbreak. Dr Zhong had risen to fame during the SARS (Severe Acute Respiratory Syndrome) fight in 2002–03. Just three days later, with little warning, the entire province of Hubei was put in quarantine – from a buffet dinner attended by tens of thousands to complete lockdown in ninety-six hours.

We only know these facts thanks to the brave Chinese journalists who were reporting relentlessly from Wuhan's ground zero. That they were able to do so wasn't by accident. The central government in Beijing has often deliberately granted limited space to the media in times of crisis. Doing so serves at least two purposes: it releases a pressure valve that aids in assuaging public anger, and it helps the central government identify the source of the problem when under-fire provincial officials are likely to be hiding facts to save their careers.

Of course, all this is possible because Beijing temporarily sees it as in its interest to project what the scholar Maria Repnikova calls 'an image of managed transparency'.[5] Unfortunately, the space for such reporting is usually fleeting, as was the case after the Sichuan earthquake in 2008 and the high-speed railway accident in Wenzhou in 2011 that claimed forty lives. By March, media outlets were ordered to cease independent reporting and follow Party guidelines on reporting on the pandemic.

The death of the whistle-blower doctor Li Wenliang on 7 February, after he had contracted the coronavirus, unleashed a wave of public rage on Chinese social media that was unprecedented on many levels. I had personally never seen anything like it. The social media noise underlined public anxiety over the outbreak, anger at the system, and the sense of immediacy of this crisis: anyone could be affected. On WeChat, everyone – from businessmen and academics to taxi drivers and primary school teachers – posted tributes to Li. The lyrics of 'Do you hear the people sing' from *Les Misérables* went viral, and the phrase 'freedom of speech' trended briefly on Weibo before censors stepped in.

If this appeared to be a tipping point, the Party, once again, fought back. As the crisis subsided in China, thanks to sweeping measures – from building temporary hospitals in Wuhan to deploying technology to track every single person's movements – the war against the virus was now turned into a rallying call ahead of the Party's 100th anniversary in 2021.

* * *

What the pandemic has appeared to do is accelerate trends that are already shaping China's political landscape, rather than altering them, such as the move towards greater control and centralization. Indeed, the lesson the Party seems to have drawn is that greater control is the answer. This is very different from the view of some Chinese: that it is a systemic culture of secrecy that prides security above all else that explains the initial failures in dealing with COVID-19; it is a culture that incentivizes local officials to cover up, control the media and maintain 'stability' at all costs, until a crisis has spiralled beyond control.

Moreover, they see the continued stifling of independent Chinese voices as hurting the government's own mission of trying to convince the world of its response. When much of the media is state controlled and there are few independent outlets mediating China's rapidly expanding engagement with the world, scepticism will likely abound overseas; this is even though China was, ironically, more transparent in its handling of the COVID-19 outbreak than it was during the SARS crisis in 2002.

Dali Yang at the University of Chicago, who is one of the sharpest political scientists studying China, told me that the pandemic had, in one sense, provided the perfect snapshot of the

Chinese system – of its strengths and weaknesses. If the biggest error, in his view, was the crackdown on Wuhan's doctors, telling them to keep silent about the crisis they were witnessing in their wards, it was also an error, he said, that this system would keep repeating as long as control remained its abiding objective.

'It appears that from the start everything was done to downplay the severity of the situation rather than, say, let's err on the side of caution,' he said. 'Wuhan having its annual political congress in early January was crucially important. This system has gotten used to the idea that you cannot allow anything to upset the political atmosphere during those times. Accidents in such systems are bound to happen again and again. It cannot become fail-safe. There were major missed opportunities in this case, but in the future there will still be a problem. The nature of the Chinese system is you tend to have this kind of shirking, but when things escalate it is capable of decisive action, as in this case it did by locking down a city with 9 million people.

'That's not a decision that most other countries could have taken, which is why the Chinese are actually congratulating themselves, but the problem is by the time they locked Wuhan down, 5 million people had left. When China did respond nationally after 20 January, they were able to get a lot of people who dealt with SARS involved and that mattered hugely in their response. Only, it was too late for the [rest of the] world. The most important lesson is that there has to be more transparency – an open environment for sharing and discussion. It was remarkable how doctors were cowed into not speaking. It became almost like a groupthink situation where even when everyone saw it was contagious, there was no public airing. No one was willing to shout this was contagious, and that we have to take action in Wuhan. That, to me, is just tragic.'

The challenges unleashed by the pandemic have by no means been vanquished, even if China may be emerging from it. For the Party leadership, COVID-19 has been the biggest crisis since Tiananmen, Richard McGregor, author of *The Party: The Secret World of China's Communist Rulers*, told me.[6] 'We've not only got what is going to be an extended economic downturn, but we have also a global political crisis over the origins of the virus, and responsibility and accountability for it. China is a much bigger economy, and a much more powerful country. That doesn't mean that it can sail through something like this, and they are fighting on a number of fronts.'

For McGregor too, the pandemic exposed both the deep weaknesses and strengths of the Chinese model. 'First of all, there's absolutely no doubt that China mishandled the early stages of this crisis. Now, we don't quite know exactly what happened. There was certainly a cover-up at some levels. There was a bureaucratic mess, fighting between the localities and the centre. There were all sorts of things happening and that, I think, was a show of China's weaknesses. In other words, a lack of openness, lack of transparency, endemic bureaucratic problems, and a fear of offending and reporting to the centre.

'Now, once China started to take it seriously, we did see a quite remarkable demonstration of the power of the Party-state. When you think what they managed to do, in a short period of time – no discussion like we have in messy democracies – they locked down in residences up to 700 million people, they mobilized the army, they mobilized the paramilitary, they commandeered businesses to make personal protective equipment for the state, they shut factories, they shut businesses. So we did see a real display of what the state in China can do. And, on its own terms, it was effective.'

* * *

If the pandemic is accelerating existing political trends in China, it is also sharpening the debate about the China model – a debate that is unfolding both within the country and around the world. For supporters of the model, it has underlined the strengths of centralized authoritarianism. For detractors, it has showed why a system that views transparency as a threat failed at a very crucial test. This was a debate that, in the spring of 2020, was heating up within China too. In the aftermath of the initial response, real estate tycoon Ren Zhiqiang penned a searing essay criticizing the political path under Xi, voicing a sentiment I heard in Beijing, from academic and business circles, deeply uncomfortable with what they saw as political regression.

Ren wrote of the Politburo meeting that was held in February: 'People used all manner of empty boosts and flattery to talk about this meeting's great significance', praising it for its 'wise and correct strategic vision'. People were told 'the Party's decision about the virus was correct' and 'it showed the significant advantages of the Central Party leadership and Socialism with Chinese Characteristics'. He wrote that when it seemed 'the entire country was cheering madly about the Great Leader's speech' he felt like China had returned to the era of the Great Leap Forward, 'when everyone was waving their red flags, holding up their Little Red books, shouting "10,000 years, 10,000 years, 10,000 years" for the Leader'. But when Ren studied the speech, what he saw 'standing there was not some Emperor showing us his "new clothes", but a clown with no clothes on who was still determined to play emperor'.[7]

The other view that the pandemic has accelerated in China is that the country now has a moment of strategic opportunity to push its global ambitions – a dominant goal of the Xi era, as we have seen – and that it must continue challenging the US. As the leading Chinese strategic affairs thinker Yan Xuetong of Tsinghua University told me, the global response to the pandemic had 'shown the lack of global leadership'. His view, which is being echoed in Beijing, is that regardless of China's initial missteps, the chaotic US response, followed by the spread of protests over the summer of 2020 ignited by the Black Lives Matter movement, had ultimately bolstered China's position in the world.

'A world without global leadership may last for a decade or more,' Yan told me. 'The competition between China and the US prevents the collective leadership of major powers. Therefore, although there is a vacuum for global leadership, no country seems ready to fulfil it in the near future. Henry Kissinger said that the pandemic will alter the world. Nevertheless, I would argue that it only strengthens the existing international political trends rather than change them.

'Most of the current international trends occurred before the pandemic. For instance, the anti-globalization trend started since Eastern European states adopted an anti-immigration policy in 2015, the decentralization of the EU has started since Brexit in 2016, China–US bipolar competition started since 2017, and some industrial chains have broken since [the US–China trade war in] 2018. The pandemic will escalate these trends, rather than reverse them.'

The Party is convinced it is still on track to achieve its goals for the 'two centenaries': to build what it calls 'a moderately prosperous society' by the time the Party marks its 100th anniversary in 2021, and have in place 'a modern socialist country that is prosperous, strong, democratic, culturally advanced and harmonious' by 2049, when the PRC turns 100. The Party is also working to build a 'world-class military' by 2050 – in other words, one that will be able to rival the US militarily.[8]

The Party may be convinced of it, but that by no means implies that China's forward march is an inevitability. The CPC faces serious challenges, both at home and abroad. Some are of its own making. The political transformations we have seen may have confirmed Xi's unrivalled standing in the Party – elevating his status to that of Mao Zedong and Deng – but it also signalled the dismantling of the model of collective leadership that Deng had left as his legacy. It was a model that many even in the Party believe allowed China to escape the fate of other authoritarian and communist states; it was an authoritarian country without a dictator, a communist nation that embraced state-led capitalism, and gave its citizens economic and social liberties lacking even in some democracies.

This has created its own stresses that aren't often easy to see from the outside. On the economic front, the Party has to steer a slowing economy that is diluting what has been one of its key sources of legitimacy. China has made huge strides in creating an innovation economy, but the next steps are getting ever harder, particularly as it confronts an increasingly difficult external environment. Globally, the pushback against China has been growing. The country's global aspirations depend as much on its own ambitions as they do on how the rest of the world, including India, chooses to accommodate them, and most importantly, whether a credible alternative emerges for countries that are drifting deeper into China's orbit.

The political scientist David Shambaugh has suggested China is now akin to a car approaching a roundabout in the road ahead, with four paths heading in different directions.[9] Turn left, and it would head down the road of neo-totalitarianism, where the modest liberties that today's China affords would be further constricted. The car could also carry on driving straight, on the path that Shambaugh describes as hard authoritarianism – the politics of the Xi era. He suggests two other possibilities. The car could turn slightly away, towards a soft authoritarianism reflecting the politics of the 2000s, during the Jiang Zemin and early Hu Jintao periods. The last option, he suggests, would be semi-democracy, a limited political liberalization in the mode of Singapore, where the existence of other political parties and some free expression are allowed, but ultimately, Party control prevails.

Perhaps when the car is as hard to drive as this one, driving straight ahead would be the likeliest option. These four choices, of course, are all predicated on the Party being in control of the vehicle, which is not a foregone conclusion.

If it's foolhardy to predict China's future, one thing that 2020 has reminded us, perhaps not in the most ideal way, is how the country impacts our lives. It shouldn't have to take crises to tell us that, but alas, we in India don't otherwise seem to pay enough close attention to our biggest neighbour, whose political, economic and social transformations will continue to affect our lives, in ways we might not always realize.

Acknowledgements

I WAS LUCKY TO ARRIVE in Beijing in what seemed to be a golden age for journalism in China, in the summer of 2009. Heading into the 2008 Olympics, the Communist Party had loosened up many controls, not only on how foreign journalists reported and travelled in China, but on the domestic media as well. While Facebook and Twitter were banned the year I arrived, Chinese social media began to boom. Weibo was a revelation. Stories abounded on Weibo, from land grabs to tales of local-level corruption. Even the greatest political scandal in many years in China, the fall of Bo Xilai, first unfolded on Weibo, with a real-time account of how his police chief fled to seek refuge in an American Consulate. Weibo was a fantastic tool to find stories and reach out to people. Of course, this golden age turned out to be fleeting, and by the time I left in 2018, the Party had struck back and muzzled the media once again.

This book would not have been possible without the fantastic journalists I came to know in Beijing, some of whom became dear friends. When I first landed in Beijing, and felt more than a little overwhelmed, Angela Bao, wise beyond her years, showed me the ropes, and was an anchor I was so lucky to be able to count on. I am grateful beyond words to Hu Yinan, Li Boya, Ma Zheng, Qu Ang, Sisi Tang, Hu Chao, Vincent Tang, Deng Wenjie, Cici Chen and Yu Bokun for their unflinching kindness, for everything that they taught me, and above all, for their friendship.

In Beijing, the folks at the International Press Centre at the Ministry of Foreign Affairs (MFA) have always treated journalists from India with warmth and kindness, regardless of the vicissitudes of the India–China relationship. My thanks to Zhou Li, Wang Huan, Lv Yongxiu, Xu Xinxin, and many others for their help over the years. At the MFA Information Department, I will always be indebted to Yan Jiarong, Liu Wenjia and Liu Jing for their kindness. My gratitude also to Zou Yonghong, Xie Liyan and Ji Rong at the Press Section of the Chinese Embassy in New Delhi, for always going out of the way to be of help.

My fellow members of the Indian press corps in Beijing became a family away from home. I consider myself fortunate to have shared the company of K.J.M. Varma, Saibal Dasgupta and Sutirtho Patranobis for so many years. I often wondered how different my experience of China may have been in their absence. No matter how difficult the situation, our friendship was a source of strength. Ours has been such a unique and long-lasting bond. For a bunch of highly competitive journalists on the same story, that is no small thing. A Chinese journalist once described us in an article as a 'Gang of Four'. She wasn't wrong. In Beijing, I was so fortunate to receive the boundless generosity and friendship of Mehernosh and Wen Pastakia, who always treated me like family. A travel tip: if you ever find yourself in Beijing and missing a slice of India, the Taj Pavilion should be your first port of call.

If there is one person who is responsible for making my China experience possible, that is N. Ram at *The Hindu*. Ram encouraged me to move to Shanghai in 2008 – and most importantly, to learn the language – and later gave me a once-in-a-lifetime opportunity to report for *The Hindu* from Beijing. There is no better newspaper in India to work for, and none that comes close when it comes to the seriousness with which the paper takes its foreign coverage. I have had the good fortune to work with, and come to know, so many fantastic colleagues at *The Hindu*, in Chennai, Mumbai and

New Delhi, who are too many to name here. I learnt everything about how to report at the Chennai bureau, and continue to learn every day from the incredible reporters who make the newspaper what it is.

My gratitude and thanks to the editors I worked with at *The Hindu* – N. Ravi, Malini Parthasarathy, Siddharth Varadarajan, Mukund Padmanabhan and Suresh Nambath – for their support. To S. Ramanujam, the Regional General Manager of *The Hindu* in New Delhi, I will need an entire book to list the number of ways you have been such an incredible source of help over the years. I am always in your debt.

A lot of reporting that appears in this book came from stories I pursued for *India Today*. And many of those story ideas came from Aroon Purie, whose deep interest and razor sharp sense of what was happening in China never ceased to amaze me. It was Mr Purie who pushed me to extend my time in China when I thought of packing my bags in 2014. I stayed reluctantly, and in many ways, that decision changed my life, both professionally and personally. Mr Purie also convinced me, despite my deep reluctance, to embrace television as a medium. As much as I disliked lugging around that JVC camera when I reported – there is perhaps no greater magnet for the local police in China - I learnt a lot from the experience, and am so much the better for it. At *India Today*, Raj Chengappa was much, much more than my Editor. I am lucky to count on him as a friend and mentor, someone who I have always turned to for advice when I most needed it. Ranjit Sahaya, more than anyone, made every day at *India Today* a pleasure, and has been a constant source of encouragement. I am grateful to Kalli Purie and Rahul Kanwal at *India Today TV* for their patience with a reporter who was clueless about the world of television (and is only slightly less clueless today), and most importantly, for giving more space to the China story than any other network in India. I will forever be grateful to Shekhar Gupta and Pranab Dhal Samanta for their trust and continued support, both when I first moved to *India Today* and more than that, in the years since.

Most of this book was written in 2019, a year I spent as a visiting fellow first at Brookings India and then at the University of Hong Kong. When I moved back to India, Brookings India gave me the perfect platform to pause, take a deep breath, and try and make sense of my time in China. I am indebted to Vikram Singh Mehta, Shamika Ravi, Kabir Vasudeva, and above all, to Dhruva Jaishankar, for bringing me on board. Most of the research that you will find in Chapter 6 on Chinese investments in India derives from a paper that I worked on for Brookings India, which was published in March 2020. A lot of work went into making that paper a reality, and it wouldn't have been possible without the help and guidance of Dhruva, Constantino Xavier, Zehra Kazmi and Nitika Nayar at Brookings India.

The Asia Global Institute at the University of Hong Kong, where I spent three months towards the end of 2019, provided me the perfect environment to work on this book. Those three months coincided with the peak of the Hong Kong protest movement, which I write about in Chapter 17. Every day was stimulating at Hong Kong U, whose faculty, and more importantly, brilliant and passionate students I came to know, gave me so much food for thought. My deep gratitude to Chen Zhiwu, K.C. Kwok, Yvonne Mak, and Joyce Yan at the Asia Global Institute for all their generosity and kindness.

This book was vastly improved by feedback from a number of people who were kind enough to read the first draft, or sections of it. Some requested to stay anonymous. You know who you are, and I am so grateful for your advice. I am grateful to Shivshankar Menon, who has always been so generous in sharing his unparalleled knowledge of China, and, of course, with his time. His deep insights on the boundary question have greatly enriched this book. At the very start of this book project in late 2018, when I was unsure of how to even begin what seemed to be an impossible task, a conversation with S. Jaishankar helped set me on the right track. His advice was invaluable, and I am so grateful for his encouragement and generosity over the years.

I have benefited enormously from the kindness and support of a number people who have not only helped me in the process of writing this book, but in making sense of the China story over many years. This book wouldn't have been possible without you. My heartfelt gratitude to Indrani Bagchi, Gautam Bambawale, M. Taylor Fravel, Kai Friese, Han Hua, Ma Jiali, Manoj Joshi, Ashok Kantha, S.L. Narasimhan, Nirupama Rao, Shyam Saran, Zorawar Daulet Singh, Jeffrey Wasserstrom, and Chen Zhiwu.

To Swati Chopra at HarperCollins, this book is as much yours as it is mine. This book would not have happened without Swati, who first suggested I try and attempt and put down my China experience on paper. I was extremely hesitant, but it was her encouragement that helped me get over my reluctance. Swati has travelled with me every step of the way on this two-year journey; in many ways, I followed her. She has been an incredible editor to work with. She has devoted so much time, attention and care towards making this book possible. At HarperCollins, I am also deeply grateful to Shatarupa Ghoshal for her work on the book, and to Saurav Das who gave this book a beautiful cover. The cover image, from Nanchang in Jiangxi province, appealed to me on many levels. It shows the Tengwang Pavilion, or the Pavilion of Prince Teng, a beautiful structure on the banks of the Yangtze river that goes back to the seventh century. It was destroyed and rebuilt some two dozen times over the years. Nanchang is also a place of historical importance, where the Chinese civil war essentially began with an uprising led by the Communists in 1927 that triggered events that would ultimately, twenty-two years later, result in the Communist Party coming to power. The image on the cover is one of restoration and renewal, of history and modernity, and encompassing all of that, a sense of mystery, hidden in the light and shadow. It also appealed to me on a personal level. Jiangxi happens to be one of the three provinces in China I'm yet to visit – a reminder that there is so much more of this story that I must still discover.

This book is dedicated to my wife and to my parents. My father still likes to joke that I conned him into agreeing to my leaving home for the US at the age of seventeen, on a promise to follow my passion and study microbiology. I ended up falling in love with history, which led me to a career in journalism. My mother and father have backed me through all my career choices with unconditional love. I owe everything to them.

Not a word in this book would have been possible without the unbelievable support and encouragement from my wife for every day these past nine years that we have known each other. Embarking on a book project, especially during the roller-coaster that the last two years have been, was an utter luxury. Through all the ups-and-downs, from moving our entire life from Beijing to India – in the company of an infant and two dogs, no less – to then confronting an even more chaotic move to Hong Kong in the midst of the protests – which finally didn't happen, leaving us apart for three months – and topping all that off with an unforgettable journey from China to India in the midst of the coronavirus pandemic (which ended with fourteen days in quarantine), she handled every twist and turn with the most unimaginable sense of poise and equanimity. I have learnt so much, and continue to learn, every day, from you. This book is, above all else, for you.

Notes

Introduction

1. Xinhua, 'Xi chairs leadership meeting on epidemic control', 3 February 2020, http://www.xinhuanet.com/english/2020-02/03/c_138753250.htm, accessed on 1 July 2020.

1: In Mao's Shadow

1. Cato Institute, https://www.cato.org/friedman-prize/mao-yushi, accessed on 1 June 2020.
2. Ananth Krishnan, 'The fallen god', *The Hindu*, 31 December 2011, https://www.thehindu.com/features/magazine/the-fallen-god/article2763305.ece, accessed on 1 June 2020.
3. Xinhua, 'Socialism with Chinese Characteristics enters a new era: Xi', 18 October 2017, http://www.xinhuanet.com/english/2017-10/18/c_136688475.htm, accessed on 1 June 2020.
4. Richard McGregor, *The Party: The Secret World of China's Communist Rulers*, Allen Lane, 2010, p. xiii.
5. Ibid., p. 17.
6. Jonathan D. Spence, *The Search for Modern China*, Second Edition, Norton, 1999, pp. 489–90.
7. John Garnaut, *Engineers of the Soul: What Australia Needs to Know about Ideology in Xi Jinping's China*, Asian Strategic and Economic Seminar Series, https://sinocism.com/p/engineers-of-the-soul-ideology-in, accessed on 1 June 2020.
8. Ibid.

9. Spence, op. cit., pp. 489–94.
10. Yang Jisheng, *Tombstone: The Great Chinese Famine 1958–1962*, Farrar Strous and Giroux, 2012.
11. Choi Chi-Yuk, 'Outspoken liberal magazine stops publication', *South China Morning Post*, 18 July 2016, https://www.scmp.com/news/china/policies-politics/article/1991412/outspoken-liberal-chinese-magazine-yanhuang-chunqiu, accessed on 1 June 2020.
12. Tania Branigan, 'Red songs ring out in Chinese city's new Cultural Revolution', *Guardian*, 22 April 2011, https://www.theguardian.com/world/2011/apr/22/red-songs-chinese-cultural-revolution, accessed on 1 June 2020.
13. Constitution of the Communist Party of China, http://www.xinhuanet.com/english/download/Constitution_of_the_Communist_Party_of_China.pdf, accessed on 1 June 2020.
14. Ibid.

2: The Rise of Xi

1. Francois Bougon, *Inside the Mind of Xi Jinping*, Westland Publications, 2018, p. 50.
2. Austin Ramzy, 'China's Cultural Revolution explained', *New York Times*, 14 May 2016, https://www.nytimes.com/2016/05/15/world/asia/china-cultural-revolution-explainer.html, accessed on 1 June 2020.
3. Bougon, op. cit., p. 51.
4. Ibid.
5. Ibid., pp. 44–45.
6. Ananth Krishnan, 'The princeling from the grassroots', *The Hindu*, 5 November 2012, https://www.thehindu.com/opinion/op-ed/the-princeling-from-the-grass-roots/article4064948.ece, accessed on 1 June 2020.
7. Xinhua, 'CPC has 89.6 million members', 30 June 2018, http://www.xinhuanet.com/english/2018-06/30/c_137292146.htm, accessed on 1 June 2020.
8. Minxin Pei, *China's Crony Capitalism: The Dynamics of Regime Decay*, Harvard University Press, 2016, p. 261.
9. Xinhua, 'Zhou Yongkang arrested, expelled from CPC', http://en.people.cn/n/2014/1206/c90000-8819004.html, accessed on 1 June 2020.
10. Ananth Krishnan, 'Is China more corrupt than India?', *India Today*, 16 December 2014, https://www.dailyo.in/politics/is-china-more-corrupt-than-india/story/1/1098.html, accessed on 1 June 2020.
11. Li Hongwei, 'Chindia: Home to a third of humanity', *Global Times*, 11 August 2011, http://www.globaltimes.cn/content/670503.shtml, accessed on 1 June 2020.

12. Ananth Krishnan, 'Death in Beijing', *India Today*, 24 February 2018, https://www.indiatoday.in/magazine/the-big-story/story/20180305-death-in-beijing-chinese-officials-suicide-xi-jinping-1176000-2018-02-22, accessed on 1 June 2020.
13. Human Rights Watch, 'Special Measures: Detention and Torture in the Chinese Communist Party's Shuanggui System', 6 December 2016, https://www.hrw.org/report/2016/12/06/special-measures/detention-and-torture-chinese-communist-partys-shuanggui-system, accessed on 1 June 2020.
14. Sutirtho Patranobis, 'China must conform to Xi, says Communist Party', *Hindustan Times*, 2 March 2016, https://www.hindustantimes.com/world/mar-2-chinaxijinpingsong/story-mdSRgpr27PBlvnxVU6g0IK.html, accessed on 1 June 2020.
15. Bougon, op. cit., p. 51.
16. Zhu Guanglei, *Governing China: Decision Making and Implementation: Interpretation of the Processes of the Chinese Government*, Foreign Languages Press, 2013, p. 24.
17. Pankaj Mishra, 'China's New Leftist', *New York Times Magazine*, 15 October 2006, https://www.nytimes.com/2006/10/15/magazine/15leftist.html, accessed on 1 June 2020.
18. Gao Yu, 'Xi Jinping: The Man', 26 January 2013, https://chinachange.org/2013/01/26/beijing-observation-xi-jinping-the-man-by-gao-yu/, accessed on 1 June 2020.
19. Ibid.
20. Ibid.
21. Cheng Li, *Chinese Politics in the Xi Jinping Era: Reassessing Collective Leadership*, Brookings Institution Press, 2016, p. 4.

3: A Battle of Ideas

1. Ananth Krishnan, 'Smooth transition', *Frontline*, December 2012, https://frontline.thehindu.com/world-affairs/article 30168640.ece, accessed on 1 June 2020.
2. Ibid.
3. 'Communiqué on the Current State of the Ideological Sphere', http://www.chinafile.com/document-9-chinafile-translation, accessed on 1 June 2020. The quotations that follow are from this document.
4. Li Junru, *Governing China in the New Era*, Foreign Languages Press, 2018, p. 57.
5. Ibid., p. 58.
6. Ananth Krishnan, 'Oxfords of the East', *India Today*, 11 April 2017, https://www.indiatoday.in/magazine/neighbours/story/20170417-china-world-class-universities-ivy-league-east-communist-party-of-china-986140-2017-04-11, accessed on 1 June 2020.

7. Louisa Lim, *The People's Republic of Amnesia: Tiananmen Revisited*, Oxford University Press, 2014, p. 201.
8. Ibid., p. 15.
9. Xu Zhangrun, 'Imminent Fears, Immediate Hopes', translated by Geremie R. Barmé, July 2018, http://chinaheritage.net/journal/imminent-fears-immediate-hopes-a-beijing-jeremiad/, accessed on 1 June 2020.
10. Ibid.
11. Jiang Shigong, 'Philosophy and History: Interpreting the Xi Jinping Era through Xi's Report to the Nineteenth National Congress of the Chinese Communist Party', *Open Times*, January 2018, https://www.thechinastory.org/cot/jiang-shigong-on-philosophy-and-history-interpreting-the-xi-jinping-era-through-xis-report-to-the-nineteenth-national-congress-of-the-ccp/, accessed on 1 June 2020.
12. Ibid.

4: The Manufacturing Miracle

1. Dipanjan Roy Choudhary, 'Yiwu keen to invite big Indian names', *Economic Times*, 7 May 2017, https://economictimes.indiatimes.com/news/economy/foreign-trade/yiwu-worlds-largest-small-commodity-wholesale-market-keen-to-invite-big-indian-business-names/articleshow/58562137.cms?from=mdr, accessed on 1 June 2020.
2. Ananth Krishnan, 'Indian traders begin legal battle to clear their names, *The Hindu*, 4 February 2012, https://www.thehindu.com/news/international/indian-traders-in-china-to-begin-legal-battle-to-clear-their-names/article2860840.ece, accessed on 1 June 2020.
3. Tim Maughan, 'Yiwu: The city where Christmas is made and sold', BBC News, 18 December 2014, https://www.bbc.com/future/article/20141218-the-hidden-home-of-christmas, accessed on 1 June 2020.
4. Press Trust of India, 'India China trade dips in 2019', *The Hindu BusinessLine*, 4 January 2020, https://www.thehindubusinessline.com/economy/india-china-trade-dips-by-nearly-3-billion-in-2019/article30567975.ece, accessed on 1 June 2020.
5. Huang Yasheng, 'Just How Capitalist is China?' 4 April 2008, MIT Sloan Research Paper No. 4699-08. Available at SSRN: https://ssrn.com/abstract=1118019, accessed on 1 June 2020.
6. Ibid.
7. Huang Yasheng, 'China's Other Path', *The Wilson Quarterly*, Spring 2010, https://www.wilsonquarterly.com/quarterly/spring-2010-the-entrepreneurial-edge/chinas-other-path/, accessed on 1 June 2020.

8. Ibid.
9. Arthur R. Kroeber, *China's Economy: What Everyone Needs To Know*, Oxford University Press, 2016, p. 8.
10. Arthur R. Kroeber, *China's Economy: What Everyone Needs To Know*, Oxford University Press, 2016, p. ix.
11. Ibid., pp. 8, 18, 30, 76, 98.
12. He Huifeng, 'Crackdown on Dongguan sex trade leaves wider economy in slump', *South China Morning Post*, 7 April 2014, https://www.scmp.com/news/china/article/1466356/crackdown-dongguan-sex-trade-leaves-wider-economy-slump, accessed on 1 June 2020.
13. Tom Phillips, 'Inside Dongguan: China's Sin City', *The Telegraph*, 1 May 2013, http://www.telegraph.co.uk/news/worldnews/asia/china/10030014/Inside-Dongguan-Chinas-Sin-City.html, accessed on 1 June 2020.
14. Glenn Leibowitz, 'Apple CEO Tim Cook: This is the number one reason we make iPhones in China', 21 December 2017, https://www.inc.com/glenn-leibowitz/apple-ceo-tim-cook-this-is-number-1-reason-we-make-iphones-in-china-its-not-what-you-think.html, accessed on 1 June 2020.
15. Press Trust of India, 'India not to import power equipment from China: R.K. Singh', *The Hindu*, 4 July 2020, https://www.thehindu.com/news/national/india-not-to-import-power-equipment-from-china-r-k-singh/article31978555.ece, accessed on 10 July 2020.
16. Amitendu Palit, *China–India Economics: Challenges, Competition and Collaboration*, Routledge, 2012, pp. 66–72.
17. Biswajit Dhar, 'Chinese cheer for Indian exports', *The Hindu BusinessLine*, 4 March 2019, https://www.thehindubusinessline.com/opinion/chinese-cheer-for-indian-exports/article26431736.ece, accessed on 1 June 2020.
18. Press Information Bureau, Government of India, http://pib.nic.in/newsite/PrintRelease.aspx?relid=187994, accessed on 1 June 2020.
19. Palit, op. cit.
20. Kroeber, op. cit., p. 45.
21. Ibid., p. 55.
22. Yasheng, 2010, op. cit.

5: From Countryside to Megacities

1. McKinsey & Company, *Comparing Urbanization in China and India*, 1 July 2010, https://www.mckinsey.com/featured-insights/urbanization/comparing-urbanization-in-china-and-india, accessed on 1 June 2020.
2. Ibid.

3. Kroeber, op. cit., p. 4.
4. Kroeber, op. cit., p. 83.
5. Chen Xiwen, *China's Agriculture, Rural Areas and Farmers*, Foreign Languages Press 2018, p. 195.
6. Lakshman Krishnamurthi and Sugandha Khandelwal, 'Agriculture journal: China versus India by the numbers', *The Wall Street Journal*, 20 September 2011, https://blogs.wsj.com/indiarealtime/2011/09/20/agriculture-journal-china-versus-india-by-the-numbers/, accessed on 1 June 2020.
7. Xinhua, 'China's high-speed railway length to top 30,000 km in 2019', 1 March 2019, https://www.chinadaily.com.cn/a/201901/03/WS5c2d7755a310d91214053454.html, accessed on 1 June 2020.
8. Martha Lawrence, Richard Bullock and Ziming Liu, *China's High-Speed Rail Development*, World Bank Group, 2019, http://documents.worldbank.org/curated/en/933411559841476316/pdf/Chinas-High-Speed-Rail-Development.pdf, accessed on 1 June 2020.
9. For more on China's ballooning debt problem, see Dinny McMahon, *China's Great Wall of Debt: Shadow Banks, Ghost Cities, Massive Loans and the End of the Chinese Miracle*, Little Brown, 2018.
10. Bloomberg News, 'Li Keqiang urges more urbanization to support growth', 21 November 2012, https://www.bloomberg.com/news/articles/2012-11-21/li-keqiang-urges-deeper-urbanization-to-support-china-s-growth, accessed on 1 June 2020.

6: The Next Tech Giant

1. Joyce Chepkemoi, 'The 25 largest internet companies in the world', *WorldAtlas*, 25 April 2017, https://www.worldatlas.com/articles/the-25-largest-internet-companies-in-the-world.html accessed on 1 June 2020.
2. Press Trust of India, 'China's internet users reach 854 million', *The Hindu Business Line*, 29 August 2019, https://www.thehindubusinessline.com/news/world/chinas-internet-users-reach-854-million/article29300988.ece, accessed on 1 June 2020.
3. The White House, 'The administration's report on the future of artificial intelligence', 12 October 2016, https://obamawhitehouse.archives.gov/blog/2016/10/12/administrations-report-future-artificial-intelligence, accessed on 1 June 2020.
4. Full text of Xi Jinping's report to the nineteenth CPC national congress, 2 November 2017, http://www.xinhuanet.com/english/special/2017-11/03/c_136725942.htm, accessed on 1 June 2020.
5. Ananth Krishnan, 'The rise of a science superpower', *India Today*, 9 February 2018, https://www.indiatoday.in/magazine/technology/

story/20180219-china-technology-artificial-intelligence-smart-manufacturing-1166259-2018-02-09, accessed on 1 June 2020

6. For more on China's AI policies and the AI race with America, see Kaifu Lee, *AI Superpowers: China, Silicon Valley and the New World Order*, Houghton Miffin Harcourt, 2018.
7. Parts of this section on Chinese investments in India are derived from a report I authored for Brookings India, called 'Following the money: China Inc's growing stake in India China relations', published in March 2020, https://www.brookings.edu/research/following-the-money-china-incs-growing-stake-in-india-china-relations/, accessed on 1 June 2020.
8. Rebecca Fannin, 'China's tech giants are pouring billions into US startups', CNBC, 8 March 2017, https://www.cnbc.com/2017/03/08/chinas-tech-giants-are-pouring-billions-into-us-start-ups.html, accessed on 1 June 2020.
9. Simon Mundy, 'Alibaba to invest $177 million in Paytm', *Financial Times*, 3 March 2017, https://www.ft.com/content/5cbb69bf-a2ae-3288-8500-27656a12067b, and Press Trust of India, 'Paytm says it never shares user data with investors', 26 July 2018, https://www.thehindubusinessline.com/info-tech/paytm-says-it-never-shares-user-data-with-investors-external-party/article24520612.ece, accessed on 1 June 2020.
10. Mihir Dalal and Anirban Sen, 'Tencent's $1 billion India bet', *Mint*, 13 October 2017, https://www.livemint.com/Companies/lQToylXzcrYd4MgLBGlplK/Tencents-billiondollar-India-bet.html, accessed on 1 June 2020.
11. Embassy of India, Beijing, https://www.eoibeijing.gov.in/economic-and-trade-relation.php, and General Administration of Customs, China www.customs.gov.cn, accessed on 1 June 2020.
12. Ministry of External Affairs, India, https://mea.gov.in/Portal/ForeignRelation/China-January-2012.pdf, accessed on 1 June 2020.
13. Figures from Ministry of Commerce (MOFCOM) China and State Administration for Foreign Exchange, cited in Ernst & Young, *Belt and Road: Exploring a Blueprint for Steady Growth in Overseas Investment*, April 2018, p. 6, https://ey.com/Publication/vwLUAssets/ey-china-overseas-investment-report-issue-7-en/$FILE/ey-china-overseas-investment-report-issue-7-en.pdf, accessed on 1 June 2020.
14. Shelley Singh and Venkat Ananth, 'Tiktok's relentless growth in India is hitting Facebook', *Economic Times*, 21 May 2019, https://economictimes.indiatimes.com/small-biz/startups/features/bytedance-bets-big-on-short-videos-to-engage-indian-market-takes-on-facebook/articleshow/69422493.cms, accessed on 1 June 2020.

15. Amrita Nair-Ghaswalla, 'Of India's top 100 apps, 44 are Chinese', *The Hindu BusinessLine*, 16 April 2019, https://www.thehindubusinessline.com/info-tech/of-indias-top-100-apps-44-are-chinese/article26857166.ece, accessed on 1 June 2020.
16. Yuthika Bhargava, 'Government bans 59 apps including China-based TikTok, WeChat', *The Hindu*, 29 June 2020, https://www.thehindu.com/news/national/govt-bans-59-apps-including-tiktok-wechat/article31947445.ece?homepage=true, accessed on 29 June 2020.
17. Pankaj Doval, '5G panel head wants Chinese vendors excluded from 5G trials,' *The Times of India*, 2 July 2019, https://timesofindia.indiatimes.com/business/india-business/5g-panel-head-wants-chinese-vendors-excluded-from-trials/articleshow/70032601.cms, accessed on 1 June 2020.

7: Building a Chinese Order

1. Jonathan D. Spence, *The Search for Modern China*, Second Edition, Norton, 1999, pp. 7–8.
2. Xinhua, 'Full text: List of deliverables from Belt and Road forum', 15 May 2017, http://www.xinhuanet.com//english/2017-05/15/c_136286376.htm, accessed on 1 June 2020.
3. Spence, op. cit., p. 192.
4. Tom Miller, *China's Asian Dream: Empire Building along the New Silk Road*, Zed Books, 2017, p. 8.
5. Ananth Krishnan, 'What Xi Jinping's nationalistic, proactive Beijing will mean for India and the world', *India Today*, 26 April 2018, https://www.indiatoday.in/magazine/cover-story/story/20180507-xi-jinping-beijing-nationalistic-proactive-means-for-india-world-1221305-2018-04-26, accessed on 1 June 2020.
6. Zheng Bijian, *Economic Globalization and China's Future*, Foreign Languages Press, 2018, pp. 13–30.
7. Joe Bavier, Cheng Leng and Andrea Shalal, 'China in driver's seat amid calls for Africa debt relief', Reuters, 12 April 2020, https://www.reuters.com/article/us-health-coronavirus-africa-china-analy/china-in-the-drivers-seat-amid-calls-for-africa-debt-relief-idUSKCN21V0CS, accessed on 1 June 2020.
8. Peter Frankopan, *The New Silk Roads: The Present and Future of the World*, Bloomsbury Publishing 2018, pp. 100–104.
9. Sebastian Horn, Carmen Reinhar, and Christoph Trebesch, 'China's Overseas Lending', Kiel Institute for the World Economy, June 2019, https://www.ifw-kiel.de/fileadmin/Dateiverwaltung/IfW-Publications/Christoph_Trebesch/KWP_2132.pdf, accessed on 1 June 2020.

10. Iain Marlow, 'Backlash could cost Xi's Belt and Road $800 billion', *Bloomberg*, 11 September 2019, https://www.bloomberg.com/news/articles/2019-09-11/backlash-could-cost-xi-s-belt-and-road-800-billion-report-says, accessed on 1 June 2020.
11. Bruno Macaes, *Belt and Road: A Chinese World Order*, Penguin Random House India, 2019, p. 6.
12. Ibid. p. 29
13. Ibid., pp. 34–35.
14. Yan Xuetong, *Ancient Chinese Thought, Modern Chinese Power*, Princeton University Press, 2011, pp. 65–66.
15. Ibid., pp. 219–20.
16. Spence, op. cit., pp. 123, 129.

8: Competition and Collaboration

1. Ben Blanchard, 'Xi Jinping's journey from China's party elite to party leader', Reuters, 15 November 2012, https://www.reuters.com/article/us-china-congress-xi-idUSBRE8AE0BZ20121115, accessed on 1 June 2020.
2. Wang Xinyi, Zhong Ya, 'How Xiplomacy pushes change in global governance', Xinhua, 15 December 2018, http://www.xinhuanet.com/english/2018-12/15/c_137676261.htm, accessed on 1 June 2020.
3. Pankaj Mishra, 'A Poet Unwelcome', *Outlook*, 18 August 2012, https://www.outlookindia.com/magazine/story/a-poet-unwelcome/281819, accessed on June 1 2020.
4. Li Hongmei, 'Indian media stinks up public opinion', *People's Daily*, 15 September 2009, http://en.people.cn/90002/96417/6758363.html, accessed on 1 June 2020.
5. Hu Xijin, 'De-escalating tensions on China-India border paramount', *Global Times*, 22 June 2020, https://www.globaltimes.cn/content/1192382.shtml, accessed on 1 July 2020.
6. Press Trust of India, 'India China trade dips in 2019', *The Hindu Business Line*, 4 January 2020, https://www.thehindubusinessline.com/economy/india-china-trade-dips-by-nearly-3-billion-in-2019/article30567975.ece, accessed on 1 June 2020.
7. Ananth Krishnan, 'Modi can rewrite ties, says Chinese expert', *The Hindu*, 17 May 2014, https://www.thehindu.com/news/international/world/modi-can-rewrite-ties-says-chinese-expert/article6017528.ece, accessed on 1 June 2020.
8. *Global Times*, 'Article on Qixi festival highlights softer side of President', 7 August 2017, http://www.globaltimes.cn/content/1160679.shtml, accessed on 1 June 2020.
9. Ministry of External Affairs, 'Joint Statement during Prime Minister's visit to China', 15 May 2015, https://www.mea.gov.in/

bilateral-documents.htm?dtl/25240/Joint_Statement_between_the_India_and_China_during_Prime_Ministers_visit_toChina, accessed on 1 July 2020

9: Where China Meets India

1. China Tibet Online, 'China-Nepal international border trade market opens in Gyirong, Tibet', 5 November 2018, http://eng.tibet.cn/eng/economy/news/201811/t20181105_6374148.html, accessed on 1 June 2020.
2. Agreement on the Maintenance of Peace and Tranquility along the Line of Actual Control in the India-China Border Areas, https://peacemaker.un.org/sites/peacemaker.un.org/files/CN%20IN_930907_Agreement%20on%20India-China%20Border%20Areas.pdf, accessed on 1 July 2020.
3. Agreement Between the Government of the Republic of India and the Government of the People's Republic of China on Confidence-Building Measures in the Military Field Along the Line of Actual Control in the India-China Border Areas, https://peacemaker.un.org/sites/peacemaker.un.org/files/CN%20IN_961129_Agreement%20between%20China%20and%20India.pdf, accessed on 1 July 2020.
4. Ministry of External Affairs, Government of India, 'Address by Prime Minister at Tsinghua University, Beijing', 15 May 2015, https://www.mea.gov.in/Speeches-Statements.htm?dtl/25242, accessed on 1 June 2020.
5. Press Trust of India, 'China for freeze in infrastructure along LAC', *Economic Times*, 10 July 2013, https://economictimes.indiatimes.com/news/politics-and-nation/china-for-freeze-on-infra-development-on-lac-india-to-reject/articleshow/21004221.cms?from=mdr, accessed on 1 June 2020.
6. Sutirtho Patranobis, 'China continues to play down border spat with India', *Hindustan Times*, 7 May 2013, https://www.hindustantimes.com/world/china-continues-to-play-down-border-spat-with-india/story-8joysCdJslgM30IAaTCAhN.html, accessed on 1 June 2020.

10: From Doklam to Galwan

1. Ananth Krishnan and Sandeep Unnithan, 'Will there be an India China war?', *India Today*, 28 July 2017, https://www.indiatoday.in/magazine/cover-story/story/20170807-doklam-stand-off-india-china-dispute-will-china-go-to-war-1026539-2017-07-28, accessed on 1 June 2020.

2. Tu Ling and Ge Xiangran, Joint Staff of the Western Theater, 'A rational victory from the Donglang confrontation', *Huanqiu* (Chinese), 26 October 2017, https://mil.huanqiu.com/article/9CaKrnK7fLc, accessed on 1 June 2020.
3. Xinhua, 'Military reorganization "a historic step": PLA Daily', *People's Daily*, 2 February 2016, http://en.people.cn/n3/2016/0202/c90780-9012742.html, accessed on 1 June 2020.
4. Ananth Krishnan, 'China scraps GDP target, hikes defence spending', *The Hindu*, 22 May 2020, https://www.thehindu.com/news/international/china-scraps-gdp-target-hikes-defence-spending/article31652992.ece, accessed on 1 June 2020.
5. M. Taylor Fravel, *Strong Borders, Secure Nation: Cooperation and Conflict in China's Teritorrial Disputes,* Princeton University Press, 2008.
6. Jeff M. Smith, *Cold Peace: China-India Rivalry in the Twenty-first Century*, Ingram, 2015.
7. Ananth Krishnan and Sandeep Unnithan, 'Will there be an India China war?', *India Today*, 28 July 2017, https://www.indiatoday.in/magazine/cover-story/story/20170807-doklam-stand-off-india-china-dispute-will-china-go-to-war-1026539-2017-07-28, accessed on 1 June 2020.
8. Ibid.
9. Ananth Krishnan, 'Beijing think-tank links scrapping of Article 370 to LAC tensions', *The Hindu*, 12 June 2020, https://www.thehindu.com/news/national/beijing-think-tank-links-scrapping-of-article-370-to-lac-tensions/article31815266.ece, accessed on 15 June 2020.

11: The China–Pakistan Nexus

1. Khurram Husain, 'CPEC Masterplan revealed', *Dawn*, 21 June 2017, https://www.dawn.com/news/1333101, accessed on 1 June 2020.
2. Tanvi Madan, *Fateful Triangle: How China Shaped US–India Relations During the Cold War*, Penguin Random House, 2020, p. 175.
3. Drazen Jorgic, 'Pakistan FDI seen surging, but some Western investors fret over Chinese influence', Reuters, 21 March 2018, https://www.reuters.com/article/us-pakistan-economy-investment/pakistan-fdi-seen-surging-but-some-western-investors-fret-over-chinese-influence-idUSKBN1GX0QO, accessed on 1 June 2020.
4. S. Akbar Zaidi, 'Has China taken over Pakistan?', The News, 18 June 2017, https://www.thenews.com.pk/tns/detail/563509-china-taken-pakistan-cpec, accessed on 1 June 2020.

5. Ananth Krishnan, 'Pakistan: China's new colony?', *India Today*, 21 July 2017, https://www.indiatoday.in/magazine/cover-story/story/20170731-china-pakistan-relations-implication-for-india-cpec-obor-1025308-2017-07-21, accessed on 1 June 2020.
6. Ibid.
7. Khurram Husain, op. cit.
8. Liu Xuanzun, 'PLA Navy to have at least 5 carriers', *Global Times*, 5 December 2018, http://www.globaltimes.cn/content/1130535.shtml, accessed on 1 June 2020.

12: Original Sins

1. *Business Standard*, 'PoK, Aksai Chin part of Jammu and Kashmir, ready to die for it: Amit Shah', 22 November 2019, https://www.business-standard.com/article/politics/j-k-including-pok-and-aksai-chin-is-inseparable-part-of-india-shah-119080600327_1.html, accessed on 1 June 2020.
2. For the full text of the 1842 treaty between Tibet and Ladakh, see A.G. Noorani, *India–China Boundary Problem 1846–1947: History and Diplomacy*, Oxford University Press, 2011, p. 236-238
3. A.G. Noorani, *India–China Boundary Problem 1846–1947: History and Diplomacy*, Oxford University Press, 2011, p. 212.
4. Arunabh Ghosh, 'Why India and China see any border breach as a threat to identity', The Quint, 20 June 2020, https://www.thequint.com/voices/opinion/india-china-border-history-relationship-military-rise-of-ethno-nationalism-modi-govt-xi-jinping, accessed on 1 July 2020.
5. Noorani, op. cit., p. 221.
6. Noorani, op. cit., p. 223.
7. Parshotam Mehra, *Essays in Frontier History: India, China and the Disputed Border*, Oxford University Press, 2007, pp. 18–31.
8. A.G.Noorani,'FatefulNote',*Frontline*,14July2012,https://frontline.thehindu.com/static/html/fl2914/stories/20120727291409100.htm, accessed on 1 June 2020.
9. Xinhua, 'China voices firm opposition to Indian leader's visit to disputed border area', 20 November 2017, http://www.xinhuanet.com//english/2017-11/20/c_136766508.htm, accessed on 1 June 2020.
10. For a history of the McMahon Line, see J.J. Singh, *The McMahon Line: A Century of Discord*, HarperCollins, 2019.
11. Noorani, 2011, op. cit., p. 202.
12. Neville Maxwell, *India's China War*, Natraj Publishers, 2013, p. 45.
13. Ibid., p. 47.
14. Mehra, op. cit., p. 36.

15. Ibid., p. 171.
16. Noorani, 2011, op. cit., p. 229.
17. The full account of the negotiations between India and China from 1960 onwards until the 1962 war is documented in Avtar Singh Bhasin, *India–China Relations 1947–2000: A Documentary Study*, Volume IV, Geetika Publishers, 2018.
18. Ibid., pp. 3146, 3183.
19. Ibid., pp. 3189, 3171, 3172.
20. Ibid., pp. 3145, 3328.
21. Ibid., p. 3354.
22. Shivshankar Menon, *Choices: Inside the Making of India's Foreign Policy*, Penguin Random House India, 2016, pp. 13–14.

13: Ghosts of 1962

1. John Keay, *China: A History*, HarperCollins, 2008, pp. 243–244.
2. John W. Garver, 'China's Decision for War in India in 1962', p. 2. in Alastair Iain Johnston and Robert S. Ross (eds), *New Directions in the Study of China's Foreign Policy*, Stanford University Press, 2006.
3. Maxwell, op. cit., p. 510.
4. See Bertil Lintner, *China's India War: Collision Course on the Roof of the World*, Oxford University Press, 2018.
5. Ibid., pp. xiv, 6–12.
6. Ananth Krishnan, 'China documents reveal ignored warnings, missed opportunities', *The Hindu*, 9 October 2012, https://www.thehindu.com/news/national/china-documents-reveal-ignored-warnings-missed-opportunities/article4013815.ece, accessed on 1 June 2020.
7. A.G. Noorani, 2012, op. cit.
8. Michael Fathers, 'His Brother's Keeper', *The Wall Street Journal*, 10 May 2015, https://www.wsj.com/articles/his-brothers-keeper-1431299979, accessed on 1 June 2020.
9. Garver, op. cit. p. 6.
10. Ibid.p. 12.
11. Ibid.p. 16.
12. For a military perspective of the failures in the lead-up to the war, see Brig J.P. Dalvi, *Himalayan Blunder: The Curtain-Raiser to the Sino-Indian War of 1962*, Natraj Publishers, 1969.
13. Part One of the Henderson Brooks–Bhagat Report (HBR) was uploaded in 2014 by Neville Maxwell on his website, www.nevillemaxwell.com, and was accessed by the author on 16 March 2014. The quotes attributed to the HBR in this chapter are sourced from the document uploaded by Maxwell.
14. Mohan Guruswamy and Zorawar Daulet Singh, *India-China Relations: The Border Issue and Beyond*, Viva Books, 2009, p. 75.

15. Garver, op. cit., pp. 46–48.
16. Ibid., p. 26
17. Ibid., pp. 46–48.
18. Ibid., pp. 36–37.
19. Ibid., pp. 46–48.

14: The Case for Settling

1. Noorani, 2011, op. cit., p. 230.
2. Menon, op. cit., pp. 21–22.
3. The quotes attributed to Dai Bingguo in this chapter are sourced from Dai Bingguo, *Strategic Dialogue: Reminiscences of Dai Bingguo* (Chinese), chapter 7, 'A Dance of Dragon & Elephant', People's Publishing House, 2016.
4. Declaration on Principles for Relations and Comprehensive Cooperation Between the Republic of India and the People's Republic of China, 23 June 2003 https://www.mea.gov.in/in-focus-article.htm?7679/Declaration+on+Principles+for+Relations+and+Comprehensive+Cooperation+Between+the+Republic+of+India+and+the+Peoples+Republic+of+China accessed on 1 June 2020
5. Documents signed between India and China during Prime Minister Vajpayee's visit to China, 23 June 2003, https://www.mea.gov.in/bilateral-documents.htm?dtl/7692/Documents+signed+between+India+and+China+during+Prime+Minister+Vajpayees+visit+to+China accessed on 1 June 2020
6. Press Trust of India, 'India, China can quickly resolve boundary dispute: Shivshankar Menon', 2 December 2014, https://economictimes.indiatimes.com/news/politics-and-nation/india-china-can-quickly-resolve-boundary-dispute-shivshankar-menon/articleshow/45347664.cms?from=mdr, accessed on 1 June 2020.
7. Agreement between the Government of the Republic of India and the Government of the People's Republic of China on the Political Parameters and Guiding Principles for the Settlement of the India-China Boundary Question, 11 April 2005, https://www.mea.gov.in/bilateral-documents.htm?dtl/6534/Agreement+between+the+Government+of+the+Republic+of+India+and+the+Government+of+the+Peoples+Republic+of+China+on+the+Political+Parameters+and+Guiding+Principles+for+the+Settlement+of+the+IndiaChina+Boundary+Question accessed on 1 June 2020
8. Jyoti Malhotra, 'Soft border pill to break China logjam', *The Telegraph*, 18 January 2007, https://urldefense.proofpoint.com/v2/url?u=https-3A__www.telegraphindia.com_india_soft-2Dborder-2Dpill-2Dto-

2Dbreak-2Dchina-2Dlogjam_cid_739580&d=DwIFaQ&c=hh7v4vz1gCZ__1Ci-hUEVZfsSwlOcPhT2q8Zs1ka6Ao&r=l2v_94nmzrG2OXdLcXHZgXE1-0WyOl7SBDFTYvFEPnoMiveoo_wEcOHGrzOixcOH&m=k67Vr2vzT9LzxhSrS3BhY86_vkOVfxZw3HFIfEmXJvQ&s=Usmzl86KkT8kuta1V5-q6Pb-B93w3U_S8n_1xxF8ux4&e=, accessed on 1 June 2020.

9. Ananth Krishnan, 'China ready to do a deal with India for concessions on Tawang?', *India Today*, 2 March 2017, https://www.indiatoday.in/world/story/aksai-chin-china-india-tawang-dai-bingguo-963639-2017-03-02, accessed on 1 June 2020.
10. Zhang Jiadong, 'Challengers linger in China India border talks', *Global Times*, 26 November 2018, http://www.globaltimes.cn/content/1129040.shtml, accessed on 1 June 2020.
11. Noorani, 2011, op. cit., p. 229.
12. Garver, op. cit., pp. 2–3.
13. Admiral Arun Prakash (retd), 'India will need to bring order and alacrity to crisis management', *Indian Express*, 25 June 2020, https://indianexpress.com/article/opinion/columns/india-china-border-stand-off-line-of-actual-control-galwan-valley-6474725/, accessed on 30 June 2020.

15: Tibet: Past and Present

1. Ananth Krishnan, 'Trust deficit in Tibet', *India Today*, 12 July 2015, https://www.indiatoday.in/magazine/cover-story/story/20150713-tibet-lhasa-dalai-lama-deyang-shar-courtyard-potala-palace-820009-2015-07-02, accessed on 1 June 2020.
2. Ibid.
3. Ananth Krishnan, 'Fiery protest spreads beyond the walls of Tibetan monasteries', *The Hindu*, 5 May 2012 https://www.thehindu.com/news/international/fiery-protest-spreads-beyond-the-walls-of-tibetan-monasteries/article3388168.ece, accessed on 1 June 2020.
4. For a history of Tibet and a detailed account of these events, see Tsering Shakya, *The Dragon in the Land of Snows: A History of Modern Tibet Since 1947*, Penguin, 2000.
5. See Parshotam Mehra, *Tibet: Writings on History and Politics*, Oxford University Press, 2012, pp. 302–26.
6. Human Rights Watch, 'China's bilingual education policy in Tibet', March 2020, https://www.hrw.org/report/2020/03/04/chinas-bilingual-education-policy-tibet/tibetan-medium-schooling-under-threat, accessed on 1 June 2020.
7. Ananth Krishnan, 'China to reconsider language policy', *The Hindu*, 23 October 2010, https://www.thehindu.com/news/international/

China-to-reconsider-language-policy/article15789567.ece, accessed on 1 June 2020.

16: Restless in Xinjiang

1. For a history of Xinjiang, see James A. Millward, *Eurasian Crossroads: A History of Xinjiang*, Columbia University Press, 2007.
2. Ananth Krishnan, 'Xinjiang's cycle of violence', *The Hindu*, 24 March 2014, https://www.thehindu.com/opinion/lead/xinjiangs-cycle-of-violence/article5822979.ece, accessed on 1 June 2020.
3. Tania Branigan, '21 killed in Kashgar clashes', *Guardian*, 24 April 2013, https://www.theguardian.com/world/2013/apr/24/chinese-gangsters-police-shootout, accessed on 1 June 2020.
4. Austin Ramzy and Chris Buckley, 'Leaked files show internment camps are run by secrecy and spying', *New York Times*, 24 November 2019, https://www.nytimes.com/2019/11/24/world/asia/leak-chinas-internment-camps.html, accessed on 1 June 2020.
5. Alim is not being identified by his real name. I first wrote about his journey in Angilee Shah and Jeffrey Wasserstrom (eds), 'The Road to a Better Life', *Chinese Characters: Profiles of Fast-Changing Lives in a Fast-Changing Land*, pp. 135-144, University of California Press, 2012.
6. For a history of the Hui and Islam's journey to China, see M.A. Aldrich and Lukas Nikol, *The Perfumed Palace: Islam's Journey from Mecca to Peking*, Garnet Publishing, 2010.
7. Human Rights Watch, 'A timeline of Ilham Tohti's case', 15 September 2014, https://www.hrw.org/news/2014/09/15/timeline-ilham-tohtis-case, accessed on 1 June 2020.
8. Radio Free Asia, 'Uyghur scholar Ilham Tohti speaks about his concerns before detention', 7 February 2014, https://www.rfa.org/english/news/uyghur/interview-02072014182032.html, accessed on 1 June 2020.

17: The Fight for Hong Kong

1. Clara Ferreira Marques, 'Hong Kong is showing symptoms of a failed state', *Bloomberg*, 9 February 2020, https://www.bloomberg.com/opinion/articles/2020-02-09/coronavirus-hong-kong-shows-symptoms-of-a-failed-state, accessed on 1 June 2020.
2. For a history of Hong Kong's protest movement, see Jeffrey Wasserstrom, 'Vigil: Hong Kong on the Brink', Columbia Global Reports, 2020.

3. Chris Buckley and Keith Bradsher, 'Law will tighten Beijing's grip on Hong Kong with security force', *New York Times*, 20 June 2020, https://www.nytimes.com/2020/06/20/world/asia/china-hong-kong-security-law.html, accessed on 30 June 2020.
4. Ananth Krishnan, 'New security law will tighten Beijing's grip on Hong Kong', *The Hindu*, 22 May 2020, https://www.thehindu.com/news/international/new-security-law-will-tighten-beijings-grip-on-hong-kong/article31653094.ece, accessed on 1 June 2020.
5. Lily Kuo, 'Tsai Ing-wen wins landslide in rebuke to China', *Guardian*, 11 January 2020, https://www.theguardian.com/world/2020/jan/11/taiwan-re-elects-tsai-ing-wen-as-president-in-clear-message-to-china, accessed on 1 June 2020.
6. Phila Siu and Tony Cheung, 'Chinese President Xi Jinping holds up 'one country, two systems' as only way forward for Hong Kong and Macau', *South China Morning Post*, 20 Dec 2019, https://urldefense.proofpoint.com/v2/url?u=https-3A__www.scmp.com_news_hong-2Dkong_politics_article_3042920_chinese-2Dpresident-2Dxi-2Djinping-2Dheaps-2Dpraise-2Dmacau-2Dciting&d=DwIFaQ&c=hh7v4vz1gCZ__1Ci-hUEVZfsSwlOcPhT2q8Zs1ka6Ao&r=l2v_94nmzrG2OXdLcXHZgXE1-0WyOl7SBDFTYvFEPnoMiveoo_wEcOHGrzOixcOH&m=k67Vr2vzT9LzxhSrS3BhY86_vkOVfxZw3HFIfEmXJvQ&s=QfqFNCIjnYUOMUAtp3PNnZbHici4rWVEZqMG_RaVfZU&e=, accessed on 1 June 2020.
7. Russell Hsiao, 'New polling data reveal deepening Taiwan identity', *CommonWealth Magazine*, 2 August 2019, https://english.cw.com.tw/article/article.action?id=2502, accessed on 1 June 2020.
8. Kris Cheng, 'Hongkongers identifying as Chinese at record low', Hong Kong Free Press, 28 June 2019, https://hongkongfp.com/2019/06/28/hongkongers-identifying-chinese-record-low-10-youth-proud-citizens-poll/, accessed on 1 June 2020.

18: Renewing Links

1. Alec Ash, *Wish Lanterns: Young Lives in New China*, Picador, 2016, p. 315.

19: The Discoverer

1. For a history of the contacts between India and China in this period, see Tansen Sen, *India, China and the World: A Connected History*, Rowman & Littlefield, 2017.

2. Ministry of External Affairs, 'Transcript of briefing by foreign secretary after Chennai informal summit', 12 October 2019, https://www.mea.gov.in/media-briefings.htm?dtl/31935/Transcript_of_Media_Briefing_by_Foreign_Secretary_during_Chennai_Informal_Summit_October_11_2019, accessed on 1 June 2020.

20: The Treasure Hunter

1. For a history of the work done by the Library of Tibetan Works and Archives, see https://tibetanlibrary.org/history-of-ltwa/.

21: The Interpreter

1. Ananth Krishnan, 'Lost in translation', *India Today*, 18 January 2016, https://www.indiatoday.in/magazine/books/story/20160118-feng-tang-lost-in-translation-828268-2016-01-06, accessed on 1 June 2020.

23: The Green Warrior

1. Elizabeth C. Economy, *The River Runs Black: The Environmental Challenge to China's Future*, Cornell University Press, 2004, pp. 157–58.
2. Ibid.
3. 'Obituary, Wu Dengming', *The Economist*, 10 August 2013, https://www.economist.com/obituary/2013/08/10/wu-dengming, accessed on 1 June 2020.
4. Nectar Gan, 'Trial by fire: three years on from the crackdown that put China's nascent human rights law movement to the test', *South China Morning Post*, 9 July 2018, https://www.scmp.com/news/china/policies-politics/article/2154278/trial-fire-three-years-crackdown-put-chinas-nascent, accessed on 1 June 2020.
5. Economy, op. cit., p. 169
6. Mu Lan, 'Farewell Wu Dengming', *Probe International*, 25 July 2013, https://journal.probeinternational.org/2013/07/25/farewell-wu-dengming-chinas-green-hero/, accessed on 1 June 2020.

Epilogue: China After the Pandemic

1. Philip Pan, 'The land that failed to fail', *New York Times*, 18 November 2018, https://www.nytimes.com/interactive/2018/11/18/world/asia/china-rules.html, accessed on 1 June 2020.

2. Figures compiled using World Bank data.
3. Xinhua, 'Xi chairs leadership meet on epidemic control', 3 February 2020, http://www.xinhuanet.com/english/2020-02/03/c_138753250.htm, accessed on 1 June 2020.
4. Gao Yu, Xiao Hui, Ma Danmeng, Cui Xiankang and Han Wei, 'How Wuhan lost the fight to contain the coronavirus', *Caixin* 3 February 2020, https://www.caixinglobal.com/2020-02-03/in-depth-how-wuhan-lost-the-fight-to-contain-the-coronavirus-101510749.html, accessed on 1 June 2020.
5. Maria Repnikova, 'The subtle muckrakers of the coronavirus', *New York Times,* 5 February 2020, https://www.nytimes.com/2020/02/05/opinion/coronavirus-china-news-journalism.html, accessed on 1 June 2020.
6. McGregor, op. cit.
7. Ren Zhiqiang's essay, 5 April 2020, http://credibletarget.net/notes/RZQ, accessed on 1 June 2020.
8. Xinhua, 'What are the two centenary goals?', 17 October 2017, http://www.xinhuanet.com/english/2017-10/17/c_136686770.htm, accessed on 1 June 2020.
9. David Shambaugh, *China's Future*, Polity, 2016, pp. 2–4.

Bibliography

Aldrich, M.A. and Lukas Nikol. *The Perfumed Palace: Islam's Journey from Mecca to Peking*. Reading: Garnet Publishing, 2010.

Ash, Alec. *Wish Lanterns: Young Lives in New China*. London: Picador, 2016.

Bhasin, Avtar Singh. *India–China Relations 1947–2000: A Documentary Study*, Volume IV. New Delhi: Geetika Publishers, 2018.

Bougon, Francois. *Inside the Mind of Xi Jinping*. New Delhi, Westland Publications, 2018.

Chen, Xiwen. *China's Agriculture, Rural Areas and Farmers*. Beijing: Foreign Languages Press, 2018.

Dai, Bingguo. *Strategic Dialogue: Reminiscences of Dai Bingguo* (Chinese). Beijing: People's Publishing House, 2016.

Dalvi, Brig J.P. *Himalayan Blunder: The Curtain-Raiser to the Sino-Indian War of 1962*. Dehradun: Natraj Publishers, 1969.

Economy, Elizabeth C. *The River Runs Black: The Environmental Challenge to China's Future*. Ithaca, NY: Cornell University Press, 2004.

Frankopan, Peter. *The New Silk Roads: The Present and Future of the World*. London: Bloomsbury Publishing 2018.

Fravel, M. Taylor. *Strong Borders, Secure Nation: Cooperation and Conflict in China's Territorial Disputes*. Princeton, NJ: Princeton University Press, 2008.

Guruswamy, Mohan and Zorawar Daulet Singh. *India-China Relations: The Border Issue and Beyond*. New Delhi: Viva Books, 2009.

Johnston, Alastair Iain and Robert S. Ross, eds, *New Directions in the Study of China's Foreign Policy*. Stanford, CA: Stanford University Press, 2006.

Keay, John. *China: A History*. London: HarperCollins Publishers, 2008.

Kroeber, Arthur R. *China's Economy: What Everyone Needs to Know*. New York: Oxford University Press, 2016.

Lee, Kaifu. *AI Superpowers: China, Silicon Valley, and the New World Order*. Boston: Houghton Mifflin Harcourt, 2018.

Li, Cheng. *Chinese Politics in the Xi Jinping Era: Reassessing Collective Leadership*. Washington, DC: Brookings Institution Press, 2016.

Li, Junru. *Governing China in the New Era*. Beijing: Foreign Languages Press, 2018.

Lim, Louisa. *The People's Republic of Amnesia: Tiananmen Revisited*. New York: Oxford University Press, 2014.

Lintner, Bertil. *China's India War: Collision Course on the Roof of the World*. New Delhi: Oxford University Press, 2018.

Macaes, Bruno. *Belt and Road: A Chinese World Order*. Gurugram: Penguin Random House India, 2019.

Madan, Tanvi. *Fateful Triangle: How China Shaped US–India Relations During the Cold War*. Gurugram: Penguin Random House India, 2020.

Maxwell, Neville. *India's China War*. Dehradun: Natraj Publishers, 2013.

McGregor, Richard. *The Party: The Secret World of China's Communist Rulers*. London: Allen Lane, 2010.

McMahon, Dinny. *China's Great Wall of Debt: Shadow Banks, Ghost Cities, Massive Loans and the End of the Chinese Miracle*. London: Little, Brown, 2018.

Mehra, Parshotam. *Essays in Frontier History: India, China and the Disputed Border*. New Delhi: Oxford University Press, 2007.

——. *Tibet: Writings on History and Politics*. New Delhi: Oxford University Press, 2012.

Menon, Shivshankar. *Choices: Inside the Making of India's Foreign Policy*. Gurugram: Penguin Random House India, 2016.

Miller, Tom. *China's Asian Dream: Empire Building along the New Silk Road*. London: Zed Books, 2017.

Millward, James A. *Eurasian Crossroads: A History of Xinjiang*. New York: Columbia University Press, 2007.

Noorani, A.G. *India–China Boundary Problem 1846–1947: History and Diplomacy*. New Delhi: Oxford University Press, 2011.

Palit, Amitendu. *China–India Economics: Challenges, Competition and Collaboration*. Abingdon: Routledge, 2012.

Pei, Minxin. *China's Crony Capitalism: The Dynamics of Regime Decay*. Cambridge, MA: Harvard University Press, 2016.

Sen, Tansen. *India, China and the World: A Connected History*. New York: Rowman & Littlefield, 2017.

Shah, Angilee and Jeffrey Wasserstrom, eds. *Chinese Characters: Profiles of Fast-Changing Lives in a Fast-Changing Land*. Berkeley, CA: University of California Press, 2012.

Shakya, Tsering. *The Dragon in the Land of Snows: A History of Modern Tibet Since 1947*. New York: Penguin Books, 2000.

Shambaugh, David. *China's Future*. London: Polity Press, 2016.

Singh, J.J. *The McMahon Line: A Century of Discord*. Noida: HarperCollins Publishers, 2019.

Smith, Jeff M. *Cold Peace: China–India Rivalry in the Twenty-first Century*. Maryland: Lexington Books, 2014.

Spence, Jonathan D. *The Search for Modern China*. New York: Norton, 1999.

Wasserstrom, Jeffrey. *Vigil: Hong Kong on the Brink*. New York: Columbia Global Reports, 2020.

Yan, Xuetong. *Ancient Chinese Thought, Modern Chinese Power*. Princeton, NJ: Princeton University Press, 2011.

Yang, Jisheng. *Tombstone: The Great Chinese Famine 1958–1962*. New York: Farrar, Straus and Giroux, 2012.

Zheng, Bijian. *Economic Globalization and China's Future*. Beijing: Foreign Languages Press, 2018.

Zhu, Guanglei. *Governing China: Decision Making and Implementation: Interpretation of the Processes of the Chinese Government*. Beijing: Foreign Languages Press, 2013.

About the Author

ANANTH KRISHNAN is the China correspondent for *The Hindu* and lives in Beijing. In 2019, he was a Visiting Fellow at Brookings India. He was previously the Beijing-based Associate Editor at the India Today Group until August 2018. He has lived in Beijing since 2009, earlier reporting for *The Hindu*. His reporting in China has taken him to all but three of China's thirty-three provinces and regions. Before moving to China, Ananth was based at *The Hindu's* headquarters in Chennai. Ananth holds a master's degree in the social sciences from the University of Chicago.

